AQUINAS ON HUMAN
SELF-KNOWLEDGE

Self-knowledge is commonly thought to have become a topic of serious philosophical inquiry during the early modern period. Already in the thirteenth century, however, the medieval thinker Thomas Aquinas developed a sophisticated theory of self-knowledge, which Therese Scarpelli Cory presents as a project of reconciling the conflicting phenomena of self-opacity and privileged self-access. Situating Aquinas's theory within the mid-thirteenth-century debate and his own maturing thought on human nature, Cory investigates the kinds of self-knowledge that Aquinas describes and the questions they raise. She shows that to a degree remarkable in a medieval thinker, self-knowledge turns out to be central to Aquinas's account of cognition and personhood, and that his theory provides tools for considering intentionality, reflexivity, and selfhood. Her engaging account of this neglected aspect of medieval philosophy will interest readers studying Aquinas and the history of medieval philosophy more generally.

THERESE SCARPELLI CORY is Assistant Professor of Philosophy at Seattle University.

AQUINAS ON HUMAN SELF-KNOWLEDGE

THERESE SCARPELLI CORY

CAMBRIDGE
UNIVERSITY PRESS

CAMBRIDGE
UNIVERSITY PRESS

University Printing House, Cambridge CB2 8BS, United Kingdom

Cambridge University Press is part of the University of Cambridge.

It furthers the University's mission by disseminating knowledge in the pursuit of education, learning and research at the highest international levels of excellence.

www.cambridge.org
Information on this title: www.cambridge.org/9781316502334

First published 2014
First paperback edition 2015

A catalogue record for this publication is available from the British Library

Library of Congress Cataloguing in Publication data
Cory, Therese Scarpelli, 1982–
Aquinas on human self-knowledge / Therese Scarpelli Cory.
pages cm
Includes bibliographical references and index.
ISBN 978-1-107-04292-6 (hardback)
1. Thomas, Aquinas, Saint, 1225?–1274. 2. Self–knowledge, Theory of. I. Title.
B765.T54C653 2013
126.092–dc23
2013018456

ISBN 978-1-107-04292-6 Hardback
ISBN 978-1-316-50233-4 Paperback

To David

nec ego ipse capio totum, quod sum.
Ergo animus ad habendum se ipsum angustus est:
ut ubi sit quod sui non capit?
Numquid extra ipsum ac non in ipso?
Quomodo ergo non capit?
Multa mihi super hoc oboritur admiratio, stupor apprehendit.
Et eunt homines mirari alta montium,
et ingentes fluctus maris,
et latissimos lapsus fluminum,
et Oceani ambitum,
et gyros siderum,
et relinquunt se ipsos.

St. Augustine, Confessiones

Contents

Acknowledgments

On the long road to completing this project, I have been fortunate to have had the philosophical guidance and companionship of very many wise and kind people. This book began its journey as a master's thesis (2007) and then a doctoral dissertation (2009) under the direction of Msgr. John F. Wippel at The Catholic University of America, to whom I owe an immense debt of gratitude for his unfailing patience, wisdom, and generosity. Fr. Mark Henninger, SJ, of Georgetown University, provided an invaluable opportunity to rework and expand the project during a postdoctoral fellowship year at the Georgetown University Center for Medieval Philosophy, 2009–10. I have benefited at various stages of the project from the incisive comments and critique of Kevin White, Greg Doolan, Tim Noone, Bernd Goehring, J.T. Paasch, Susan Brower-Toland, Daniel De Haan, Brian Carl, and two reviewers. In particular, I owe many thanks to my husband David for his enthusiasm for puzzling over problems in medieval philosophy at any time of the day or night – not to mention his stoicism in reading and commenting on a seemingly endless series of drafts.

The research and writing of this project was generously funded by Mrs. Catharine Ryan and the Georgetown University Martin Center for Medieval Philosophy, whose support I gratefully acknowledge. And last but certainly not least, I recall with grateful affection the guidance and support of the late Dean of the School of Philosophy at The Catholic University of America, Fr. Kurt Pritzl, OP.

Abbreviations

Titles of works in Latin

Abbreviations given are for the works of Aquinas, unless otherwise stated. Since many medieval authors wrote a commentary on the *Sentences*, I use the same abbreviation for all such commentaries (*Sent*).

In references to these works, internal divisions such as books, distinctions, questions, and articles, or lectiones or chapters, are given in Arabic numerals, separated by periods, without preceding designations unless these are necessary for clarity (e.g., *Sent* 1.3.4.5). Book numbers of commentaries and the parts of the *Summa theologiae*, however, are given in Roman numerals according to standard practice.

CT	*Compendium theologiae*
DeCar	*Quaestio disputata de caritate*
DeTrin	*De Trinitate* (Augustine)
DeVirtCom	*Quaestio disputata de virtutibus in communi*
DEE	*De ente et essentia*
DeHom	*De homine* (Albert)
DM	*Quaestiones disputatae de malo*
DP	*Quaestiones disputatae de potentia*
DUI	*De unitate intellectus*
DV	*Quaestiones disputatae de veritate*
InCor I	*Super primam epistolam ad Corinthios lectura*
InDA	*Sentencia libri De anima* (also Albert)
InDivNom	*In librum Beati Dionysii De divinis nominibus expositio*
InDMR	*Sentencia libri De memoria et reminiscencia*
InDSS	*Sentencia libri De sensu et sensato*
InEthic	*Sententia libri Ethicorum*
InIoan	*Super Evangelium S. Ioannis lectura*

InMeta	*In duodecim libros Metaphysicorum Aristotelis expositio*
InMeteor	*Expositio in libros Meteorologicorum*
InPerierm	*Expositio libri Peryermenias*
InPhys	*In VIII libros Physicorum*
InPsalm	*In Psalmos*
InPostAn	*Expositio libri Posteriorum*
QDDA	*Quaestiones disputatae de anima*
QDSC	*Quaestio disputata de spiritualibus creaturis*
Quodl	*Quaestiones de quolibet*
SCG	*Summa contra gentiles*
Sent	*Scriptum super libros sententiarum magistri Petri Lombardi* (also Bonaventure and Albert)
SBDE	*Super Boetii De ebdomadibus*
SBDT	*Super Boetii De Trinitate*
SLDC	*Super Librum de causis expositio*
ST	*Summa theologiae*

Editions of the works of Aquinas

Leon.	*Sancti Thomae Aquinatis, Doctoris Angelici, opera omnia, iussu impensaque Leonis XIII P.M. edita.* Rome: S.C. de Propaganda Fide, 1882–.
Mand./Moos	*Scriptum super libros Sententiarum magistri Petri Lombardi.* 4 vols. 1–2, ed. R.P. Mandonnet; 3–4, ed. R.P. Maria Fabianus Moos. Paris: Lethielleux, 1929–47.
Marietti	*Thomae Aquinatis, opera omnia.* Turin/Rome: Marietti (dates vary).
Parma	*Sancti Thomae Aquinatis, Doctoris Angelici, ordinis Praedicatorum opera omnia.* Parma: Typis Petri Fiaccadori, 1852–73.
Saffrey	*Sancti Thomae de Aquino super Librum de causis expositio,* ed. H.-D. Saffrey. Louvain: Nauwelaerts, 1954.

Other frequently referenced editions

Borgnet	Albert the Great. *B. Alberti Magni Ratisbonensis episcopi, ordinis Praedicatorum, opera omnia.* Paris: Vivès, 1890.
Bougerol	Jean de la Rochelle. *Summa de anima.* Ed. Jacques Guy Bougerol. Paris: Vrin, 1995.

CCSL	*Corpus Christianorum series latina.* Turnholt: Brepols, 1953–.
Col.	Albert the Great. *Alberti Magni opera omnia.* Aschendorff: Monasterium Westfalorum, 1951–.
Crawford	Averroes. *Commentarium magnum in Aristotelis De anima.* Ed. F. Stuart Crawford. Cambridge, Mass.: The Mediaeval Academy of America, 1953.
Michaud-Quantin	Jean de la Rochelle. *Tractatus de divisione multiplici potentiarum animae.* Ed. Pierre Michaud-Quantin. Paris: Vrin, 1964.
Paris	William of Auvergne. *Guilielmi Alverni Episcopi Parisiensis opera omnia.* 2 vols. Paris: Pralard, 1674.
Pattin	Anonymous. *Liber de causis.* Vol. I of *Miscellanea,* ed. Adriaan Pattin. Leuven: Bibliotheek van de Faculteit der Godgeleerdheid, 2000.
Quar.	Bonaventure. *Doctoris seraphici S. Bonaventurae opera omnia.* 9 vols. Quaracchi: Collegium S. Bonaventurae, 1882–1902.
	Also Alexander of Hales. *Glossa in quatuor libros Sententiarum Petri Lombardi.* 4 vols. Quaracchi: Collegium S. Bonaventurae, 1951–7.
Van Riet	Avicenna Latinus. *Liber de anima seu sextus De naturalibus.* Ed. S. Van Riet. 2 vols. Louvain: Peeters, 1972 and 1968.

Introduction

What could be more familiar and yet more obscure than one's own self? Although I depend on other people's reports to know what they are thinking or feeling, I seem to have "VIP backstage access" to my own mental states, experiencing them from the inside with a sense of unshakeable certitude: "I am thinking; I exist!" Yet when I try to get a closer look, my own familiar mind is transformed into something elusive, remote, mysterious. Extramental objects dominate conscious experience to such an extent that it seems impossible to achieve an experience of myself or my mind isolated from their clamorous presence. And the very things that ought to be most intimately familiar to me – my own motivations, choices, character traits, justifications for firmly held beliefs, and especially what the mind itself is – are instead the most obscure.

This recurring tension between privileged self-access and self-opacity was cast into dramatic relief by early modern thinkers. A deeply-rooted sense of intimate presence to myself underlies, for instance, Descartes's assertion that one cannot doubt one's own existence, or Locke's claim that one need only turn one's attention inward to notice oneself and one's mental acts. But this initial confidence is shaken when one actually attempts a perception of the bare self isolated from the experience of extramental objects – hence the plausibility of Hume's claim that the self is merely posited and not experientially perceived. The tension between these compelling but conflicting aspects of our experience of ourselves is perhaps one of the most difficult problems that any theory of self-knowledge faces, and these early modern battle-lines continue to guide contemporary investigations into the very possibility of self-knowledge.[1]

It is not well known, however, that this same experienced tension between privileged self-access and self-opacity inspired a lively debate

---

[1] For example, see the arguments for and against privileged self-access in *Self-Knowledge*, ed. Quassim Cassam (Oxford University Press, 1994).

among medieval Latin thinkers, under the innocuous guise of questions such as "Whether the mind always understands itself," or "Whether the mind cognizes itself by itself or by a species." These questions emerged as part of the thirteenth-century conversation between the Neoplatonic and Aristotelian psychological traditions, the former stressing that self-knowledge is natural to the human mind, and the latter asserting the dependence of self-knowledge on cognition of other things.

The flagship source for the Neoplatonic perspective on self-knowledge in the thirteenth century was Augustine's *De Trinitate*, which describes the mind as always understanding itself even if it is not always thinking about itself. A similar line of thought was further developed in texts introduced to the Latin West from the Islamic world during the Arabic-to-Latin translation project of the twelfth and thirteenth centuries. One bulwark of the debate was the *Liber de anima* (translated into Latin around 1152–66), in which the great Persian philosopher Avicenna deftly blends Aristotelian and Neoplatonic thought into a single original doctrine on the soul. Another was the anonymous *Liber de causis* (translated into Latin sometime between 1167 and 1187), a work inspired by Proclus but which its Latin readers initially believed to be a report of Aristotle's teaching on the first causes. These sources impressed upon thirteenth-century Latin minds the notion that it belongs to the nature of intellectual beings to be perpetually engaged in self-knowing. Self-opacity is thus only a superficial phenomenon, the result of inattention. The Islamic Neoplatonic perspective was perhaps especially attractive since it provided a more systematic psychological account of self-opacity, reinforcing a preexisting Latin theological interest in self-opacity as an ethical problem.

In contrast to the Neoplatonic tendency to blame self-opacity on sensory distraction, the newly translated Aristotelian commentary tradition defended a positive role for sensation and abstracted intelligibles. Expounding Aristotle's cryptic claim that "mind is intelligible like other things" (*De anima* 430a2), Greek and Arabic commentators such as Alexander of Aphrodisias, Themistius, and Averroes insisted that cognition of extramental intelligibles mediates and limits human self-knowledge (or at least some kinds of self-knowledge). Sensory activity is thus not the cause of, but the cure for the mind's native self-opacity, since sensation is a precondition for receiving the extramental intelligibles that reveal the mind to itself. Nevertheless, self-opacity can never be completely eliminated, because the mind can only understand itself within the framework provided by each specific act.

As these newly translated texts gained in popularity during the first half of the thirteenth century, a number of prominent thinkers at the University of Paris took the Neoplatonic route of emphasizing the mind's privileged self-access over its self-opacity. For mid-century thinkers such as the theologian and bishop of Paris William of Auvergne (*c.* 1180/90–1249), the Franciscan thinker Jean de la Rochelle (d. 1245), and Aquinas's own teacher Albert the Great (d. 1280), it is *a priori* impossible for a mind to be ignorant of itself. Self-opacity is merely a failure to attend to a more basic condition of self-knowing. For these thinkers, the Aristotelian proposal that self-knowledge depends on acts of cognizing extramental objects is either absurd (Jean de la Rochelle, William of Auvergne), or restricted to one specific kind of self-knowledge that does not conflict with the soul's more basic condition of perpetual self-knowing (Albert).

Thomas Aquinas (1225–1274) challenges this trend with a theory that ignited considerable controversy among his contemporaries. Of any thirteenth-century thinker, Aquinas appears to be most impressed by the phenomenological experience of self-opacity: the indissociability of self-awareness from cognition of extramental objects, the difficulty of grasping the mind's nature, and the frequency with which we misidentify our true motivations and impulses. For him, these phenomena suggest that the human mind is naturally ignorant of itself, a condition that can only be relieved when the mind is actualized by thinking about something else. Nevertheless, he is also keenly aware of the need to account for privileged self-access: the feeling of comfortable self-familiarity, the awareness of oneself as subject that seems to frame all our acts of thinking, the certitude that I am the one thinking my own thoughts.

Aquinas thus sets himself the task of grounding both an ineliminable self-opacity and a limited privileged self-access in the structure of human cognition. With Augustine and other Neoplatonic sources, he argues that the mind has special, intimate self-familiarity, while rejecting their view of the human mind as pure self-thinking in favor of a (broadly) Aristotelian concept of the human intellect that makes all our self-knowledge depend on the senses. Careful to protect privileged self-access, however, he denies that the latter should be interpreted as implying that everything we know about ourselves is derived abstractively or discursively from sensory experiences of our bodies.

The result is the strikingly sophisticated theory of self-knowledge that is the topic of this book. Three key features of this theory stand out as particularly noteworthy; indeed they are not features that one might have expected to find in a medieval thinker:

- *A layering of self-opacity in the mind.* For Aquinas, there are certain things that the mind can grasp about itself prephitosophically when it glimpses itself acting (i.e., its own existence, its singular self, the fact that it *is* acting), and other things that it can only understand about itself after a tedious process of reasoning (its own essential properties, or what kinds of acts it is performing and why). His account suggests an intriguing way of accommodating rich descriptive content in prephilosophical self-knowledge without having to explain away self-opacity.

- *The first-person subject-as-agent.* As de Libera has noted, Aquinas's theory of soul is partly responsible for the thirteenth-century shift towards the notion of subject-as-agent.[2] A parallel development, however, takes place in Aquinas's account of the way in which I experience myself, not as a pure "mind" or "self," but as a first-person agent-in-act. Consequently, for Aquinas, self-awareness is neither the Cartesian introspection of a transcendent, self-seeing "I," nor the Humean positing of a cause of impressions, but an experience of oneself-thinking-about-something.

- *A linking of intentionality, conscious thought, and selfhood.* At the heart of Aquinas's account of intellectual cognition is his view that self-awareness is intrinsic to every intellectual act. To think about myself is always to apprehend myself as a first-person agent actually engaging with the extramental world. Conversely, to think about something is to apprehend it as manifested to me, the cognizing subject. This position (anticipating the views of Franz Brentano and recently, Uriah Kriegel[3]) provides Aquinas with a mechanism to account for the ephemeral yet privileged character of self-awareness. We will also find in it the key to Aquinas's little-known accounts of certain phenomena typically associated with human selfhood, such as unity of consciousness, first-person perspective, and subject–object duality.

In light of its sophistication and its overlap with themes of interest to contemporary philosophy of mind, it is surprising that Aquinas's theory of self-knowledge has received so little scholarly attention. In fact, self-knowledge in Aquinas is generally treated – when it is mentioned at all – either as an insignificant appendage to his account of cognition, or as an isolated curiosity. Hardly any of the twentieth century's monographs on

---

[2] See Alain de Libera, *Archéologie du sujet*, vol. 1, *Naissance du sujet* (Paris: Vrin, 2007), ch. 4.
[3] See Chapter 6.

Aquinas's theory of cognition even mention self-knowledge (with the notable exceptions of Kenny's *Aquinas on Mind* and Pasnau's *Thomas Aquinas on Human Nature*).[4] As for articles, after a brief flurry of interest in France in the 1920s and 1230s,[5] subsequent decades have seen only a few publications, usually aimed at specific aspects of his account.[6] Putallaz's 1991 monograph *Le sens de la réflexion en Thomas d'Aquin* took strides toward rehabilitating Aquinas's theory of self-knowledge.[7] Despite these efforts, Aquinas's thought on self-knowledge – like that of medieval thinkers generally – remains woefully understudied and generally not well known.

One reason for this neglect is that self-knowledge is still widely considered to be a "modern" problem, to such an extent that even dedicated followers of Aquinas have assumed that he could have little of interest to say about it. In fact, a tendency among many early twentieth-century

---

[4] See Anthony Kenny, *Aquinas on Mind* (New York: Routledge, 1993), 119–27; and Robert Pasnau, *Thomas Aquinas on Human Nature: A Philosophical Study of* Summa theologiae *1A 75–89* (Cambridge University Press, 2002), 330–55. For instance, self-knowledge or reflexion upon oneself is mentioned in *The Cambridge Companion to Aquinas* and more recently in *The Oxford Handbook of Aquinas* only briefly in connection with the verification of judgments, and not at all as a theme in its own right. It is entirely absent from such older classic Thomistic studies of cognition theory as Robert Edward Brennan, *Thomistic Psychology: A Philosophic Analysis of the Nature of Man* (New York: Macmillan, 1941); Joseph Moreau, *De la connaissance selon S. Thomas d'Aquin* (Paris: Beauchesne, 1976).

[5] For references, see pp. 92–3, note 2.

[6] To mention a few noteworthy examples: John D. McKian, "The Metaphysics of Introspection According to St. Thomas," *The New Scholasticism* 15 (1941): 89–117; Joseph de Finance, "Cogito cartésien et réflexion thomiste," *Archives de philosophie* 16.2 (1946): 3–185; John Ruane, "Self-Knowledge and the Spirituality of the Soul in St. Thomas," *The New Scholasticism* 32 (1958): 425–42; Jaume Bofill y Bofill, "Para una metafísica de sentimiento," in *Obra filosófica* (Barcelona: Ariel, 1967), 107–61; James Reichmann, "The 'Cogito' in St. Thomas: Truth in Aquinas and Descartes," *International Philosophical Quarterly* 26 (1986): 341–52; Deborah L. Black, "Consciousness and Self-Knowledge in Aquinas's Critique of Averroes's Psychology," *Journal of the History of Philosophy* 31 (1993): 349–85, and most recently, Susan Brower-Toland, "Self-Knowledge, Self-Consciousness, and Reflexivity," in *Companion to Cognitive Theory in the Later Middle Ages*, ed. Russell Friedman and Martin Pickavé (Leuven University Press, forthcoming). Two insightful dissertations on the topic are: Mariasusai Dhavamony, *Subjectivity and Knowledge in the Philosophy of Saint Thomas Aquinas* (Rome: Typis Pontificiae Universitatis Gregorianae, 1965); and Carl N. Still, "Aquinas's Theory of Human Self-Knowledge" (PhD diss., University of Toronto, Centre for Medieval Studies, 1999). Finally, parts of the following works treat self-knowledge or selfhood in Aquinas: Estanislao Arroyabe, *Das Reflektierende Subjekt: zur Erkenntnistheorie des Thomas von Aquin* (Frankfurt am Main: Athenäum, 1988); R. Fetz, *Ontologie der Innerlichkeit: Reditio completa und processio interior bei Thomas von Aquin* (Fribourg: Universitätsverlag Freiburg Schweiz, 1975); and Stephen Wang, *Aquinas and Sartre on Freedom, Personal Identity, and the Possibility of Happiness* (Washington, DC: The Catholic University of America Press, 2009).

[7] François-Xavier Putallaz, *Le sens de la réflexion chez Thomas d'Aquin* (Paris: Vrin, 1991), followed by *La connaissance de soi au XIIIe siècle: De Matthieu d'Aquasparta à Thierry de Freiberg* (Paris: Vrin, 1991). There is also Richard T. Lambert's *Self Knowledge in Thomas Aquinas: The Angelic Doctor on the Soul's Knowledge of Itself* (Bloomington, Ind.: AuthorHouse, 2007), but this work has significant deficiencies.

neo-Thomists to overstate Aquinas's differences from Kant and Descartes resulted in a preference for treating intellectual self-knowledge as exactly parallel to cognition of extramental objects. This preference was bolstered by the Aristotelian maxim that "The intellect is intelligible like other things" and the scholastic maxim that "Nothing is in the intellect that was not first in the senses."[8] Aquinas was even said to hold that one perceives one's own existence "superficially, and by non-intellectual means" (Sertillanges)[9] or that one infers one's own existence from one's acts (Roland-Gosselin and Grabmann).[10] While such interpretations were later disproven, their atmospheric influence has been remarkably persistent, leaving a lingering impression that Aquinas's theory of self-knowledge is crude, primitive, and insensitive to the phenomena.

Aquinas complicates matters by scattering discussions of self-knowledge throughout his corpus in a way that makes consolidation difficult.[11] Although he discusses human self-knowledge obliquely or directly nearly a hundred times in twenty-two works (not counting passing references, or texts on divine or angelic self-knowledge), most of these references highlight only parts or implications of his theory. In addition, it is hard to evaluate how well Aquinas's account lines up with ordinary experience, because it is not always evident what kinds of phenomena he is trying to explain in the first place. Does an assertion like "the soul perceives itself by its act" refer to a sensory consciousness, or to a unitary perception of the self as the subject of all one's actions, or to conscious reflection on one's own actions and motivations, or to some other experience altogether?

My hope is that the present study will dispel these lingering misperceptions and textual ambiguities.[12] Over the course of the next few chapters,

---

[8] This scholastic maxim is often wrongly taken as the structuring principle of Aquinas's theory of cognition, but he uses it only once, in *DV* 2.3, ad 19, where it appears as a rule about cognizing essences of material objects, not as a general rule. He prefers the weaker and more ambiguous "formulation principle of all our cognition is in the senses"; see for instance *SBDT* 6.2; *DV* 12.3, ad 2; *DV* 18.2, ad 7; and *ST* Ia.84.6.

[9] A. D. Sertillanges, *Foundations of Thomistic Philosophy*, trans. Godfrey Anstruther (St. Louis: Herder, 1931), 34. A recent proponent of this reading is Lambert, *Self Knowledge in Thomas Aquinas*, 133–52.

[10] Marie-Dominique Roland-Gosselin, "Peut-on parler d'intuition intellectuelle dans la philosophie thomiste?" in *Philosophia Perennis*, ed. F.-J. von Rintelen, vol. II (Regensburg: Habbel, 1930), 729–30; and Martin Grabmann, *Thomas Aquinas: His Personality and Thought*, trans. Virgil Michel (New York: Longmans, Green, & Co., 1928), 148.

[11] Once one begins to look for references to self-knowledge, one finds them everywhere, even in unexpected contexts, such as in questions on the cognition of singulars, divine and angelic modes of knowing, reflexive cognition of second intentions, knowledge of one's moral state, the presence of God to the soul, the metaphysics of immaterial being, the problem of multiple intellects, prelapsarian life, truth-judgments, and Trinitarian processions.

[12] I thus adopt the practice of "clarification before resolution" recently proposed by Jeffrey Brower and Susan Brower-Toland: "Although Aquinas's commentators often make bold claims about how

it will become evident that Aquinas has left us, not a primitive account of self-knowledge, but a sophisticated and compelling theory attuned to the phenomena, which grapples with many of the issues that continue to occupy contemporary philosophers. One of the main contentions of this book is that self-knowledge is central to Aquinas's conception of human cognition and personhood, to a degree that is unexpected for a medieval thinker. One cannot make complete sense of his views on intentionality, attention, personal identity, the "identity" of intellect and object in cognition, or even the nature of the human soul, without reference to his theory of self-knowledge.

This book adopts a two-pronged approach to the problem of self-knowledge in Aquinas's thought. Part I narrates the tale of the mid-thirteenth-century debate on self-knowledge, tracing the concepts and problems that it generated, together with Aquinas's appropriation and modification of these concepts throughout his career. One of the biggest challenges facing the modern reader of scholastic texts is that in the larger scheme of things, whole treatises are scarcely more than a sentence overheard from the middle of a conversation into which we are just entering. These texts were composed amidst vibrant, ongoing discussions (many of them originated from day-to-day university instruction and disputation), and they assume their audience's familiarity with a certain set of concepts, vocabulary, and problems. And despite scholasticism's legendary systematicity, a thinker's views were not set in stone, but often developed over time – or even changed completely – in response to new challenges, new insights, and newly translated sources. Thus for hermeneutic purposes, the reader must be able to distinguish cases of internal development from cases of inconsistency and from normal contextual or terminological variation.

This first part, then, aims to familiarize the reader with the "skeletal structure" of Aquinas's theory of self-knowledge – his basic assumptions, the concepts he inherits, the concerns that motivate his reshaping of the existing medieval debate, the views against which he defines his own position, and the overarching structure and development of his own theory. Chapter 1 sketches the mid-thirteenth-century Parisian debate about

his views can be used to resolve long-standing difficulties in contemporary philosophy of mind, our own view is that any such assessment is premature and must await further clarification of the views themselves" ("Aquinas on Mental Representation: Concepts and Intentionality," *Philosophical Review* 117 [2003]: 195). Consequently, I do not intend to argue for using Aquinas's theory to resolve problems in contemporary theories of self-knowledge – a project that could occupy an entire study in itself – although I will highlight relevant connections to themes in contemporary debates on self-knowledge as reference points.

self-knowledge that Aquinas inherited, with the key themes and sources that shape the landscape of debate. Chapter 2 lays the groundwork for Part II with an overview of Aquinas's theory of self-knowledge as it develops over a twenty-year period, tracing how he works through the issues raised by his predecessors and reshapes their conceptual frameworks for his own purposes.

In contrast, Part II is thematically organized around the phenomena of self-knowledge that Aquinas addresses and the problems that his explanations raise. In order to create a theory of human self-knowledge that is responsive both to the phenomena and to the constraints of a hylomorphic anthropology, his strategy is to distinguish different kinds of self-knowledge and trace each back to the nature of the human intellect. Part II thus unpacks each of these kinds of self-knowledge with reference to the philosophical problems and phenomena they are designed to address. Chapter 3, on the content of actual self-awareness, examines what is included in a "perception of one's own existence" and why day-to-day self-awareness nevertheless leaves the mind largely opaque to itself. Chapter 4, on the mode of actual self-awareness, argues that for Aquinas, prephilosophical self-awareness is a genuine intuition of myself, i.e., a direct and immediate perception of myself in my acts. Chapter 5, on habitual self-awareness, explores how the fact that *the mind already is itself* affects its self-knowledge. Chapter 6, on implicit and explicit self-awareness, argues that, for Aquinas, self-awareness is integral to the very structure of intellectual cognition, and discusses how he handles the Humean problem of the imperceptible self. Chapter 7, on quidditative self-knowledge, explores the degree to which self-opacity can be overcome by philosophical inquiry. In Chapter 8, we step back to explore the implications of Aquinas's theory of self-knowledge for his view on human personhood, focusing on three problems: subjectivity, first-person perspective, and diachronically unified consciousness.

Now one might question the practicality of combining in a single volume these two approaches, namely, the historical narrative of Part I and the problem-centered analysis of Part II. Could not the task of historical and textual contextualization have been reserved for a history-of-ideas study, in order to proceed directly to a consideration of Aquinas's arguments? In my view, this kind of methodological segregation, although commonly practiced, is risky when attempting to retrieve the philosophical insights of medieval thinkers, who were often operating under paradigms very different from our own. By setting Aquinas's arguments in the context of a historical narrative (both the broader narrative of the mid-thirteenth-century debate and the more specific narrative of the development of his own thought in response to changing conceptions of the human soul), we get a much "cleaner" portrait of the theoretical concerns that guided his treatment of self-knowledge. The historical narrative in Part I, then, makes the arguments in Part II easier to follow by clarifying these theoretical concerns, together with the terminology and conceptual framework that would have been familiar to Aquinas's audience. Likewise, it prevents us from importing foreign paradigms into his arguments or getting bogged down in false problems originating in unfamiliarity with the context.

Nevertheless, those who must go straight to Part II should at least familiarize themselves with the concepts outlined in the final sections of Chapters 1 and 2. In particular, only in the final section of Chapter 2 will the reader find a sketch of Aquinas's entire theory of self-knowledge all in the same place. One should have this sketch in hand before embarking on Part II.

Aquinas's general cognition theory

For those unfamiliar with Aquinas's cognition theory, the following summary provides a brief overview of its main points, by way of background to his theory of self-knowledge. Many aspects of this theory remain the subject of considerable debate, and I shall attempt to present them in the least controversial form possible, but it is impossible to summarize an author who has received as much scholarly attention as Aquinas without making at least a few disputed claims. So the reader should keep in mind that the following summary is an interpretation, and refer for further discussion to the extensive scholarly literature.

Aquinas's theory of cognition is grounded in an anthropological theory sometimes known as "Thomistic hylomorphism": namely, the human individual is a matter–form composite in which soul and body constitute a single substance with a single act of existing. Like plant and animal souls, the human soul is the substantial form or life-principle of an organic body. But unlike them, it survives physical death because, as an intellectual being, it is immaterial and self-subsistent. For Aquinas, the hylomorphic character of human nature is reflected in the mode of human cognition: The embodied human intellect is naturally directed toward the quiddities or essences that are in material objects, and it depends on the senses for access to such objects. Thus the senses are not the obstacle, but the vehicle, for human intellectual cognition.

But the intellect cannot simply receive raw data from the senses without some process of translation, as it were, because an enmattered

essence cannot be received into an immaterial entity like the intellect
(similarly, I cannot hear light because my eardrums are not structured as
light-receptors). In order to bridge the gap between immaterial intellect
and material realities, Aquinas posits a complex psychological process of
dematerialization. This process is accomplished by a hierarchy of cognitive powers, each grasping a different aspect of experienced reality, with
higher powers receiving content from lower powers in an increasingly
dematerialized way.

For example, suppose that as I am walking down the street, a barking dog rushes out of a yard at me. Information about the dog's sensible
attributes, such as color and the pitch of bark, are "received" by the bodily
organs (eyeball, eardrum, etc.) of my external senses. Each sense relays this
impressed sensory data, known as "sensible species," to the brain, which
is the organ of the four internal senses: common sense, imagination, esti-
mation, and memory. The common sense perceives the acts of the external
senses and bundles their disparate species, allowing me to recognize the
barking and the bristling brown fur as belonging to a single perceptual
object.[13] From this unified bundle of sense impressions, the imagination
produces and stores a mental image or "phantasm" of *this particular dog*.
The remaining two internal senses detect additional content in my sensory
experience of the dog, which they add to the stored phantasm. Memory
tracks the temporal order and duration of perceptions, so that I can later
recognize this dog as the one that *previously* attacked me. And estima-
tion (i.e., animal instinct, which Aquinas calls the "cogitative sense" in
humans) perceives harmfulness or beneficence, impelling me either to run
away or to stop and pat the dog.

So far, we have only described what Aquinas would call sensory cognition, which takes place in material cognitive powers using bodily organs
(the exterior sense-organs and the brain), and which humans and animals
share. But in humans, a further step occurs, in which I understand something universal and intelligible about the furry thing rushing toward me:
its nature, dogness. Now for Aquinas, my understanding of dogness has an

---

[13] The common sense thus is responsible for sensory consciousness, i.e., the state of communication between senses and brain. We might be tempted to see in the common sense some sort of
self-awareness, but for Aquinas, although it provides the most basic form of consciousness, one
which we share with animals, the common sense is only a sensible power of a material organ (the
brain). Therefore, it cannot fully bend back upon *itself*, which, for Aquinas, is what is properly
required for self-awareness. For further discussion, see Putallaz, *Le sens de la réflexion*, 53–4; and
Michael Stock, "Sense Consciousness According to St. Thomas," *The Thomist* 21 (1958): 415–86,
esp. 418–22.

active and a passive dimension, on account of which one must posit two intellectual powers, the "agent intellect" and the "possible intellect." The agent intellect is a creative intellectual "light" that strips away the material characteristics from the phantasm of *this dog*, producing the "intelligible species," which is an intramental likeness of the essence dogness.[14] In contrast, the possible intellect is a pure intellectual potency, awaiting the species as its form. The operation of intellectual thinking occurs when the possible intellect is "informed" by the intelligible species of dogness illuminated by the agent intellect. At that moment, my possible intellect is actually formally united with the essence in that individual dog, which is to say that I understand dogness.

For Aquinas, this intellectual grasp of essences is not a detached abstraction directed away from sensed reality, but an insight into the natures of the concrete individuals that we experience on a day-to-day basis (as when I recognize the thing rushing toward me as a dog). Our intellectual attention, he explains, is "turned toward the phantasms," so that sense and intellect are unified in my perceiving *this-sensory-individual-as-dog*. This "turn" secures a unified experience of the world in which sense and intellect cooperate, in consonance with the hylomorphic soul–body unity that is the human individual.

Later we will have the opportunity to discuss some of these features of Aquinas's cognition theory in more depth. For now, however, I want to anticipate two misconceptions that could hamper the project of determining how self-knowledge fits into this theory. First of all, one might be tempted to broaden the parameters of his account of human cognition (in the hope that doing so would open up more possibilities for self-knowledge) by appealing to the fact that he permits the disembodied soul to have a radically different kind of cognition and self-knowledge after death. But it would be a mistake to use this account of disembodied cognition to draw any conclusions about embodied human cognition. For Aquinas, one's mode of action follows one's mode of being. The embodied soul's mode of cognition thus suits its status as the form actualizing a material body: i.e., it thinks in an "embodied" way, with the cooperation of the senses. Conversely, the disembodied soul's mode of cognition suits

---

[14] Aquinas's notion of intelligible species is particularly hard to express in contemporary terms, since today terms like 'idea' or 'concept' come preloaded with implications that Aquinas might not have accepted. He insists that it is not the *object* of cognition, but only the *means* or instrument. For further discussion of his position and the scholarly debate thereon, see p. 98, note 18, pp. 109–10, and p. 141, note 22–3.

its new status as a separate substance, i.e., it thinks in the higher mode that is proper to angels. But it does so imperfectly and awkwardly, like a beginner trying to play a Mozart concerto, because its intellectual weakness makes it ill-equipped for such an exalted mode of cognition. In fact, for Aquinas this weakness is precisely why God created human intellects to be embodied in the first place. Consequently, Aquinas's account of the separated soul's mode of self-knowledge sheds no light on his thought on embodied self-knowledge.

Secondly, because Aquinas focuses so much attention on the abstractive mechanisms for dematerializing and universalizing the essences of material objects, it is easy to assume that he thinks the human mind cannot cognize immaterial singulars – such as "separate substances" (i.e., God and angels) and its own singular self.[15] If this were true, of course, self-knowledge would be impossible. But in fact, this abstractive procedure is required only when an intelligible object must be dematerialized for compatibility with the immaterial intellect: "The singular is not incompatible with intelligibility insofar as it is a singular, but insofar as it is material, because nothing is known except immaterially. And therefore if there is some immaterial singular, such as the intellect, it is not incompatible with intelligibility."[16]

Immaterial singulars, then, do not have to undergo abstraction in order to be cognized. But if they cannot be sensed, how do we encounter them so as to cognize them? Aquinas holds that in our embodied state we cannot directly cognize God and angels, but are severely limited by whatever sensible objects reveal about them (for instance, we can only reason to God's existence from his created material effects). But this solution seems inapplicable to self-knowledge; since the human mind *already is itself*, it hardly seems plausible that it would cognize itself by gleaning information about itself from sensory objects.

Here we encounter the central difficulty that Aquinas faces in making his theory of embodied human cognition accommodate self-knowledge. On the one hand, *all* embodied human thought originates in the senses, a condition imposed by human hylomorphism. On the other hand, the immaterial human mind is obviously inaccessible to the senses; and since the mind *is itself*, surely it should not have to cognize itself by reasoning from its sensory effects, as it does in cognizing other non-sensible beings, like God. We will see that his resolution of this dilemma is quite ingenious.

---

[15] See for instance Kenny, *Aquinas on Mind*, 122.
[16] *ST* Ia.86.1, ad 3; Ia.88.1, ad 5; and *DUI* 5.

Notes on terminology, texts, and translations

All translations are my own, unless otherwise indicated. Due to considerations of space, when translating medieval authors into English for in-line
citation, I include the original Latin text in a footnote when it would be
especially useful to the reader, for instance (a) when the original text is
not readily available in most libraries; or (b) in the case of short in-line
citations, when the reader might find it helpful to be able to refer immediately to a fuller version; or (c) when there are nuances in the Latin that
could be lost in translation.

The Latin terminology of Aquinas's theory of cognition poses special
challenges to the modern translator. Aquinas does not always employ a
rigorously consistent technical philosophical vocabulary, although one
can often discern overarching patterns in his usage of a given term.
Many of the most important Latin terms like *species*, *intentio*, or *ratio*
carry multiple shades of meaning that cannot be captured perfectly by
any English term. Conversely, much of our contemporary philosophical
idiom – developed within conceptual frameworks foreign to medieval
thinkers – carries definitions or atmospheric connotations that make
it difficult to repurpose for communicating medieval concepts. Many
relevant terms have no universally agreed-upon definition (e.g., 'self-
awareness,' 'self-consciousness,' etc.).

These difficulties have no perfect solution. To avoid the subtle pre-inter-
pretations that creep in when assigning English "matches" to medieval
terms, I have used ordinary everyday language as much as possible when
translating Aquinas's concepts and vocabulary. Where technical vocabulary was indispensable, I have employed contemporary philosophical ver-
nacular when the relevant terms have a single well-established meaning
and can convey his meaning without anachronism. When this is not possible, I usually translate using the closest English cognate and provide a
definition.

In particular, the following conventions should be noted. Aquinas distinguishes two main types of self-knowledge: cognition of oneself as the
first-person agent of one's acts, and cognition of the soul's nature. But
he does not assign them technical names, referring to them instead by
somewhat cumbersome descriptions. It will be convenient, then, simply
to designate the first type as 'self-awareness' and the second type as 'quidditative self-knowledge.' 'Self-awareness' is said in many ways in contemporary philosophical discourse, but I rely here on the everyday meaning
that grounds other more specific meanings – i.e., 'self-awareness' as used

here will refer to any sort of ordinary first-person cognition of "myself," as distinct from philosophical modes of self-knowledge. In addition, to translate Aquinas's term *reflexio*, I use 'reflexion' rather than 'reflection,' since in English the latter has connotations of prolonged meditation or consideration, which are unhelpful to us here.

Further, Aquinas refers to the subject and object of self-knowledge interchangeably as the soul, the intellect, the mind, or simply the individual human (e.g., Socrates). He does not make a strong distinction between the soul's cognition of itself vs. the mind's cognition of itself vs. Socrates' cognition of himself. He has certain phenomenological reasons for this that will become evident in Chapter 3 (where we will also discuss difficulties arising from this usage).[17] For convenience, I follow his practice throughout.

---

[17] Speaking precisely, Aquinas designates the soul as a metaphysical part of the individual Socrates, and the intellect as a power of the soul. But he also uses "mind" and "intellect" loosely to refer to the human soul under the aspect of its chief power, as explained in *DV* 10.1 and *ST* Ia.79.1, ad 1. Moreover, while strictly speaking "what" is performing a given act is the individual human, he allows the internal principle of action (the soul or a specific power) to stand in as the subject of a given act; see the opening paragraphs of *DUI* 3; and the justification in *ST* Ia.77.1, ad 1 [Leon. 5.237]: "Totum vero potentiale adest singulis partibus secundum totam suam essentiam, sed non secundum totam virtutem. Et ideo quodammodo potest praedicari de qualibet parte; sed non ita proprie sicut totum universale."

PART I

Historical and textual origins

CHAPTER ONE

The development of a medieval debate

The roots of the problem of self-knowledge

Aquinas's theory of self-knowledge has been broadly characterized as aiming to supplant an "Augustinian" intuitive self-knowledge in favor of an "Aristotelian" self-knowledge by abstraction.[1] But this narrative caricatures Aquinas's participation in what is in fact a much more complex historical drama unfolding in the mid-thirteenth century. The celebrity presence of Augustine and Aristotle should not overshadow the key contributions of other sources, including the Neoplatonic Christian theologian Pseudo-Dionysius and the Islamic philosophers whose writings were disseminated in the Latin West during the great translation efforts of the twelfth and thirteenth centuries. (In fact, these lesser-known sources were often responsible for shaping medieval interpretations of Augustine and Aristotle.) Nor should one underestimate the influence of Aquinas's immediate Parisian predecessors: When he first addressed the topic of self-knowledge at Paris in the early 1250s, he was not reading a set of ancient sources in a vacuum, but engaging with a living debate about self-knowledge that had already

---

[1] For a number of scholars, Aquinas's account of self-knowledge is predominantly "Aristotelian," with any references to Augustine explained as mere concessions to the latter's authoritative status. See for instance Richard T. Lambert, "Nonintentional Experience of Oneself in Thomas Aquinas," *New Scholasticism* 59 (1985): 261, n. 33; Lambert, *Self Knowledge in Thomas Aquinas*, 21–4; Jan Szaif, "Selbsterkenntnis: Thomas contra Augustinum," *Theologie und Philosophie: Vierteljahresschrift* 74 (1999): 321–37; Reginald Garrigou-Lagrange, "Utrum mens seipsam per essentiam cognoscat, an per aliquam speciem," *Angelicum* 5 (1928): 43; Mark Jordan, *Ordering Wisdom: The Hierarchy of Philosophical Discourses in Aquinas* (Notre Dame, Ind.: University of Notre Dame Press, 1986), 124–35; Olivier Boulnois, *Être et représentation: une généalogie de la métaphysique moderne à l'époque de Duns Scot, XIIIe–XIVe siècle* (Paris: Presses universitaires de France, 1999), 160; and Christopher J. Martin, "Self-Knowledge and Cognitive Ascent: Thomas Aquinas and Peter Olivi on the KK-Thesis," in *Forming the Mind: Essays on the Internal Senses and the Mind/Body Problem from Avicenna to the Medical Enlightenment*, ed. H. Lagerlund (Dordrecht: Springer, 2007), 93–108 (here 97). In reaction, some interpreters have described Aquinas's view as predominantly Augustinian; see Johannes Brachtendorf, "Selbsterkenntnis: Thomas von Aquin als Kritiker Augustins?" *Philosophisches Jahrbuch* 109.2 (2002): 255–70; Ambroise Gardeil, "La perception expérimentale de l'âme par elle-même d'après saint Thomas," in *Mélanges Thomistes* (Le Saulchoir: Kain, 1923), 219–36 (here 219).

established its own way of describing the relevant phenomena, its own vocabulary, and its own set of polarizing themes.

Most importantly, the mid-thirteenth-century debate that Aquinas inherited was not some sort of pitched battle between intuitionism and abstractionism. Rather, it is more accurate to speak of two general notions of self-knowledge that shaped the landscape of the debate, loosely associated, respectively, with Augustinianism (or Neoplatonism more generally) and Aristotelianism. The first is the notion of self-knowledge as something that naturally belongs to the mind (natural self-knowledge). For thirteenth-century thinkers, this notion was encapsulated in two maxims from Augustine's *De Trinitate*, interpreted through the lens of other Neoplatonic sources, such as Pseudo-Dionysius's *De divinis nominibus*, the anonymous Arabic *Liber de causis*, and Avicenna's *Liber de anima*. The second notion is of self-knowledge as dependent on cognition of extramental objects (dependent self-knowledge), a notion that medieval thinkers encountered in Aristotle's *De anima*, as read through the lens of an extensive commentary tradition.

By themselves, these two broad notions were not necessarily in competition, but various attempts to flesh out the details resulted in either explicit reconciliation or explicit conflict. Driven by these evolutions, a fascinating debate on self-knowledge unfolded throughout the 1230s to 1250s. Since I cannot comprehensively discuss all the relevant theories of self-knowledge, I will here pursue the more modest goal of sketching the overarching structure and key trends of the debate as a whole, to provide a clearer picture of the intellectual climate in which Aquinas's own theory of self-knowledge developed. Let us begin with the historical sources for these two central notions of self-knowledge, before turning to the mid-thirteenth-century debate itself.

Two Augustinian maxims

The story, unsurprisingly, begins with Augustine,[2] who arguably exercised the most significant influence on the mid-thirteenth-century debate by introducing themes such as the certitude of self-knowledge (via what is

---

[2] A few of the studies that focus on self-knowledge in Augustine are: Edward Booth, "St. Augustine's *'notitia sui'* Related to Aristotle and the Early Neo-Platonists," 4 pts., *Augustiniana* 27 (1977): 70–132, 364–401; 28 (1978): 183–221; 29 (1979): 97–124; Rowan Williams, "The Paradoxes of Self-Knowledge in the De Trinitate," in *Augustine: Presbyter factus sum*, ed. J.T. Lienhard (New York: Lang, 1993), 121–34; Phillip Cary, *Augustine's Invention of the Inner Self: The Legacy of a Christian Platonist* (Oxford University Press, 2000). On the purifying character of self-knowledge in Augustine and its relation to cognition of God, see John M. Rist, *Augustine: Ancient Thought*

known as Augustine's *Cogito*),[3] the special difficulty of self-knowledge,[4] the relationship between incorporeality and self-knowing,[5] the unique properties of reflexive beings,[6] and the special self-presence of the mind.[7] With his "psychological model" of the Trinity, which cast self-knowledge and self-love as images of the Trinitarian processions, Augustine also gave medieval authors a theological motivation for inquiring into self-knowledge.[8]

Most importantly for the present purposes, Augustine is the source of two maxims that his medieval readers treated as authoritative, and that effectively secured their universal commitment to some sort of natural self-knowledge. Their pithy formulation, however, left ambiguous *what kind* of self-knowledge naturally belongs to the mind (even though Augustine himself attempted to settle this question), creating an environment ripe for disagreement.

> Maxim 1: The mind knows itself by itself (*per seipsam*) because it is incorporeal.

This maxim originates in *DeTrin* 9.3.3: "Just as the mind itself gathers knowledge (*notitias*) of corporeal things through the senses of the body, so [it gathers knowledge] of incorporeals through its own self. Therefore it also knows (*nouit*) itself through itself (*per se ipsam*) because

---

Baptized (Cambridge University Press, 1996), 146–7; Gerard Verbeke, "Connaissance de soi et connaissance de Dieu chez saint Augustin," *Augustiniana* 4 (1954): 495–515; Booth, "St. Augustine's '*notitia sui*'," pt. 3, 206; Lewis Ayres, "The Discipline of Self-Knowledge in Augustine's *De trinitate* Book X," in *The Passionate Intellect: Essays on the Transformation of Classical Traditions*, ed. Ayres (London: Transaction Publishers, 1995), 261–96; and Luigi Gioia, *The Theological Epistemology of Augustine's* De Trinitate (Oxford University Press, 2008), ch. 9–10. For a more general analysis of Augustine's account of human cognition, see Gerard O'Daly, *Augustine's Philosophy of Mind* (Berkeley: University of California Press, 1987).

[3] See *De civitate Dei* 11.26 [*CCSL* 48.345:18]: "Si fallor, sum"; and *DeTrin* 10.10.14 [*CCSL* 50.327]: "Vivere se tamen et meminisse et intellegere et uelle et cogitare et scire et iudicare quis dubitet?" For comparison of Augustine and Descartes, see Étienne Gilson, *The Christian Philosophy of St. Augustine*, trans. L.E.M. Lynch (New York: Vintage, 1967), 41–3; Gareth B. Matthews, "Si Fallor, Sum," in *Augustine: A Collection of Critical Essays*, ed. R.A. Markus (New York: Anchor Books, 1972), 151–67; Stephen Menn, *Augustine and Descartes* (Cambridge University Press, 1988), 247–54; Gareth B. Matthews, *Thought's Ego in Augustine and Descartes* (Ithaca, N.Y.: Cornell University Press, 1992), 29–38; and Wayne J. Hankey, "Between and Beyond Augustine and Descartes: More Than a Source of the Self," *Augustinian Studies* 32 (2001): 65–88.

[4] *DeTrin* 10.12.19 and 10.11.17–18.

[5] See note 9 below.   [6] *DeTrin* 10.11.18.

[7] *DeTrin* 14.4.7 [*CCSL* 50A.429]: "[N]ec menti magis quidquam praesto est quam ipsa sibi."

[8] See *DeTrin* 9.2.2. Self-knowledge in Augustine thus has both theological and ethical import, i.e., it is the basis for investigating the Trinity and establishing a relationship with God (the latter is emphasized in *DeTrin* 14.12.15). For a study of the "psychological analogy" in medieval Trinitarian theology, see Russell L. Friedman, *Medieval Trinitarian Thought from Aquinas to Ockham* (Cambridge University Press, 2010).

it is incorporeal."⁹ The mind already possesses within itself everything it needs for self-knowledge: it is the sole "parent" or "generator" of its own knowledge.¹⁰ So it need not search for knowledge of itself outside in the realm of sensory experience; in fact, self-knowledge perfects and purifies the mind precisely by drawing it *away* from external things back into its inner self.

If the mind self-sufficiently generates its own self-knowledge, then there seems to be no obstacle to its doing so perpetually. Hence the second maxim, from *De Trin* 14.6.9:

> Maxim 2: The mind always remembers, always understands, and always loves itself, although it does not always think of itself as distinct from other things.¹¹ (The two halves of this maxim are often cited separately by medieval thinkers.)

This maxim encapsulates Augustine's attempt to reconcile the conflicting experiences of self-opacity and intimate self-familiarity. Earlier, in *De Trin* 10.9.12, he had described this conflict most memorably as a paradox arising from the Delphic command, "Know thyself." I recognize the command's applicability to myself because I do not yet know myself – but how did I understand the command at all unless I already knew myself? The quest for self-knowledge apparently presupposes self-knowledge!¹² The above maxim encapsulates his eventual solution: The mind always knows itself indistinctly, although it is not always attentively thinking about itself (*se cogitare*¹³). But this solution merely substitutes a puzzle for a paradox: In what sense does the mind always know itself?

Augustine's struggles to explain how the mind always knows itself result in his positing two distinct kinds of natural self-knowledge. First, in *De Trin*

---

⁹ *De Trin* 9.3.3 [*CCSL* 50.296]: "Mens ergo ipsa sicut corporearum rerum notitias per sensus corporis colligit sic incorporearum per semetipsam. Ergo et se ipsam per se ipsam nouit quoniam est incorporea. Nam si non se nouit, non se amat."

¹⁰ *De Trin* 9.12.18.

¹¹ See *De Trin* 14.6.9 [*CCSL* 50A.432]: "Sed quoniam mentem semper sui meminisse semperque se ipsam intelligere et amare, quamuis non semper se cogitare discretam ab eis quae non sunt quod ipsa est, quaerendum est quonam modo ad cogitationem pertineat intellectus, notitia uero cuiusque rei quae inest menti etiam quando non de ipsa cogitatur ad solam dicatur memoriam pertinere"; as well as the texts cited in note 14 below.

¹² *De Trin* 10.9.12; see Brian Stock, *Augustine the Reader: Meditation, Self-Knowledge, and the Ethics of Interpretation* (Cambridge, Mass.: Belknap Press, 1996), 266ff.; and Booth, "Augustine's *notitia sui*," pt. 3, 203.

¹³ Verbeke notes that *se cogitare* "indicates an actual, explicit knowledge, while [*se nosse*] designates an implicit and latent knowledge, which is the indispensable condition for explicit knowledge" ("Connaissance de soi," 505). Rist adds that *cogitare* indicates a "knowing about" which has not yet achieved the perfection of quidditative knowledge, whereas *scire* or *intellegere* signify true and full understanding (*Augustine*, 87).

10 he describes a permanent dispositional or habitual self-knowledge that naturally belongs to the power of memory – a sort of perpetual self-familiarity (*notitia, se nosse*).[14] The mind always knows itself (*nosse*) even when not thinking about itself (*cogitare*), just as a doctor "knows" grammar while thinking about medicine. Because the doctor already knew grammar all along, it seems familiar to him when he begins thinking about it again.[15] In the same way, I experience a sense of familiar recognition when I turn my attention to myself.[16] Second, in *De Trin* 14.6.9–7.10 (in a discussion that opens with the second maxim), Augustine additionally attributes to the mind a perpetual self-understanding (*se intellegere*) that naturally belongs to the power of intelligence.[17] This self-understanding is neither a habitual self-knowledge (*se nosse*) nor an attentive thought about oneself (*se cogitare*). Rather, it is a kind of peripheral, pre-conscious cognition in which the cognized entity (in this case, the mind itself) is brought out of the storehouse of memory and made present to the intellect without yet being the object of conscious cogitation.[18] He refers back to an earlier example from *De Trin* 11, in which a weary reader's eyes travel down the page, "seeing" the words without consciously registering them.[19] Similarly, the intelligence always grasps or understands itself (*se intellegere*) even when it is not turning its attention inward upon itself.[20] It is not clear, however, what phenomenon (if any) is supposed to correspond to this perpetual self-understanding, or how exactly it differs from a habitual self-cognition.

Augustine thus differentiates what one might call a "weak" kind of natural self-knowledge (*se nosse*, a disposition for thinking about oneself) and

---

[14] See *De Trin* 10.5.7, 14.6.9, and 15.15.25 (the latter using *scire* rather than *nosse*). *Nosse* is the decayed perfect of *noscere* and signifies "to be familiar with something." Augustine connects *se nosse* and self-memory especially in *De Trin* 14.6.8–9 and 10.12.19.

[15] *De Trin* 10.5.7; likewise 14.5.7 and 14.6.8.

[16] *De Trin* 14.6.8; for comments see Gilson, *Christian Philosophy of St. Augustine*, 221.

[17] *De Trin* 14.6.9 [*CCSL* 50A.432]: "[Q]uaerendum est quonam modo ad cogitationem pertineat intellectus, notitia uero cuiusque rei quae inest menti etiam quando non de ipsa cogitatur ad solam dicatur memoriam pertinere. Si enim hoc ita est, non habebat haec tria ut sui meminisset et se intellegeret et amaret, sed meminerat sui tantum, et postea cum cogitare se coepit tunc se intellexit atque dilexit."

[18] *De Trin* 14.7.10 [*CCSL* 50A.435]: "Hanc autem nunc dico intellegentiam qua intellegimus cogitantes, id est quando eis repertis quae memoriae praesto fuerant sed non cogitabantur cogitatio nostra formatur, et eam uoluntatem siue amorem uel dilectionem quae istam prolem parentemque coniungit."

[19] See the whole of book 11, especially 11.8.15. I am grateful to Susan Brower-Toland for drawing my attention to this passage.

[20] Gioia has argued that for Augustine "the mind *is* self-knowledge," to the extent that "it is even inadequate to say that the mind knows itself through itself" (*Theological Epistemology of Augustine*, 206).

a "strong" kind (*se intellegere*, a mysterious perpetual self-understanding). This distinction, however, was not captured in the two maxims above, which merely hint vaguely at *some* sort of natural self-knowledge. As we shall see in the next section, a "strong" notion of natural self-knowing would eventually enter the medieval debate, but as the result of certain Islamic influences.

Greek and Islamic Neoplatonic influences

Augustine shrouds the notion of natural self-knowledge in poetry and high flights of rhetoric, allowing the reader quick mysterious glimpses of it as he works his way through a series of often aporetic arguments in *De Trin* books 9–14. Unsurprisingly, then, twelfth-century followers of Augustine (many of whom may have only read quotes from his texts in florilegia) apparently missed the point, citing him instead in support of the attenuated claim that the incorporeal soul is teleologically oriented toward self-knowledge as its most proper activity.[21] Less concerned with explaining self-knowledge as a psychological phenomenon, they sought to teach the soul to reflect on the nobility of its immaterial being so that it can achieve this teleological goal of knowing itself and ultimately God. The notion of self-knowledge as "natural" in the sense of "teleologically perfective" also appears in Pseudo-Dionysius' *De divinis nominibus*, a work of Christian Neoplatonism familiar to Latin theologians since the ninth century, which describes circular motion as the proper motion of an intellectual being.[22] The imagery of circular motion and associated terms like *reflexio*,[23] "bending back," or *conversio*, "turning back," depicted self-knowledge as a

---

[21] See for instance the treatises on the soul by three twelfth-century Cistercian thinkers, William of St. Thierry's *De natura corporis et anima*, Isaac of Stella's *Epistola de anima*, and the anonymous *Liber de spiritu et anima*, all translated in Bernard McGinn's *Three Treatises on Man: A Cistercian Anthropology* (Kalamazoo, Mich.: Cistercian Publications, 1977). For details on the *Liber de spiritu et anima*, see note 25 below.

[22] Pseudo-Dionysius, *De divinis nominibus* 4. For historical background on Pseudo-Dionysius and his influence on medieval thought, see Beate Regina Suchla, *Dionysius Areopagita: Leben, Werk, Wirkung* (Freiburg: Herder, 2008); Tzotcho Boiadjiev, Georgi Kapriev, and Andreas Speer, eds., *Die Dionysius-Rezeption im Mittelalter: Internationales Kolloquium in Sofia vom 8. bis 11. April 1999* (Turnhout: Brepols, 2000).

[23] It is sometimes claimed that *reflexio* is an Aristotelian notion (see Dhavamony, *Subjectivity and Knowledge*, 79; George P. Klubertanz, "St. Thomas and the Knowledge of the Singular," *New Scholasticism* 26 [1952]: 135–66 [here at 146]). But while the phenomenon indicated by *reflexio* is also arguably described by Aristotle (see Lloyd P. Gerson, "*Epistrophe pros heauton*: History and Meaning," *Documenti e studi sulla tradizione filosofica medievale* 8 [1997]: 1–32 [here at 10–12]), the term *reflexio* has a Neoplatonic pedigree among thirteenth-century authors.

self-unification, in which the mind does not stray restlessly outside itself but rotates stably around its own inner core.[24]

In the late twelfth century, however, two philosophical images from the Arabic-speaking world reintroduced the notion of self-knowledge as "natural" in the sense of *embedded in the soul's very nature*, not merely in the sense of a teleological perfection. One was the *reditio completa*, or "complete return to one's essence," described in the anonymous Arabic *Liber de causis*, a work based on Proclus that reached Latin readers under an Aristotelian attribution. The other was the "Flying Man" from the *Liber de anima* of the great Persian philosopher Avicenna, an original treatise on the soul combining Aristotelian and Neoplatonic insights.[25] Together, these texts promoted the notion that self-knowledge is natural to the mind in the sense that *an incorporeal being necessarily cognizes itself just by being itself.*

The *Liber de causis*, prop. 15, describes this natural self-knowledge as a "complete return to one's essence":

> Every knower who knows his own essence is returning to his essence with a complete return (*reditione completa*) ... The reason is that, because knowledge is the knowledge of a knower, and the knower knows his essence, his operation is returning to his essence again.[26]

---

[24] See Richard Sorabji, *The Philosophy of the Commentators 200–600* AD: *A Sourcebook*, vol. I, *Psychology (with Ethics and Religion)* (Ithaca, N.Y.: Cornell University Press, 2005), 161–81. Thirteenth-century authors applied this vocabulary of turning and returning to many different kinds of cognitive phenomena, including a natural self-knowledge, an implicit or concomitant self-awareness, or a turning of one's mental attention inward.

[25] For background on these texts and their transmission in the Latin West, see respectively Richard C. Taylor, "A Critical Analysis of the Structure of the *Kalām fī mahd al-khair* (*Liber de causis*)," in *Neoplatonism and Islamic Thought*, ed. Parviz Morewedge (Albany, N.Y.: State University of New York Press, 1992), 11–40; *Von Bagdad nach Toledo: Das "Buch der Ursache" und seine Rezeption im Mittelalter*, ed. Alexander Fidora and Andreas Niederberger (Mainz: Dieterich'sche Verlagsbuchhandlung, 2001), which includes Taylor's corrections to Pattin's critical edition; and Dag Nikolaus Hasse, *Avicenna's De anima in the Latin West: The Formation of a Peripatetic Philosophy of the Soul 1160–1300* (London: The Warburg Institute, 2000), 1–12. Another important influence is the widely quoted *Liber de spiritu et anima*, which emphasizes the independence of self-knowledge from bodily sensation and the radical difference between knowing oneself and knowing other things, e.g., I.2: "Animus corporis dominator, rector, habitator videt se per se: per se ipsum semetipsum videt. Non quaerit auxilium corporalium oculorum, imo vero ab omnibus corporis sensibus tanquam impedientibus et perstrepentibus abstrahit se ad se, ut videat se in se, ut noverit se apud se" (in *Patrologia cursus completus, series Latina*, ed. J.P. Migne, vol. 40 [Paris: Garnier, 1844], 781). The text was wrongly attributed to Augustine by some medieval thinkers, but it is likely the work of Alcher of Clairvaux (Étienne Gilson, *History of Christian Philosophy in the Middle Ages* [New York: Random House, 1955], 169). I will not discuss it here, as it is mainly a pastiche of earlier sources. Aquinas not only denies its Augustinian authorship but criticizes it for saying "many things that are false and inappropriate"; see *QDSC* 11, ad 2; *DV* 15.1, ad 1; *InIoan* 10.2; *QDDA* 9, ad 1; and *QDDA* 12, ad 1.

[26] *Liber de causis*, prop. 15 [Pattin, 79–80]; for discussion, see Fidora and Niederberger, *Von Bagdad nach Toledo*, 178–9.

The "complete return to oneself" is the natural birthright of every incorporeal, intellectual entity. The return begins ontologically in self-subsistence and "completes" psychologically with self-knowledge. Now the restrictive clause in the first line ("Every knower who knows his own essence") suggests that the "complete return" is only achieved by some knowers, resonating with the twelfth-century Latin notion of self-knowledge as the teleological goal of intellectual beings. But a variant text was circulating without the restriction: "Every knower knows his own essence, and therefore is returning to his essence with a complete return."[27] This variant suggests the stronger claim that intellectual entities know themselves just by being themselves.

This stronger claim was reinforced by the dramatic image of the "Flying Man" in Avicenna's *Liber de anima* I.1, a thought-experiment designed to "awaken" the reader to the soul's distinctness from the body.[28] Avicenna asks the reader to consider an adult man instantaneously created in a state of total sensory deprivation, floating in air "in such a way that the sensible density of the air does not touch him," and with no limb touching another. Nevertheless, Avicenna insists, despite his ignorance of all extramental reality, this so-called flying man would still cognize his own self. The self or "I" that he grasps cannot be something sensible, since he lacks sensation. It must therefore be the soul, distinct from the body.[29]

---

[27] This reading appears in MS Toledo *Bibl. dei Cabildo* 97–1 (see Pattin, 14, for details). Aquinas cites this variant in *SLDC* 15 and *DV* 8.6, ad 5 s.c.; elsewhere, he cites the version in Pattin's edition. See also Bonaventure's paraphrase in *Collationes De septem donis Spiritus Sancti* 8 [Quar. 5.498]: "Omnis substantia intellectualis est sciens et rediens supra se reditione completa."

[28] Like the *Liber de causis*, then, Avicenna's "Flying Man" appeals to self-knowledge to demonstrate the immateriality of the soul. For literature on the Flying Man, see S. Pines, "La conception de la conscience de soi chez Avicenne et chez Abū'l-Barakāt al-Baghdādī," *Archives d'histoire doctrinale et littéraire du moyen âge* 29 (1954): 21–56; M.E. Marmura, "Avicenna's 'Flying Man' in Context," *Monist* 69 (1986): 383–95; T.-A. Druart, "The Soul and Body Problem: Avicenna and Descartes," in *Arabic Philosophy and the West: Continuity and Interaction*, ed. Druart (Washington, DC: Center for Contemporary Arab Studies, Georgetown University, 1998), 27–48; Mehdi Aminrazavi, "Avicenna's (Ibn Sīnā) Phenomenological Analysis of How the Soul (Nafs) Knows Itself ('ilm al-hūdūri), in *The Passions of the Soul in the Metamorphosis of Becoming*, ed. Anna-Teresa Tymieniecka (Dordrecht: Kluwer, 2003), 91–100; Ahmed Alwishah, "Avicenna's Philosophy of Mind: Self-Awareness and Intentionality" (PhD diss., University of California, Los Angeles, 2006); Jari Kaukua, "Avicenna on Subjectivity: A Philosophical Study" (PhD diss., University of Jyväskylä, 2007); Deborah Black, "Avicenna on Self-Awareness And Knowing that One Knows," in *The Unity of Science in the Arabic Tradition*, ed. S. Rahman, T. Hassan, T. Street (Dordrecht: Springer Science, 2008), 63–87; and Luis Xavier López-Farjeat, "Self-Awareness (Al-Shu'Ūr Bi-Al-Dhât) in Human and Non-Human Animals in Avicenna's Psychological Writings," *in Oikeiosis and the Natural Bases of Morality: From Classical Stoicism to Modern Philosophy*, ed. Alexander Vigo (New York: Georg Olms Verlag, 2012), 121–40. For a comparison of Avicenna's intended purpose for the "Flying Man" to its use by the early medievals, see Hasse, *Avicenna's De anima*, 80–92.

[29] See Avicenna, *Liber de anima* I.1 [Van Riet 1.36–7]: "[N]on enim dubitabit affirmare se esse, nec tamen affirmabit exteriora suorum membrorum, nec occulta suorum interiorum nec animum nec

This thought-experiment has important implications for self-knowledge.[30] It suggests, for instance, that to apprehend "myself" is to apprehend my existing soul:

> The intention of that which I cognize to be myself is that which I designate in speech when I say "I sensed," "I cognized," "I did" – properties that are conjoined in one thing that is myself. If someone should say, "You do not know that this is the soul," I would say that I always scientifically know it, and that this is the intention that I call "soul," but perhaps I do not know that it is named "soul."[31]

Avicenna even argues that behind all the layers of bodily consciousness, my soul is *never ignorant of its own existence and incorporeality*. Self-ignorance is a superficial failure to attend to a self that is always already known:

> And because I inquire whether [the soul] exists and whether it is not a body, I am not therefore ignorant of it with an absolute ignorance, although I disregard it. Often indeed the cognition of a thing is nearby, but because it is disregarded, it becomes unknown and afterwards is sought from more remote places; but sometimes in order to cognize a thing it is sufficient that one be awakened (*excitari*). Yet because it is easy, man neglects it and his mind does not notice (*animadvertit*) it.[32]

For Avicenna, then, a non-conscious self-knowing is built into the very essence of the soul. As Black explains: "If the soul is essentially immaterial and rational, then there can be no point in its existence at which it is not in some sense actually cognitive. To the extent that the human soul is truly an intellective soul, it must have the characteristic property of all

---

cerebrum, nec aliquid aliud extrinsecus, sed affirmabit se esse, cuius non affirmabit longitudinem nec latitudinem nec spissitudinem … [I]mmo non eget corpore ad hoc ut sciat animum et percipiat eam"; V.7 [Van Riet 2.162]. For discussion, see Druart, "The Soul and Body Problem," 28 and 38–44. I cite the Latin Avicenna since this is the version with which the medievals were familiar.

[30] Deborah Black, for instance, has convincingly argued that Avicenna's ultimate goal here is to establish a ground for the unity of consciousness ("Avicenna on Self-Awareness," 23; see also Druart, "The Soul and Body Problem," 33).

[31] Avicenna, *Liber de anima* V.7 [Van Riet 2.164]: "[U]nde ipsum membrum essentialiter non est id quod percipio esse ego essentialiter, sed accidentaliter; intentio autem de eo quod cognosco quod sit ego est id quod designo mea dictione cum dico 'sensi,' 'cognovi,' 'feci': quae proprietates coniunctae sunt in uno quod est ego. Si quis autem dixerit: 'nescis quia hoc anima est', dicam me semper scire, et quia haec est intentio quam voco animam, sec fortassis nescio illam appellari animam."

[32] Avicenna, *Liber de anima* V.7 [Van Riet 2.166–7]: "Et quia inquiro eius esse, et an sit non corpus, non ideo sum ignarus eius ignorantia absoluta, quamvis negligam illud: plerumque enim cognitio rei in proximo est, sed quia negligitur, fit ignota et postea requiritur ex locis remotioribus; aliquando autem ad cognoscendum rem sufficit excitari, sed quia est facile, homo negligit illud et eius ingenium non animadvertit illud." Hasse (*Avicenna's De anima*, 84–7) and Marmura ("The Flying Man in Context," 390–3) have noted the role of the "Flying Man" thought-experiment as a *tanbīh* or "awakening" to a reality that the soul already knows.

subsistent intellects, that of being actually intelligible to itself."[33] Just by being a soul, it knows not only its existence, but also its essential properties like incorporeality.[34]

Avicenna was enormously influential on early thirteenth-century thought on the soul, and his "Flying Man" cleared a conceptual space for a "strong" notion of natural self-knowledge as an *actual, non-conscious self-knowing that is built into the very nature of the soul*. We can call this "natural supraconscious self-knowing." Reinforced by the two authoritative maxims from Augustine (as well as by certain readings of the *Liber de causis*), natural supraconscious self-knowing became a staple of mid-thirteenth-century theories. It is particularly important for our purposes, because it will be the main opposing theory that Aquinas targets in his theory of self-knowledge.

Aristotle and his commentators

A new strain of influence entered the medieval self-knowledge debate with the Latin translation of Aristotle's *De anima* and parts of the attendant Greek and Arabic commentary tradition.[35] This sprawling Aristotelian tradition affected the mid-thirteenth-century conversation about self-knowledge in the same way that it affected cognition theories generally – by modeling a more analytical and less analogy-driven approach to human psychology.

---

[33] Black, "Avicenna on Self-Awareness," 23; Kaukua, "Subjectivity in Avicenna," 118ff.; Farjeat, "Self-Awareness." In *Notes* Avicenna goes so far as to assert: "Our awareness of ourselves is our very existence ... Self-awareness is natural to the self, for it is its existence itself, so there is no need of anything external by which we perceive the self. Rather, the self is that by which we perceive the self" (trans. in Black, "Avicenna on Self-Awareness," 65). This text, however, was not available to thirteenth-century Latin thinkers.

[34] This notion could have been reinforced by a mistake in the Latin translation of Avicenna's *Liber de anima* V.2 [Van Riet 2.95]: "[A]nima enim apprehendit essentiam suam semper, quamvis plerumque apprehendit eam separatam a corporibus cum quibus est ipsa, sicut iam ostendimus." Where the Latin has "separate" (*separatam*), the Arabic reads "conjoined," as Van Riet's critical apparatus points out.

[35] For information on which texts were available in Latin and when, see Charles Burnett, "Arabic into Latin: The Reception of Arabic Philosophy into Western Europe," in *The Cambridge Companion to Arabic Philosophy*, ed. Peter Adamson and Richard C. Taylor (Cambridge University Press, 2005), 370–404. On Aristotle's treatment of intellectual self-knowledge, see for instance Joseph Owens, "A Note on Aristotle, *De anima* 3.4, 429b9," *Phoenix* 30, no. 2 (1976): 107–18; and Charles Kahn, "Aristotle on Thinking," in *Essays on Aristotle's De anima*, ed. M.C. Nussbaum and A.O. Rorty (Oxford: Clarendon Press, 1992), 359–79. For an overview comparing Aristotle and some Arabic thinkers (Avicenna and Averroes) in the history leading up to the late thirteenth-century Franciscan theories of self-knowledge, see Boulnois, *Être et représentation*, ch. 3.

But Aristotle also made an important doctrinal contribution by spurring his medieval readers to consider a new notion of self-knowledge as dependent on cognition of extramental objects, requiring the intellect's reception of a "species" or "likeness" or "intention." This notion was associated with a maxim taken from *De anima* III.4.430a2:

> The intellect is intelligible like other intelligibles.[36]

This notion of dependent self-knowledge was integrated unevenly into the thirteenth-century debate under a wide variety of interpretations. One strand of discussion centered on two ways in which the intellect could be said to cognize itself: by a species or "intention" (*per speciem, per intentionem*, generally taken to be the Aristotelian position), vs. by its essence (*per essentiam, per se*, associated with Neoplatonic sources such as Augustine).[37] This distinction relies on a view, common at the time, that a thing is cognized according to the mode of being that it has in the soul. Some things (such as virtues, thoughts, passions, and the soul itself) exist *in* the soul "in their essence," i.e., in their real being, and are therefore cognized by their own being (*per seipsam, per praesentiam, per essentiam*).[38] Other things, however (birds, trees, rocks) exist in their real being *outside* the soul: i.e., the proper ontological place for this bird, that tree, is in the extramental realm. Such things can only be made present to the soul by a likeness or species existing in the soul, so they are cognized by that likeness (*per similitudinem, per speciem, per intentionem*). When "cognizing *per speciem*" is construed as referring to the mode in which extramental objects are made present to the intellect, the notion of cognizing oneself *per speciem* seems absurd. The mind is by definition not an extramental object and it already *is* itself, so surely it does not require a species to make itself intramentally present?

---

[36] In the Latin *nova translatio* which Aquinas was using after 1265, this passage reads, "Et ipse autem intelligibilis est sicut intelligibilia" [430a2, in Leon. 45/1.214].

[37] For instance, see Averroes, *Commentarium magnum in Aristotelis De anima* III.15 [Crawford, 434:6–20], relying perhaps on an earlier form of this distinction in Alexander of Aphrodisias's *De anima* 3.17.86.14–23, between knowing oneself "essentially" vs. knowing oneself "accidentally" in one's actualization by an intelligible species (ed. Athanasios P. Fotinis [Washington, DC: University Press of America, 1979], 112).

[38] Sometimes, however, something is said to be known *per essentiam* when the known object is present to the intellect by *the intellect's very essence* (as when God knows all things by *his* essence; this usage of the phrase *per essentiam* appears most commonly in discussions of divine and angelic knowledge). See Bonaventure, *De scientia Christi* 2, ad 11 [Quar. 5.10]: "[T]unc autem est immediata coniunctio secundum rationem *cognoscendi*, quando cognoscens cognoscit cognoscibile vel per essentiam cognoscentis, vel per essentiam cogniti."

But another strand of discussion emerged from a more sophisticated way of thinking about what it means to cognize oneself *per speciem*, transmitted to Latin medieval readers via the Greek and Arabic Aristotelian commentary tradition.[39] According to this view, the intellect does use a species to cognize itself – not an abstracted species of itself, but the abstracted species of its extramental object. This species does not make an absent intellect vicariously present to itself, but rather actualizes the intellect, making the intellect manifest to itself. The *locus classicus* for discussing this theme in the Aristotelian commentary tradition was *De anima* III.4.429b5–10:[40]

> Once the mind has become each set of its possible objects, as a man of science has … its condition is still one of potentiality, but in a different sense from the potentiality which preceded the acquisition of knowledge by learning or discovery: the mind too is then able to think *itself*.[41]

For commentators, this text suggests that since the mind and its object are one in the act of understanding, sharing one and the same form,[42] the mind's own intelligibility depends on its reception of intelligible forms. For instance, the Arabic philosopher Averroes argues that once the intellect has been perfected by acquiring intelligible forms, "then it will understand itself insofar as it is nothing else but the forms of the things, inasmuch as it draws them out from matter. It is as if it understands itself in an accidental way."[43] Alexander of Aphrodisias, Themistius, and others

---

[39] A major source for their information about untranslated sources in this tradition seems to have been Averroes' *Commentarium magnum in Aristotelis De anima*.

[40] The same theme appears in *Met.* XII.9.1072b19–21 and 1074b35–1075a5.

[41] *De anima* III.4.429b5–10, trans. J.A. Smith in *The Basic Works of Aristotle*, ed. Richard McKeon (New York: Random House, 1941), 590. There is a scholarly dispute over the placement of the last phrase, 429b9–10, for which Bekker gives καὶ αὐτὸς δὲ αὑτὸν τότε δύναται νοεῖν (accurately reproduced in the Latin text that Aquinas was following as: "Et ipse autem se ipsum tunc potest intelligere"; *InDA* III.2 [Leon. 45/1.208, at 429b9]). Owens ("Note on *De anima* 429b9," 107–18) and Kahn ("Aristotle on Thinking," 373) argue that the reading as given here is correct. In addition, sometimes δὲ αὐτὸν is read as δι' αὐτοῦ ("The mind too is then able to think *through* itself"), as in *De anima Books II and III*, trans. D.W. Hamlyn (Oxford University Press, 1993), 58; and *Aristotelis De anima*, ed. W.D. Ross (Oxford University Press, n.d.), 70. According to this alternate reading, the closing remark at 429b9–10 has nothing to do with self-knowledge, but rather describes a facility for thinking about what one has previously learned.

[42] See *De anima* III.4.430a3–4; and III.5.430a19–20, where thought is said to be identical with its object.

[43] Averroes, *Commentarium magnum in Aristotelis De anima* III.8 [Crawford, 420:19–24]: "Idest, et cum intellectus fuerit in hac dispositione, tunc intelliget se secundum quod ipse non est aliud nisi forme rerum, inquantum extrahit eas a materia. Quasi igitur se intelligit ipse modo accidentali, ut dicit Alexander, idest secundum quod accidit intellectis rerum quod fuerint ipse, idest essentia eius"; here trans. Richard Taylor, in *Long Commentary on the De anima* (New Haven: Yale University Press, 2009), 335. For a similar interpretation in recent Aristotle scholarship, see Kahn, "Aristotle on Thinking," 373.

even argue that acts of cognizing extramental objects are *necessarily* acts of cognizing oneself: "When [intellect] thinks these objects it thinks itself, if that is, the things that it thinks become intellect when they are thought. For if the actual intellect is [in actuality] the things that are thought and it does think them, then it comes to think itself."[44]

Thus Aristotle's medieval readers had a number of strategies available for dealing with the Aristotelian maxim and the associated claim that the intellect cognizes itself *per speciem*. Those less committed to a charitable reading of Aristotle vis-à-vis Neoplatonic sources could flatly reject self-knowledge *per speciem*, on the grounds that it would be absurd for self-knowledge to depend on anything that the mind receives from outside itself. Or, they could distinguish different kinds of self-knowledge, arguing that the intellect is manifested to itself on a conscious level only in cognizing extramental objects *per speciem*, while agreeing with the Neoplatonic tradition that the intellect also always cognizes itself supraconsciously *per essentiam*. We will see that William of Auvergne, Jean de la Rochelle, and Bonaventure take the first path, and Albert the Great takes the second.

The mid-thirteenth-century debate

The medieval debate on self-knowledge emerges at the intersection of these influences. We will focus here on the discussion centered at Paris from the 1230s to 1250s, which provides the immediate context for Aquinas.[45] He studied with Albert the Great from 1245 to 1252 in Paris and then in Cologne; commented on the *Sentences* at Paris from 1252 to 1256 (a project that saw his first attempt to explain self-knowledge); and occupied his first magistral chair there from 1256 to 1259. In 1257–58 he disputed *De veritate*

---

[44] Alexander of Aphrodisias, *De intellectu* 109.7, trans. Frederic M. Schroeder and Robert B. Todd, in *Two Greek Aristotelian Commentators on the Intellect: The* De intellectu *Attributed to Alexander of Aphrodisias and Themistius' Paraphrase of Aristotle* De anima *3.4–8* (Toronto: Pontifical Institute of Mediaeval Studies, 1990), 50; see also his *De anima* 3.18.86.23–8. Likewise, see Themistius, *Paraphrase of* De anima 95.9, trans. Schroeder and Todd, 82: "In this way the intellect too, when inactive, is said to have the state of possessing thoughts, but when active towards one of its thoughts is at that time identical with what is being thought, and by thinking that thing thinks itself too"; Simplicius, *On Aristotle's* On the Soul *3.1–5*, at 429b9, trans. H.J. Blumenthal (Ithaca, N.Y.: Cornell University Press, 2000), 94; and Philoponus, *In de intellectu*, in *Commentaire sur le* De anima *d'Aristote, traduction de Guillaume de Moerbeke*, ed. G. Verbeke, Corpus Latinum Commentariorum in Aristotelem Graecorum 3 (Paris: Éditions Béatrice-Nauwelaerts, 1966), 20–1. For self-awareness among Neoplatonic commentators, see Matthias Perkams, *Selbstbewusstsein in der Spätantike: Die neuplatonischen Kommentare zu Aristoteles'* De anima (Berlin: de Gruyter, 2008).

[45] For basic biographical, bibliographical, and doctrinal information about the authors discussed here, see *A Companion to Philosophy in the Middle Ages*, ed. Jorge J. Gracia and Timothy B. Noone (Oxford: Blackwell, 2003).

q. 10 there, whose eighth article presents for the first time his full-fledged theory of self-knowledge.[46]

In the early stages of the debate, during the 1230s, we find a group of thinkers looking to Avicenna's "Flying Man" to shed light on the second Augustinian maxim's reference to the mind's perpetual self-understanding,[47] a procedure that is typical of a broader thirteenth-century trend known as "Avicennizing Augustinianism."[48] This group included two of Avicenna's most enthusiastic thirteenth-century proponents at the University of Paris: Jean de la Rochelle in his *Tractatus de divisione multiplici potentiarum animae* (1233–39) and *Summa de anima* (1235–36), and William of Auvergne in his *De anima* (1235–40).[49]

Following the trail of Avicenna's "Flying Man," Jean and William posit two kinds of human self-knowledge: a perpetual natural supraconscious self-knowing and intermittent acts of thinking about oneself. Their descriptions of supraconscious self-knowing are frustratingly imprecise. They are content to insist that genuine self-ignorance is impossible, without ever

---

[46] For a detailed history of this period in Aquinas's life, see Jean-Pierre Torrell, *Saint Thomas Aquinas*, vol. I, *The Person and His Work*, rev. edn., trans. Robert Royal (Washington, D.C.: The Catholic University of America Press, 2005), 18–74. For dating of *DV* 10, see James A. Weisheipl, *Friar Thomas d'Aquino: His Life, Thought, and Works*, 2nd edn. (Washington, D.C.: The Catholic University of America Press, 1983), 126.

[47] For the use of Avicenna's *Liber de anima* by Jean de la Rochelle, William of Auvergne, and Albert the Great, see Hasse, *Avicenna's* De anima, 42–51 and 60–9.

[48] The name was coined by Étienne Gilson in "Les sources gréco-arabe de l'augustinisme avicennisant." *Archives d'histoire doctrinale et littéraire du moyen âge* 4 (1929–30): 5–149. Boulnois mentions self-knowledge as one of the themes affected by this trend (see *Être et représentation*, 165–7).

[49] I set aside Alexander of Hales, since his position on self-knowledge is similar to and less well developed than Jean de la Rochelle's. Jean has received very little scholarly attention. For recent studies of his life and writings, see Jacques Guy Bougerol, "Jean de la Rochelle: Les oeuvres et les manuscrits," *Archivum Franciscanum historicum* 87 (1994): 205–15; Jörg Alejandro Tellkamp, "Einleitung," in *Johannes von la Rochelle, Summa de anima, Tractatus de viribus animae, Lateinisch–Deutsch* (Freiburg: Herder, 2010), 9–43. On his approach to the soul and his use of sources, see P. Michaud-Quantin, "Les puissances de l'âme chez Jean de la Rochelle," *Antonianum* 24 (1949): 489–505; and on the relationship between his *Summa* and *Tractatus*, see Odon Lottin, *Psychologie et morale aux XIIe et XIIIe siècles*, vol. VI (Gembloux: Duculot, 1960), 181–206. In contrast, William of Auvergne is one of the better-known early thirteenth-century authors; see Ernest A. Moody, "William of Auvergne and His Treatise *De anima*," in his *Studies in Medieval Philosophy, Science, and Logic, Collected Papers 1933–1969* (Berkeley: University of California Press, 1975), 1–109; Steven P. Marrone, *William of Auvergne and Robert Grosseteste: New Ideas of Truth in the Early Thirteenth Century* (Princeton University Press, 1983); Roland Teske, "William of Auvergne's Spiritualist Concept of the Human Being," in *Autour de Guillaume d'Auvergne († 1249)*, ed. Franco Morenzoni and Jean-Yves Tilliette (Turnhout: Brepols, 2005), 35–53. Teske documents Avicenna's influence on William in "William of Auvergne's Debt to Avicenna," in *Studies in the Philosophy of William of Auvergne, Bishop of Paris 1228–1249*, ed. Roland Teske (Milwaukee, Wis.: Marquette University Press, 2006): 217–37. An English translation of William's *De anima*, with notes and corrections of the corrupted Latin text, can be found in *The Soul*, trans. Roland J. Teske (Milwaukee, Wis.: Marquette University Press, 2000).

specifying the status of the self-knowledge the soul *does* have, or explaining what it means to cognize oneself without being conscious of oneself.[50]

Despite their shared commitment to a supraconscious self-knowing, these two thinkers diverge on an important point. According to Jean, the soul always knows its *existence* as something numerically distinct from its body, but he apparently does not think it thereby always knows *what it is*, i.e., an incorporeal being.[51] It is not clear why Jean thinks that the soul's self-identity would give it permanent privileged access to its own existence but not its own essence. Nevertheless this unusual attempt to accommodate self-opacity will later be repeated in Aquinas's key distinction between cognizing the soul's existence vs. essence.

William has no such scruples, appealing to Avicenna's "Flying Man" to support the claim that the soul can never be ignorant, not only of its own existence, but of *anything that is essential to itself,* including its immateriality, or even its own genus and species.[52] In constructing an unimpressive proof for the immateriality of the soul, he argues that the soul knows its entire being independently from sensation. Since "separation and conjunction are contraries," he reasons, "it is impossible for the human soul to think of itself as separate from anything to which it is essentially conjoined" – or vice versa.[53] If the human soul were corporeal, it could not conceive of itself as separate from matter; thus, since some philosophers have conceived of the soul as immaterial, it must be immaterial. (One might well object, however, that this reasoning equally supports the opposite conclusion: Some have conceived of the soul as corporeal, so it is corporeal.) William concludes that denial of the soul's incorporeality is caused by inattention to what one already knows.[54] Self-ignorance, in his

---

[50] See Jean de la Rochelle, *Summa de anima* 1.1 [Bougerol, 51–2]: "Impossibile est igitur quod ignoret se esse"; and William of Auvergne, *De anima* 1.4 and 2.13–14. On ambiguity as a didactic strategy in William, see Marrone, *William of Auvergne and Robert Grosseteste*, 68–9.

[51] In the *Summa de anima* he separates his brief argument "that the soul is" (*quod sit anima*) in 1.1 from the inquiry into "what the soul is" (*quid sit anima*) introduced in 1.2 and developed subsequently. Interestingly, at the end of 1.1, he explicitly casts the former as the ground for the latter.

[52] William, *De anima* 2.13 [Paris 2.83]: "Procul dubio dicet se non habere corpus, et eodem modo negabit de se partes omnes et singulas corporis humani … [A]liud autem erit apud ipsum esse quod concedet de se, aliud vero quod negabit de se: quia igitur negabit de se esse corpus, concedet autem de se esse suum, sive quod habet et sentit se habere, necesse est eam habere esse quod non est corporis et propter hoc necesse est ipsam non esse corpus."

[53] William, *De anima* 2.14. This unusual claim is predicated on a widely held premise that William states in *De anima* 3.12 (note 59 below): namely, that whatever exists in the soul is cognized by its very presence. William thus reasons, if the soul were composed of matter, that composition would necessarily be cognized from its presence in the soul.

[54] William, *De anima* 2.14 [Paris 2.84]: "[E]ssentialia sua ignorare non est possibile eidem"; and 3.13 [Paris 2.104]: "Declaratum igitur est tibi per hoc propter quod difficile valde est animabus

view, amounts to a sort of insanity, a lapse into contradiction caused by excessive sensory distraction.

Another important feature of Jean's and William's theories of self-knowledge is the way that they apply the distinction mentioned earlier, between things like virtues that are cognized by their ontological inherence in the soul (*per seipsam/essentiam*) vs. things like horses or dogs that are made present to the mind by abstracted species (*per speciem*).[55] Jean insists that the soul cognizes itself by turning inwards, without the assistance of an "extrinsic light." "By an innate light it cognizes that it exists, that it can reason and sense, that it has scientific knowledge of something or is ignorant thereof, that it is just or unjust – by turning to itself."[56] In the *Tractatus* he is still more explicit: The soul cognizes itself, not by an abstracted species or form, but simply by turning its attention inwards.[57] He even says that the soul *is* the form or species by which it cognizes itself, a formulation that will reappear in Albert.[58]

William likewise asserts that the soul cognizes itself simply by looking to itself, but the details of his account reveal the surprisingly blurry boundary between this assertion and the assertion of some sort of cognition-dependent self-knowledge. In *De anima* 3.12 he argues that just as individual human beings are revealed by their sensible accidents to the observer, so too my soul is manifested to me by its accidents – its "science, doubts, opinions, joys, sorrows, fears, and courage." It is absurd to deny that I can grasp such accidents: indeed, Socrates' accidents are only accessible to me "by their image or sign" (i.e., their impression existing accidentally in my soul). Since accidents like doubt and joy inhere in

---

nostris semetipsas vere, ac pure seorsum a fantasiis sensibilibus cogitare: quamquam sicut tibi multipliciter praeostensum est impossibile sit eidem veritatem vel essentiam suam ignorare ... cogitare autem se difficillimum est eidem."

[55] See p. 27 above.

[56] Jean, *Summa* 2.116 [Bougerol, 279]: "Ad cognoscenda uero ea que sunt intra animam, ut est ipsa anima et potencia ipsius et habitus sciencie et uirtutes, non indiget anima lumine extrinseco; sed lumine innato cognoscit se esse, se posse ratiocinari, sentire, se scire aliquid uel ignorare, iustam uel iniustam esse, per conuersionem ad se". Compare Bonaventure, note 66 below, and Albert, note 71 below.

[57] Jean, *Tractatus* 2.22 [Michaud-Quantin, 94]: "Est autem alius modus operationis respectu formarum, que non indigent abstractione, sicut sunt virtutes et scientie et alia, que sunt in anima sicut in subiecto ... cum sint in anima aut possint esse secundum rem, non indigent speciebus, quibus cognoscuntur, que non sint ipse res, ideo ad cognoscenda hec non requiritur nisi conuersio intellectus possibilis cum illuminatione intellectus agentis"; see also 2.20 [Michaud-Quantin 90–1]."

[58] Jean, *Summa* 2.113 [Bougerol, 270–1]: "Forma ergo qua cognoscitur ipsa anima uel angelus est ipsa anima racionalis que, cum utitur se ut similitudine, cognoscit se et intelligit referendo ad se.... Vnde ibi differens est solum secundum racionem, et non secundum rem, res que cognoscitur et forma qua cognoscitur"; see also *Tractatus* 2.15 [Michaud-Quantin, 82–3]. Compare Albert in note 72 below.

my soul in a superior mode (i.e., in their real being), I cognize them "by themselves" with "incomparably greater" certitude. William concludes: "No man is permitted to be ignorant of his soul, because he necessarily has to cognize so many and so great and such things about it on account of the very presence of their truth that in no way can he be ignorant that his very soul is undergoing them."[59] This passage is especially perplexing, since it is unclear what kind of self-knowledge he is describing. Despite the comparison to seeing visible objects, he cannot be describing acts of attentively thinking about oneself – otherwise, his concluding comment would mean, absurdly, that one attentively thinks about every mental act. Nor is he describing a supraconscious self-knowing, since the latter is perpetual, while mental acts come and go. Rather, he is arguably hinting at the notion that an agent is aware of acting because of the internally felt presence of the act. If so, even though this kind of self-knowing is said to occur "by itself," it must have a certain dependence on cognition of extramental realities (at least in most instances), since these internally felt acts are usually caused by extramental objects.

Over the next two decades, the 1240s and 1250s, a new approach to self-knowledge emerged in a second group of thinkers, who sought to resolve the ambiguities in earlier theories by applying Aristotelian psychology more rigorously and by specifying precisely *what kinds* of self-knowledge the soul already has. Most notably, they introduced into the debate a distinction between habitual and actual self-knowledge. Two such thinkers were Bonaventure (commentary on the *Sentences*, written 1250–52 and revised 1254–57) and Albert the Great (*De homine, c.* 1241–42, commentary on the *Sentences*, 1243–49, and commentary on *De anima*, 1254–57), who exemplify two different methods of resolving the ambiguities endemic to earlier theories.[60]

---

[59] William, *De anima* 3.12 [Paris 2.103]: "Jam igitur declaratum est tibi per hoc quod incomparabiliter major est unicuique homini cognitio animae suae sive de anima sua quam possit esse eidem cognitio sensibilis cujuscumque alterius hominis. Declaratum etiam est tibi quod nullus homo permittitur ignorare animam suam, cum tot et tanta ac talia de ipsa cognoscere necesse habeat propter ipsam suae praesentiam veritatis quae nullo modorum ipsam ignorare animam suam pati possunt." See also 2.10.

[60] For a summary of the psychological and anthropological principles underlying Albert's theory of self-knowledge, see Leonard A. Kennedy, "The Nature of the Human Intellect According to St. Albert the Great," *Modern Schoolman* 37 (1960): 121–37; and, in more depth, Arthur Schneider, "Die Psychologie Alberts des Grossen," Beiträge zur Geschichte der Philosophie des Mittelalters 4, parts 5–6 (Münster: Aschendorff, 1903/1906), especially the second section, on the Neoplatonic elements in Albert's thought; as well as Bernhard Blankenhorn, "How the Early Albertus Magnus Transformed Augustinian Interiority," *Freiburger Zeitschrift für Philosophie und Theologie* 58 (2011): 351–86; and Markus Führer, "Albertus Magnus' Theory of Divine Illumination," in *Albertus Magnus: Zum Gedenken nach 800 Jahren: Neue Zugänge, Aspekte und Perspektiven*, ed. Walter Senner *et al.*

Bonaventure's theory of self-knowledge is clear and simple. He admits just two kinds of self-knowledge corresponding roughly to Augustine's *se nosse* and *se cogitare*:[61]

(1) an innate, habitual aptness for thinking about oneself;
(2) intermittent acts of thinking about oneself by turning one's attention inward.

Bonaventure apparently does not endorse a supraconscious self-knowing.[62] Instead, he holds that the soul always cognizes itself "from its birth" or "by its heritage" (*a sui ipsius origine*) only in the sense of having an "innate disposition" for self-knowledge. The soul has this habit simply because *it is itself* and is therefore always self-present.[63] Interestingly, Bonaventure often avoids the term "habit" altogether, preferring to use adjectives: The soul is "apt" (*habilis*) to know itself,[64] or naturally ready to reflect upon itself (*nata est super se reflecti*).[65] This usage, perhaps, betrays a preference for thinking of habitual self-knowledge as part of the soul's essential being, rather than as something innate but accidental to the soul.

Although Bonaventure is not a proponent of the soul's *actually* cognizing itself by its nature (i.e., supraconscious self-knowing), it is not because he defends the notion of dependent self-knowledge. Quite the contrary: For him, the soul thinks of itself whenever it wants, just by turning its

(Berlin: Akademie Verlag, 2001), 141–55. For an introduction to Bonaventure's thought, see Étienne Gilson's *The Philosophy of St. Bonaventure*, trans. Illtyd Trethowan and Frank J. Sheed (Paterson, N.J.: Desclée, 1965).

[61] Bonaventure, *Sent* III.27, dub. 3 [Quar. 3.618]: "[I]lla tria, quae tanguntur in littera, dupliciter possunt attribui animae, videlicet *actu* vel *habitu*. Si *habitu*, sic vere et semper attribuuntur ei, quoniam anima per se ipsam nata est sui meminisse, se intelligere et se diligere. Si autem intelligatur in *actu*; sic non semper sibi attribuuntur, quia non semper se cogitat nec semper super se convertitur"; as well as I.3.2.1.2, ad 4.

[62] In two theological texts, Bonaventure says that "the eye of the mind sees itself first, and other things afterwards," which at first glance suggests some sort of supraconscious self-knowing (see *Collationes in Hexaëmeron* V.23–24 [Quar. 5.357–8] and *Tractatus de plantatione paradisi* 14 [Quar. 5.578]). But the context suggests that Bonaventure is merely describing a habitual self-knowledge.

[63] See Bonaventure, *Sent* I.3.2.2.1, ad 1 [Quar. 1.89–90]: "Quendam enim habitum habet animae potentia ab *acquisitione*, quendam ab innata *dispositione*, tertium habet a *sui ipsius origine* ... [Anima est facilis] ad diligendum se ipsum per sui naturalem originem ... *Similiter*, cum *intellectus* noster semper sit sibi praesens, semper est habilis sibi ad se cognoscendum." See also I.37.1.3.2; and I.3.2.2.2, ad 3 [Quar. 1.92, appearing in the edition as the second half of ad 2]: "Per hoc enim, quod anima sibi praesens est, habet notitiam; per hoc, quod est unum sibi, habet habitum amoris: et ideo, sicut potentiae sunt consubstantiales animae, ut supra visum est, ita et huiusmodi habitus"; II.3.2.2.2, arg. 3 and ad 3; I.17.1.1.2, ad 4; and for a parallel innate cognition of God, see *Quaestiones disputatae de mysterio Trinitatis* 1.1.

[64] See Bonaventure, *Sent* I.3.2.2.1, ad 1, and I.3.2.2.2, ad 2.

[65] See Bonaventure, *Sent* II.19.1.1, arg. fund. 7 [Quar. 3.459]: "[A]nima rationalis secundum actum proprium nata est super se reflecti cognoscendo se et amando"; I.17.1.1.2, ad 4; III.27, dub. 3.

attention inward. Acts of thinking about oneself occur intermittently, not because they await the fulfilment of some external condition, but because they depend on a choice to think about oneself. In fact, when the soul does think about itself, it does so "by its essence" (*per essentiam*) because it already is itself. It does not need "the assistance of the senses" or any "similitude received from outside."[66] Interestingly, he traces the capacity for this inward turn again to the nature of the soul, noting that the soul's ability to reflect on itself is based in its self-presence and simplicity.[67]

Bonaventure thus exemplifies a minimalist solution to the ambiguities inherent in earlier theories of self-knowledge: He discards the troublesome notions of supraconscious self-knowing and dependent self-knowledge, in favor of a natural disposition for self-knowledge and intermittent, voluntarily elicited acts of thinking about oneself. His theory, and its anthropological foundation, can be tidily summarized as follows: On account of their self-presence and simplicity, intellectual, immaterial entities are naturally suited to think about themselves independently from sensation.

The characteristically eclectic Albert adopts the opposite strategy for resolving the same ambiguities, positing multiple kinds of self-knowledge to accommodate all the insights of all his sources:

(1) an innate habit for cognizing oneself (Augustinian *se nosse*);
(2) intermittent acts of consciously thinking about oneself (Augustinian *se cogitare* and, nominally, Aristotelian self-cognition *per speciem*);
(3) an intermittent implicit or concomitant "vision" of oneself in every thought (Aristotelian dependent self-knowledge);
(4) an indeterminate actual self-vision (Augustinian *se intellegere* and Avicenna's supraconscious self-knowing).

First, Albert attributes to the mind a "consubstantial" habit for cognizing itself,[68] which he identifies with the self-familiarity (*notitia*, from

---

[66] Bonaventure, *Sent* II.39.1.2 [Quar. 2.904]: "Si qua autem sunt cognoscibilia, quae quidem cognoscantur per *sui essentiam*, non per *speciem*, respectu talium poterit dici conscientia esse habitus *simpliciter innatus*, utpote respectu huius quod est Deum amare et Deum timere ... Quid autem sit *amor* et *timor*, non cognoscit homo per *similitudinem exterius acceptam*, sed per *essentiam;* huiusmodi enim affectus essentialiter sunt in anima. Ex his patet responsio ad illam quaestionem, qua quaeritur, utrum omnis cognitio sit a sensu. Dicendum est, quod non. Necessario enim oportet ponere, quod anima novit Deum et se ipsam et quae sunt in se ipsa, sine adminiculo *sensuum exteriorum*."

[67] See Bonaventure, *Sent* III.33.1.3, ad 3.

[68] Albert, *DeHom* [Col. 27/2.553:56–9]: "Dictum Augustini non extenditur ad omnem notitiam, sed tantum ad illam qua mens novit se et deum secundum habitus insertos sibi a natura" (note that due to the excessively complex subdivisions in Albert's *De homine*, it is usually referenced by the Cologne edition, rather than by its internal parts); and *Sent* I.3.X.36 [Borgnet 25.145–6].

nosse) of Augustinian memory.[69] This habit presumably disposes the mind for a second kind of self-knowledge, i.e., occurrent acts of thinking about oneself, in which the mind "understands itself as an intelligible distinct from others."[70] Like Jean and Bonaventure, Albert holds that thinking about oneself is simply a matter of turning one's attention inward "at will" (*quando voluerit*).[71] But curiously, he equates this view with a version of "Aristotelian" cognition *per speciem*, arguing that the "species" by which the intellect thinks about itself is just the intellect itself: "The intellect itself is the intention [in the sense of a species] by which it is understood."[72]

Albert's third type of self-knowledge is a dependent self-knowledge that is implicit in the very structure of the intellectual act. Citing Alexander of Aphrodisias, Albert states that the mind "understands itself with all intelligibles as their subject, not distinct from them,"[73] insofar as the agent intellect "sees itself" when it illuminates intelligibles and the possible intellect "receives itself" when it receives the intelligible.[74] The mind thus concomitantly understands itself in understanding anything at all.

Albert's fourth type of self-knowledge is a natural supraconscious self-knowing, which he identifies with Augustine's mysterious perpetual *se intellegere* and seeks to explain in terms of Aristotelian psychology.[75] In *De*

Interestingly, Albert identifies this habit with the substance of the mind in a certain sense as the "praesentia [mentis] sui sibi; et tunc notitia materialiter accepta, idem erit quod mens nota" (*Sent* I.3.X.39 [Borgnet 25.150]). See Schneider, *Die Psychologie Alberts*, 510 and 524–31.

[69] Albert, *DeHom* [Col. 27/2.551:52–7]: "Sic enim [memoria] non est nisi conservatio habituum insertorum nobis a natura, sicut notitia veri et boni, quod deus est, et notitia veri et boni, quod mens est sive anima, et notitia veri et boni, quod iustitia tenenda est, et huiusmodi quae per naturam sciuntur a quolibet."

[70] Albert, *DeHom* [Col. 27/2.422:26–30], responding to the claim that the agent intellect always knows itself because it is conjoined to itself: "[I]ntellectus agens semper intelligit se aliquo illorum modorum praehabitorum, sed non semper intelligit se ut intelligibile distinctum ab aliis. Ad hoc enim non sufficit sola praesentia sui apud se, sed etiam exigitur, ut convertatur supra se per actum intelligendi"; see also Col. 27/2.549:64–550:15.

[71] Albert, *DeHom* [Col. 27/2.426:62–427:4; and see 422:26–30].

[72] Albert, *InDA* III.2.17 [Col. 7/1.203:27–9]: "[I]pse intellectus est intentio, per quam intelligitur." Compare to Jean in note 58 above.

[73] Albert, *DeHom* [Col. 27/2.427:4–8]: "Alio modo intelligit se cum omnibus intelligibilibus ut subiectum ipsorum non distinctum ab ipsis, et sic iterum in potentia non est ad se, sed ad intelligibilia. Et hoc patet per verba Alexandri in libro De intellectu et intelligibili"; *Sent* I.3.H.29 [Borgnet 25.129–30]; *InDA* III.2.15 [Col. 7/1.199:45–55].

[74] The respective roles of agent and possible intellects are made especially clear in Albert's *Sent* I.I.3.H.29. For texts focusing on the agent intellect, see *DeHom* [Col. 27/2.421:39–50 and 549:64–550:19]; and *De intellectu et intelligibili* 2.5 [Borgnet 9.510–11]; and see Lawrence Dewan, "St. Albert, St. Thomas, and Knowledge," *American Catholic Philosophical Quarterly* 70 (1996): 121–35. For discussions focusing on the possible intellect, see *DeHom* [Col. 27/2.427:4–15]; and *InDA* 3.2.15 [Col. 7/1.199:45–50]. *DeHom* [Col. 27/2.422:6–17] mentions both agent and possible intellects.

[75] See *Sent* I.I.3.H.29 [Borgnet 25.130], where he makes the connection to Augustine and differentiates this fourth type of self-knowledge from the first three types especially clearly; see also *DeHom* [Col. 27/2.421:51–422:17].

homine, he depicts the agent intellect always understanding itself indeterminately as "the act of the possible intellect," even when it is not illuminating any specific intelligible. The situation is "as if light, through itself alone, were in the eye without color – then the eye would be affected by the act of colors [viz., light], but there would not be a distinct affectation with respect to some determinate species of color."[76] A few years later in his commentary on the *Sentences* he describes the same phenomenon slightly differently as the possible intellect's always beholding itself because it is "always presented to itself (*objicitur sibi*, literally: made an object to itself) in the light of the agent intellect."[77] When he returns a decade later in the commentary on *De anima* to the question of the intellect's natural knowledge, he still seems to be defending a natural supraconscious self-knowing, but he no longer mentions the agent intellect. Instead, he states tersely that the intellect is always intelligible to itself and "must understand itself," because it is by its nature both immaterial and present to itself.[78]

Aquinas will be influenced by Albertist eclecticism, inasmuch as he too seeks to maintain some sort of natural self-knowledge *together with* a dependent self-knowledge. But he will also adopt elements of Bonaventurean minimalism, in his rejection of natural supraconscious

---

[76] Albert, *DeHom* [Col. 27/2.421:51–64]: "Ad hoc quod quaeritur, utrum semper intelligat se, dicimus quod sic, eo modo quo improprie dicimus intellectum agentem intelligere se; hoc enim est intelligere se ut actum possibilis; suum enim intelligere est suum esse, cum semper sit in actu. Et hoc est quod sit actus possibilis, sed ille actus non perficit possibilem nisi secundum quid, sicut si lumen per se solum esset in oculo sine colore, tunc enim esset immutatus oculus ab actu colorum, sed non esset distincta immutatio ad aliquam speciem coloris determinatam. Similiter quando solum lumen agentis est in possibili, tunc possibilis est in actu indistincto secundum aliquam speciem intelligibilis, et intellectus agens intelligit se ut talem actum semper." For discussion of the implications, see Blankenhorn, "The Early Albertus Magnus."

[77] Albert, *Sent* I.3.H.29 [Borgnet 25.130]: "Cum igitur lumen intellectus agentis semper splendeat super possibile, eo quod agens sit forma et actus possibilis, intellectus possibilis semper objicitur sibi in lumine illo: et cum hoc sit intelligere se secundum Augustinum, semper intelligit se." For Albert's view of the agent intellect as the Augustinian "higher part of the soul" and a "separated light," see Kennedy, "The Nature of the Human Intellect," 121–37; for its curious relationship to the possible intellect, see Jörn Müller, "La vie humaine comme un tout hiérarchique: Félicité contemplative et vie active chez Albert le Grand," in *Vie active et vie contemplative au Moyen Age et au seuil de la Renaissance*, ed. C. Trottmann (Rome: École Française de Rome, 2009), 241–63; and for its role in this fourth type of self-knowledge, see Markus L. Führer, "The Contemplative Function of the Agent Intellect in the Psychology of Albert the Great," in *Historia Philosophiae Medii Aevi: Studien zur Geschichte der Philosophie des Mittelalters*, ed. B. Mojsisch and O. Pluta (Amsterdam: Grüner, 1991), 305–19; Führer, "Albertus Magnus' Theory of Divine Illumination," 141–55.

[78] Albert, *InDA* III.2.17 [Col. 7/1.203:68–76]: "Et quia illa quae abstrahit, ante abstractionem sunt in *potentia intelligibilia*, ideo non semper praesentia sunt in anima, et *ideo intellectus non* semper *est* de *illis*, quia *intellectus* non est *talium* intellectorum, nisi quando sunt *sine materia*, non autem semper sunt sine materia; *illi autem* intellectui, scilicet possibili, convenit semper *intelligibile esse*, eo quod semper denudatus semper praesens est sibi, et quia immaterialis est, habet intelligere seipsum."

self-knowing, and in his mature attempt to provide a unified account of all the types of self-knowledge in terms of the nature of the human soul.

Aquinas vs. his predecessors

The debate over self-knowledge in the 1230s to 1250s can thus be characterized as a project of refining the central notions of natural and dependent self-knowledge and assessing their compatibility. The discussion revolved around maxims taken from Augustine and Aristotle, interpreted through conceptual frameworks contributed by Avicenna, Averroes, and the Greek commentators on Aristotle. The 1230s saw an "Avicennizing" development that denied the possibility of self-ignorance and hinted at supraconscious self-knowing. Thinkers in the 1240s and 1250s pursued greater precision by distinguishing different kinds of self-knowledge and applying the tools of Aristotelian psychology.

Amid all their diversity, mid-thirteenth-century theories of self-knowledge share a common assumption: *The soul cognizes itself by its essence or by itself (per essentiam, per seipsam), since the soul is itself and must therefore be more present to itself than anything else.* This natural self-knowledge is typically conceived (except by Bonaventure) as a supraconscious self-knowing perpetually actualized outside the realm of conscious attention, although its proponents have trouble articulating how it is supposed to work. Dependent self-knowledge is frequently rejected; when it is affirmed (e.g., by Albert), its scope is restricted so that it cannot compete with natural self-knowledge.

Where, then, will Aquinas fit into this historical picture? From the late 1250s onward, Aquinas explicitly challenges the above assumption, to the extent that this self-knowledge is identified with a supraconscious self-knowing (as in Albert) or described as wholly independent from cognition of sensed extramental objects (as in Bonaventure).[79] He thus insists that all actual human self-knowledge depends on cognition of extramental objects, although he provocatively casts this claim as a new and more sophisticated way of affirming that the soul cognizes itself by itself.

But Aquinas does more than merely propose a new theory. He reshapes the framework of debate, focusing on two issues that had received little

[79] See for instance the questions formulated in *DV* 10.8: "Utrum mens seipsam per essentiam cognoscat, aut per aliquam speciem"; *SCG* 3.46: "Quod anima in hac vita non intelligit seipsam per seipsam"; and *ST* 1a.87.1: "Utrum anima intellectiva seipsam cognoscat per suam essentiam"; similar questions are raised with respect to the soul's knowledge of its own habits in *DV* 10.9 and *ST* 1a.87.2.

attention from his predecessors. The first concerns the content of self-knowledge: What kinds of things does the soul cognize about itself? With the exception of Jean de la Rochelle, previous authors did not address whether the soul might have special access to some aspects of its being and not others (reasonably enough, since if the soul cognizes itself just by being itself, it is hard to see why such knowledge would not encompass its entire being).[80] Aquinas, however, admits a privileged access only to certain aspects of the soul's being, placing his distinction between cognizing one's existence vs. one's essence at the heart of his theory early on.

The second issue concerns the anthropological implications of self-knowledge. While the differing accounts of self-knowledge sketched above obviously flow from diverging views about the relation between soul and body, Aquinas's immediate predecessors do not make much of this connection. In contrast, Aquinas distinguishes different modes of self-knowledge appropriate to different kinds of intellectual beings (humans, angels, God), and he commonly rejects supraconscious self-knowing on the grounds of its incompatibility with a hylomorphic account of human nature.[81] He conceives of his theory of human self-knowledge as an integral part of his anthropology, inextricably bound up with the soul's relation to the body, the nature of its rational powers, and the nature of human cognition.

---

[80] Albert apparently holds that the soul naturally cognizes its entire essence; see *DeHom* [Col. 27/2.420:54–62 and 422:20–5 = arg. 7 and ad 7], echoing William, *De anima* 2.13–14.

[81] For Aquinas's belief that supraconscious self-knowing would require conceiving the human soul as a separate substance, see Black, "Consciousness and Self-Knowledge," 362.

CHAPTER TWO

The trajectory of Aquinas's theory of self-knowledge, 1252–72

Against the background of this thirteenth-century debate, Aquinas unfolds his own theory of self-knowledge, tentatively and incompletely in earlier writings, and then later with increasing confidence and originality. A study of its trajectory over the course of twenty years (1252–72) reveals that: (1) While Aquinas remains indebted to his predecessors, his concern to legitimate self-opacity leads him to seek a way to make all acts of self-knowledge dependent on cognition originating in sensation; (2) Although his theory of self-knowledge remains fairly consistent across his lifetime after his commentary on the *Sentences*, it does undergo considerable maturation. In fact, one can distinguish three main phases in this maturation, which I suspect follow a gradual maturing of his anthropological thought.

To dramatize his thought in these three phases, we will study seven representative texts that contain Aquinas's most important treatments of self-knowledge: from the initial immature phase, two texts from his commentary on the *Sentences* (I.3.4.5 and III.23.1.2, ad 3); from a subsequent phase of systematicization, *De veritate* 10.8 and *Summa contra gentiles* 3.46; and from a final, mature phase, *Summa theologiae* Ia.87.1 and the comments on the Aristotelian and Proclean doctrines of self-knowledge in *In De anima* III, c. 3 and *Super librum De causis*, prop. 15.[1] These assembled

---

[1] In my view, the commentaries on *De anima* and the *Liber de causis* offer authentic insight into Aquinas's own position on self-knowledge; he relies on both sources as authorities in developing his position on self-knowledge elsewhere, and his discussions of self-knowledge in these commentaries are in line with his own position as expressed in other contexts. The disputed question *Utrum anima coniuncta cognoscat seipsam per essentiam*, discovered by F. Pelster in Bodleian MS Laud Misc. 480 and subsequently published by L.A. Kennedy, will not be included, since it is probably not authentic. See F. Pelster, "Eine ungedruckte Quaestio des hl. Thomas von Aquin über die Erkenntnis der Wesenheit der Seele," *Gregorianum* 36 (1955): 618–25; L.A. Kennedy, "The Soul's Knowledge of Itself: An Unpublished Work Attributed to St. Thomas Aquinas," *Vivarium* 15 (1977): 31–45. Pelster's arguments for its authenticity were accepted by Weisheipl, *Friar Thomas d'Aquino*, 367. The first dissenter was A.M. Kenzeler, who suggests Bernard of Trilia as a more likely author (see "Une prétendue dispute de saint Thomas," *Angelicum* 33 [1956]: 172–81). More recently, Putallaz has

texts provide a bird's-eye view of Aquinas's theory of self-knowledge as a whole, revealing how he sought to distinguish his views from those of his predecessors, which aspects of self-knowledge he found especially intriguing or troubling, and which key anthropological and phenomenological concerns motivated him to develop his theory as he did.

This narrative not only provides a new perspective on Aquinas's approach to self-knowledge, it also sheds light on the growth and development of his anthropology in general. Over this twenty-year period, his position on self-knowledge is guided by an increasingly refined insight into the phenomena of self-opacity and privileged self-access and their implications for human nature. Eventually Aquinas comes to consider self-knowledge as a test case for theories of what it means to be intellectual in a *human* way, with important repercussions for the status of the human soul and its relationship to the body.

An immature first phase: Aquinas's commentary on the Sentences

Aquinas's first phase of thinking about self-knowledge can be characterized as one in which he is gathering together the components of what will become his own theory of self-knowledge, without having quite worked out how to fit them all together. We can see this phase unfolding in the pages of his mammoth commentary on the *Sentences* (*c.* 1254–56) which offers a glimpse of a scholar beginning to develop his own thought, yet still strongly influenced by his Dominican teacher, Albert the Great.[2] By the time Aquinas arrived at the University of Paris, bachelors were required to comment on Peter Lombard's *Sentences* (a theological compendium composed *c* 1157) in order to qualify for the rank of master. The genre of *Sentences* commentaries quickly became a framework for discussion of particular problems loosely connected to the original text. Commentators unabashedly drew considerable amounts of material, often verbatim, from other *Sentences* commentaries in constructing their own works. Therefore, considerable information about an author's philosophical commitments can be gleaned by comparing his solution to parallel passages in other contemporary commentaries. (For instance, when an author is closely following a source text but then abruptly diverges from the source with a

detailed what I believe to be strong arguments for inauthenticity (see *Le sens de la réflexion*, Annexe, 305–10); Torrell concurs in *Saint Thomas Aquinas* 1:430.

[2] Torrell dates the teaching of the commentary on the *Sentences* to around 1252–54, and its written composition around 1254–56, noting that its written version was still incomplete in 1256 (*Saint Thomas Aquinas* 1:332).

new and original solution, these divergences provide clues about his distinctive concerns and motivations.)

By the time of Aquinas, there were two *loci classici* for treating self-knowledge in commentaries on the *Sentences*: the discussion of the Trinitarian image in the human mind (Book I, d. 3), and the discussion of whether one can know with certitude that one has charity (Book III, d. 23). When Aquinas's treatment of these themes is compared to parallel texts in earlier *Sentences* commentaries – especially Albert's and Bonaventure's[3] – the result is surprising. In his earliest treatment of the theme in Book I, d. 3, q. 4, Aquinas repeats Albert's doctrine, including a defense of perpetual supraconscious self-knowledge. But in Book III, d. 23, q. 1, a. 2, he breaks with the traditional way of answering the question and sets up a new approach, introducing the main distinctions and ideas that will serve as the basic framework for his unique theory of self-knowledge, as articulated shortly thereafter in *DV* 10.8.

An Albertist account: Sent 1.3.4.5

The Albertist elements in Aquinas's first in-depth treatment of human self-knowledge in *Sent* bk. I, d. 3, q. 4, a. 5 are best appreciated against the backdrop of the preceding articles 1–4 in question 4. This question as a whole discusses Augustine's psychological model of the Trinity, which images the Trinitarian processions through the relationship among the acts of the mind's three powers, i.e., the acts of memory, intellect, and will.[4] The main focus is on the relationship of the acts of memory and intellect. When these acts are directed to extramental objects, the act of intellect generates the act of memory, since I must first cognize something before I can remember it. But when these acts are directed to the mind itself, the order is reversed, representing the order of Trinitarian processions: The act of self-memory generates the act of self-understanding (corresponding to the Father generating the Son).[5]

---

[3] For the corresponding texts see Albert, *Sent* I.3.G–H and III.23.G.15; Bonaventure, *Sent* I.3.2 and III.23, dub. 4. Bonaventure's and Albert's commentaries are well documented as key sources in Aquinas's commentary; see Torrell, *Saint Thomas Aquinas* 1:42–3; and M.-D. Chenu, *Das Werk des Hl. Thomas von Aquin*, trans. Otto M. Pesch (Heidelberg: Kerle, 1960), 309.

[4] Later Aquinas insists that memory is not a separate power from intellect but just the retentive aspect of the intellect (*DV* 10.6 and *ST* 1a.79.6). Here, however, perhaps in deference to the Augustinian context, he treats it as a separate power, while making clear that it does not have acts or habits of its own; see below.

[5] *Sent* I.3.4.4 [Mand. 1.120]: "In illis enim quae per habitum acquisitum discuntur, non servatur ordo, ut dictum est supra, quia intelligendi actus praecedit actum memorandi ... Si autem considerentur istae potentiae respectu hujus objecti quod est anima, sic salvatur ordo, cum ipsa anima naturaliter

In this discussion, Aquinas adopts Augustine's distinction between the "act of memory" and the "act of intellect" (*nosse* vs. *intellegere* – see Chapter 1). Nevertheless, in a. 1 he notes that technically speaking there is no such thing as an act of memory; rather, "in the place of an act, it belongs to memory to hold."[6] The idea seems to be that memory, as a retentive power, does not have its own proper acts and habits. Rather, its function is related to that of intellect: It "holds" permanently a habitual knowledge (*notitia*) from which the power of intellect generates corresponding acts of understanding.[7] (Notice that memory's "act" of holding something habitually is associated with the term *nosse* or *notitia*.) Aquinas takes these distinctions and explanation directly, sometimes verbatim, from Albert's *Sentences*.[8]

Throughout q. 4, aa. 1–4, then, Aquinas is already distinguishing the habit for self-knowledge (namely, memory's "act of holding" knowledge of oneself), from the intellect's act of self-understanding. So when he asks in a. 5 whether "those powers are always in their acts with respect to those objects [i.e., the mind and God itself] in which the [Trinitarian] image is especially to be found," it is clear that he is asking whether memory always holds a habitual self-knowledge, intellect is always actually self-understanding (an act perpetually generated from self-memory), and will is always actually self-loving. Surprisingly, he answers in the affirmative; it is the opposing arguments that reject the possibility of a perpetual actual self-understanding. His explanation of the intellect's perpetual actual

---

sit sibi praesens; unde ex notitia procedit intelligere, et non e converso ... Maxime autem servatur ordo, quia ex memoria procedit intelligentia, eo quod ipse est per essentiam in anima, et tenetur ab ipsa non per acquisitionem."

[6] *Sent* I.3.4.1, ad 3 [Mand. 1.113]: "[P]hilosophi accipiebant potentias illas tantum quae ordinantur ad aliquem actum. Proprietas autem retentiva ipsius animae non habet aliquem actum; sed loco actus habet hoc ipsum quod est tenere; et ideo de memoria sic dicta non fecerunt mentionem inter potentias animae."

[7] *Sent* I.3.5.1, ad 5 [Mand. 1.124]: "[H]abitus est principium elicitivum operationis. Unde, quia memoria non habet per se actum qui sit simpliciter operatio, non respondet sibi aliquis habitus, sed eodem habitu, scilicet notitia, memoria et intelligentia reducuntur in unam operationem"; and I.3.4.1, ad 5. Compare Albert, *Sent* I.3.X.36; and Bonaventure, *Sent* I.3.2.2.1, ad 2 [Quar. 1.90]: "Et ipsa praesentia et oblatio, qua anima offert se semper suae intelligentiae, tenet locum habitus et actus memoriae."

[8] *Sent* I.3.4.1, ad 5 [Mand. 1.114]: "[I]ntelligere et nosse differunt: nosse enim est notitiam rei apud se tenere; intelligere autem dicit intueri." See Albert, *Sent* I.3.G.27 [Borgnet 1.126–7], esp. corp: "[N]on idem est notitiam rei apud se tenere, et intueri rem cujus est species illa vel notitia: et ideo aliud est intelligere se, et aliud nosse se," as well as his *DeHom* [Col. 27/2.548:23–30 and 549:51–67 = arg. 5 and ad 4–6]. Bonaventure, however, rejects this distinction and the account of supraconscious self-knowing that it grounds; see note 13 below and Chapter 1 for details. There is also a rather muddled distinction between *nosse* and *intelligere* in the somewhat earlier *Glossa Sententiarum* of Alexander of Hales, I.3, no. 44 [Quar. 1.62], though Alexander seems to be more interested in the distinction between *nosse* and *cogitare*.

self-understanding has strong links to Albert. In fact, the article reads like a paraphrase of Albert's parallel *Sent* 1.3.H.29, repeating several of the same objections and responses, and, most importantly, Albert's two solutions to the problem of whether the intellect is always in the act of self-understanding.

Albert's first solution, borrowed from "a philosopher expositing Aristotle," posited a dependent self-knowledge whereby the intellect sees its own light and receives its own intelligibility whenever it cognizes any intelligible object – in other words, a self-awareness implicit in all one's cognitive acts.[9] His second solution posited a natural supraconscious self-knowing, alleging the authority of Augustine[10] "who means that the intellect is always understanding itself beneath every other intelligible." This self-understanding (*se intelligere*) is "nothing other than a simple gaze" on what is held in memory. It is neither conscious nor determinate, but must be distinguished from attentive acts (*se cogitare, se discernere*).[11]

In *Sent* 1.3.4.5, Aquinas repeats both solutions in reverse order. His second solution (Albert's first) is that the intellect is "always" actually self-understanding, in the sense that it understands itself whenever it is actualized in understanding other things, "because everything that is understood is only understood as illuminated by the light of the agent intellect and received into the possible intellect."[12] Here he endorses the dependent self-knowledge that will become an enduring feature of his mature theory; in fact, this solution constitutes his earliest account of implicit self-awareness

---

[9] Albert, *Sent* 1.3.H.29 [Borgnet 25.129]: "[I]ntellectus intelligit se in omni intelligibili. Sicut enim lux videtur in omni colore, eo quod color sit motivum visus secundum actum lucidi: ita dicit, quod intellectus videtur in omni intelligibili, quia ipse est id quod facit actu aliquid intelligibile … Quia vero intellectus possibilis … cum accipit intelligibile in se, accipit subjectum intelligibilis cum intelligibili simul, licet non accipiat ut subjectum." This is his third type of self-knowledge; see p. 38.

[10] Interestingly, Albert presents Augustine's doctrine of the circumincession of the powers as the reason for attributing to Augustine a theory of perpetual actual self-knowing; see the beginning of *Sent* 1.3.H.29 [Borgnet 25.128].

[11] Albert, *Sent* 1.3.H.29 [Borgnet 25.130]: "[Augustinus] vult, quod sub omni intelligibili alio intellectus semper intelligat se, et alia duo: et memoria semper meminerit sui, et aliorum duorum: et voluntas semper vult se, et ali duo. Unde sine praejudicio dico secundum praedicta, quod meminisse nihil aliud est quam notitiam rei apud se retinere. Intelligere vero *nihil aliud quam notitiae specie vel essentia notitiae se intueri simpliciter sine consideratione sui et discretione suae naturae*, quia hoc vocat Augustinus 'intelligere se': et discernere se et cogitare se plus secundum eum dicunt quam intelligere se." Emphasis mine (compare with Aquinas in note 13 below). This is Albert's fourth type of self-knowledge; see pp. 36–7.

[12] *Sent* 1.3.4.5 [Mand. 1.122]: "Alio tamen modo, secundum philosophos, intelligitur quod anima semper se intelligit, eo quod omne quod intelligitur, non intelligitur nisi illustratum lumine intellectus agentis, et receptum in intellectu possibili. Unde sicut in omni colore videtur lumen corporale, ita in omni intelligibili videtur lumen intellectus agentis; non tamen in ratione objecti sed in ratione medii cognoscendi."

(see Chapter 6). When he later abandons supraconscious self-knowing, he will argue that the human mind *only* grasps itself insofar as it is actualized in cognizing other things.

More intriguing from the perspective of doctrinal development is Aquinas's first solution (repeating Albert's second), which is the only place where he defends a natural supraconscious self-knowing. Taking up Albert's distinction between *cogitare, discernere, intelligere*, he argues that the mind does not always think about its parts and properties (*cogitare*) or "cognize itself by its difference from other things" (*discernere*). But the mind does always actually "understand" (*intelligit*) itself – meaning that it beholds itself with a gaze (*intuitum*) that is "nothing other than an intelligible presence to the intellect in some sort of way."[13]

Some of Aquinas's readers have interpreted this definition of *se intelligere* as a "presence to the intellect" as an early reference to habitual self-awareness, which he associates in *DV* 10.8 with the soul's self-presence.[14] But at this point, Aquinas is simply reiterating Albert's notion of a natural supraconscious self-knowing, which in turn reiterates Augustine's notion of perpetual self-understanding (*se intellegere*), the state in which the mind is brought forth from the storehouses of memory and presented to itself without being the object of attention. As we can see from the above discussion of the textual context and comparison to Albert, Aquinas clearly differentiates this supraconscious self-knowing or perpetual self-understanding (*se intelligere*) from memory's "act of holding" (*se nosse*); it is an

---

[13] *Sent* I.3.4.5 [Mand. 1.122]: "Dico ergo, quod anima non semper cogitat et discernit de Deo, nec de se, quia sic quilibet sciret naturaliter totam naturam animae suae, ad quod vix magno studio pervenitur: ad talem enim cognitionem non sufficit praesentia rei quolibet modo; sed oportet ut sit ibi in ratione objecti, et exigitur intentio cognoscentis. Sed secundum quod intelligere *nihil aliud dicit quam intuitum*, qui nihil aliud est quam praesentia intelligibilis ad intellectum quocumque modo, sic anima semper intelligit se et Deum." Aquinas borrows these definitions of *cogitare* and *discernere* from Albert (*Sent* I.3.G.27; compare *DeHom* [Col. 27/2.550:13–15]). For *cogitare* and *discernere* in other thinkers in the 1230s to 1250s, see William of Auvergne, *De anima* 3.12–13; Bonaventure, *Sent* III.23, dub. 4, and III.27, dub. 3; and Alexander of Hales, *Glossa Sententiarum* I.3, no. 44, though compare his definition of *cernere* in his *Summa theologica*, Tract. Int., q. 2, no. 15. The listing of *intelligere, cogitare, discernere*, and sometimes *nosse* is standard in treatments of this theme from the 1230s to the 1250s (see the texts just listed by Albert, William, and Alexander). Mandonnet [1.122] erroneously cites Augustine's *De utilitate credendi* 11.25 as the source; the more likely source is *De Trin* 10.12.19 and/or 14.6.9–7.10, paraphrased and expanded. Interestingly, in the parallel text from his own commentary on the *Sentences* (I.3.2.2.1), Bonaventure jettisons these traditional distinctions in favor of a distinction between actual and habitual self-knowledge; in *Sent* III.27, dub. 3, and III.23, dub. 4, he explicitly maps the traditional terminology onto actual and habitual self-knowledge.

[14] Compare *DV* 10.8, resp. and ad 11; and see Gardeil, "La perception expérimentale," 225, n. 3, who is opposed by D. Juvenal Merriell, *To the Image of the Trinity: A Study in the Development of Aquinas' Teaching* (Toronto: Pontifical Institute of Mediaeval Studies, 1990), 73–6. Lambert presents evidence for both sides in *Self-Knowledge in Thomas Aquinas*, 111–12.

act of intellect generated by memory.[15] This interpretation is confirmed by his responses to the second and third arguments, which had argued that a perpetual self-understanding would make it impossible to attend to anything other than oneself. If Aquinas had wanted to appeal to habitual self-awareness, the answer would have been easy: Obviously habitual cognition of A does not compete with actual cognition of B! Instead, he responds by distinguishing "understanding as we have here defined it" from "a complete operation of the distinguishing or cogitating intellect," and arguing that the former "does not require an intention."[16] These responses apparently assume some sort of distinction between conscious and non-conscious intellectual acts, in the footsteps of Augustine and Albert. Nevertheless, Aquinas does tone down or omit some of Albert's strongest formulations (though it is impossible to know whether these differences are philosophically motivated or not). Most notably, he referes to the perpetual shining of the agent intellect as the source of supraconscious self-knowing only in passing, in arg. 1 s.c. In any case, he never endorses a natural supraconscious self-knowing again. In *DV* 10.8, he will explicitly reject it; in *SCG* 3.46, he transforms the notion of an indeterminate self-awareness into an indistinct (but not perpetual) actual self-awareness.

A new distinction: Sent *III.23.1.2, ad 3*

In *Sent* I.3.4.5, the bachelor Aquinas was hewing close to the Albertist line, but already in *Sent* III.23.1.2, we find him moving in a new direction.[17] The context is the discussion of whether one can know one's habits – a question of great interest to commentators at the time, since it has bearing on the theological problem of whether believers can be sure of possessing the theological virtues (i.e., the habits of faith, hope, and charity), and thus be sure of being in a state of grace (i.e., in a right relationship with God). In earlier commentaries such as Bonaventure's and Albert's, this question

---

[15] See also the *sed contra* arguments by which Aquinas supports his own position, i.e., s.c. 1: "Contra, Philosophus dicit quod intellectus agens semper intelligit. Maxime autem hoc videtur respectu eorum quae semper sibi sunt praesentia, sicut anima et Deus. Ergo videtur quod intellectus, horum respectu, semper sit in actu"; s.c. 2: "Praeterea, dicit Augustinus quod quidquid est in memoria mea, illud memini. Sed anima et Deus semper est praesens memoriae. Ergo memoria semper est in actu eorum, et similiter est in aliis" [Mand. 1.121–2].

[16] *Sent* I.3.4.5, ad 2 [Mand. 1.122]: "Philosophus loquitur de intelligere, secundum quod est operatio intellectus completa distinguentis vel cogitantis, et non secundum quod hic sumitur intelligere"; ad 3 [Mand. 1.122]: "[I]ntentio intelligentis non requiritur ad tale intelligere, sicut dictum est."

[17] Note that according to Torrell (*Saint Thomas Aquinas* 1:42–3), Albert's influence, strong throughout the first three books of Aquinas's *Sent*, becomes less pronounced in the fourth book. *Sent* III.23.1.2, then, may exemplify the waning of Albertist influence.

of cognizing habits had been treated as a parallel to *Sent* I.3's question of how the mind always cognizes itself, since in both cases the cognized object is present to the mind in its real being rather than by a likeness. Consequently, both questions had typically been answered in the same way, i.e., by appealing to the "Augustinian" distinction between types of cognition (*nosse, intelligere, cogitare, discernere*) to identify which kinds of cognition can be generated merely by the mental presence of the object.[18]

Whereas Aquinas had been content to adopt this traditional approach in his *Sent* I.3.4.5, here in *Sent* III.23.1.2 he strikes out in a new direction. In the body of his solution, he distinguishes two kinds of things that the soul can know about a habit it possesses, i.e., that the habit exists (*an est*) and what the habit is (*quid est*). In the article's lengthy response to the third argument, he goes on to apply the same distinction to the soul's cognition of itself, thus laying out the earliest version of his trademark distinction between quidditative self-knowledge (cognizing what the soul is) and self-awareness (here, cognizing the soul's own acts, which in later texts is identified with cognizing that the soul exists):

> It happens that through cognition the soul is bent back (*reflectitur*) upon itself or upon those things which are its own, in two ways. In one way, inasmuch as the cognitive power cognizes its own nature, or [the nature] of those things which are in it … But the intellect, as is said in III *De anima*, cognizes itself like other things – by a species, not of itself, but of the object which is its form, from which it cognizes the nature of its act, and from the nature of the act, the nature of the cognizing power, and from the nature of the power, the nature of the essence … In another way, the soul is bent back (*reflectitur*) upon its own acts by cognizing that these acts are (*esse*) … [The intellect] can cognize its act, insofar as it is affected in some way by the object and informed by the species of the object.[19]

In this text, Aquinas shifts the traditional focal point of discussion from *which kinds of intellectual acts are involved in self-knowledge* to *what the soul cognizes about itself* and *whether this cognition depends on the senses*. His answers to the latter two questions are likewise unique, not only in the theological context of *Sentences* commentaries, but also in philosophically oriented treatises on the soul. As we saw in Chapter I, none of his predecessors had proposed a distinction between quidditative self-knowledge and self-awareness as the solution to problems concerning self-knowledge.

---

[18] See Albert, *Sent* III.23.G.15; Bonaventure, *Sent* III.23, dub. 4; and to some extent Alexander of Hales, *Glossa Sententiarum* III.23(L), no. 17.

[19] *Sent* III.23.1.2, ad 3.

Nor had they made acts of *attentively thinking about oneself* dependent on cognizing extramental things.

These innovations are the mainstays of Aquinas's own idiosyncratic theory of self-knowledge, and he here introduces them in an apparently deliberate departure from traditional approaches. It is not clear what motivates this shift. One possibility is concern for self-opacity: In the body of the same article, Aquinas had discussed the ethical phenomenon of self-opacity at length, insisting on the agent's inability to know the nature of the habit, virtuous or vicious, from which she is acting. Alternatively, perhaps he is influenced by Aristotle, whose *De anima* is quite prominent in this response.[20] In any case, this shift does not necessarily indicate an abandonment of the perpetual supraconscious self-knowing defended in *Sent* I.3.4.5. In fact, nothing in III.23.1.2 explicitly conflicts with his earlier remarks. If his distinction between "two ways in which the soul reflects upon itself" refers to conscious acts of thinking about oneself – as seems likely – it does not necessarily exclude non-conscious self-knowledge, which would simply fall outside the scope of debate in this article.

While the building-blocks of Aquinas's trademark theory of self-knowledge in *DV* 10.8 are mostly already arrayed in *Sent* III.23.1.2, ad 3, this text lacks the sophistication and nuance of later treatments. For instance, the formulation of his main distinction here (cognizing one's acts vs. cognizing the soul's nature) is philosophically less solid than the subsequent formulation (cognizing that the soul exists vs. cognizing what it is). The former leaves Aquinas open to the objection often leveled at Descartes: In merely perceiving the existence of a cognitive act, how do I know that this act is *mine*?[21] Moreover, it will take Aquinas another decade or so to settle on a satisfactory explanation of why the soul can cognize its intellectual acts. In Chapter 1, we saw William of Auvergne arguing that the soul necessarily grasps its "accidents" by their internal presence. But for Aquinas, presence alone cannot suffice for cognition, because vital acts of nutrition and growth (not to mention habits) are present in the soul without being grasped. In *Sent* III.23.1.2, ad 3, he reasons that the soul can perceive its understanding and willing because in their independence from a

---

[20] Aquinas here cites two Aristotelian maxims that he will use repeatedly thereafter, i.e., that the mind cognizes itself like other things, and that the soul's essence is grasped by reasoning from object to acts to powers. Avicenna and/or the *Liber de causis* are behind his comment that only immaterial acts can reflect on themselves (*Liber de causis* 7 and 15, and Avicenna Latinus, *De anima* V.2 [Van Riet, 2.93–4]) – a claim that Aquinas seems to be using here to account for privileged self-access. The *Liber de causis*, of course, was at the time thought to be a report of Aristotle's teaching on first causes.

[21] See Chapter 4.

corporeal organ, these acts are reflexive. A different explanation appears in *Sent* IV.49.3.2: We only notice our acts of thinking, sensing, and desiring because they change, attracting attention – but we do not notice stable acts such as nutrition and growth.[22] In his mature account, the intentionality of the intellectual act (related to its immateriality) rather than its variability will be the reason that we are aware of our thoughts but not our acts of growth.

The second phase: innovation and systematization in the late 1250s–1260s

Around 1257, Aquinas's theory of self-knowledge enters a new phase with the detailed treatments of self-knowledge in *Quaestiones disputatae de veritate* 10.8 and *Summa contra gentiles* 3.46, where he deftly fuses his sources' insights into a single, complete, original theory. While many elements of this theory were already present in the commentary on the *Sentences*, Aquinas now clarifies the parameters of his account of self-knowledge and explicitly addresses the tension among the approaches taken by his authoritative sources, rejecting supraconscious self-knowing. In addition, he now grounds his account of quidditative self-knowledge anthropologically in the passivity of the human possible intellect.

The fourfold division: De veritate, q. 10, a. 8

The *Quaestiones disputatae de veritate*, the written version of a private oral disputation given at the Dominican convent of Saint-Jacques in 1257–58, contains Aquinas's longest and most detailed treatment of self-knowledge in its q. 10, a. 8.[23] He now finally presents his full-fledged distinction between cognizing *that* the soul is (self-awareness) and cognizing *what* the soul is (quidditative self-knowledge). The first is the prephilosophical cognition of one's own personal inner life; the second is a philosophical grasp of the definition of the human soul:

---

[22] *Sent* IV.49.3.2 [Parma 7.1217]: "Dispositio autem quae est jam inhaerens, a nobis non apprehenditur ita sicut dum est in fieri, ut Avicenna dicit in 6 de Naturalibus ... Unde cum esse nostrum et vivere nostrum, et omnes actus proprii insint nobis ut in nobis quiescentes, sola autem operatio insit in nobis ut in fieri existens; in ipsa operatione percipimus et esse nostrum et vivere nostrum." See Avicenna, *De medicinis cordialibus*, printed in the appendix to *Liber de anima* [Van Riet 2.193]. I am grateful to Kevin White for bringing these texts to my attention.

[23] Torrell dates *De veritate* to 1256–59; see *Saint Thomas Aquinas* 1:62. Weisheipl clarifies that q. 10 was disputed during the academic year 1257–58; see *Friar Thomas d'Aquino*, 126.

A twofold cognition of the soul can be had by everyone, as Augustine says in Book 9 of the *De Trinitate*: one whereby the soul of each man cognizes itself only with respect to that which is proper to it; and another whereby the soul is cognized with respect to that which is common to all souls. The latter cognition, therefore, which concerns every soul in common, is that by which the nature of the soul is cognized; but the cognition which someone has of the soul insofar as it is proper to himself, is the cognition of the soul insofar as it exists (*habet esse*) in this individual. Thus, through this cognition, one cognizes that the soul is (*an est anima*), as when someone perceives that he has a soul. By the other type of cognition, however, one scientifically knows what the soul is (*quid est anima*) and what its proper accidents are.[24]

Only in *DV* 10.8 does Aquinas explicitly subdivide further, for a total of four types of self-knowledge representing four modes whereby the soul cognizes itself (by its act, by its essence, by a species, and by beholding inviolable truth):

(1) actual self-awareness, in which the soul perceives itself by its acts (*per actus suos*). "One perceives that he has a soul and lives and is, because he perceives that he senses and understands and exercises other vital operations of this kind";

(2) habitual self-awareness, in which "the soul sees itself by its essence (*per essentiam*) – that is, from the fact that its essence is present to itself, it has the power to go forth into an act of cognizing its own self";

(3) apprehension of the soul's immaterial essence, by reasoning from the nature of the intelligible object and the nature of the intelligible species (*per speciem*);

(4) judgment "by beholding inviolable truth" (*intuendo inviolabilem veritatem*) that this essence has been correctly apprehended.

This fourfold distinction represents a considerable advancement over Aquinas's first-phase treatment of self-knowledge. Instead of speaking of self-awareness as cognizing *one's acts*, he now speaks of cognizing *oneself by one's acts*, a formulation more sensitive to the requirements for first-person cognition (see Chapter 4). He now also broadens the scope of dependent self-knowledge,[25] stating that *all* human self-knowledge depends on the intellect's receiving abstracted intelligibles. In support of this claim, he seeks to reconcile his sources, appealing to Aristotle's *Nicomachean Ethics* 9.9 to show that a theory of dependent self-awareness is designed to

24 *DV* 10.8. For this distinction see Augustine, *De Trin* 9.6.9 and, tentatively, Jean de la Rochelle, *Summa de anima* 1.1–2, discussed in Chapter 1, p. 31.
25 See Chapter 1, p. 81.

explain the very phenomenon of experiencing oneself in the first person that Augustine describes in *De Trin* 9.6.9.[26] Finally, and significantly, he now attempts to ground self-knowledge – though at this point only quidditative self-knowledge – in the human possible intellect's sheer potency to intelligible form, "like prime matter."[27]

Despite its schematic simplicity, however, the solution in *DV* 10.8 already raises some of the most pressing philosophical questions about Aquinas's theory of self-knowledge. Do all four types of self-knowledge fulfil an important role in Aquinas's account of self-knowledge, or does he include them merely to reconcile various authorities?[28] Which psychological experiences is he trying to explain? In arguing that the soul only perceives itself "by its act," does he mean that it never really perceives *itself*, but only extramental intelligibles? Why does he use the terminology of "perceiving" with reference to self-awareness? Why does quidditative self-knowledge require reasoning to the soul's immateriality? We will return to these questions in Part II.

Does the mind know itself by itself? Summa contra gentiles, *bk. 3, ch. 46*

In Aquinas's next in-depth foray into human self-knowledge, *SCG* 3.46,[29] the phenomenon of self-opacity takes center stage. His motivation for discussing human self-knowledge in this text originates in ch. 45, where he denies that the embodied human intellect can have direct knowledge of separate substances (i.e., pure subsistent intellects that Aquinas identifies with God and angels). In ch. 46, he addresses an objection to this position: Augustine says that the incorporeal mind knows itself by itself (*per seipsam*), so the human mind is able to grasp the incorporeal essences of separate substances by its likeness to them.[30] Aquinas's strategy for dismissing

---

[26] See *DV* 10.8 [Leon. 22/2.321:200–34].

[27] *DV* 10.8 [Leon. 22/2.322:258–77]: "Anima enim nostra in genere intellectualium tenet ultimum locum, sicut materia prima in genere sensibilium … Unde mens nostra non potest se intelligere ita quod se ipsam immediate apprehendat, sed ex hoc quod apprehendit alia devenit in suam cognitionem, sicut et natura materiae primae cognoscitur ex hoc ipso quod est talium formarum receptiva. Quod patet intuendo modum quo philosophi naturam animae investigaverunt." For discussion, see Richard T. Lambert, "A Textual Study of Aquinas' Comparison of the Intellect to Prime Matter," *The New Scholasticism* 56 (1982): 80–99.

[28] The *responsio* in *DV* 10.8 ties together the views of Augustine, Aristotle, and Averroes [Leon. 22/2.322:311–17]: "Sic ergo patet quod mens nostra cognoscit seipsam quodammodo per essentiam suam, ut Augustinus dicit: quodam vero modo per intentionem, sive per speciem, ut philosophus et Commentator dicunt; quodam vero intuendo inviolabilem veritatem, ut item Augustinus dicit."

[29] The date of this text is uncertain. Although some chapters of *SCG* 3 can be precisely dated, it is unclear whether 3.46 was written closer to *De veritate*, or overlaps with the composition of the *Prima Pars*. Torrell dates *SCG* 3 to 1260–64 (*Saint Thomas Aquinas* 1:102).

[30] This is the first Augustinian maxim (*De Trin* 9.3.3); see p. 19.

the objection is to deny that Augustine could have meant that the intellectual soul grasps its own incorporeal essence by itself. In a striking defense of the reality of self-opacity, he argues that if the soul cognized its own essence by itself, our experience of ourselves would be entirely different: (1) Each person would always actually understand the soul's essence; (2) Knowledge of the soul's essence would be universally distributed; (3) The soul would be known naturally and indemonstrably, rendering disputes about its definition futile; and (4) The soul would be known as a first principle from which other things are cognized.[31]

When he presents his own position on how the soul *does* cognize itself, Aquinas's approach is similar to that of *DV* 10.8. He distinguishes what the soul cognizes about itself (that it exists vs. what it is) and how (by itself/its essence vs. by a species). The Augustinian maxim that the mind "cognizes itself by itself," he explains, is meant to apply only to the mind's cognition of its own existence: "Our mind knows itself by itself inasmuch as it cognizes *that it exists*. From the fact that it perceives itself acting, it perceives itself existing; but it acts by itself; therefore it cognizes by itself that it exists."[32] Interestingly, Aquinas is now explicitly equating the mind's "cognizing itself by its act" with "cognizing itself by itself." Still, his interpretation of Augustine seems broadly consistent with that of *DV* 10.8, ad 1 s.c.: namely, the mind cognizes itself "by itself" in the sense that it has within itself what it takes to engage spontaneously in the act that manifests it to itself.[33]

There is a problem here, however. At the beginning of *SCG* 3.46, Aquinas had identified four hypothetical characteristics of a cognition of an object "by itself" (*per seipsam*), which all run contrary to the experience of self-opacity. In particular, he had used the first characteristic to make the following argument: Whatever is actually present to the soul and cognized by itself must be actually perpetually understood; but "the soul is always actually present to itself, so if it cognized by itself *what it*

---

[31] For a similar line of reasoning, see *InDA* II.6 [Leon. 45/1.94:173–90].

[32] *SCG* 3.46 [Leon. 14.123]: "Sic igitur, secundum intentionem Augustini, mens nostra per seipsam novit seipsam inquantum de se cognoscit *quod est*. Ex hoc enim ipso quod percipit se agere, percipit se esse; agit autem per seipsam; unde per seipsam de se cognoscit quod est ... Sicut autem de anima scimus quia est per seipsam, inquantum eius actus percipimus; quid autem sit, inquirimus ex actibus et obiectis per principia scientiarum speculativarum: ita etiam de his quae sunt in anima nostra, scilicet potentiis et habitibus, scimus quidem quia sunt, inquantum actus percipimus; quid vero sint, ex ipsorum actuum qualitate invenimus."

[33] Compare *DV* 10.8, ad 1 s.c. [Leon. 22/2.324:441–7]: "[V]erbum Augustini est intelligendum quod mens se ipsam per se ipsam cognoscit, quia ex ipsa mente est ei unde possit in actum prodire quo se actualiter cognoscat percipiendo se esse; sicut etiam ex specie habitualiter in mente retenta inest menti ut possit actualiter rem illam considerare"; and *ST* Ia.87.1 (note 45 below).

is, it would always actually understand what it is."[34] But if we apply this argument to his subsequent assertion that the soul cognizes its own exist-ence "by itself," it seems that we must conclude that the soul always actu-ally understands its own existence. Is Aquinas here affirming the natural supraconscious self-knowing that *DV* 10.8 had rejected? We will return to this puzzle in the final section of the chapter.

The final mature phase: from the late 1260s onward

The third and final phase of Aquinas's treatment of self-knowledge is one of refinement or maturation rather than doctrinal change, and seems to be part of a focused inquiry into anthropology in the second half of the 1260s.[35] In this phase, his entire account of self-knowledge – not only quidditative self-knowledge but also self-awareness – solidifies around the anthropological thesis that the human intellect is by default unactualized, and the resulting psychological thesis that all self-know-ing depends on intellectual actualization. In this psychological thesis, Aquinas discovers a nexus of compatibility among apparently compet-ing paradigms of self-knowledge: the Aristotelian paradigm of depend-ent self-knowing, and the Neoplatonic paradigm of intellectual being as naturally self-knowing (see Chapter 1). Whereas in the second phase he had tried to salvage and recombine parts of each theory, he now unites them in the single insight that the intellect cognizes itself by its own actualized being.

Knowing my soul by its act: Sententia libri De anima *III, c. 3* *and* Summa theologiae *Ia, q. 87, a. 1*

It is generally agreed that Aquinas wrote his commentary on *De anima* alongside the "treatise on human nature" (*Prima Pars*, qq. 75–89) of the *Summa theologiae*, as a preparatory study for his treatment of human

---

[34] *SCG* 3.46 [Leon. 14.122]: "Per hoc enim fit potentia cognoscitiva actu cognoscens, quod est in ea id quo cognoscitur. Et si quidem sit in ea in potentia, cognoscit in potentia; si autem in actu, cognoscit actu; si autem medio modo, cognoscit habitu. Ipsa autem anima semper sibi adest actu, et nunquam in potentia vel in habitu tantum. Si igitur per seipsam anima seipsam cognoscit quid est, semper actu intelliget de se quid est. Quod patet esse falsum." Note that Aquinas's Avicennian opponents could have retorted, however, that this actual self-knowing is supraconscious, a claim that by definition cannot be experientially shown to be "clearly false."

[35] Between 1266 and 1269, for instance, he writes the *Quaestiones disputatae de anima, Quaestio dispu-tata de spiritualibus creaturis*, the commentary on *De anima*, and the treatise on human nature from the *Prima Pars* of the *Summa theologiae*.

nature in the latter.[36] These works describe nearly identical accounts of
human self-knowledge, so it makes sense to discuss them together.

Aquinas's commentary on *De anima* III, c. 3 (on 429b22–430a9 of
Aristotle's text) gives us a unique glimpse into his interpretation of the
"Aristotelian" approach to self-knowledge, without any of the hedging
and rephrasing involved when he places it into dialogue with Neoplatonic
perspectives. In the source text, Aristotle is discussing the implications of
characterizing the intellect as "a tablet on which as yet nothing is actually written" – one of which is that the intellect is intelligible "like other
things"[37] (the Aristotelian maxim of dependent self-knowledge discussed
in Chapter 1). Aquinas takes this passage to indicate that the parameters
for *both* self-knowledge *and* cognition of extramental objects are set by the
nature of the possible intellect. Because "the thing actually understood
and the one actually understanding" (*intellectum in actu et intelligens in
actu sunt unum*), the received species is that by which not only the cognized object, but the cognizing intellect is cognized. In this way, the intellect "cognizes itself like other things":

> Therefore he says first of all that the possible intellect is intelligible, not
> by its essence, but by some intelligible species, just like other intelligibles.
> This is proved from the fact that what is understood-in-act and what actu-
> ally understands are one ... Therefore the species of the thing understood
> in act is the species of the intellect itself, and thus by it, the intellect can
> understand itself; whence the Philosopher says above that one examines the
> nature of the possible intellect[38] by [the act of] understanding itself and by
> that which is understood; for we do not cognize our intellect except insofar
> as we understand ourselves understanding.[39]

He goes on immediately to tie the mode of human self-knowledge to the
nature of the possible intellect as a sheer potency for intelligible form:

---

[36] This commentary can be precisely dated to 1268–69 because Aquinas is using Moerbeke's *nova
    translatio* of the *De anima*, which was available only at the end of 1267 (Torrell, *Saint Thomas
    Aquinas* 1:341 and 172–3). The *Prima Pars* of the *Summa theologiae* dates to 1265–68 (ibid., 1:333).

[37] In the Latin translation that Aquinas was using: "Oportet autem sic sicut tabula nichil est actu
    scriptum, quod quidem accidit in intellectu. Et ipse autem intelligibilis est sicut intelligibilia" (*De
    anima* 429b30–430a2 [Leon. 45/1.213]).

[38] When Aquinas cites the maxim that "the intellect cognizes itself like other things," he often goes
    on to apply it to quidditative self-knowledge, though without explicitly restricting its application
    to quidditative self-knowledge; see in addition *Sent* III.23.1.2.3, ad 3; *DV* 10.8; *SCG* 3.46; *QDDA* 3,
    ad 4; *QDDA* 16, ad 8. He applies the maxim specifically to quidditative self-knowledge alone in *DV*
    10.8, ad 6 (see perhaps also *DV* 10.8, ad 9 s.c.; and *DV* 10.9, ad 4 and 10). In *SCG* 2.98, however,
    he applies the maxim broadly to human self-knowledge without specifying which kind of self-
    knowledge is involved. In *ST* Ia.14.2, ad 3, and Ia.87.1, it is clearly applied to both self-awareness
    and quidditative self-knowledge.

[39] *InDA* III.3 [Leon. 45/1.216:65–86].

This accrues to the possible intellect – namely, that it is understood not by its essence but by an intelligible species – for this reason: that it is a mere potency in the order of intelligibles: for the Philosophy shows in *Metaphysics* IX that nothing is understood except insofar as it is in act.

He concludes that just as prime matter "has no action by its essence, but only by the form conjoined to it," so too the possible intellect, "which is solely in potency in the order of intelligibles, neither understands nor is understood except by a species received in it."[40]

What is interesting here is that in tracing the structure of human quidditative self-knowledge to the potency of the possible intellect, Aquinas now for the first time also draws actual self-awareness (understanding oneself understanding, *intelligimus nos intelligere*) into the anthropological story.[41] Self-awareness is here presented as the basis for inquiry into the soul's nature. The scope of the immediately ensuing explanation of the mode of human self-knowledge – namely, that the possible intellect has no intelligible actuality of its own, but is in sheer potency to intelligible form – therefore seems to include both types of self-knowledge. Intelligibility accrues to the human intellect when it is actualized by extramental forms (*per speciem*).[42] In receiving a species in some act of cognition, the intellect is gaining its own actuality and thus its own intelligibility. Because the species of oakness received into the intellect is *the only actuality that the intellect has*, it is just as much the intelligible form of the intellect as of oakness. It will become even clearer in the nearly contemporaneous *ST* Ia.87.1 that this account grounds both actual self-awareness and quidditative self-knowledge.

In this text, then, we find Aquinas's detailed exposition of exactly how he understands the Aristotelian maxim "The intellect is intelligible like other things" (*sicut alia*). It does not mean "The intellect is cognized by an

---

[40] See *InDA* III.3 [Leon. 45/1.216:87–217:106].
[41] In earlier texts such as *Sent* III.23.1.2; *SCG* 2.98 and 3.46; *QDDA* 3, ad 4; and *QDDA* 16, ad 8, when Aquinas had grounded quidditative self-knowledge in the nature of the possible intellect, he typically mentioned cognition of one's act as a key element in the process of reasoning to quidditative self-knowledge. In these texts it was quite clear, however, that the cognition in question was an inquiry into the nature of the intellectual act as an object of philosophical consideration (*suum actum, suam operationem, suum intelligere*). Here in *InDA* III.3, he is clearly referring to actual self-awareness with the accusative-and-infinitive *intelligimus nos intelligere*, presenting the possible intellect's actualization as not only the reason that the intellect can cognize its own nature by a species, but *also* the explanation for understanding that one understands. (*DV* 10.8, ad 8 s.c. had already identified self-awareness as the experiential basis for quidditative self-knowledge, but did not make a connection to the nature of the possible intellect.)
[42] Intelligibility, for Aquinas, is a thing's truth, an objective metaphysical property belonging to anything that could be or is cognized (see *DV* 1.1, ad 4–5, and *InMet* IX.10–11). Something that is potentially intelligible can be cognized (once it is dematerialized by the agent intellect); something that is actually intelligible is currently being cognized. See Chapter 6, pp. 156–8.

abstracted species of itself just as it cognizes other things by abstracted species of those things." Rather it means something like "A species makes the intellect intelligible, just as that same species makes other things intelligible." One oak-species does double duty: it both makes the *oak* intelligible by informing the intellect immaterially and makes the *intellect* intelligible by informing the intellect immaterially. As we will see in Chapter 6, this position grounds Aquinas's defense of the duality of conscious thought.[43]

In the roughly contemporary *Summa theologiae* Ia, q. 87, a. 1, Aquinas places these psychological insights into dialogue with Augustinian concepts[44] and applies them to the phenomenological experience of self-knowledge. Like anything else, he explains, the intellectual soul is intelligible only to the extent to which it is actual.[45] Thus it cognizes *both its existence and its essence* solely "by its act" (*per actum*):

> Our intellect understands itself as follows: insofar as it is rendered into act by a species abstracted by the light of the agent intellect, which is the act of those intelligibles, and with them mediating, [the act] of the possible intellect. Therefore our intellect cognizes itself not by its essence, but by its act (*non per essentiam, sed per actum suum*). This happens in two ways: in the first way, which is particular, insofar as Socrates or Plato perceives that he has an intellective soul from perceiving that he understands; and in the second way, which is universal, insofar as we consider the nature of the human mind from the act of the intellect. But it is true that the judgment and efficacy of this cognition by which we cognize the nature of the soul belongs to us according to the derivation of the light of our intellect from divine truth, in which the reasons (*rationes*) of all things are contained ... There is, however, a difference between these two kinds of cognition. To have the first cognition of the mind, the very presence of the mind suffices, which is the principle of the act from which the mind perceives itself. And therefore the mind is said to know itself by its own presence (*per suam praesentiam*). But to have the second cognition, [the mind's] presence does not suffice, but a diligent and subtle inquiry is required. Whence not only are many ignorant of the soul's nature, but many also err regarding the soul's nature.

This text draws an especially sharp contrast between that to which the mind has privileged access "by its own [actualized] presence" (such as the reality of

---

[43] Compare Alexander of Aphrodisias, Themistius, Simplicius, Philoponus, Averroes, and Albert, as discussed above in Chapter 1, pp. 26–9 and 36.
[44] The first Augustinian maxim (*De Trin* 9.3.3) is cited in arg. 1. The text also includes an implicit reference to *De Trin* 9.6.9 in the framing of the main types of self-knowledge as "particular" vs. "universal" and the reference to judgment by divine truth; and perhaps *De Trin* 10.9.12 in the reference to the mind's cognizing itself "by its presence."
[45] *ST* Ia.87.1 [Leon. 5.355]: "[U]numquodque cognoscibile est secundum quod est in actu, et non secundum quod est in potentia, ut dicitur in IX Metaphys., sic enim aliquid est ens et verum, quod sub cognitione cadit, prout actu est." For this principle see also for instance *SCG* 3.46; *QDDA* 16, ad 8; *InDA* III.3; *InMet* IX.10; for its historical background see p. 104, note 36.

one's own mind and its acts) and that which is accessed only by the "diligent and subtle inquiry" of reason (such as the nature of the mind or soul).

Much of this account is familiar from as far back as *DV* 10.8. But there are two apparent discontinuities. First, Aquinas now categorically denies that the soul cognizes itself *per essentiam*, whereas in *DV* 10.8 he had allowed for habitual self-awareness *per essentiam*. Second, in explaining how the soul perceives its existence in its acts, he states that, for this kind of cognition, "the very presence of the mind suffices, which is the principle of the act from which the mind perceives itself." The phrasing is similar to *SCG* 3.46, where Aquinas identifies self-awareness "by one's acts" with self-awareness "by oneself" ("it acts by itself; therefore it cognizes by itself that it exists"). But if the soul only cognizes itself in its act, how can the soul's self-presence "suffice" for self-awareness? We will address these problems in the final section of this chapter.

Returning to one's essence: Super Librum de causis, *prop. 15*

Toward the end of his life, Aquinas broached the theme of self-knowledge again in his commentary on the *Liber de causis*, prop. 15,[46] which he interprets as containing an argument from self-knowledge to the soul's immateriality.[47] His comments on prop. 15 are especially interesting, not only because they constitute his last in-depth treatment of self-knowledge, but also because they help check the impulse to over-Aristotelianize his position, showing that he shares common ground with his Neoplatonizing contemporaries.

This text reveals the extent to which, in this mature phase, Aquinas is willing to accommodate the view that, for an intellectual being, to be is to know oneself. He was familiar with at least two versions of prop. 15's opening thesis, but here he comments on the variant that more strongly suggests a supraconscious self-knowing: "Every knower knows his essence; therefore, he is returning to his essence with a complete return (*reditione completa*)."[48] He explains the *Liber*'s "complete return" as the teleological completion of a "substantial return to one's essence" (the self-subsistence characterizing

---

[46] Gauthier dates this work to the Paris–Naples period, 1272–73 (*Index scriptorum ab ipso Aquinas nominatorum*, in Leon. 25/2.498), a dating that Torrell accepts in the "Additions and Corrections to the Second Edition" of *Saint Thomas Aquinas* 1:434. Aquinas was familiar with prop. 15 from his earliest days in Paris, and quoted it at least six times throughout his career; *Sent* I.17.1.5, ad 3; *Sent* II.19.1.1; *DV* 1.9; *DV* 2.2, ad 2; *DV* 8.6, arg. 5 s.c.; *DV* 10.9; *ST* Ia.14.2, ad 1.

[47] For similar arguments, see *Sent* II.19.1.1 and *SCG* 2.49.

[48] See p. 24, note 27. This variant appears only one other time in Aquinas, i.e., *DV* 8.6, arg. 5 s.c., where the wording probably came from the objector. Elsewhere, Aquinas cites or paraphrases the version that is reproduced in Pattin's edition of *Liber de causis*, prop. 15: "Omnis sciens qui scit essentiam suam est rediens ad essentiam suam reditione completa" (79–80). The restrictive clause in the latter version, of course, is more conducive to Aquinas's own theory of self-knowledge.

intellectual entities) by an "operational return to one's essence" (the act of
thinking about one's essence, i.e., quidditative self-knowledge).[49] The ontological independence of a self-subsisting being is completed and manifested
by the psychological independence of self-knowledge, in which knower and
known are numerically one.[50]

Now it is hard to overlook the fact that this variant of prop. 15, "Every
knower knows his essence," seems to present quidditative self-knowledge
as following necessarily upon intellectual being. Curiously, however, while
Aquinas does not draw attention to this conclusion, he neither critiques it
nor even attempts a friendly reinterpretation. This striking neutrality can
give the impression that this text is merely a detached historical exposition.[51]
But I would argue that Aquinas finds prop. 15 more useful to his campaign
against natural supraconscious self-knowing if he can identify a degree of
common ground with "the Platonists" (among whom he includes the author
of the *Liber*)[52] even while admitting certain disagreements with them. In
this way, he can show that the *Liber* and Aristotle together stand against the
view that the soul cognizes itself by its essence. Although his textual interpretation involves some sleight-of-hand, the resulting philosophical synthesis is
remarkable.

This strategy becomes clear at the end of his comments on prop. 15,
where Aquinas proposes two different ways of explaining the basic premise on which prop. 15's argument depends, i.e., "The soul scientifically
knows its own essence." For the Platonists, the soul cognizes itself "by
higher intellects in which it participates." For Aristotle, the soul cognizes
itself "by intelligible species that are made [its] forms in some way, insofar

[49] There are no grounds for associating the "operational return" as Dhavamony does (*Subjectivity and Knowledge*, 79) with the awareness of oneself acting. It is even going too far, I think, to argue as Still does ("Aquinas's Theory of Human Self-Knowledge," 129–31; see also Fetz, *Ontologie der Innerlichkeit*, ch. 4) that the text obliquely refers to self-awareness as the basis for cognizing one's own essence. Nor can the "complete return" be some sort of basic reflexive self-awareness intrinsic to all truth-judgments, as Putallaz proposes (*Le sens de la réflexion*, 182–202); for my critique of the latter view see Chapter 7, pp. 195–8.

[50] *SLDC* 15 [Saffrey, 90]: "Et quod hoc debeat vocari reditus vel conversio, manifestat per hoc quod, cum anima scit essentiam suam, *sciens et scitum sunt res una.*"

[51] As Jourdain Wébert concludes in "'*Reflexio*': Études sur les opérations réflexives dans la psycholo-gie de saint Thomas d'Aquin," in *Mélanges Mandonnet*, vol. 1 (Paris: Vrin, 1930), 323. For a bal-anced assessment of Aquinas's procedure in *SLDC*, see Vincent A. Guagliardo, "Introduction," in *Commentary on the Book of Causes*, trans. Vincent A. Gualiardo, Charles R. Hess, and Richard C. Taylor (Washington, D.C.: The Catholic University of America Press, 1996).

[52] In fact, there is considerable evidence – too complex to review here – to suggest that Aquinas's commentary on the *Liber de causis* is not merely expository, but at least sometimes serves to put his own thought in dialogue with that of "the Platonists." In addition, his thought on the nature of intellectual being is far more influenced by this work than is generally recognized.

as it is actualized by them." Aquinas traces both explanations to a shared anthropological premise: Whereas the Divine and angelic intellects cognize themselves insofar as they are "intelligible forms," the human intellect (a mere intellectual power) can cognize itself only when it gains intelligible actuality accidentally from an external source. He triumphantly concludes that Platonists and Aristotle agree that the soul cognizes itself only as actualized, and that it receives this actualization from an external source (though they disagree on the source).[53]

Aquinas's claim that, for "the Platonists," the human intellect is merely an "intellectual power" is hard to justify historically, but it serves his purposes admirably. In a single stroke, Aquinas maneuvers Aristotle and the *Liber* into the same camp, marshalling these divergent authorities against the theory that the human soul cognizes itself by its essence (i.e., the theory of natural supraconscious self-knowing). Now we see why Aquinas was so little disturbed by the *Liber*'s claim that "every knower knows its essence." He takes this to mean that, although the soul has perpetual quidditative self-knowledge, it enjoys such self-knowledge *by receiving illumination from a higher intellect*, rather than just by being itself. Consequently, he can appeal to the *Liber* as evidence that even "the Platonists," who treated the soul as a separate substance and granted it perpetual self-knowledge, did not hold that the soul could know itself just by being itself (by its essence). A theory of natural supraconscious self-knowing, then, finds no support in Aristotle, nor even in the Platonists who otherwise share so many of its intuitions.

Here, towards the end of his life, the full ingenuity of Aquinas's mature thought on self-knowledge is on display. Key is his assertion that *intellects cognize themselves only insofar as they have actuality as intellects* (i.e., insofar as they are actually cognizing). While this principle had been operative to some extent from *Sent* to *SCG*, it now emerges as not only the central principle in Aquinas's mature theory of self-knowledge, but also the unifying thread connecting all his sources' theories of self-knowledge. As we

---

[53] *SLDC* 15 [Saffrey, 91–2]: "Ubi diligenter considerandum est quod supra, cum de intellectuum cognitione ageret, dixit quod primus intellectus intelligit seipsum tantum, ut in 13ª propositione dictum est, quia scilicet est ipsa forma intelligibilis idealis; alii vero intellectus tamquam ei propinqui participant a primo intellectu et formam intelligibilitatis et virtutem intellectualitatis, sicut Dionysius dicit IVº capitulo *De divinis nominibus* quod supremae *substantiae* intellectuales sunt et *intelligibiles et intellectuales*; unde unusquisque eorum intelligit et seipsum et superiorem quem participat. Sed quia anima intellectiva inferiori modo participat primum intellectum, in substantia sua non habet nisi vim intellectualitatis; unde intelligit substantiam suam, non per essentiam suam, sed, secundum Platonicos, per superiora quae participat, secundum Aristotelem autem, in IIIº *De anima*, per intelligibiles species quae efficiuntur quodammodo formae in quantum per eas fit actu."

will see in subsequent chapters, this reading of his sources frees him to incorporate Neoplatonic insights about privileged self-access and the intuitive, first-personal character of self-awareness into a broadly Aristotelian psychological framework. The theory he develops is governed by a single guiding insight: Self-knowledge hinges on intellectual actualization.

The "big picture" view

We can now take a closer look at the apparent discrepancies observed earlier among Aquinas's statements on whether the soul can cognize itself "by itself" (*per seipsam*) or "by its essence" (*per essentiam*). The four problematic claims are as follows:

(1) The mind cognizes itself by its essence *only* habitually (*DV* 10.8, resp.).
(2) The soul does not cognize itself by its essence at all (*ST* Ia.87.1).
(3) Whatever is cognized by itself is always actually cognized, universally cognized, grasped as indemonstrable, and cognized as the first principle from which other things are cognized (*SCG* 3.46, first four arguments from self-opacity).
(4) The soul cognizes by itself that it exists (*SCG* 3.46, solution).

In my view, the discrepancies among these claims result from different meanings that the phrases 'by its essence' and 'by itself' take on in different texts, not from any change in Aquinas's underlying account of self-knowledge.[54] But these are not whimsical, insignificant changes in meaning. Rather, they shed light on Aquinas's shifting construal of the flashpoint of disagreement with a theory of supraconscious self-knowing (the latter being associated with the claim that the soul cognizes itself by its essence or by itself). This shift, which took place toward the end of the second phase, is connected to his maturing practice of grounding his account of self-knowledge anthropologically in the human intellect's native lack of form.

We can observe the results of this shift in the different meanings of 'cognizing something by its essence' (*per essentiam*) in (1) and (2). In *DV* 10.8 the flashpoint of disagreement is *the sufficiency of intellectual self-presence in producing actual self-knowledge*, with the defenders of supraconscious self-knowing arguing for sufficiency and Aquinas himself arguing for mere necessity. Accordingly, he here defines 'by its essence' as referring to a cognized object's mode of presence to the intellect:

[54] See Jordan, *Ordering Wisdom*, 126–8. My interpretation of these meanings, however, differs from Jordan's.

E₁: "Something is cognized by its essence when its essence is that by which it is known."[55]

This usage relies on the common medieval distinction between two modes of mental presence: Some things (mental acts, habits, virtues, the intellect itself) are present in the intellect in their real being (by its essences, *per essentiam*), whereas others (trees, rocks, cats) can only be present to the intellect by a species (*per speciem*).[56] (1) thus makes the following case against supraconscious self-knowing: Since the mind *is itself*, it is present to itself "by its essence" (in the sense of E₁); but this presence only disposes the mind habitually to self-awareness, and is therefore not sufficient for actual self-knowledge.

By *ST* Ia.87.1, however, Aquinas has relocated the flashpoint of disagreement to *the source of the intellect's intelligibility* (this is important because, as we shall see in Chapter 6, he thinks actual self-intelligibility is sufficient for actual self-knowledge, even if presence is not). He thus recenters the debate on whether the intellect is naturally actually self-intelligible (as the defenders of supraconscious self-knowing must hold), or whether it acquires actual intelligibility from outside itself (his own view). Accordingly, 'by its essence' does not refer to a mode of presence, but to the way in which a thing is intelligible:

> E₂: Something is cognized by its own essence if it belongs to its essence to be actually intelligible[57] (which for Aquinas would entail that it would always be actually understood).

Of course it makes no sense to describe a habitual cognition of oneself as occurring "by one's essence" in the sense of E₂, since habitual cognition has to do with an object's presence in an intellect, not the status of its intelligibility (an object is either actually intelligible or potentially intelligible). Hence (2) denies categorically that the human mind has any sort of self-knowledge by its essence in this sense. The assertion of a merely habitual self-presence in (1) is fully compatible with the denial of any native actual intelligibility in the human intellect in (2). In fact, for Aquinas, the intellect's lack of actual intelligibility is precisely *why* its self-presence merely disposes it habitually to self-knowledge (see Chapter 5).

---

[55] Verbatim from the beginning of *DV* 10.8, resp.

[56] See Chapter 1, pp. 27 and 32. Aquinas adopts this distinction in *Sent* 1.3.5.1, ad 1; *SBDT* 1.2; and more remotely, *ST* Ia.57.1, ad 2.

[57] *ST* Ia.87.1 [Leon. 5.355]: "Unde et in substantiis immaterialibus, secundum quod unaquaeque earum se habet ad hoc quod sit in actu per essentiam suam, ita se habet ad hoc quod sit per suam essentiam intelligibilis."

Bridging the gap between *DV* 10.8 and *ST* Ia.87.1, we find *SCG* 3.46 – a text that, in my view, shows Aquinas grappling with the notion of the soul's cognizing itself 'by itself,' while shifting the center of gravity in the self-knowledge debate away from intellectual presence toward intellectual intelligibility. There are three senses of cognizing something 'by itself' in this one short text.

> S_1: Something is cognized by itself if it is actually intelligible by itself (used in the first and second arguments from self-opacity in *SCG* 3.46 – equivalent to E_2).
> S_2: Something is cognized by itself if it is self-evident, like an indemonstrable first principle (used in the third and fourth arguments from self-opacity in *SCG* 3.46).
> S_3: The mind cognizes something by itself if the mind is self-sufficient for eliciting the relevant act of cognition spontaneously (used to interpret the Augustinian maxim that the mind cognizes itself by itself, in Aquinas's own solution in *SCG* 3.46).

The resulting equivocation on 'by itself' explains why (3) and (4) can be consistent with each other. Recall that, as summarized in (3), Aquinas began by describing four ways in which the soul could not be opaque to itself if it cognized itself by itself. But he goes on to state in (4) that the soul cognizes its existence by itself – and the reader is left to wonder how (3) and (4) are consistent with the act-dependence of actual self-awareness. His procedure makes more sense, though, if 'by itself' is construed in the sense of S_1 and S_2 in the opening arguments, whereas S_3 is introduced only subsequently, to articulate how the soul grasps its own existence. Although self-awareness is dependent on cognition of extramentals, Aquinas still holds that the mind, due to its natural self-presence, is properly equipped to engage in self-awareness when the right conditions are met (see Chapter 5). Thus (4)'s assertion that the mind cognizes its own existence 'by itself' merely means that, insofar as the mind has within itself the power to engage spontaneously in acts of thinking, it has the power to perceive its own existence in those acts – but it cannot perceive its own existence *independently from* those acts (more on this in Chapter 4). This way of defining 'by itself' had also appeared in *DV* 10.8, ad 1 s.c. Arguably *ST* Ia.87.1's claim that the mind's presence "suffices" for self-awareness could be interpreted the same way.[58]

---

[58] Compare *DV* 10.8, ad 1 s.c., interpreting the same Augustinian maxim, in note 33 above, and *ST* Ia.87.1 [Leon. 5.356]: "Nam ad primam cognitionem de mente habendam, sufficit ipsa mentis praesentia, quae est principium actus ex quo mens percipit seipsam. Et ideo dicitur se cognoscere per suam praesentiam" (see p. 56 above). Note that in *ST* Ia.87.1, ad 1, Aquinas adopts a different strategy for reading the same Augustinian maxim, distinguishing two meanings of *per se notum*: S_2 and a second meaning

Furthermore, notice that S₁ and S₂ have to do with an object's intelligibility (including self-evidence), whereas S₃ refers only obliquely to presence – not exactly to an *object's* mode of mental presence, but to a facility of action that the object's mental presence confers on the *intellect*. *SCG* 3.46 thus seems to have a transitional character. The sufficiency of self-presence has lost its prominence as a central component in Aquinas's argument against supra-conscious self-knowing, replaced by a defense of self-opacity that highlights the human intellect's native lack of actual intelligibility. But he has not yet explicitly identified this lack of actual intelligibility as the single anthropological foundation for the mode of both self-awareness and quidditative self-knowledge.[59]

***

Setting aside the immature texts from the commentary on the *Sentences*, then, Aquinas's theory can be sketched in broad strokes as follows. Its central claim is that all self-knowledge is dependent on cognizing extramental intelligibles – a radical claim at the time, which appears to be motivated especially by a concern to save the phenomenon of self-opacity. Its central questions concern what the soul cognizes about itself (i.e., its existence, its essence) and how it cognizes them (i.e., by a species, by its essence, by itself, by its act, etc.). To address these new questions, Aquinas divides human self-knowledge into two main types, each of which can be further subdivided:

(1) cognition of oneself as an individual, i.e., cognition "that the soul exists" (*quia/an/quod est*), which we call self-awareness. There are two kinds of self-awareness:
  (a) habitual self-awareness, which is the soul's essential self presence;
  (b) actual self-awareness, which is a prephilosophical cognition of oneself acting;

---

that we could call S₄ (i.e., items are *per se notum* if they fall within the proper scope of the relevant cognitive power; I thus disagree with Jordan, who takes Aquinas to be describing here a mode of cognition that contrasts with cognizing oneself "through [one's] activities" [*Ordering Wisdom*, 128]). Aquinas does not specify which meaning of *per se* applies to the mind's "knowing itself by itself," but we can get a clue from his statement that the mind "arrives at last" (*tandem pervenit*) to this self-knowledge, obviously indicating quidditative self-knowledge. Now we know that Aquinas does not hold that the soul's essence is cognized *per se* in the sense of S₂, because the definition of the soul is not self-evident. So it remains that the soul's essence is cognized *per se* in the sense of S₄, because the soul is a being and therefore is included in the proper object of intellectual cognition. Here in *ST* Ia.87.1 ad 1, then, *per seipsam* would likely be better translated "in itself" or "in its own right" rather than "by itself."

[59] His discussions of self-knowledge in *SCG* and the somewhat later *QDDA* seem to come close; but the identification only becomes explicit in *InDA* III.3 and *ST* Ia.87.1. See references in note 41 above.

(2) cognition of the soul under a universal aspect, i.e., cognition of "what the soul is" (*quid est*), which we call quidditative or scientific self-knowledge. It can have two components:
   (a) apprehension of the soul's essence, attained by argumentation;
   (b) judgment affirming that the apprehended essence does exist in reality.

In its actual self-awareness, the actualized mind has intimate access to its existence and its acts, which it cognizes "from the inside" in the first person. In contrast, quidditative self-knowledge is reached only by a long and difficult process of reasoning, because prephilosophical self-awareness does not include a grasp of one's own nature, acts, or powers.

Now what about development? Can Aquinas's texts all be trusted to tell this same story about self-knowledge over the twenty-year period from 1252 to 1272? If we understand 'development' in the sense of changing one's philosophical position, Aquinas's theory undergoes development only from the first to the second phase of his writing on self-knowledge. His initial dalliance with an Albertist theory of supraconscious self-knowing in *Sent* I, and the fact that he does not repudiate this theory explicitly until *DV* 10.8 (even though in *Sent* III he is already laying the groundwork for his own opposing position), suggest that one should exercise caution when using texts from the *Sentences* to interpret later texts. Aquinas's own views on self-knowledge crystallize in *DV* 10.8 and remain stable throughout the rest of his career.

But if we understand 'development' in the sense of a maturation in which an author increasingly masters his own theory, refining his grasp of what is at stake and working toward a clearer view of the principles required to support his argumentation – then we can say that such a development occurs throughout the second and third phases of Aquinas's writing on self-knowledge. The texts tell the story of an increasingly sophisticated appraisal of the phenomena and their anthropological implications. In the second phase, he had sought to preserve the insights from various sources by matching different traditions to different phenomena of self-knowledge, recognizing that although Aristotle best safeguards self-opacity with his claim that the mind cognizes itself "like other things" (or by a species), thinkers like Augustine, Avicenna, and the *Liber de causis* have something important to say about the feeling of privileged access to one's own mental acts. His reflection on the reality of self-opacity culminates with *SCG* 3.46 and its four opening arguments about what ordinary experience would be like if the mind, simply by being itself, intuited

itself completely. In the third phase, he explicitly connects all the phenomena of self-knowledge to each other and cements them onto a unified
anthropological foundation: Due to its sheer potency for intelligible form,
the human intellect is made intelligible only by acting. This insight allows
him to streamline his account in an original way. Whereas in the second
phase self-awareness occurs "by one's act" and quidditative self-knowledge
occurs "by a species," in the third phase these distinct accounts are reduced
to one that applies to all types of self-knowledge. "The intellect cognizes
itself by the species that become its forms insofar as it is actualized by
them" (*SLDC* 15) – and it can only cognize itself in this way because of its
essential potency to intelligible form, as the intellectual power of a hylomorphic form. Self-knowledge comes into its own as a test case for a hylomorphic anthropology.[60]

---

[60] *DUI* 3 [Leon.43.307:402–10]: "[S]i hoc intellectiuum principium quo nos intelligimus, esset secundum esse separatum et distinctum ab anima que est corporis nostri forma, esset secundum se intelligens et intellectum, et non quandoque intelligeret, quandoque non; neque etiam indigeret ut
se ipsum cognosceret per intelligibilia et per actus, sed per essentiam sum sicut alie substantie
separate."

PART II

Phenomena and problems

CHAPTER THREE

Perceiving myself
The content of actual self-awareness

Self-awareness: an everyday phenomenon

Aquinas's effort to reconcile self-opacity and privileged access leads his theory of actual self-awareness into territory yet uncharted in the thirteenth century: How can one affirm the dependence of actual self-awareness on cognition of extramental objects without undermining the intimate, first-person character of our ordinary self-awareness? Aquinas's strategy is to argue that one's existence is manifested to oneself only "by one's acts," thereby limiting the content of self-awareness while in the same stroke securing its intuitive, first-person mode.[1] Throughout the next two chapters, we will be exploring how this strategy plays out in two closely intertwined areas: (1) his quasi-phenomenological reflection on the content of actual self-awareness, which seeks to establish precisely *what* someone knows about herself in self-awareness, and (2) his psychological analysis of the mode of actual self-awareness, which seeks to describe *how* this act takes place. These two strands are too closely connected to separate completely, so although I will examine content first, I will occasionally have to fill in some gaps by referring to the mode of self-awareness. Detailed argument about the latter, however, will be left for the next chapter.

In a sense, it is a little misleading to use the term 'content' in connection with Aquinas's cognition theory, because the model that he uses for cognition is not one of containment, but one of intellectual actualization

---

[1] It can be difficult to identify texts that are specifically focused on self-awareness, since in his shorter references to self-knowledge, Aquinas often does not specify whether he means self-awareness, quidditative self-knowledge, or both. Still, the texts in which he most clearly outlines the differences between self-awareness and quidditative self-knowledge (*Sent* III.23.1.2; *SBDT* 1.3; *DV* 10.8 and 10.9; *SCG* 2.75 and 3.46; *ST* Ia.87.1 [and with respect to the will, 87.4], and III.1, ad 3; *DM* 16.8, ad 7; *DUI* 5) offer a number of clues to help interpret other passages. Descriptions of self-awareness are characterized by: (1) use of verbs of sensation such as *percipere*; (2) emphasis on the singularity of the object, whether the soul itself, its existence, or its acts; (3) use of accusative-and-infinitive constructions that show the intellect grasping a state of affairs (*intelligit se intelligere*).

(intellectual "matter" actualized by intelligible "form").[2] Properly speaking, Aquinas does not view the mind as a "container" for thoughts or ideas, themselves serving as "containers" for information about the world. Rather, he thinks of the mind as formally shaped according to the likeness (species) of the cognized object and actualized by thinking about that object. Thus for Aquinas, one ought properly to say that "the mind is assimilated to and engaged in thinking about some object," rather than that "it has a thought with such-and-such a content." Nevertheless, with this caveat we can still use the term 'content' as a convenient way of referring to what is being manifested or made present in a given species-informed act.

In inquiring into the content of actual self-awareness, then, we are asking about *what, for Aquinas, is made manifest to the thinker in actual self-awareness*. This is an important question, because it has to do with how he construes the basic phenomena that his theory of self-awareness aims to explain. Now Aquinas himself describes the content of actual self-awareness variably. Sometimes it seems to be the mere fact of the soul's existence, i.e., "that it exists" (*se esse, an est, quia est, quod est*).[3] But Aquinas also says that the soul or mind understands itself (*seipsam*) or its thinking (*suum intelligere*)[4] or itself doing something (indicated with an accusative-and-infinitive construction, *percipit se intelligere*).[5] In *DV* 10.8 and *ST* Ia.87.1, we even find phrases like "Socrates perceives that he has an intellective soul" or "Someone perceives that he has a soul, that he lives, and that he exists."[6] These formulations suggest a fairly rich content – certainly more than just sheer facticity.

I will address the differences among these formulations in a moment. But in the collective, they already reveal what phenomenon Aquinas is seeking to explain: namely, self-awareness is an ordinary, first-personal

---

[2] For detailed discussion, see Chapter 6.

[3] The examples are too numerous to list. For *se esse*, see for instance *DV* 10.8 [Leon. 22/2.312–6, lines 224, 233, 241, etc.]. For *an est*, see ibid., line 213. For *quia est*, see *SCG* 3.46. For *quod est*, see *DM* 16.8, ad 7.

[4] For instance, *Sent* IV.49.3.2; *SCG* 2.75 and 3.46; *DV* 10.8; *ST* Ia.79.6, ad 2 [Leon. 5.271]: "[S]icut intelligit seipsum intellectus, quamvis ipse sit quidam singularis intellectus, ita intelligit suum intelligere"; Ia.87.1–3; *DUI* 3 and 5; *DM* 6, ad 18.

[5] For instance *DUI* 5 [Leon. 43.312:234–8]: "Unde et intellectus meus quando intelligit se intelligere, intelligit quendam singularem actum"; *Sent* I.1.2.1, ad 2; *DV* 10.8 and 10.10, ad 5; *ST* Ia.76.1; Ia.79.6, ad 2; Ia.87.1–3; Ia.93.7, ad 4; *InDA* III.3 [Leon. 45/1.216:84–6]; *InEthic* IX.11 [Leon. 47/2.540.96–104]; *DM* 16.8, ad 7. See also *InDA* I.1 [Leon. 45/1.5:94–5]: "[E]xperitur in se ipso, quod habeat animam et quod anima uiuificet."

[6] *ST* Ia.87.1 [Leon. 5.356]: "[Intellectus noster cognoscit se uno modo] particulariter, secundum quod Socrates vel Plato percipit se habere animam intellectivam, ex hoc quod percipit se intelligere"; *DV* 10.8 [Leon. 22/2.321:222–4]: "[A]liquis se percipit animam habere et vivere et esse."

awareness of myself, my own existence, my mental acts. Aquinas generally conveys this intimate, first-personal character with the reflexive pronouns *se* and *seipsam*. But in some instances, he even adopts the first-person perspective of the self-knower: "I understand myself to understand,"[7] equating such personal self-understanding with cognition of one's own intellect: "We do not cognize our intellect except insofar as we understand ourselves to understand."[8] Self-awareness is simply an everyday concrete prephilosophical experience of oneself, and not some detached philosophical endeavor to examine "the I." It is an everyman's phenomenon, a common experience whose veracity cannot be doubted.[9]

Aquinas's choice of verbs to designate the act of self-awareness underscores the intimacy of the experience (here we must look ahead briefly to the mode of self-awareness, which will be discussed in more detail in Chapter 4). While he sometimes uses general verbs of cognition for self-awareness, such as *intelligere*, *cognoscere*, and *scire*,[10] the verb he most often uses is *percipere* (to perceive), a term more often used for sense-cognition. He describes self-awareness as a "perception" in at least twenty-two different texts from nine works,[11] most frequently in *De veritate* – where it

---

[7] *Sent* I.1.2.1, ad 2 [Mand. 1.38]: "[E]adem operatione intelligo intelligibile, et intelligo me intelligere"; I.3.3, prooem.; I.3.4.4; I.3.4.5, arg. 3; IV.50.1.1; *SBDT* I.3, ad 2; *DV* 10.9 [Leon. 22/2.328:159–61]: "Non enim possum scire me habere castitatem, nisi sciam quid est castitas"; *DUI* 3 [Leon. 43.303:27–31]: "Manifestum est enim quod hic homo singularis intelligit: nunquam enim de intellectu quaeremus, nisi intelligeremus; nec cum quaerimus de intellectu, de alio principio quaerimus, quam de eo quo nos intelligimus"; and texts cited in note 8. Aquinas is, of course, also familiar with first-person-perspective discussions of self-knowledge from Augustine's *De Trin*.

[8] *InDA* III.3 [Leon. 45/1.216:84–6]: "Non enim cognoscimus intellectum nostrum nisi per hoc, quod intelligimus nos intelligere"; *DM* 16.8, ad 7. The third person gives way seamlessly to the first person in *InEthic* IX.11 [Leon. 47/2.540:96–101]: "Ille enim qui videt se videre sentit suam visionem, et similiter est de illo qui audit se audire; et similiter contingit in aliis quod aliquis sentit se operari. In hoc autem quod nos sentimus nos sentire et intelligimus nos intelligere, sentimus et intelligimus nos esse."

[9] See *DV* 10.8, ad 2 [Leon. 22/2.323:335–9]: "[N]ullus unquam erravit in hoc quod non perciperet se vivere, quod pertinet ad cognitionem qua aliquis singulariter cognoscit quid in anima sua agatur"; and ad 8 s.c. [Leon. 22/2.325:521–4]: "Secundum hoc scientia de anima est certissima quod unusquisque in se ipso experitur se animam habere et actus animae sibi inesse"; *InDA* I.1; *InEthic* III.3 [Leon. 47/1.127:165–7]: "[M]anifestum est, quod non potest ignorare quis sit operans, quia sic ignoraret se ipsum, quod est impossibile."

[10] For *intelligere*: *Sent* I.1.2.1, ad 2; I.3.4.5; *DV* 10.8; *QDDA* 2.5; *InDA* III.3; *ST* Ia.79.6, ad 2. For *cognoscere*: *ST* Ia.III.1, ad 3; *DM* 16.8, ad 7. For *scire*: *Sent* I.17.1.4, ad 2; IV.49.3.2; *DV* 10.9 and 10.10, ad 5, etc.

[11] See *Sent* I.17.1.4, III.23.1.2, III.39.1.5.1, and IV.49.3.2; *DV* 10.8–10; *SBDT* I.3; *SCG* 2.75 and 3.46; *ST* Ia.76.1, 79.4, 82.4, 87.1, 87.2, 87.4, and 93.7, ad 4; Ia–IIae.112.5; *DM* 16.8, ad 7; *DeCar* 1, ad 7; *Quodl* 8.2.2; *InEthic* IX.11. Aquinas often uses *percipere* nontechnically with reference to "noticing" something, without specifying whether the perception is sensory or intellectual, though it is impossible to verify whether he always uses it in this sense. When it is used technically to refer to a particular cognitional act, *percipere* most often describes sensation. For instance, in Deferrari's *Lexicon*, which indexes the vocabulary of the *Summa theologiae* "and selected passages of [Aquinas's] other works,"

is applied to self-awareness thirty-nine times in the questions relating to self-knowledge alone (q. 10, aa. 8–10) – but also as late as *De malo*. Other terms borrowed from the vocabulary of sense-cognition also make an appearance, such as *experiri* (to experience)[12] and *visio intellectualis* (intellectual vision).[13]

In general, of course, it is not unusual to find Aquinas drawing comparisons between intellectual and sensory cognition. But the frequency with which he describes self-awareness as a "perceiving" or "experiencing" (instead of using terms like "understanding" or "cognizing") *is* unusual enough to attract attention. Black suggests that such vocabulary indicates the "vague, inchoate nature [of self-awareness], its lack of any real content."[14] Jordan likewise describes the term *percipere* as "looser" than *cognoscere*, such that self-awareness is a mere "affirmation of one's own activity," lacking "theoretical content."[15] Putallaz, however, glosses *percipere* as an "experiential consciousness,"[16] an interpretation that is supported by an examination of Aquinas's broader usage of verbs of sensation for acts of

---

the literal meaning of the verb *percipere*, consistent with classical Latin usage, is "to get, obtain, receive." Under the figurative meanings, the first pertains to sensation ("to perceive, observe, to obtain knowledge through the senses"); the second pertains to intellection ("to apprehend, with the mind; to recognize the nature of; to comprehend, understand, note"). See Roy J. Deferrari and M. Inviolata Barry, *A Lexicon of St. Thomas Aquinas* (Washington, D.C.: The Catholic University of America Press, 1949), s.v. *percipere*, p. 818. An examination of the approximately 1,200 occurrences of the various forms of *percipere* in Aquinas's writings via the *Index Thomisticum* (www.corpusthomisticum.org/it/index.age) bears out this analysis. Note, however, that although Aquinas tends to use *percipere* slightly more often in the context of sensation, its intellectual meaning appears nearly as often; and it is used equally frequently as a general term of cognition

[12] *DV* 10.8, ad 2 and ad 8 s.c.; *DV* 18.4, ad 12; *SCG* 2.76; *QDDA* 5 and 15; *ST* 1a.76.1, 79.4, 81.3, 84.7, 89.1; 1a–IIae.112.5, ad 1 and ad 5; *DM* 16.8, ad 7; *InDA* I.1, and other texts in which Aquinas appeals to an inner "experience" of our own acts to justify his cognition theory. This term should be interpreted with caution since the verb *experiri* and the related nouns *experientia* and *experimentum* have a broad array of extended meanings for internal and external sensation as well as intellection. Sometimes it can refer to an inner intellectual perception, but sometimes it refers to the "experience" (usually, *experientia*) or practical wisdom gained over time at the end of a series of experiences (usually, *experimenta*) by creatures possessing memory. The texts listed here refer exclusively to an internal experience of phenomena which could only be perceived intellectually. My analysis of this term, derived from a review of nearly 600 instances of *experiri* and derivative terms throughout the Thomistic corpus, substantially differs from the analysis in Deferrari's *Lexicon*, s.v. *experientia, experimentalis, experimentum,* and *experior*, p. 398. Deferrari treats *experimentum* and *experientia* as synonyms, and gives the primary meaning of *experior* as "to try a thing, either by way of testing it or attempting it" – a meaning which, as far as I can tell, applies in fact only to a very small percentage of instances.

[13] *ST* 1a.57.1, ad 2 [Leon. 5.69]: "Quaedam vero sunt quae sunt in intellectu vel in anima secundum utrumque esse. Et utrorumque est visio intellectualis"; compare *DV* 10.8, ad 2 s.c.

[14] "Consciousness and Self-Knowledge" 357–8. At n. 17 on p. 358, she adds: "The use of *percipere* here probably reflects the parallel use of αἰσθάνεσθαι in Greek as a general verb of consciousness."

[15] *Ordering Wisdom*, 129 and 133.

[16] *Le sens de la réflexion*, 106.

intellect. Interestingly, when Aquinas uses verbs of sensation (perceiving, experiencing, seeing, intuiting) with reference to specific intellectual acts, he does so typically in order to underscore the intelligible object's intimate presence to the intellect, analogous to the here-and-now experience of individual sensory objects.[17] The implied comparison to sensation draws attention to the fact that a certain intelligible reality is directly present to the intellect, i.e., grasped instantaneously without discursion,[18] or that it is present in its singular being.[19] For Aquinas, then, verbs like *percipere* and *experiri* serve as general verbs of cognition (like *intelligere* or *cognoscere*) to denote sensory or intellectual operations or some cognitive operation in general, but they carry an additional connotation of the object's intimate presence to the intellect, perhaps even in its singular being.

Thus when Aquinas describes the mind "perceiving that it exists," he is emphasizing the "feel" of self-awareness as an intimate internal experience of myself as an existing individual, concretely present to myself in my acts.[20] He is identifying self-awareness with a common, prephilosophical experience of oneself that is woven into one's daily life, and that allows the proverbial Man on the Street to use the first-person pronoun in conversation. The content of this experience is "myself," encountered as an existing individual. (We will see in Chapters 4 and 8 how Aquinas accounts for the experiential, first-personal character of self-awareness, but for now it is enough simply to note that this is the phenomenon he has in mind.)

---

[17] Aquinas explains this usage in *DM* 16.1, ad 2 [Leon. 23.283:375–84]: "[E]xperientia proprie ad sensum pertinet. Quamuis enim intellectus non solum cognoscat formas separatas ut Platonici posuerunt set etiam corpora, non tamen intellectus cognoscit ea prout sunt hic et nunc, quod est proprie experiri, set secundum rationem communem: transfertur enim experientie nomen etiam ad intellectualem cognitionem sicut et ipsa nomina sensuum ut uisus et auditus."

[18] *ST* Ia.58.3, ad 3 [Leon. 5.84]: "[E]xperientia in Angelis et Daemonibus dicitur secundum quandam similitudinem, prout scilicet cognoscunt sensibilia praesentia; tamen absque omni discursu." Aquinas speaks of the intellect "perceiving" complexes instantaneously all at once in a single glance, as in the case of cognizing one thing as manifest in another (*Sent* II.10.1.1; II.11.2.2; IV.49.2.5, ad 1), *per se* known propositions (*ST* Ia–IIae.57.2, *QDDA* 14, ad 16, etc.) or arguments (*SBDT* 1.3, ad 6).

[19] *ST* Ia.54.5, ad 1 [Leon. 5.52–3]: "*Experientia* vero angelis attribui potest per similitudinem cognitorum, etsi non per similitudinem virtutis cognoscitivae. Est enim in nobis experientia, dum singularia per sensum cognoscimus: angeli autem singularia cognoscunt, ut infra patebit, sed non per sensum." Aquinas also often describes our cognition of God as a "perceiving" and of course even as a "beholding" in the case of the beatific vision (see for instance *SCG* 3.24, 25, 47, and 154).

[20] This makes sense given formulations such as *ST* Ia.87.1 [Leon. 5.356]: "[Intellectus noster cognoscit se] dupliciter. Uno quidem modo, particulariter, secundum quod Socrates vel Plato percipit se habere animam intellectivam, ex hoc quod percipit se intelligere"; and *ST* Ia.87.2, ad 1, which explicitly describes self-awareness as a perception from the inside [Leon. 5.360]: "Etsi fides non cognoscatur per exteriores corporis motus, percipitur tamen etiam ab eo in quo est, per interiorem actum cordis. Nullus enim fidem se habere scit, nisi per hoc quod se credere percipit."

As applied to self-awareness, then, the term 'perception' has to do with the cognitive experience of a particular phenomenon with first-personal content. Consequently, it is important to be clear that the term 'perception' as used here to translate Aquinas's term *percipere* has quite a different meaning from the contemporary usage of the term in connection with an explicit awareness, often higher-order, of sensory input. For one thing, it is not clear whether *percipere* or *experiri* in Aquinas even specially connote explicit awareness in intellectual or sensory acts; I have seen no evidence that they do. Moreover, *percipere* in Aquinas – like *intelligere* or *cognoscere* – is a general term that can apply either to the intellect's "first operation" of apprehending simple intelligibles[21] or to its "second operation" of judging complex propositions,[22] whereas 'perception' in the contemporary sense would be associated with apprehension. In line with his usage, when I describe self-awareness as a 'perception' or 'experience' of oneself, I use these terms as *descriptions* of a certain kind of phenomenon, not as *explanations* of that phenomenon. (For instance, in describing self-awareness in Aquinas as a "perception of one's acts," I do not mean that self-awareness is a higher-order monitoring of one's mental states.)

We have now taken an important step toward understanding the content of self-awareness, but we are still a long way from a complete picture. First, what should we make of the differences among Aquinas's descriptions of the content of self-awareness? Is this content supposed to be purely existential, focused on the sheer fact of my existence, or does it also include essential content such as 'I' or 'mind' or 'soul' or 'thinking, living, existing being'? Either option brings its own problems. On the one hand, if self-awareness already includes essential content, Aquinas's foundational distinction between cognizing that the soul exists and cognizing what the soul is seems a mere difference in degree. And it seems implausible that ordinary prephilosophical self-perception should include a *recognition* of my soul or my mind as such, or even of characteristics like 'living' and 'thinking.' On the other hand, it is hard to reconcile the claim that self-awareness is merely a perception of sheer facticity with Aquinas's broader position on how a thing's essence and existence are cognized.

---

[21] See *DV* 28.3, ad 6; and *ST* IIa–IIae.45.2, ad 3, where he distinguishes between "percipere et iudicare."

[22] Aquinas speaks of "perceiving" complexes, propositions, and intelligible truth, which is the work of judgment. For complexes and propositions, see the texts in note 18 above. For perceiving truth, see *QDDA* 2, ad 15. For *percipere* as affirming existence or truth, see *InPostAn* II.7 [Leon. 1*/2.199:151–2]: "[S]i aliquis percipiat *hominem* esse, propter hoc quod *est quoddam animal*"; *Sent* III.39.1.5.1 – and many of the texts in notes 3 and 6 above (especially *DV* 10.8), in which Aquinas speaks of "perceiving oneself to exist."

In the first intellectual operation, apprehension, the possible intellect receives an abstracted likeness of a thing's essence, cognizing *what* a thing is ('human,' 'being'). In the second intellectual operation, judgment or "composition and division," the intellect grasps the real existence of the corresponding thing (*esse rei*)[23] and pronounces a propositional judgment, such as "Man is a rational animal," "Socrates is not sitting," "Socrates exists."[24] Although these operations need not have a distinct temporal sequence, for Aquinas apprehension has ontological priority. Some degree of essential content is always necessary as the grounding for a judgment of existence,[25] so there can be no grasp of facticity without some apprehended essential content.

Second, can Aquinas account for the limited content of self-awareness, such that in grasping my own existence I do not thereby instantaneously know the nature of the mind?[26] If self-awareness is an *experience of myself*, it is not clear what prevents me from cognizing myself completely in such experiences. Confusion about this content-related question bleeds into discussions of the mode of self-awareness. For instance, one argument

---

[23] It is significant that Aquinas makes judgment, and not apprehension, responsible for grasping a thing's real existence; see *SBDT* 5.3 [Leon. 50.147:101–2]: "Secunda vero operatio respicit ipsum esse rei." Since apprehension concerns universalized essences, it would only grasp existence universally as 'existence as such' – in which case judging that "this man really exists" would involve remotely recombining the universalized concepts 'man' and 'existence.' For Aquinas, however, the human intellect is oriented, not toward abstractions, but toward the essences of real things – the actually existing trees and buildings in our sensory environment, whose existence is not grasped abstractly by apprehension, but rather affirmed concretely by judgment (on this point, see the studies by Owens, Knasas, Maritain, Gilson, and Wippel in note 24).

[24] On these two operations see *SBDT* 5.3; *InPerierm* I.1 and 1.3; *ST* Ia.16.2; *ST* Ia.85.2, ad 3; *InDA* III.5. For the Aristotelian texts from which Aquinas derives this theory, see Aristotle *De anima* 430a26–b30; *De interpretatione* 1.16a9–12. There has been considerable scholarly controversy about which operation grasps existence. For some of the main proponents of the view that I adopt here, see Jacques Maritain, *Existence and the Existent*, trans. Lewis Galantiere and Gerald B. Phelan (New York: Pantheon Books, 1948), 25; Étienne Gilson, *Being and Some Philosophers* (Toronto: PIMS, 1949), 203–9; Joseph Owens, *An Interpretation of Existence* (Milwaukee, Wis.: Bruce Publishing Co., 1968), ch. 2; Joseph Owens, *An Elementary Christian Metaphysics* (Milwaukee, Wis.: Bruce Publishing Co., 1963), ch. 3; John F. Wippel, *The Metaphysical Thought of Thomas Aquinas: From Finite Being to Uncreated Being* (Washington, D.C.: The Catholic University of America Press, 2000), 24–31; John F.X. Knasas, *Being and Some Twentieth-Century Thomists* (New York: Fordham University Press, 2003), 182–202. An opposing view, according to which a thing's existence and its essence are each grasped separately by the operation of apprehension and then joined by the operation of judgments, is defended by L.-M. Régis, *Epistemology*, trans. Imelda Choquette Byrne (New York: Macmillan, 1959), especially 312–32; and Francis A. Cunningham, *Essence and Existence in Thomism* (Lanham, Md.: University Press of America, 1988), 47.

[25] For articulation of this principle, see for instance *SBDT* 6.3 and *InPostAn* II.7 [Leon. 1*/2.199:127–54]; and Joseph de Finance, *Connaissance de l'être: traité d'ontologie* (Paris: Desclée de Brouwer, 1966), 47: "We only grasp existence through the existent, *esse* through *ens*" (translation mine).

[26] See the discussion of *SCG* 3.46 in Chapter 2, pp. 51–3 and 62.

frequently raised against the intuitive character of self-awareness (to be discussed in Chapter 4) relies on the following major premise:

> Since the soul *is itself*, if the soul intuitively perceived *its own singular self*, it would necessarily "see" its whole essence in the first instant of self-perception.[27]

This premise takes for granted that the content of self-awareness is all-or-nothing, so that if the mind were directly manifested to itself *at all* in the act of self-awareness, it would cognize itself comprehensively.[28] (And thus, the argument continues, since we obviously do not comprehend the essence of the mind in the moment of actual self-awareness, the latter cannot be an experiential cognition of *oneself*.[29]) So it seems as though Aquinas must choose between accounting for the privileged self-access and first-personal character of self-awareness, or the experience of self-opacity in self-awareness.

The key to answering these questions – and thus the key to elucidating the content of self-awareness – lies in the fact that for Aquinas, self-awareness belongs to a group of cognitive phenomena that we can call "indistinct perceptions," in which an object of sensory or intellectual experience is grasped in such a way that its essence cannot be properly distinguished from that of other things. This solution is suggested in *SCG* 3.46 and *ST* Ia.87.1:

> Augustine says in the tenth book on the Trinity [*De Trin* 10.9.12] that "the soul, when it seeks knowledge of itself, does not seek to grasp itself as though it were absent, but present [to itself] it strives to discern itself – not so that it might cognize itself as though it did not know itself, but so that it might distinguish itself from that which it knows to be other." By this, he indicates that the mind cognizes itself by itself as present, not as distinct from other things. Whence he says that some erred in that they did not distinguish the soul from other things that were diverse from it. But by knowing scientifically what a thing is, the thing is scientifically known insofar as it is distinct from others; whence, too, the definition, which signifies what

---

[27] See Roland-Gosselin, "Peut-on parler d'intuition intellectuelle," 729; and Garrigou-Lagrange, "Utrum mens," where this unstated premise guides the analysis, coupled with an assumption that no cognition *per speciem* can be intuitive. More recently, see Martin, "Self-Knowledge and Cognitive Ascent," 98–9; Lambert, "Nonintentional Experience of Oneself," 272; Reichmann, "The 'Cogito' in St. Thomas," 348; and Francisca Tomar Romero, "La *memoria* como conocimiento y amor de sí," *Revista española de filosofía medieval* 8 (2001): 95–110 (here at 102).

[28] Sertillanges even goes so far as to argue, "Were we able to discover ourselves we should discover everything. To comprehend ourselves in our knowing states would be to comprehend the world" (*Foundations of Thomistic Philosophy*, 34).

[29] For further argumentation against intuitive self-awareness, see pp. 101–2, below.

a thing is, distinguishes the definitum from all others ... Thus Augustine's intention [in *De Trin* 9.3.3] was to say that our mind knows itself by itself insofar as it cognizes that it exists. For from perceiving that it acts, it perceives that it exists ...[30]

Augustine [*De Trin* 10.9.12] says regarding such inquiry [into the soul's nature]: "Let the mind seek, not to see itself as though absent, but to discern its present self," i.e., to cognize its difference from other things; which is to cognize its essence and nature.[31]

Notice that in appealing to Augustine, Aquinas is contrasting self-awareness and quidditative self-knowledge as an "indistinct" perception of the present, existing soul and a "distinct" knowledge of the soul's essence.[32] This designation provides an important clue to the content of self-awareness, since in his general cognition theory, the difference between indistinct and distinct cognition has to do with content. Thus we must briefly investigate Aquinas's general theory of indistinct cognition[33] in order to ascertain what kind of content he attributes to the indistinct perception of existents. We can then show that self-awareness is an indistinct self-perception with both existential and essential content.

Indistinct cognition

Cognitive indistinctness in Aquinas is traceable to the weak human intellect's incapacity for full and instant comprehension, compounded in some

---

[30] *SCG* 3.46 [Leon. 14.123]: "[Augustinus] dicit in X libro *de Trin*. quod *anima, cum sui notitiam quaerit, non velut absentem se quaerit cernere, sed praesentem se curat discernere: non ut cognoscat se, quasi non novit; sed ut dignoscat ab eo quod alterum novit.* Ex quo dat intelligere quod anima per se cognoscit seipsam quasi praesentem, non quasi ab aliis distinctam. Unde et in hoc dicit aliquos errasse, quo animam non distinxerunt ab illis quae sunt ab ipsa diversa. Per hoc autem quod scitur de re quid est, scitur res prout est ab aliis distincta: unde et definitio, quae significat quid est res, distinguit definitum ab omnibus aliis ... Sic igitur, secundum intentionem Augustini, mens nostra per seipsam novit seipsam inquantum de se cognoscit quod est."

[31] *ST* 1a.87.1 [Leon. 5.356]: "Propter quod Augustinus dicit, X *de Trin*., de tali inquisitione mentis [quidditative self-knowledge]: *Non velut absentem se quaerat mens cernere; sed praesentem quaerat discernere*, idest cognoscere differentiam suam ab aliis rebus, quod est cognoscere quidditatem et naturam suam"; see also *DM* 16.8, ad 7. In *ST* 1a.93.7, ad 4, Aquinas interprets a similar Augustinian comment about "thinking of oneself as discrete from things that are not itself" as a reference to actual self-awareness (*De Trin* 14.6.9 [*CCSL* 50A.432]: "Sed quoniam mentem super sui meminisse semperque se ipsam intelligere et amare, quamuis non semper se cogitare discretam ab eis quae non sunt quod ipsa est"; the second Augustinian maxim from Chapter 1). The reason is probably that Aquinas interprets the first half of this maxim as a reference to habitual self-awareness, so it made sense to treat the second half as a reference to actual self-awareness.

[32] For the definition of *discernere* in Aquinas and other thirteenth-century thinkers, see p. 45, note 13.

[33] This area of his cognition theory has received surprisingly little attention; but see Pasnau, *Thomas Aquinas on Human Nature*, 318–29.

cases by incomplete sensory data or confusion in the imagination.[34] His theory of indistinct cognition originates in Aristotle's claim in *Physics* I.I that we first cognize things confusedly and generally, and then proceed to a more perfect, specific knowledge of them.[35] Following Aristotle, he takes up a classic example that we can call "indistinct perception," in which the essence of a singular object of perception is grasped at a too-universal level: "When someone is seen from a distance, we first perceive that it is a body before perceiving that it is an animal – and this, before perceiving that it is a man, and finally that it is Socrates."[36]

Now Aquinas is here using the term 'perceive' (*percipere*) in the non-standard sense that I have just defined, i.e., as a general term for intellectual or sensory cognition that emphasizes experiential directness. Here, the term encompasses the whole cognitive experience of this faraway individual, which is manifested to the viewer on multiple cognitive levels. Whereas a dog's perception of the individual Socrates is purely sensory, a human's perception of the individual Socrates is both intellectual and sensory: namely, it includes intelligible content concerning his essence and sensible content concerning his color, shape, etc., so that he is perceived as having certain sensory features and belonging to a certain kind, humanity.[37]

For humans, then, there are two reasons that in perceiving Socrates, one might grasp his essence indistinctly. (1) Confused sensory data leads to an indistinct grasp of this entity's essence,[38] perhaps because of my own visual inadequacies (I misplaced my glasses or am blinded by the sun), or because of obstacles in the intervening medium (the air is foggy), or because the object is not clearly displaying its distinguishing characteristics (Socrates is wearing a disguise or crawling around in a way that is not typical of adult humans). (2) My prior understanding of the essence 'man' is indistinct (e.g., my concept of 'human' is really just a concept of 'primate'), so that even if I recognize Socrates as a human, I do not properly understand the essence that I am ascribing to him.[39]

---

[34] *Sent* II.II.2.2 and II.20.2.2; *ST* Ia.89.1; and Aquinas's curious comments about demonic assistance (*Sent* II.7.2.2) or divine assistance (*ST* Ia.12.13, ad 2) in unfolding the implications of what one cognizes.

[35] See also *Categories* 5.

[36] *InPhys* I.I [Leon. 2.6]: "[C]um aliquis a remotis videtur, prius percipimus ipsum esse corpus quam esse animal, et hoc prius quam quod sit homo, et ultimo quod sit Socrates."

[37] See for instance *ST* Ia.84.7, and for discussion, Klubertanz, "St. Thomas and the Knowledge of the Singular," 162–6; and Eleonore Stump, *Aquinas* (New York: Routledge, 2003), 260–2 and 270–3.

[38] See *Sent* II.20.2.2 and *InDMR* 7.

[39] See *ST* Ia.55.3, ad 2; *ST* Ia.85.3; and *InPhys* I.I.

Either way, the result is the same: The intellectual content of this per-ception of Socrates (i.e., my understanding of his essence) is insufficient to distinguish Socrates' essence properly from all other essences. This resulting indistinctness can manifest itself in two ways.[40] In one way, my understanding of Socrates's essence may not be specific enough, as when I conceive of 'man' in a too-universal way as 'animal' or 'creature' – or, at the most indistinct level, merely as 'a being.'[41] In fact, for Aquinas, every-thing I perceive must *at minimum* be grasped as a being.[42] Even if my sensory data is so impoverished that the perceptual object appears as a blur in the distance, I still grasp it as 'a thing' (*res*) or 'indivisible whole' (*unum*) – which for Aquinas is just to say I have grasped it as 'a being' in the sense of an individual.[43]

In another way, indistinctness can be traceable to the disorganization of intellectual content, i.e., the failure to distinguish between essential and merely descriptive content. For instance, in perceiving Socrates indistinctly as 'an animal,' I may notice that this animal is white, moving erratically, and speaking Greek. I may even append the name 'man' to the complex 'white, erratically moving, Greek-speaking animal.' In practice, this descriptive content helps to differentiate humans and bears. A more refined descrip-tion may even enable me to use 'human' correctly and consistently. But for Aquinas this descriptive content is only accidentally unified "in the way that the *Iliad*, i.e., the poem about Trojan history, has unity. And in this way an account is said to be one, when it explains the name or manifests

---

[40] For a summary of both, see *InPostAn* II.7 [Leon. 1*/2.199:126–35]: "[Aristotiles] dicit quod rem aliquam esse possumus scire absque eo quod sciamus perfecte quid est, dupliciter: uno modo secundum quod cognoscimus aliquod *accidens* eius, puta si per uelocitatem motus estimemus leporem esse; alio modo per hoc quod cognoscimus *aliquid* de essencia eius (quod quidem est possibile in substanciis compositis, ut puta si comprehendamus hominem esse per hoc quod est rationalis, nondum cognitis aliis, quae complent essenciam hominis)."

[41] See for instance *SBDT* 1.3; *DV* 10.6, ad 4; *ST* 1a.85.3.

[42] *DV* 1.1 [Leon. 22/1.5:100–2]: "Illud autem quod primo intellectus concipit quasi notissimum, et in quod conceptiones omnes resoluit, est ens ... unde omnes aliae conceptiones intellectus accipi-antur ex additione ad ens." This well-known text is a *locus classicus* for Aquinas's thought on the origin of the metaphysical concept of being *qua* being (see for instance Maritain, *Existence and the Existent*, 26; Gilson, *Being and Some Philosophers*, 204; Wippel, *Metaphysical Thought*, 40–4); but I would suggest that it also has less-often-discussed implications for 'being' as necessarily included indistinctly in all intellectual content. For being as that which is first apprehended, see for instance *DEE*, prooem.; *SBDT* 1.3, ad 3; *InMet* X.4 (for a more extensive list, see Wippel, *Metaphysical Thought*, 41).

[43] See *InMet* IV.2, no. 553 [Marietti, 155]: "[H]oc nomen Res imponitur a quiddidate tantum; hoc vero nomen Ens, imponitur ab actu essendi: et hoc nomen Unum, ab ordine vel indivisione. Est enim unum ens indivisum. Idem autem est quod habet essentiam et quiddidatem per illam essentiam, et quod est in se indivisum. Unde ista tria, res, ens, unum, significant omnino idem, sed secun-dum diversas rationes"; and *DV* 1.1 (which makes the same point, adding "aliquid"); see Wippel, *Metaphysical Thought*, 193 and 470.

the denominated thing through various accidents – as when someone says, 'Man is a risible animal able to be educated.'"[44] Such descriptions, while useful, fail to identify 'man' as something "one," distinct from all other things, since they fail to identify what is central to *being human*.

Now if either kind of indistinctness is merely traceable to inadequate sensory data in this particular situation, there is an easy solution: I can put on my glasses or wait for Socrates to get close enough to be recognizably human. But if my understanding of 'human' is *still indistinct in itself* (as is very likely unless I have learned how to define 'human'[45]), the solution is more difficult. The first step – if applicable – is to introduce specification into the indistinct essential content. According to Aquinas, the reason that intellectual content does not self-differentiate is that the universal wholes we grasp contain their parts only potentially. Because this indistinct essential content, such as undifferentiated 'animal,' is partly actual and partly potential,[46] I can actually grasp the universal without actually grasping its parts. To acquire distinct essential content, I actualize the potential parts of the universal whole 'animal' so as to distinguish 'human,' 'bear,' 'raccoon,' etc.[47] The more parts I actualize, the more distinct the content of my knowledge is. Learning about essences, then, is a process of differentiation-by-actualizing, which requires reasoning, further experience, and perhaps assistance from teachers.[48] The second step is to determine *why* humans are distinct from other animals, by selecting the specifying difference 'rationality' from among all the other accidents in the descriptive content. It is not sufficient to include 'rationality' in my descriptive understanding of humanity; I must recognize it as the feature

---

[44] *InPostAn* II.8 [Leon. 1*/2.203:92–124]; see also *SBDT* 6.3.

[45] *InPhys* I.I [Leon. 2.6]: "[D]efinientia secundum se sunt prius nota nobis quam definitum; sed prius est notum nobis definitum, quam quod talia sint definientia ipsius: sicut prius sunt nota nobis animal et rationale quam homo; sed prius est nobis notus homo confuse, quam quod animal et rationale sint definientia ipsius."

[46] *InMeteor* I.I [Leon. 3.326]: "Scientia autem quae habetur de re tantum in universali, non est scientia completa secundum ultimum actum, sed est medio modo se habens inter puram potentiam et ultimum actum. Nam aliquis sciens aliquid in universali, scit quidem aliquid eorum actu quae sunt in propria ratione eius: alia vero sciens in universali non scit actu, sed solum in potentia. Puta, qui cognoscit hominem solum secundum quod est animal, solum scit sic partem definitionis hominis in actu, scilicet genus eius: differentias autem constitutivas speciei nondum scit actu, sed potentia tantum. Unde manifestum est quod complementum scientiae requirit quod non sistatur in communibus, sed procedatur usque ad species"; *InPhys* I.I.

[47] *DV* II.I; *DV* 18.4 [Leon. 22/2.541:171–9]: "Principium autem [naturalis cognitionis] est in quadam confusa cognitione omnium: prout scilicet homini naturaliter inest cognitio universalium principiorum, in quibus, sicut in quibusdam seminibus, virtute praeexistunt omnia scibilia quae ratione naturali cognosci possunt. Sed huius cognitionis terminus est quando ea quae virtute in ipsis principiis insunt, explicantur in actum"; *InPhys* I.I; *ST* Ia.85.3 and Ia–IIae.27.2, ad 2.

[48] For discussion, see Pasnau, *Thomas Aquinas on Human Nature*, 324–9.

that properly distinguishes humanity from all other essences in the same genus – the "specific difference" in the definition.[49] When my grasp of an essence meets both of these conditions,[50] the content of my knowledge is distinct, properly distinguishing that essence from all other essences. At this moment I have achieved "quidditative knowledge" of the essence, articulable in a definition.[51]

***

A picture is now emerging of what kinds of content are included in the first indistinct perception that I have of a perceptual object like Socrates. Such a perception necessarily includes some indistinct essential content (at minimum, "a whole" or "a being"), as well as descriptive content taken from the object's sensible characteristics or from my stored knowledge of that essence. And – perhaps most importantly – unless a thing's essence is recognized as previously known, my initial perception of that thing *must* be indistinct. For Aquinas, the proper subdivisions of genera are not immediately evident to us. It takes experience and reasoning to reach distinct, quidditative knowledge of an essence. We can already begin to see what this account will entail for self-awareness as an indistinct perception. But since Aquinas so often describes self-awareness as perceiving "that one exists," a crucial piece of the puzzle is still missing: Where does perception of facticity (that something exists) fit into this account?

As mentioned above, for Aquinas essence and real existence are grasped respectively by the operations of apprehension and judgment. But when I perceive *a concrete object present to sense and intellect* in a maximally indistinct way as 'a being,' the apprehension of the object's essence and the judgment of its existence occur inseparably. As we have already seen, the minimal essential content for every perception, even the most indistinct, is 'a being.' But for Aquinas, a being is simply "that which is (*id quod est*)" or "something having

---

49 *InPostAn* II.8 [Leon. 1*/2.203:124–30]: "[A]*lia vero* ratio est una in quantum simpliciter significat unum de re una, cuius est ratio, et hoc non *secundum accidens*; et talis ratio est diffinitio significans 'quid est', quia essencia cuiuslibet rei est una"; with detailed discussion of how to achieve a definition in II.14–15.

50 There is no reason to think that for Aquinas these conditions are impossible to meet. His famously pessimistic statement that "nullus philosophus potuit unquam perfecte investigare naturam unius muscae" (*In symbolum Apostolorum*, prooem., no. 864 [Marietti, 194]) presumably applies to comprehension, i.e., perfect and complete knowledge. Quidditative knowledge is not necessarily comprehensive, but merely definitive.

51 *InPostAn* II.2 [Leon. 1*/2.180:65–6]: "[D]iffinitio est indicatiua eius 'quod quid est'"; see also *SBDT* 6.3, where Aquinas distinguishes a "perfect cognition" of the definition from a "confused cognition" in which one conceives 'man' "secundum cognitionem alicuius generis proximi uel remoti, et aliquorum accidentium que extra apparent de ipso" [Leon. 50.167:114–168:129].

existence (*habens esse*)," so that to call a concrete, presently perceived entity 'a being' is already to signify that it exists.[52] Thus if I am already perceiving the faraway Socrates as 'a being,' nothing is added to my knowledge of that being if someone says, "Also, whatever that is, it exists." To perceive something as a being is *already* to grasp it as real, existing, something that *is* – and vice versa. Thus the first and most foundational thing that we know about every perceived object is that it is a being and that it exists.[53] In fact, when our knowledge of some perceived object is most indistinct, we generally say that all we know about it is that it exists (its facticity), i.e., "that there is something there."

Now of course, Aquinas does not mean that merely to conceive of an essence is to attribute to it real existence.[54] To conceive of something we have never encountered ('platypus,' 'chimera') as 'a being' is to conceive of it as existing in some way, but we must subsequently judge whether the essence has real extramental existence or merely intramental existence. Nevertheless, ordinarily our knowledge of essences derives from encountering them instantiated in concrete, really existing individuals like dogs and frogs and apple pie, i.e., in the course of a sensory-intellectual perception, as defined above. In these usual cases, apprehending a *concretely present perceptual object* as 'a being' arguably entails judging that it has real existence, unless one suspends judgment, distrusting conscious experience.[55] To put it another way, while the concept 'a being' necessitates no judgment of facticity, to grasp *this perceptual object concretely present here and now as* 'a being' is already to judge that it exists.[56] And interestingly, Aquinas appeals to the same mechanism

---

[52] *SBDE* 2 [Leon 50.271:52–9]: "[S]et id quod est significatur sicut subiectum essendi, uelud id quod currit significatur sicut subiectum currendi; et ideo … possumus dicere quod ens siue id quod est sit inquantum participat actum essendi"; *ST* Ia–IIae.26.4 [Leon. 6.190]: "[E]ns simpliciter est quod habet esse"; see also *DV* I.I.

[53] Régis, *Epistemology*, 304; and Gilson, *Being and Some Philosophers*, 209: "[B]eing itself is neither existence nor essence; it is their unity, and this is why it is whole and sound. Since an *ens* is an *esse habens*, all that which is conceived as a being is also judged to be an is. It must be so, since 'to be' is part of 'being.'"

[54] I.e., the conceptual content 'a being' does not necessarily include the content 'existing'; see *InPerierm* I.5 [Leon. I*/I.31:358–60]: "[N]on solum uerbum non significat rem esse uel non esse, set nec ipsum 'ens' significat rem esse uel non esse."

[55] To put it another way, to affirm the object's temporal presence is to affirm its *esse simpliciter*, in contrast to the qualified affirmation of *esse* for past or future objects: "[N]on est *uerum uel falsum*, nisi quando additur *esse uel non esse*, uel secundum presens tempus, quod est esse uel non esse in actu, et ideo hoc dicit esse *simpliciter, uel secundum tempus* preteritum aut futurum, quod non est esse simpliciter, set secundum quid" (*InPerierm* I.3 [Leon. I*/I.18:230–5]).

[56] Owens, *An Interpretation of Existence*, 25: "A nature in abstraction from existence is just not there to be grasped, and existence apart from something it actuates is nowhere found in the range of human experience. Both appear and are grasped as different aspects of the one existent thing … they are aspects known through two different kinds of intellectual activity, one of which is communicated

(grasping an essence as existing in a real extramental – which he elsewhere calls the "turn to phantasms"[57]) to explain how the intellect can obliquely cognize extramental singulars like Socrates: The judgment that an essence exists in a real thing yields an oblique intellectual cognition of that singular thing.[58]

In sum, to cognize something "as present, not as though distinct from other things," as Aquinas says of self-awareness in *SCG* 3.46, is just to perceive it indistinctly in its sheer manifest reality (its presence), as belonging to the most universal whole of "being." Here we must be careful to distinguish the respective contributions of apprehension and judgment: Apprehension grasps 'a being' as the subject of real existence, and judgment affirms that real existence. But in this most indistinct perception of a concrete existent, these two operations are simultaneous, inseparable, and co-dependent. A maximally indistinct apprehension of essence and a judgment of facticity converge in my recognition that "there is something there"; "it is a being"; "it exists." In such perceptions, facticity is never divorced from a minimal essential content – we cognize facticity, not by itself, but as the existence of *some singular thing*, whose essence is indistinctly understood at least as 'something that exists.'

Making sense of the content of self-awareness

Against the background of this account of indistinct perception, we can now make sense of Aquinas's strange and apparently conflicting descriptions of the content of self-awareness: those that suggest essential content ("one perceives oneself/the intellective soul"), those that suggest facticity ("one perceives that one/the soul/the mind exists"), and those that suggest that an act is perceived ("one perceives one's understanding/that one understands"). If Aquinas thinks that actual self-awareness is simply an

through simple terms, the other through sentences"; see also Wippel, *Metaphysical Thought*, 33–5 and 44; Gilson, *Being and Some Philosophers*, 205.

[57] For just one of many examples, see *ST* 1a.84.7 [Leon. 5.325]: "[N]ecesse est ad hoc quod intellectus actu intelligat suum obiectum proprium, quod convertat se ad phantasmata, ut speculetur naturam universalem in particulari existentem." Klubertanz has argued that the judgment of real existence *is* the "turn to the phantams," by which the intellect indirectly grasps the real sensory particulars that are the objects of ordinary daily perception (see "St. Thomas and the Knowledge of the Singular," 165), but I would suggest rather that the judgment *depends* on this "turn to the phantasms."

[58] See *ST* 1a.86.1, and for discussion, Klubertanz, "St. Thomas and the Knowledge of the Singular"; Camille Bérubé, *La connaissance du singulier au moyen âge* (Paris: Presses universitaires de France, 1964), 60. For an alternative interpretation, see Stump, *Aquinas*, 272.

indistinct perception[59] of oneself "as present, not as distinct from other things," then there is nothing extraordinary in his characterization of its content. Like our indistinct perception of the distant Socrates, actual self-awareness includes three kinds of content. The first two constitute the *minimal common content* of every act of self-awareness, and the third varies from act to act and person to person:

(1) the most indistinct essential content via apprehension: 'a being,' grasped in the first person as 'I';
(2) existential content, via a judgment of facticity: 'that I exist';
(3) descriptive content taken from the particular act in which I presently perceive myself, or accumulated from previous experiences: 'a thinker-thinking-about-peaches, a sly fellow, a mind, a human, etc.'

First, self-awareness must have at least *some* essential content, because as we have seen, for Aquinas there is no such thing as a judgment of facticity entirely devoid of essential content. Nevertheless, the essential content in self-awareness is maximally indistinct; one grasps oneself simply as 'a being,' 'an existent,' 'something,' an undifferentiated 'whole.'[60] But whereas in cognition of extramental objects this maximally indistinct essential content would normally be equated with the third-person 'it,' in the case of self-awareness, it is in the first person, 'I.' (Perhaps one could say that this is an indistinct apprehension of 'a being,' not as *id quod est* but as *id quod sum*). For now we can take this first-personal character as given, but we will see in Chapter 8 how Aquinas accounts for it.

Second, self-awareness includes the existential content 'existing' or '[subject] exists,' because, as we have seen, Aquinas construes self-awareness as the cognitive encounter with oneself concretely present here and now (a "perception" or "experience"). In such encounters, it is impossible to apprehend the object as 'a being' without simultaneously judging that it exists. Thus in an act of self-awareness, (2) is necessarily packaged with (1); the judgment 'that I exist' converges with an indistinct essential grasp of myself as 'a being.' The judgment 'that I exist' is thus responsible for the individuality and concreteness of the content of self-awareness, such that the mind cognizes "what is proper to oneself ... insofar as it has existence

---

[59] Recall that as we are using it here, 'perception' is a general term of cognition, with the additional connotation of a direct experiential encounter.

[60] *ST* Ia.93.7, ad 2 [Leon. 5.409]: "Sed quia mens, etsi se totam quodammodo cognoscat, etiam quodammodo se ignorat, prout scilicet est ab aliis distincta; et sic etiam se quaerit, ut Augustinus ponit"; *SCG* 2.49 [Leon. 13.381]: "Intellectus autem supra seipsum agendo reflectitur; intelligit enim seipsum non secundum partem, sed secundum totum. Non est igitur corpus."

(*esse*) in such an individual."[61] Thus we can distinguish the contributions of apprehension and judgment in the act of self-awareness. I perceive by judgment that I exist, and I apprehend the subject of this existence essentially as a member of the class of that-which-is (*id quod est*). Nevertheless, the essential and existential content of this maximally indistinct perception is experientially indistinguishable to the thinker herself.

Third, as we have seen, all indistinct perception always includes some nominal or descriptive content. Self-awareness, too, has descriptive content taken from my experience of the acts in which I perceive myself ("One perceives that one knows ... that one has a soul, lives, exists"[62]), just as the descriptions 'white' and 'moving erratically' are taken from the visible characteristics of the indistinctly perceived Socrates. The descriptive content of self-awareness thus varies depending on the type of act in which I perceive myself and how I understand that act. If I grasp an act indistinctly only as 'an act,' then I perceive myself as 'a thing' or 'an agent'; but if I grasp it as 'an act of thinking,' then I perceive myself as 'a thinker.'[63] Moreover, the intentional object of that act is also part of the content of self-awareness. I do not merely grasp myself as 'thinking' but more precisely as 'thinking about peaches' or 'wishing for warm weather.'[64] (In Chapter 6 we will see why Aquinas thinks it is possible and even necessary for self-awareness to include this extramental content.) Over the years, the fruits of repeated experience and inquiry are stored in memory in association with the intelligible entity that I call "myself."[65] While Aquinas does not go into detail, one may reasonably suppose that this content is useful in constructing what is popularly known as a self-image, which could be included in later acts of self-awareness (for instance, I might now recognize myself as 'a mind' or 'a human,' or as having certain faults, virtues, or

---

[61] *DV* 10.8 [Leon. 22/2.321:210–12]: "[Q]uantum ad id quod est sibi proprium ... secundum quod esse habet in tali individuo"; *ST* 1a.87.1 [Leon. 5.356]: "Uno quidem modo, particulariter, secundum quod Socrates vel Plato percipit se habere animam intellectivam, ex hoc quod percipit se intelligere"; and texts in notes 4 and 5 above. Note though that the soul perceives itself directly, rather than indirectly as with material singulars, as we shall see in Chapter 4.

[62] See notes 5 and 6 above.

[63] "This concomitant cognition of self and one's own activity is not clear cognition. It makes the percipient aware that he exists and that he is performing the activity. But the kind of activity and the kind of agent can be known only through specification by the objects" (Joseph Owens, "Aquinas on Cognition as Existence," in *Thomas and Bonaventure: A Septicentenary Commemoration*, ed. George F. McLean, Proceedings of the American Catholic Philosophical Association 48 [Washington, D.C.: The Catholic University of America Press, 1974], 74–82 (here at 82)).

[64] *DV* 10.8 [Leon. 22/2.321:229–34]: "Nullus autem percipit se intelligere nisi ex hoc quod aliquid intelligit, quia prius est intelligere aliquid quam intelligere se intelligere; et ideo anima pervenit ad actualiter percipiendum se esse per illlud quod intelligit vel sentit."

[65] See Chapter 8, pp. 207–13, for the relationship of memory and self-awareness.

predilections). As we will see in Chapter 7, too, a philosopher can use this descriptive information in reasoning to a definition of the human soul.

In short, Aquinas's varying descriptions of self-awareness describe different aspects of the same basic content: The soul indistinctly perceives itself in an apprehension-*cum*-judgment as an existing singular, "a being," "something that exists." This perception may be "colored" more or less vividly with descriptive content taken from the acts in which the soul perceives itself. This descriptive content can accidentally specify the indistinct essential content 'a being' further as 'a principle of acting' or 'a thinking principle.'[66] Perhaps eventually I will even nominally recognize this principle as a 'mind' or 'soul' ("Socrates perceives that he has an intellective soul"). Nevertheless, the correct use of these names does not imply that I grasp my essence distinctly. Distinct essential content is achieved only in quidditative self-knowledge, by organizing and specifying my knowledge to attain the soul's definition (more on this in Chapter 7).

In response to our first question,[67] we can now see that there is no conflict between Aquinas's insistence that self-awareness (*an sit anima*) precedes quidditative self-knowledge (*quid est anima*), and his general rule that cognition of a thing's essence is at least logically prior to the judgment of its existence. In fact, Aquinas's main distinction between self-awareness and quidditative self-knowledge turns out not to be a distinction between a cognition of pure existence and a cognition of essence after all. Instead, it is a distinction between an indistinct essential/existential cognition of the soul as "something that exists" and a distinct essential cognition that attains the proper definition of the soul. So when Aquinas says that one cognizes "*that* the soul is" long before one cognizes "*what* it is," he simply means that one first encounters oneself as an existent in an maximally indistinct essential perception, long before one ever attains distinct quidditative self-knowledge.[68] But self-awareness is not thereby devoid of essential content; the soul must at least grasp itself as something.

---

[66] In commenting on Aristotle's famous example of the descriptive specification of "thunder" as "a sound in the clouds," Aquinas uses the soul as a further example: "Et eadem ratio est … si percipiat animam esse, propter hoc quod est aliquid seipsum movens" (*InPostAn* II.7 [Leon. 1*/2.199:151–4]; see also *ST* Ia–IIae.112.5, ad 1 [Leon. 7.327]: "[I]lla quae sunt per essentiam sui in anima, cognoscuntur experimentali cognitione, inquantum homo experitur per actus principia intrinseca, sicut voluntatem percipimus volendo, et vitam in operibus vitae").

[67] See pp. 74–5.

[68] *DV* 10.9 [Leon. 22/2.328:162–78]: "[M]ulti enim sciunt se animam habere qui nesciunt quid est anima … sed anima non est principium actuum per essentiam suam sed per suas vires, unde perceptis actibus animae percipitur inesse principium talium actuum, utpote motus et sensus, non tamen ex hoc natura animae scitur"; compare *InPostAn* II.7. Thus I would agree with Black that Aquinas defends the "vague, inchoate nature [of self-awareness]," but disagree that such

Here, Aquinas's strategy for preserving self-opacity in prephilosophical self-awareness finally comes into focus. On the one hand, every act of self-awareness, like all perceptions, includes a minimum core content: I am a being, i.e., something that exists, and I am acting. One's own reality and the reality of one's mental acts are absolutely certain, never in question. But on the other hand, because we do not instantly see which of the mind's manifested parts and properties are relevant to its definition, we only grasp ourselves indistinctly. The indistinctness of self-awareness does not result from some special mysteriousness of the human mind, but simply from the limitations inherent in the human mode of cognition.[69] The abstracted essences we cognize are manifested to us as universal wholes that contain their parts only potentially. This indistinct apprehension of essence is what grounds the initial judgment of existence.[70] The process of reaching proper definitive knowledge involves "explicating" or actualizing these parts ourselves later by reasoning, and sorting the essential from the merely accidental.[71]

The mind's essence is opaque to us in self-awareness in the same way, and for the same reason: "Although the mind cognizes itself as a whole (*totam*), nevertheless it is ignorant of itself, i.e., of how it is distinct from other things; and thus it seeks itself … as though its knowledge were not made completely equal to the mind itself (*non totaliter menti coaequetur*)."[72] This problem is exemplified in *ST* Ia.76.1, where Aquinas recognizes that although "everyone experiences himself to be the one who thinks," not everyone agrees that the agent to whom thinking is attributed is the whole

inchoateness suggests "its lack of any real content" ("Consciousness and Self–Knowledge," 357–8; compare the similar interpretation in Putallaz, *Le sens de la réflexion*, 110–13). What de Finance says with respect to indistinct essential cognition in general applies also to the content of self-awareness: "To affirm in general that there is being, is in no way to affirm an *indeterminate* being, but merely a being *whose determinations are unknown*" (*Connaissance de l'être*, 45, translation mine).

[69] See for instance *ST* Ia.89.1 on the difference between the indeterminate species that human intellects abstract from sensory information, and the fully explicit species that separate substances (angels and God) use. On ignorance vs. falsity in our understanding of essences and composition of definitions, see *InPostAn* II.7 and *InMet* IX.11.

[70] *InPostAn* II.7 [Leon. 1*/2.199:139–42]: "Oportet autem quod qui cognoscit aliquam rem esse, per aliquid rei illud cognoscat: et hoc vel est aliquid praeter essentiam rei, vel aliquid de essentia ipsius."

[71] See notes 46 and 47 above.

[72] *ST* Ia.93.7, ad 2. Interestingly, Aquinas here appeals to self-opacity in connection with a theological analogy, explaining that Augustine's triad of *mens, notitia, amor* does not represent the perfect co-equality of the Persons of the Trinity, because our self-knowledge and self-love are not adequate to our being; this co-equality is better represented by triad of *memoria, intelligentia, voluntas*, which are equal to the mind itself.

human individual (rather than, say, just the mind).[73] In accepting the need for argument here, Aquinas accepts the fact that we may describe our self-experience in the right words, while the part–whole relationships that define the intellect as a kind of thing remain obscure. Even the correct use of words like 'mind,' 'soul,' or 'thinking' does not imply quidditative knowledge of these essences.[74]

Consequently, in answer to our second question,[75] we can see that the premise "If the soul perceived *itself*, it would necessarily understand its essence" is grounded in a misunderstanding of indistinct perception in Aquinas. To cognize the soul's "very substance"[76] does not entail that one grasp the genus and specific difference that distinguish the soul's essence from other essences. It makes no difference that the soul is itself, or that it is immaterial, since its definition is still composed of parts.[77] For Aquinas, even if I grasped every characteristic of my being in the very first act of self-awareness (*per impossibile*, as we shall see in Chapter 4), the enormously rich descriptive content of such a self-perception would still have to be organized by reasoning, in order to identify the specifying difference that distinguishes human souls from other kinds of things.

The same applies to the nature of our mental acts. For instance, I may perceive myself as choosing, sensing, rejoicing, thinking, alive, behaving generously, etc., but I could be mistaken about the nature of these acts for the same reason that I can be mistaken about my own nature. For Aquinas, indistinct understanding of our own acts not only generates philosophical disputes, but lies at the root of moral self-ignorance. Because I perceive my acts indistinctly, I inerrantly recognize *that I am acting*, but without considerable reflection and reasoning, I do not know what kind of acts

---

[73] *ST* Ia.76.1. As Jordan puts it, "Whatever content is had in [self-awareness], it is not a speculative [read: quidditative] content. If it were, one could not explain how 'multi etiam circa naturam animae erraverunt'" (*Ordering Wisdom*, 127).

[74] Note that Aquinas often appeals to experience to support claims he makes about the nature and inner workings of the human mind, but he only means that we can check the reasonableness of our conclusions against our experience of what it is like to be thinking, not that these features of the mind show up as distinct items in our experience.

[75] See pp. 75–6.

[76] *ST* Ia.77.1, ad 1 [Leon. 5.237]: "Sic ergo notitia et amor, inquantum referuntur ad ipsam ut cognitam et amatam, substantialiter vel essentialiter sunt in anima, quia ipsa substantia vel essentia animae cognoscitur et amatur."

[77] By way of objection, one might point to texts like *InPostAn* II.7, where Aquinas says that one can have indistinct essential cognition of composites, but not of simple substances, "quia non potest cognosci aliquid de substantia simplicis rei, nisi tota cognoscatur" [Leon. 1*/2.199:196–8]. But nothing here suggests that Aquinas thinks this kind of simplicity accrues to the human soul. From the context, and from his comments on *Metaphysics* 1051b17–1052a4, which is his source for this claim, it seems clear that by "simple substances" he is referring to entities that are identical with their essences, i.e., angels or God (see *InMet* IX.11).

they are and from which kinds of habits (vicious or virtuous) they spring. Thus I might firmly believe myself to be generous, when in fact this "generosity" is pure self-serving.[78]

Two final problems

We have seen what the content of actual self-awareness is for Aquinas, what its common features are, and how its content can vary from act to act and person to person. But there are still two lingering worries about the relationship among his multifaceted descriptions of self-awareness.

First, Aquinas says not only that one perceives *oneself* or one's soul or intellect, but also that one perceives *one's act of understanding.*[79] But is "cognizing one's acts" necessarily equivalent to "cognizing oneself"?

Now in one sense, these are equivalent acts of self-awareness in the sense of *being the same kind of act with the same minimum common content.* As I will show in Chapter 4, for Aquinas acts cannot be experienced separately from agents. Any experiential cognition of one's cognitive act is *ipso facto* a cognition of oneself as agent. Thus whether self-awareness is described as "perceiving my act" or "perceiving myself," the minimum common content is the same: In self-awareness, what is manifested indistinctly is an existing, first-person individual-in-act. In another sense, however, Aquinas's account allows different instances of self-awareness to be "colored" by different descriptive contents. And because the content of self-awareness is complex, presumably I could direct my attention differently within that complex, focusing on the act itself and focusing on myself as agent: "I am thinking – *not just imagining, but thinking!* – about peaches" vs. "I – *I and no one else!* – am thinking about peaches." Still, the content of both acts would be the same in that they still all have to include 'I,' 'existing,' 'thinking' (and of course, 'peaches').

A second concern is that even though Aquinas seems to assume that the 'being' grasped in actual self-awareness is first-personal – 'myself,' 'that I exist' – he nevertheless frequently describes it either as the soul's perception of itself, or as someone's perception "that he has a soul." But for Aquinas, famously, the individual human person to whom the word 'I'

---

[78] See Aquinas's discussions of how we know our habits in *Sent* III.23.1.2, *DV* 10.9–10, and *ST* Ia.87.2, among others.

[79] See texts cited in note 4 above. In fact as we saw in Chapter 2 (pp. 46–9), in his initial attempt to divide the kinds of self-knowledge in *Sent* III.23.1.2, ad 3, he distinguished between the soul's "reflecting on its acts" and its "reflecting on its nature," although he uses a different formulation later.

refers is not the soul, but the human composite,[80] so it seems that perceiving my own soul cannot be equated with perceiving *myself*.[81] Is there an inconsistency here?

Now historically, the practice of using formulations like "someone perceives that he has a soul" to describe the experience of *me perceiving my own existence* would have been familiar to Aquinas from Avicenna and his thirteenth-century followers, for whom the phenomenon of ordinary first-person self-perception is the access point to an anthropological discussion about whether the human being has an immaterial soul. For these thinkers, when I perceive *myself* and recognize that I exist, I am already grasping my own soul without recognizing it *as* a soul.[82] This practice was reinforced by other sources, such as Augustine, who speaks interchangeably of cognizing myself or my mind; or Aristotle, who casts self-knowledge as the intellect's cognition of itself. Aquinas falls in line with this common thirteenth-century practice, which can be conveniently justified by his theory of indistinct cognition. When "Socrates perceives that he has a soul," he may be simply recognizing, "I exist," in which case *what* he perceives indistinctly is his existing soul, although he does not recognize it *as* a soul. Or, a more philosophically enlightened Socrates could be attaching the name 'soul' to what he perceives, but without distinctly understanding what a soul is. Aquinas's theory of indistinct cognition even has

---

80 See for instance *ST* 1a.75.4, ad 2 [Leon. 5.201]: "[N]on quaelibet substantia particularis est hypostasis vel persona, sed quae habet completam naturam speciei. Unde manus vel pes non potest dici hypostasis vel persona. Et similiter nec anima, cum sit pars speciei humanae"; *InCor I* 15.2, no. 924 [Marietti, 411]: "[A]nima autem cum sit pars corporis hominis, non est totus homo, et anima mea non est ego"; *DP* 9.2, ad 14. Aquinas's identification of the human person with the composite has received considerable attention in connection with his account of personal immortality. For a few key representative studies, see: Eleonore Stump, "Non-Cartesian Dualism and Materialism without Reductionism," *Faith and Philosophy* 12 (1995): 505–31; Eleonore Stump, "Resurrection, Reassembly, and Reconstitution: Aquinas on the Soul," in *Die menschliche Seele: Brauchen wir den Dualismus?*, ed. Bruno Niederberger and Edmund Runggaldier (Frankfurt: Ontos Verlag, 2006), 153–74; David Oderberg, "Hylemorphic Dualism," in *Personal Identity*, ed. Eleanor Franken Paul, Fred Dycus Miller, and Jeffrey Paul (Cambridge University Press, 1995), 70–99; Richard Swinburne, *The Evolution of the Soul*, rev. edn (New York: Oxford University Press, 1997); Peter van Inwagen, *Routledge Encyclopedia of Philosophy* (London: Routledge, 1998), s.v. "Resurrection"; Jason T. Eberl, "The Metaphysics of Resurrection: Issues of Identity," *Proceedings of the American Catholic Philosophical Association* 74 (2000): 215–30; Jason T. Eberl, "Do Human Persons Persist between Death and Resurrection?" in *Metaphysics and God: Essays in Honor of Eleonore Stump*, ed. Kevin Timpe (New York: Routledge, 2009), 188–205; Pasnau, *Thomas Aquinas on Human Nature*, chs. 2 and 12; and Christina Van Dyke, "Not Properly a Person: The Rational Soul and 'Thomistic Substance Dualism'," *Faith and Philosophy* 26 (2009): 186–204.

81 This concern is expressed by Putallaz, *Le sens de la réflexion*, 37, 75–92, and 294; Kenny, *Aquinas on Mind*, 119; and Black, "Consciousness and Self-Knowledge," 358.

82 See Avicenna, *Liber de anima* V.7, in p.25, note 31; a view repeated in his Latin medieval followers Jean de la Rochelle, *Summa de anima* 1.1, and William of Auvergne, *De anima* 2.13.

the resources to explain why it is psychologically possible for Socrates to conclude wrongly that the "I" he perceives just *is* his soul or mind to the exclusion of the body.

In any case, we need not worry that in identifying first-person self-awareness with a cognition of my soul or mind, Aquinas is inappropriately identifying the human "I" with the soul. After all, common usage allows one to identify oneself with various parts of the body that are not, strictly speaking, the human "I" but only parts thereof. For instance, when I complain to one person, "The cow kicked me," and to another, "The cow kicked my leg," no one would assume that I think that I *am* my leg, to the exclusion of other bodily parts. Nevertheless, it was my leg, and not another part of my body, that was injured. Similarly, I need not hold that I am my soul in order to use the statements "I perceive myself" and "I perceive my soul" interchangeably. Following Aristotle, Aquinas considers the soul to be the principle of vital acts, and he insists that self-awareness is the *intellect's* perception of itself acting, since full reflexivity cannot be achieved by any corporeal organ.[83] Therefore, just as I recognize *myself* as being-kicked when I perceive the blow to my leg, so too I recognize *myself* as intellectual agent when I perceive my soul, the internal first principle of that intellectual agency. This does not, however, entail that the agent (Socrates) is identified exclusively with the internal principle of agency (the soul).

---

[83] See *Sent* III.23.1.2, ad 3; *DV* 1.9; *SCG* 2.49; *SLDC* 7; and see Chapter 8, pp. 206–7.

CHAPTER FOUR

Perceiving *myself*
Is self-awareness an intuitive act?

"Like other things": the intuition question

From the content of self-awareness, we turn now to the mode of self-awareness. As we already know, according to Aquinas the human mind cognizes itself "by its act" or "by a species" (*per actum, per speciem*), in the same mode whereby it cognizes other things (*sicut alia*). But it is not at all clear what the implications are for privileged self-access. Does dependence on cognition of extramental objects "filter" self-awareness, making it less intimate or more remote than my experiences of other things? Or do I "intuit" myself directly or immediately in thinking about other things? We can call this the "intuition question." In various forms, it has received the most scholarly attention of all the themes in Aquinas's theory of self-awareness, partly because of interest in situating his theory in relation to Descartes's *Cogito* or Hume's imperceptible self.

Attempts to answer this question are complicated by the risk of reading a foreign conceptual framework into Aquinas, who almost never refers to self-awareness as an *intuitus*,[1] and who uses associated terms like *directe* or *immediate* in senses that may not always be relevant to the question that his modern readers are posing. So in order to attempt a solution, we will need to determine what it would even mean to ask whether self-awareness is intuitive, direct, or immediate in the framework of Aquinas's theory of cognition.[2]

---

[1] An exception is *Sent* 1.3.4.5, where he describes self-awareness as an "understanding" (*intelligere*) – a term he had just defined as a *simplex intuitus*. See *DV* 10.8, ad 2 s.c., and *ST* Ia.57.1, ad 2, for intellectual "vision" (*visio*) of intramental realities.

[2] An extended debate on the intuition question among early twentieth-century French Thomists serves as a cautionary tale in this respect. This debate, which was perhaps the most sustained scholarly inquiry into this question, ran from 1923 into the mid-1930s. Curiously, recent literature sometimes appeals to this debate as having authoritatively debunked the notion that self-awareness for Aquinas is intuitive (e.g., Still, "Aquinas's Theory of Human Self-Knowledge," 8; Jordan, *Ordering Wisdom*, 242, n. 7). But in fact, a close look at the often heated and vitriolic exchanges during that period reveals nearly identical interpretations of Aquinas on both sides. All agreed that the soul

First, though, we should address a misconception about how self-awareness is "like" cognition of extramental objects: namely, the view that for Aquinas the human mind cognizes itself by means of a species representing itself, abstracted from a phantasm of itself. This view is surprisingly common, though only rarely developed in print.[3] It originates from his references to the Aristotelian maxim, "The soul cognizes itself like other things,"[4] which is interpreted as establishing a strict parallel

can only perceive its own existence when engaged in cognizing something else. No one defended actual perpetual self-awareness (Romeyer, who was prone to exaggeration, came close in his initial interpretation of habitual self-awareness, but subsequently disavowed this view). Nearly all agreed that for Aquinas one "experiences" one's own existence; most were even willing to call self-awareness an intuition. Disagreement is typically traceable merely to lack of common definitions of terms such as "immediate," "direct," "intuitive," or "experiential," or to tangential disagreements about the natural knowledge of God or Aquinas's devotion to Augustine over Aristotle.The main disputants in this debate were as follows. On one side, defending the intuitive character of self-awareness, there was Blaise Romeyer, with a series of articles: "Notre science de l'esprit humain, d'après saint Thomas d'Aquin," *Archives de philosophie* 1.1 (1923): 32–55; "La doctrine de saint Thomas sur la vérité," *Archives de philosophie* 3.2 (1925): 1–54; "Saint Thomas et notre connaissance de l'esprit humain," *Archives de philosophie* 6.2 (1928): 1–114; "À propos de S. Thomas et notre connaissance de l'esprit humain," *Revue de philosophie* 36 (1929): 551–73; as well as Ambroise Gardeil: "Perception expérimentale"; "L'habitation de Dieu en nous, et la structure interne de l'âme," *Revue thomiste* 28 (1923): 238–60; *La structure de l'âme et l'expérience mystique*, 2nd edn, 2 vols (Paris: J. Gabalda, 1927); "Examen de conscience," *Revue thomiste* 33 (1928): 156–80; "À propos d'un cahier du R.P. Romeyer," *Revue thomiste*, n.s., 12 (1929): 520–32. Their most notable opponents were Simonne Leuret, "Saint Thomas et *Notre science de l'esprit humain*," *Revue thomiste* 28 (1923): 368–86; M.-D. Roland-Gosselin, Review of "Notre science de l'esprit humain, d'après S. Thomas d'Aquin," by Blaise Romeyer, *Bulletin thomiste* 1/4 (1924): 113–15; Review of "Saint Thomas et notre connaissance de l'esprit humain," by Blaise Romeyer, *Bulletin thomiste* 6/2 (1929): 469–74; "Peut-on parler d'intuition intellectuelle," 709–30; Garrigou-Lagrange, "Utrum mens"; and E. Peillaube, "Avons-nous expérience du spirituel?" *Revue de philosophie* 36 (1929): 245–67 and 660–85. When the debate finally wore itself out, it was recapitulated by Régis Jolivet, "Étude critique: Saint Thomas et notre connaissance de l'esprit humain," *Revue de philosophie*, n.s., 4 (1933): 295–311. Despite an incisive critique of some of Romeyer's views, Jolivet conceded that most Thomists would be amenable to the claim that for Aquinas the soul experientially "sees" itself in its acts (304).

³ Lambert defends this interpretation in *Self Knowledge in Thomas Aquinas*, 133–52. He cites four texts (*DP* 9.5; *DV* 4.2; *DV* 10.9, ad 7; and *ST* Ia.87.3, ad 2) in support of the view that self-awareness, depending on the act of thinking about some extramental, requires two species: a species of the extramental and a species of the soul itself. But none of these texts supports his position. From their context, the first three texts are apparently discussing concept-formation, not species-abstraction. The fourth text, which refers to the difference between the "act whereby the intellect understands a stone" and "the act whereby it understands itself understanding a stone," is trickier. Lambert explains that "since acts are defined by their species or objects, this statement would mean that there are distinct species for knowing the object and for knowing one's awareness of the object" (138). But for Aquinas, acts are distinguished by their *objects*, and a single species may serve to make present more than one cognitive object. So the fact that thinking about a stone and thinking about myself are two different acts does not imply that they use two different species (this point will be considered in more depth in Chapter 6).

⁴ In Gauthier's edition of Moerbeke's translation, *De anima* 430a3 reads: "Et ipse [intellectus] autem intelligibilis est sicut intelligibilia" [Leon. 45/1.214]; for the Aristotelian context, see Chapter 1. In quoting 430a3, Aquinas typically takes Aristotle's "in the same way" (*sicut et alia*) to mean "by a species"; see *Sent* III.23.1.2, ad 3; *DV* 10.8, ad 6 (in light of the description of quidditative self-knowledge

between the mode of self-awareness and the abstractive mode of ordinary cognition. But Aquinas does not interpret this maxim as literally as one might suppose; in fact, he rejects the most straightforward application of it. The structure of abstraction, as he conceives it, could technically have accommodated cognition of one's own intellect, though at the expense of explaining the phenomenon of first-person cognition. He could have taken self-awareness to be parallel to other cases in which we imaginatively construct phantasms from which we abstract intelligible species of things we do not directly experience (for instance, a wallaby, or "whoever it was that shot at me"), after reasoning to their existence or hearing them described. Such an account of actual self-awareness would have looked something like this: My imagination constructs a phantasm of 'my intellect' (or 'myself'), from which my intellect then abstracts a corresponding species and uses it to think about itself.[5]

But – perhaps to preclude this very interpretation – Aquinas repeatedly insists that the species used in self-awareness is the *species of the extramental object*. For example:

> *InDA* III.3: Therefore [Aristotle] says that the possible intellect is intelligible not by its essence, but by some intelligible species, just like other intelligibles … Therefore the species of the thing understood in act (*rei intellecte in actu*) is the species of the intellect itself, and thus by it, [the intellect] can understand itself.
>
> *ST* Ia.87.1, ad 3: And therefore the human intellect, which is in act by the species of the understood thing, is understood by the same species (*per eandem species intelligitur*), as though by its own form.[6]

The same is true even of quidditative self-knowledge (see pp. 180–1).

Now if one and the same species 'horse' serves as the principle of cognizing *extramental horseness* and of cognizing *my own intellect*, it seems that this species cannot be playing the same role in both cognitions. (We will return to this point later.) Thus we must be careful not to interpret Aquinas's maxim "The intellect is intelligible like other things, i.e., by a

---

in the *respondeo*); *SCG* 2.98 and 3.46; *QDDA* 3, ad 4; *QDDA* 16, ad 8; *InDA* III.3; *ST* Ia.14.2, ad 3; and Ia.87.1. (One exception is *Sent* 1.3.4.5, where this phrase is taken to mean "by the light of the agent intellect.") A caveat: although this maxim generally applies equally to self-awareness or to quidditative self-knowledge, its significance is somewhat different in each case; see Chapter 7 for how quidditative self-knowledge occurs "like other things."

[5] See Lambert, *Self Knowledge in Thomas Aquinas*, 133–52.

[6] For commentary, see Charles Boyer, "Le sens d'un texte de saint Thomas: 'De Veritate, q. 1, a. 9'," *Gregorianum* 5 (1924): 424–43 (here at 441–2), whom Putallaz follows in *Le sens de la réflexion*, 197–8. See also *DV* 10.8, ad 5 s.c.; *DV* 10.9, ad 4, ad 10, and ad 2 s.c.; and *SCG* 2.98; but note that in these texts Aquinas does not make clear whether he is referring to self-awareness or quidditative self-knowledge or both.

species" too stringently, then, because the mode of self-awareness appears to be different from that of cognition of extramentals.

Nevertheless, the recognition of this unique mode is still not enough to settle the question of whether self-awareness is an "intuitive" self-vision. Let us turn back to the intuition question, then, in order to determine what criteria must be satisfied in order for self-awareness to be "intuitive." The intuition question might be interpreted in a few different ways: i.e., (1) whether Aquinas thinks my own existence is self-evident to me (in the manner of the Cartesian *Cogito*), or (2) whether Aquinas thinks human self-awareness shares the *per essentiam* mode of Divine or angelic self-knowledge so that self-awareness belongs to the very being of the soul (as most of his predecessors had affirmed), or (3) whether Aquinas thinks human self-awareness has the intimate character typical of sensation. This third interpretation is the one that bests fits the intuition question as typically posed by contemporary readers of Aquinas.[7] Sensation is par excellence an "intuition" in the sense of a "direct and immediate vision of something present."[8] It provides a useful reference point for evaluating intellectual cognition, because sensation requires that the object be present *in itself* to the sense. In sensation, for Aquinas, there can be no proxies for the sensible object.[9] (For instance, if I see the curtain twitching because a mouse is running up it, I am sensing only the *curtain*, and guessing at the existence of the mouse. I only sense *the mouse* when it itself comes into view.) In fact, those who deny that self-awareness is an intuitive act in Aquinas typically mean that self-awareness lacks this paradigmatically sensory characteristic of direct and immediate presence, so that one "sees" oneself only by a proxy (the act or the species or the extramental object), as though from behind a curtain or in a mirror.[10] Conversely,

---

[7] See notes 10 and 11 below. Occasionally, in line with the second interpretation, human self-awareness in Aquinas is described as "indirect" or "mediate" because it depends on sensation and is therefore not innate (see for instance Still, "Aquinas's Theory of Self-Knowledge," 41). But this seems unhelpful; *no* human intellectual cognition in Aquinas is "intuitive" in the sense of being sense-independent and innate. So by posing the question in this way, we learn nothing new about how self-awareness does or does not differ from the mode of ordinary abstractive cognition.

[8] See the second meaning s.v. "intuition" in André Lalande's *Vocabulaire technique et critique de la philosophie*: "Vue directe et immédiate d'un objet de pensée actuellement présent à l'esprit et saisi dans sa réalité individuelle" (9th edn [Paris: Presses Universitaires de France, 1962], 538, with further discussion on 541–2). According to Lalande, this definition evokes sensation; he associates it with Kant (*Critique of Pure Reason* I.1, A320/B377).

[9] *DV* 11.1, ad 12 [Leon. 22/2.353:474–9]: "[N]on est omnino simile de intellectu et visu corporali: visus enim corporalis non est vis collativa ut ex quibusdam suorum obiectorum in alia perveniat, sed omnia sua obiecta sunt ei visibilia quam cito ad illa convertitur."

[10] E.g., Sylvester of Ferrara, Roland-Gosselin, Jordan, Grabmann, Rabeau, Kennedy, Dhavamony, Pasnau, Boulnois, Brown, and Martin, in notes 20–23, 26, and 28 below.

those who affirm the intuitive character of self-awareness in Aquinas usually mean that in that self-vision I am intimately present to myself without any intermediary.[11]

I propose, then, that the intuition question concerns the degree of similarity between actual self-awareness and sensation as the "direct and immediate vision of something present." This framing of the question avoids anachronism, since Aquinas himself frequently explains the structure of intellection by comparing it to sensation. In fact these comparisons suggest the conditions that self-awareness would have to fulfil in order to be considered "intuitive" to the same degree as sensation: Specific acts approximate the intimacy of sensory vision to greater and lesser degrees, depending on how they fulfill two criteria that I shall call "directness" and "immediacy."[12] (A word of caution: Aquinas's Latin terms *immediate* and *directe* do not always correspond to 'immediate' and 'direct' as defined here.[13] In such cases, I will use alternate translations, restricting the English terms 'direct' and 'immediate' exclusively to the meanings specified here.)

Directness

I propose to equate "direct" and "indirect" cognition with what Aquinas calls cognition of something "in itself," vs. cognition of something "from its effects." I understand dogness in itself (directly) because I have experienced the reality of dogness in real dogs, Fido and Spot. But I understand the university registrar "from her effects" (indirectly), because I only experience those effects (the grades she posts or the emails she sends). This is not to say that in attempting to think about the university registrar, I can only think about her emails. Dogness and the university registrar are equally objects of cognition for me. But I have no *experience* of the registrar in herself, so my understanding of the university registrar is limited by how well her effects indirectly convey the reality of who she is.

Of the various kinds of indirect cognition that Aquinas identifies, two are relevant to us, since as we shall see, something like them has often been used to explicate his view of self-awareness.[14] In the first kind of indirect

---

[11] E.g., Romeyer, Gardeil, Peillaube, Lonergan, Hoenen, de Finance, McKian, Pedrazzini, Ruane, and Putallaz in note 43 below, and Gaetani, Toccafondi, Reichmann, and Still in note 28.

[12] See *Quodl* 7.1.1, where Aquinas discusses the conditions controlling a given intellectual act's aptitude for being described as a "vision."

[13] E.g., in *Quodl* 7.1.1 he uses the term *mediate* to describe a kind of cognition that I will call "indirect," i.e., cognition of a thing by its effects.

[14] On both types of indirectness, see *SCG* 3.49 [Leon. 14.134]: "Contingit enim ex effectu cognoscere causam multipliciter. Uno modo, secundum quod effectus sumitur ut medium ad cognoscendum

cognition, a cause is cognized by reasoning discursively from its effect; for example, from reading emails, I infer that the university has a registrar and that she has a sense of humor. Here the cause and effect are cognized in two distinct cognitive acts. We can call this kind of indirect cognition "discursively indirect."

In the second kind of indirect cognition, the relationship of cause and effect is such that both can be cognized in a single act (this happens in the case of an exemplar cause and its image-effect). For instance, if I see a picture of the registrar in the school newsletter, I cognize *her in her picture*, in a single act without any discursion from the picture to the registrar. (Aquinas often uses the example of seeing someone's reflection in a mirror; perhaps hearing a story about the registrar could be another example.) This kind of indirect cognition can be called "representationally indirect."[15]

The reason that both these types of cognition are indirect is that in both cases, I never experience the registrar in herself, but only her effects. So we can construe the question of whether the soul cognizes itself "directly" or "indirectly" as follows: Does the soul have experiential access to itself *in itself*, or does it grasp its own existence only discursively (from another) or representationally (in another)?

Immediacy

According to the strictest standard of immediacy, an "immediate cognition" involves only the cognitive power and a present cognitive object, employing no additional psychological entities.[16] This standard is initially appealing because it reflects the prephilosophical experience of sensory objects as being "right there, before my very eyes." But such a standard is too strict for our purposes, because it precludes the use of sensible and intelligible species, which are essential to Aquinas's theory of sensory and intellectual cognition. Self-awareness in Aquinas cannot meet this

---

de causa quod sit, et quod talis sit: sicut accidit in scientiis, quae causam demonstrant per effectum [= discursive indirectness]. – Alio modo, ita quod in ipso effectu videatur causa, inquantum similitudo causae resultat in effectu: sicut homo videtur in speculo propter suam similitudinem [= representational indirectness]. Et differt hic modus a primo. Nam in primo sunt duae cognitiones, effectus et causae, quarum una est alterius causa: nam cognitio effectus est causa quod cognoscatur eius causa. In modo autem secundo una est visio utriusque: simul enim dum videtur effectus, videtur et causa in ipso"; *Quodl* 7.1.1.

[15] For this type of indirectness, see *ST* Ia.56.3.

[16] Garrigou-Lagrange apparently has this sort of criterion in mind when he says that Aquinas's adherence to a doctrine of intelligible species means that no cognitive act in this life, including self-awareness, can be intuitive; see "Utrum mens," 54.

standard of immediacy, because it relies in some way on a species – but then neither can sensation, not to mention intellectual cognition of extramental entities.

So instead, I will here adopt a more generous standard of immediacy, according to which a cognitive act can be immediate even if it employs a species, as long as the species merely facilitates cognition without interposing itself in any way between the cognitive power and the object.[17] And in fact, scholars representing diverse lines of interpretation, such as Stump, O'Callaghan, Knasas, and Dewan, have argued that intelligible and sensory species in Aquinas have precisely this sort of facilitating role: i.e., they serve to conform the cognitive powers to their objects, without behaving like intermediaries in the cognitive act.[18] If they are right, we can construe the question of whether self-awareness in Aquinas is "immediate" as follows: Is the role of the species of an extramental object in self-awareness such that self-awareness has *at least* the same degree of immediacy as sensation does?

Self-awareness as self-intuition

Arguments for indirect self-awareness and the first-person problem

When Aquinas insists that human beings become aware of themselves "by their acts" (*per actum*),[19] some of his readers have taken him to mean that I cannot *directly access my own self*, the agent performing those acts. While this view is familiar from Hume, as an interpretation of Aquinas it can be traced at least to the sixteenth-century Thomistic commentator, Sylvester

---

[17] "Immediacy" in this sense would certainly exclude representational indirectness, i.e., the species functioning crudely as an internal picture *at which* the mind or sense is looking. But it would also exclude more sophisticated accounts whereby the species interposes itself "invisibly" between sense/ intellect and object as a means of communication between the two (like a translator or a radio transmission).

[18] Stump, *Aquinas*, 245–6; John P. O'Callaghan, *Thomist Realism and the Linguistic Turn: Toward a More Perfect Form of Existence* (Notre Dame, Ind.: Notre Dame Press, 2003), 199–236, esp. 208–24; Lawrence Dewan, "Saint Thomas, Ideas, and Immediate Knowledge," *Dialogue* 18 (1979): 392–404; and Knasas, *Being and Some Twentieth-Century Thomists* – though of course these authors differ on the specifics of this interpretation. Their interpretation has been challenged by, for instance, Robert Pasnau, *Theories of Cognition in the Middle Ages* (Cambridge University Press, 1997), ch. 6; and Claude Panaccio, "Aquinas on Intellectual Representation," in *Ancient and Medieval Theories of Intentionality*, ed. Dominik Perler (Leiden: Brill, 2001), 185–202. A helpful review of various ways of thinking about the relationship of species and extramental objects is given in Brower and Brower-Toland, "Aquinas on Mental Representation."

[19] Most notably *DV* 10.8, *ST* Ia.87.1 and 87.3, and *DM* 6, ad 18.

of Ferrara.[20] This way of reading Aquinas was standard at the beginning of the twentieth century and has reappeared in various forms in more recent studies.

According to a more extreme reading, self-awareness in Aquinas is discursively indirect.[21] For instance, Roland-Gosselin argues that I directly perceive my acts and then infer my own existence from them – an inference that becomes so routine that I mistake it for an intuition.[22] A more moderate reading, recently developed in detail by Pasnau, takes self-awareness to be representationally indirect.[23] Pasnau interprets self-awareness for Aquinas as merely "a certain way of looking at external things: it is an outward look that is reflected back within." Thus, he says, the thoughts (1) "The cheese is moldy" and (2) "I am thinking that the cheese is moldy" are really just two different kinds of thoughts about the moldy cheese.[24] Thus I never catch a direct glimpse of *myself*: "There is nothing in Aquinas's account to license any sort of direct experiential awareness of the self."[25] According to this reasoning, the extramental object of thought serves as a proxy reflecting *myself, the thinker*, just as the registrar's photo serves as a proxy reflecting the registrar.

Both the discursively indirect and the representationally indirect readings, however, make it impossible to explain first-person cognition. Only one recent study, by Christopher J. Martin, has drawn out this implication. Taking Aquinas to be defending a theory of indirect self-awareness, Martin notes:

> Within Aquinas's account of the mind, the soul's proper actual cognition of itself can, however, it seems to me, be no more than the bare awareness of particular mental acts as occurring, that is to say, no more

[20] Romeyer has made an interesting case for this derivation; see his "Saint Thomas et notre connaissance," 66–70; the relevant passages appear in Sylvester's commentary on Aquinas's *SCG* 3.46, printed in the Leonine edition [Leon. 13.125b].

[21] See Roland-Gosselin, "Peut-on parler," 714–30, esp. 714–15, 721, and 728–30; and Grabmann's slightly earlier work, *Thomas Aquinas*, 148. The same view is suggested more recently in Jordan, who refers to self-awareness as an abstractive "inference" (*Ordering Wisdom*, 126).

[22] Roland-Gosselin, "Peut-on parler," 728. But somewhat incoherently, he also insists that one does not perfectly intuit one's acts, since the act itself is dependent on an abstracted species of an extramental one (726).

[23] Pasnau, *Thomas Aquinas on Human Nature*, 336–47; see also Boulnois, *Être et représentation*, 160; Deborah J. Brown, "Aquinas' Missing Flying Man," *Sophia* 40 (2001): 17–31 (here at 25–6); Dhavamony, *Subjectivity and Knowledge*, 82.

[24] Pasnau, *Thomas Aquinas on Human Nature*, 343–5, rejecting discursive indirectness at 337. Putallaz proposes a similar interpretation in his description of "pre-reflexive consciousness," which he nevertheless characterizes as experientially direct (*Le sens de la réflexion*, 109–13) and in his description of "reflexion in the strict sense" (ibid., 153–4).

[25] Pasnau, *Thomas Aquinas on Human Nature*, 349.

than an undifferentiated act of intellectual attention ... Indeed nothing
that Aquinas says shows how my awareness of my act of understanding
can be either an awareness that the act is *my* act or that it is an act of
understanding.[26]

As Martin recognizes, a theory of self-awareness in which I have no direct
access to *myself* is liable to a critique similar to the one often raised against
Descartes's *Cogito*: If I only perceive acts of thinking, how do I perceive
this act of thinking as *mine*, such that I can say, "I am thinking"? Where
does the first-person content come from? Indirect cognition can only lead
to the cognition of *some agent* in the third person. Yet I experience *myself* –
not some third-person agent that I happen to call 'me,' but something
qualitatively different, whose uniqueness I express by using the first person in speech.

Now the first-person content of self-awareness cannot be explained by
discursively indirect self-awareness. As Perry points out, if I see a trail of
sugar on the floor of the grocery store, I can reason that there is someone
making a mess – but just by reasoning from the sugar on the floor, I cannot discover whether I or someone else is that person.[27] The claim "*I* am
making a mess" is not reducible to and cannot be derived from the claim
"Someone is making a mess."

Nor can the use of the first-person pronoun be explained by representationally indirect self-awareness. If the cognized extramental object served
as a mirror in which I saw my reflection, self-awareness would be parallel to my recognizing "I am/was making a mess!" when I view the store's
closed-circuit TV footage of someone trailing sugar from a torn bag in
her cart. But once again, the footage portraying *someone* making a mess
is insufficient to ground the first-person recognition that *I* am that mess-
making agent. In order to connect the third-person agent in the video
with *myself* – in order to be able to use the first-person pronoun at all – a
prior first-person awareness is presupposed.

In short, every attempt to explain first-person cognition as a discursively
or representationally indirect cognition must presuppose some prior first-
person cognition. So in order for there to be any first-person cognition at

[26] Martin, "Self-Knowledge and Cognitive Ascent," 98–9; see also Pasnau, *Thomas Aquinas on Human Nature*, 455, n. 13. Gardeil ("Perception expérimentale," 227) and Bernd Goehring ("St. Thomas Aquinas on Self-Knowledge and Self-Awareness," *Cithara* 42 [2003]: 3–14 [here at 10–12]) raise a similar concern, but propose habitual self-awareness as the solution.

[27] See John Perry, "The Problem of the Essential Indexical," *Noûs* 13 (1979): 3–20. As his discussion is concerned with indexicals, Perry does not discuss the psychological requirements of such a claim.

all, I must have some sort of irreducibly direct self-access. (For now we will assume that direct self-access is the source of the first-person character of self-awareness; in Chapter 8 we will examine the connection between the two.)

Evidence against indirect self-awareness in Aquinas: perceiving agents in their acts

Nevertheless, the incoherence of a theory of indirect self-awareness tells us nothing about whether Aquinas himself held such a view. One might argue, for instance, that a theory in which the intellect can be aware of itself only "by its act" *must* be a theory of indirect self-awareness (however incoherent such a theory might be). In fact, the most common explicit reason given for ascribing indirectness to self-awareness in Aquinas is encapsulated in the following thesis, to which he is assumed to adhere:[28]

> The indirectness thesis: The intellect needs to be in act in order to cognize itself, *only if* the intellect cannot directly cognize itself.

So the reasoning goes, if Aquinas had thought that the mind could perceive itself directly in itself, he would not have made human self-awareness dependent on the mind's actualization in cognizing something else. The acts or the cognized extramental object, then, must serve as a proxy from/ in which the soul indirectly cognizes itself.

But this reasoning is based on the assumption that Aquinas holds an underlying premise that is in fact foreign to his view of the relationship between agents and acts:

> The separability premise: An act can be perceived without perceiving its agent, and an agent can be perceived without perceiving its act.

---

[28] Of course, the vocabulary of intuition/directness/immediacy is applied in different ways by different authors, but the idea is generally the same. See for instance Roland-Gosselin, "Peut-on parler," 726; Gaston Rabeau, Species, Verbum: *L'activité intellectuelle élémentaire selon S. Thomas d'Aquin* (Paris: Vrin, 1938), 88–9; Kennedy, "The Soul's Knowledge of Itself," 33; Richard T. Lambert, "Habitual Knowledge of the Soul in Thomas Aquinas," *The Modern Schoolman* 60 (1982): 1–19 (here at 13); and Pasnau, *Thomas Aquinas on Human Nature*, 333–6, 348, and 455–56, n. 16. This concern is raised even by authors who otherwise attribute to Aquinas what I would consider an intuitive self-awareness: F. Gaetani, "Come l'anima conosca se stesa. Controversie speculative e contributi sperimentali," *Civiltà Cattolica* 86 (1935): 465–80 (here at 466); Eugenio T. Toccafondi, "La spiritualità dell'anima e la coscienza dell'io," *Doctor communis* 11 (1958): 155–77 (here at 109); Reichmann, "The 'Cogito' in St. Thomas," 347–8; and Still, "Aquinas's Theory of Human Self-Knowledge," 26–8 and 41 (note that although he repudiates the language of intuition, it is because he defines the term very differently; see note 7 above).

According to the separability premise, perceiving an *act* is one thing, and perceiving an *agent* is quite another. Once we understand why Aquinas does not defend the separability premise, we will be in a position to see why he cannot hold the indirectness thesis.

The problem with the separability premise is that it treats acts like effects. For the medievals, however, acts are modifications of the agent-substance, whether they are what Aquinas would call "immanent acts" that remain wholly within the agent as internal perfections (e.g., thinking, desiring, sensing) or "transitive acts" that terminate in a product outside the agent (e.g., building a house, singing a song). Whereas effects have their own existence apart from the cause and can be perceived independently of the cause, for Aquinas, an agent and an act constitute just one thing, the agent acting. In fact, as De Libera has pointed out, the medieval development of the notion of subject-as-agent hinged on an increasingly prevalent view of accidental being as a determination or mode of a substance, rather than as something contained by a substance.[29]

This view has not merely ontological, but psychological import. For Aquinas, a substance and its accidents constitute a single perceptual object and are thus perceptually inseparable.[30] The substance is manifested in its accidental determinations; the accidents are manifested insofar as their being is derivative upon the substance's being.[31] Consequently, one sees, not bare "red" or bare "motion" or bare "thing," but a red, moving thing. (Interestingly, Shoemaker makes the same point against Hume: "An experiencing is something whose existence is 'adjectival on' a subject of experience. The ontological status of an experiencing, or an episode of being appeared to, is similar to that of a bending of a branch or a rising of the sun."[32])

In short, for Aquinas – *contra* the separability premise – to perceive an act is necessarily to perceive the agent directly in itself. One can perceive an effect apart from the cause, because they are two distinct entities. But one cannot perceive an act apart from the agent – to perceive the act *is* to

---

[29] De Libera, *Archéologie du sujet* 1, ch. 3 (esp. 50–1, where he lists common medieval propositions that support this narrative).

[30] See W. Norris Clarke, "What Is Most and Least Relevant in the Metaphysics of St. Thomas Today?" *International Philosophical Quarterly* 14 (1974): 411–34 (here at 419–21).

[31] The reason is that accidents are actualities that only exist in dependence on some concrete subject. See e.g., *Sent* II.26.1.2, ad 3 [Mand. 2.672]: "[A]ccidens est actus subjecti in esse accidentali"; and the discussion of the resulting logical structures in *ST* Ia.77.5 [Leon. 5.244–5]: "[I]llud est subiectum operativae potentiae, quod est potens operari, omne enim accidens denominat proprium subiectum."

[32] Sydney Shoemaker, "Introspection and the Self," in *Self-Knowledge*, ed. Cassam, 118–39 (here at 125).

perceive the agent. For instance, a student could use the university calendar without having any clue that it was compiled by the university registrar. But he cannot perceive her transitive act of "compiling" apart from perceiving *her*; to perceive this "compiling" is necessarily just to perceive "the registrar compiling."[33]

Aquinas's rejection of the separability premise is in line with ordinary intuitions; indeed, it is hard to imagine what it would be like to have discursively or representationally indirect cognition of an agent from/in its act. Discursive indirectness would entail that just as we perceive *effects* (the rustling of a page or the clink of a shovel) and infer the agent's existence, we could likewise perceive a bare act (thinking, compiling, digging), and then quickly infer the agent's existence. As for representational indirectness, when *A* is said to be seen "in *B*" rather than in itself, the indirectness obtains precisely because *A* and *B* are each independently existing substances. But when I say, "I saw the registrar compiling the calendar," I do not mean that the registrar's act of compiling served as an independently existing image in which I saw her. Rather, I saw the registrar in herself, compiling the calendar.

So much, then, for the separability premise. And since the indirectness thesis depends on the separability premise, it too is in trouble. In fact, we can now see that the indirectness thesis misses the point of Aquinas's requirement that the mind can only cognize itself "by its act." It assumes that his rationale is as follows: The intellectual soul is intellectually invisible, so it needs *something else* as a proxy from or in which it can cognize itself indirectly. When it is thinking about an extramental object, its cognitive act (or the extramental object itself) serves as this proxy; so the soul cognizes itself from/in its act indirectly.[34] The indirectness thesis is predicated on the assumption that an *act* can serve as a distinct cognitive proxy for an *agent*, per the separability premise – whereas for Aquinas an act is not an effect of an agent, but a modification or attribute of an agent. As Chisholm points out:

> From the fact that we are acquainted with the self as it manifests itself in having certain qualities, it follows that we are acquainted with the self as it is in itself. Manifestation, after all, is the converse of acquaintance: *x*

---

[33] Lambert, *Self Knowledge in Thomas Aquinas*, 160: "The subject is part of the meaning of the act"; Ruane, "Self-Knowledge and the Spirituality of the Soul," 433–4.

[34] According to this line of reasoning, Aquinas's account of self-awareness would be modeled on his account of how God is cognized in this life: Since he can never be seen "face-to-face," he can only be cognized in a discursively or representationally indirect way, from or in his effects. See texts cited above in note 14.

manifests itself to *y*, if and only if, *y* is acquainted with *x*. How can a man be acquainted with *anything* unless the thing manifests or presents itself to him? And how can the thing manifest or present itself unless it manifests or presents itself as having certain qualities or attributes?[35]

In insisting that the soul cognizes itself "by its act," Aquinas does not intend to claim that the soul is never directly cognitively accessible to itself. Rather, he is stipulating the *condition* under which the soul (*qua* cognized) becomes directly cognitively accessible to itself: namely, it must be in act. He appropriates this condition from an axiom originating in *Metaphysics* IX but more clearly articulated by Averroes: "For something is understood only to the extent to which it is in act."[36] Taken negatively, this axiom means that whatever is in any way non-existent is to that extent unintelligible. Taken positively, it means that something can be cognized only to the extent to which it has actuality. Any act renders the agent intelligible to some extent (for instance, *esse*, substantial form, and accidental forms, including immanent and transitive operations), though certain acts contribute more intelligibility than others.[37] For Aquinas, actuality is the root of intelligibility. One might say that actuality is the only language that the intellect understands. So "the intellect cognizes itself by its act" merely means that the mind, like everything else, must have some sort of actuality in order to be intelligible. And just as existence is the actuality of a material essence, so too the operation of thinking is the *intellect's own actuality*.[38] For Aquinas, to cognize myself "by my act" is to cognize myself-in-act – which is just to cognize *myself*.

Aquinas's rejection of the separability premise and consequently the indirectness thesis has important implications for the ways in which his account of self-awareness compares to later (and today better-known) early modern accounts. There are conspicuous differences between

---

[35] Roderick M. Chisholm, "On the Observability of the Self," *Philosophy and Phenomenological Research* 30 (1969): 7–21 (here at 21).

[36] *InDA* III.3 [Leon. 45/1.216:91–2]: "[N]ichil intelligitur nisi secundum quod est in actu." In the critical apparatus, Gauthier identifies this reference as a very oblique reference to *Metaphysics* IX.10, 1051a29–33, cross-referencing *SBDT* 4.2; *Sent* IV.49.2.1; *DV* 13.3; *ST* Ia.5.2, 14.3, and 87.2; *InPerierm* I.14; *DM* 16.7; and *ST* IIIa.10.3. In his "Introduction," 273*, he adds that Aquinas owes this specific formulation to Averroes (commentary on the *Metaphysics* IX.20).

[37] Even the forms left as clues in a substance's effects make that substance intelligible, though they only manifest the cause's existence, and only as absent (which is why one cannot experience a cause from its effect).

[38] *SCG* 1.45 [Leon. 13.136]: "Intelligere comparatur ad intellectum sicut esse ad essentiam"; *ST* Ia.14.4 [Leon. 13.171]: "[I]ntelligere … manet in operante sicut actus et perfectio eius, prout esse est perfectio existentis: sicut enim esse consequitur formam, ita intelligere sequitur speciem intelligibilem."

Descartes's account, according to which one can look at the subject just by turning one's attention inward,[39] and Aquinas's account, according to which there is no "bare self" to look at – only an agent that perceives itself by acting. Consequently, it is tempting to conclude that Aquinas would ally himself with Hume, for whom there is no direct cognition of "I myself," but only an indirect inference to the unperceived cause of my thoughts.[40] But the reason that Aquinas rejects the Cartesian paradigm is *not* that he agrees with the Humean notion of an imperceptible self. Rather, he rejects the assumption underlying both the Cartesian and the Humean accounts, namely, that bare subjects and bare mental acts or ideas are distinct, independently perceptible entities. For Aquinas, the subject is an agent,[41] and thoughts are acts that this agent performs by its intellectual power – acts by which the agent manifests itself. Descartes's model of the subject as an internal object among many, and Hume's model of the mind/subject as an invisible theater of ideas are thus equally foreign to Aquinas.[42]

Thus when Aquinas speaks of cognizing "oneself," the reflexive pronoun connotes not some first-person bare "I" or "self," but a first-person principle of action: "I-thinking." (Similarly, with respect to third-person agency, we describe an athlete in terms of his present action as "the runner"

---

[39] Descartes, *Discourse on Method* 4. On the relationship between Descartes's and Aquinas's views of self-awareness; see de Finance, "Cogito cartésien"; and Reichmann, "The 'Cogito' in St. Thomas." Aquinas would have been familiar with similar views in, say, Avicenna, Jean de la Rochelle, and Bonaventure; see Chapter 1.

[40] For Hume, see *Treatise on Human Nature* 1.4.6. Pasnau takes Aquinas's view to be similar to Hume's, except that he does not adopt Hume's resulting bundle theory of the self (*Thomas Aquinas on Human Nature*, 349).

[41] *ST* 1a.8/.4, ad 3 [Leon. 6.363]: "[A]ffectus animae non sunt in intellectu neque per similitudinem tantum, sicut corpora; neque per praesentiam ut in subiecto, sicut artes; sed sicut principiatum in principio, in quo habetur notio principiati." On the soul's perceiving itself prephilosophically as the first principle of vital operations, see *DV* 10.8; *ST* 1a.76.1; 1a–IIae.112.5, ad 1; *InDA* 1.1 [Leon. 45/1.5:92–5]; and *DM* 16.8, ad 7. For background on the subject-as-agent in Aquinas, see De Libera's discussion of how Aquinas revises Augustine and Averroes in his account of the relationship between the soul and its powers (*Archéologie du sujet* 1, ch. 4). This view in Aquinas is connected with his maxim "Actions belong to supposits" (*Actiones sunt suppositorum*), which De Libera discusses in "Les actions appartiennent aux sujets: Petite archéologie d'un principe leibnizien," in *Ad Ingenii Acuitionem: Studies in Honour of Alfonso Maierù*, ed. S. Caroti et al. (Louvain-La-Neuve, Fédération Internationale des Instituts d'Etudes Médiévales, 2007), 199–220; see also Richard Cross, "Accidents, Substantial Forms, and Causal Powers in the Late Thirteenth Century: Some Reflections on the Axiom *actiones sunt suppositorum*," in *Compléments de substance: études sur les propriétés accidentelles offertes à Alain de Libera* ed. C. Erismann and A. Schniewind (Paris: Vrin, 2008), 133–46.

[42] These early modern paradigms may be genealogically related to developments in Scotus's cognitive theory, which places thinking in the category of quality, rather than in the category of act, where Aquinas places it. For discussion, see Giorgio Pini, "Two Models of Thinking: Thomas Aquinas and John Duns Scotus," in *Intentionality, Cognition and Representation in the Middle Ages*, ed. Gyula Klima (New York: Fordham University Press, forthcoming); and for further discussion, p. 120, note 18.

or "the one running.") The first-person agent "I" can be perceived directly in itself, but only *as acting*.

Evidence of direct self-awareness in Aquinas

Once we realize that Aquinas's metaphysical and anthropological views preclude an indirect self-awareness in which the mind cognizes its acts but not itself, we can recognize the ample positive textual evidence for direct self-awareness.[43] This evidence can be divided into three groups, which we will briefly review here: (1) references to self-awareness as an "experience"; (2) phrases that suggest direct perception of the acting agent; (3) references to perceiving acts as *one's own*.

First, Aquinas says that one "experiences" (*experiri*) one's own acts, as well as oneself as agent.[44] For example, *ST* Ia.76.1 argues that a theory of cognition must account for what Aquinas describes as a basic fact of experience: namely, our ownership of our intellectual acts. "This act of understanding is the act of this man; for each one experiences himself to be the one understanding."[45] In *InDA* I.1, the certitude of the "science of the soul" is said to derive from the fact that "each one experiences in himself that he has a soul and that the soul is life-giving." Here, one experiences one's own soul as the principle of vital operations.[46] In *ST* Ia–IIae.112.5, ad 1 and 5, Aquinas states more broadly that when cognizing something that exists in the soul by its very essence (such as habits or cognitive and appetitive powers), we cognize it experientially as an "inner principle" manifested in action. "By willing we perceive the will, and life in vital operations"; likewise, "in the work that Abraham accomplished, he was able to cognize experientially that he had fear of the Lord."[47] The

---

[43] A theory of direct self-awareness is attributed to Aquinas by Romeyer, in the works cited in note 2 above; Gardeil, "Perception expérimentale," 220 and 227; Peillaube, "Avons-nous expérience du spirituel?" pt. 1, 261; Bernard Lonergan, "Christ as Subject: A Reply," *Gregorianum* 40 (1959): 242–70 (here at 258–59); Marten Hoenen, *Reality and Judgment according to St. Thomas*, trans. Henry F. Tiblier (Chicago: Regnery, 1952), 275–6; de Finance, "Cogito cartésien," esp. 91; McKian, "Metaphysics of Introspection," esp. 96–8 and 104; Ruane, "Self-Knowledge and the Spirituality of the Soul," esp. 432, 437–8; and Putallaz, *Le sens de la réflexion*, 109–13.

[44] See p. 72, note 12.

[45] *ST* Ia.76.1 [Leon. 5.209]: "Si quis autem velit dicere animam intellectivam non esse corporis formam, oportet quod inveniat modum quo ista actio quae est intelligere, sit huius hominis actio: experitur enim unusquisque seipsum esse qui intelligit."

[46] *InDA* I.1 [Leon. 45/1.5:92–5]: "Hec autem sciencia, scilicet de anima ... certa est (hoc enim quilibet experitur in se ipso, quod scilicet habeat animam et quod anima uiuificet)."

[47] *ST* Ia–IIae.112.5, ad 1 [Leon. 7. 327]: "[I]lla quae sunt per essentiam sui in anima, cognoscuntur experimentali cognitione, inquantum homo experitur per actus principia intrinseca: sicut voluntatem percipimus volendo, et vitam in operibus vitae"; and ad 5: "[I]llud etiam verbum Abrahae

last example is particularly telling; I experience not only my internal powers and habits, but also my *ownership* of them as the principles by which
I act – an important premise for grounding personal responsibility, not to
mention first-person cognition (see Chapter 8).

As we saw in Chapter 3, for Aquinas the verb *experiri* properly refers
to sensation of particulars "insofar as they are here and now," and by
extension to intellectual perception of essences.[48] It refers to an encounter with a present thing in itself, and precludes both discursive and representational indirectness. (For instance, in reasoning to God from his
effects, one knows that God exists, but one does not *experience* God.
Again, seeing the registrar in the mirror does not make the registrar
herself an object of experience.) Aquinas's willingness to speak of an
"experience" of one's acts and their acting principle thus suggests a direct self-awareness.

In a second group of texts supporting direct self-awareness, the perception of my own intellectual act is identified with the perception of my
own existence.[49] The following texts are typical:

> *SCG* 3.46: From the very fact that the mind perceives itself to act (*ex hoc
> ipso quod percipit se agere*), it perceives that it exists; but it acts by itself,
> whence it cognizes by itself that it exists … We have scientific knowledge of
> our soul's existence by itself insofar as we perceive its act (*scimus quia est per
> seipsam, inquantum eius actus percipimus*).
>
> *ST* Ia.93.7, ad 4: Whenever [the soul] understands something, it under-
> stands itself in perceiving its act (*percipiendo actum suum*).[50]
>
> *InEthic* IX.11: Insofar as we sense that we sense and understand that we
> understand, we sense and understand that we exist (*in hoc quod nos sentimus
> nos sentire et intelligimus nos intelligere, sentimus et intelligimus nos esse*); for
> it was said above that being and living, for humans, is principally sensing
> and understanding.[51]

---

dictum, potest referri ad notitiam experimentalem, quae est per exhibitionem operis. In opere enim
illo quod fecerat Abraham, cognoscere potuit experimentaliter se Dei timorem habere."

[48] See *DM* 16.1, ad 2; for analysis of Aquinas's usage of *experiri* and related terms, see Chapter 3,
pp. 71–3.

[49] Recall from Chapter 2 that in *Sent* III.23.1.2, ad 3, Aquinas had described the first main type of self-
knowledge as cognizing the soul's *acts*, but thereafter he describes it as cognizing (by its acts) that
the soul *exists*.

[50] For this formulation, see also *DV* 10.8, ad 5 [Leon. 22/2.323:352–5]: "[O]biectio illa procedit de
notitia actuali, secundum quam anima non percipit se esse nisi percipiendo actum suum et obiectum"; *DV* 10.8, ad 1 s.c.; *CT* I.85; *DM* 16.8, ad 7.

[51] [Leon. 47/2.540:99–103]. This text suggests an interesting anthropological reason that "perceiving
oneself to act" just *is* "perceiving oneself to exist." Viewed from the perspective of human tele-
ology, the operations of sense and understanding just *are* modes of perfected human existence, i.e.,
second acts. To perceive one's thinking is just to perceive one's own existence in second act.

With Aquinas's account of the agent–act relationship in mind, it becomes clear that the mental act is not interposed between the mind *qua* cognizer and itself *qua* cognized, as some third thing "from" or "in" which I cognize myself indirectly. Rather, mental acts have the role of *illuminating the mind to itself*, to such an extent that Aquinas uses the formulations 'perceiving the act' and 'perceiving that one acts' interchangeably in the above text from *SCG* 3.46. Since Aquinas, unlike many of his readers, does not have Hume (or more remotely, Sylvester of Ferrara![52]) hovering over his shoulder, it would not occur to him that the former formulation might be taken as non-equivalent to the latter, because he simply does not think of an act as something independently perceptible.

These texts also reinforce the previous section's argument that for Aquinas the "I" is never encountered as a bare thing, but always as a first-person agent. As *InEthic* IX.11 shows, for Aquinas to perceive one's existence *just is* to perceive oneself acting. *SCG* 3.46 likewise emphasizes that self-awareness is the mind's recognition of itself as the agent operating spontaneously ("acting by itself") from within.

The third group of texts supporting direct self-awareness includes those that present self-awareness not just as the perception of an act, but as a perception of *my* act, or *myself acting*.[53] For instance, Aquinas asserts in *DUI* 3: "For it is manifest that this singular man understands: for we would never ask about the intellect unless we understood; nor, when we ask about the intellect, do we ask about any other principle than that by which we understand."[54] It is clear that for Aquinas, in grasping my act of cognition, I grasp it as *mine*, perceiving *myself thinking* about something. This insight is neatly encapsulated in the accusative-and-infinitive construction that he often employs in these contexts: "I know that I know" (literally, "I know myself to be knowing," *intelligo me intelligere*).[55] These formulations

---

[52] See pp. 98–9 above.

[53] For texts in which the first person appears, see p. 71, notes 7 and 8. In Chapter 8, we will discuss *how* this first-personality comes about; for now we are interested only in the implied assertion that the act is perceived *as belonging to an agent* (myself).

[54] *DUI* 3 [Leon. 43.303:27–31]: "Manifestum est enim quod hic homo singularis intelligit: numquam enim de intellectu quereremus nisi intelligeremus; nec cum querimus de intellectu, de alio principio querimus quam de eo quo nos intelligimus"; *ST* Ia.79.6, ad 2 [Leon. 5.271]: "[E]t ideo sicut intelligit seipsum intellectus, quamvis ipse sit quidam singularis intellectus, ita intelligit suum intelligere, quod est singularis actus vel in praeterito vel in praesenti vel in futuro existens"; as well as many of the texts cited in the first two categories above.

[55] See *Sent* I.1.2.1, ad 1; *InDA* III.3 [Leon. 45/1.216:65–86, esp. 83–6]: "[U]nde et supra Philosophus per ipsum intelligere et per illud quod intelligitur scrutatus est naturam intellectus possibilis: non enim cognoscimus intellectum nostrum nisi per hoc quod intelligimus nos intelligere"; and the texts in p. 70, note 5.

suggest that he is thinking of actual self-awareness as a single perception of the agent acting, such that to grasp the act is to grasp the agent. Perceiving myself in my acts is not like positing the mouse's existence from the moving curtain, nor like seeing the registrar in a photograph. Rather, it is like perceiving a passing train in the sound of thundering wheels and the blur of colors and shapes speeding past.

For Aquinas, then, self-awareness must be a direct cognition of oneself. When we have either discursively or representationally indirect cognition of a thing *A*, the indirectness is due to the fact that we are "looking" at something else, *B*, that reveals *A* in some way – either by making premises available from which we can reason to *A*'s existence, or by presenting an image of *A*. Neither type of cognition can account for first-person cognition; neither can account for the personal familiarity and unshakeable certitude of our self-awareness. Instead, because of the perceptual inseparability of acts and agents, a perception of "thinking" is necessarily a perception of "me-thinking." I conclude that for Aquinas, self-awareness meets the criteria of "directness" in the sense defined earlier.[56]

The immediacy of self-awareness

Our inquiry into directness has shown that for Aquinas the soul's mode of self-awareness is *just as* direct as that of sensation – i.e., as direct as any act of clutching a pencil or seeing a tree or hearing a live concert. Turning to immediacy, our second criterion for an act's intuitive character, I now want to argue that self-awareness surpasses even sensation in its immediacy: Self-awareness involves a *more intimate union* of knower and known than does any other sensory or intellectual cognition, because of the difference between how sensible and intelligible species facilitate cognition of the horse Bucephalus, vs. how the intelligible species of horseness facilitates cognition of the mind. Although the goal here is to evaluate the immediacy of self-awareness relative to sensation, I will use intelligible species rather than sensible species as the point of comparison in order to avoid complicating and unnecessary discussions of the physiology of sense organs in Aquinas. This approach will not affect our analysis of immediacy, since intelligible and sensible species play the same role in their respective acts of intellection and sensation.

---

[56] Against this interpretation, one might cite *QDDA* 16, ad 8 [Leon. 24/1.147:397–400]: "[I]ntellectus possibilis noster intelligit se ipsum non directe, apprehendendo essentiam suam, set per speciem a fantasmatibus acceptam." But this text concerns quidditative self-knowledge, which is discursively indirect.

In ordinary abstractive cognition, the intelligible species has two roles: (1) a perfective role whereby it gives form to the intellect; (2) a presencing role as the object's "likeness" or "intentional being" whereby the object is made present to the intellect.[57] In its perfective role, the intelligible species gives the intellect a specifying form or "shape" that the intellect, as a sheer potency for intelligible form, lacks.[58] The species 'cat' makes the intellect catlike, so to speak, just as in a bronze statue of Napoleon, the form makes the bronze "Napoleon-like." Insofar as it is thus assimilated to 'catness,' the intellect is enabled to engage in an operation of thinking about cats.[59] Just as bronze existing in a certain shape is a statue of Napoleon, the intellect "shaped" by cat-species and engaging in an intellectual operation is *the intellect-in-act*, i.e., the intellect thinking about cats. In this perfective role, the species-in-act does not mediate cognition – rather, it plays a metaphysical role in constituting the intellect as the cognizer of catness.[60]

In its presencing role, the intelligible species is a vehicle for importing a foreign intelligibility into the intellect.[61] For instance, because the species 'cat' is a likeness of felinity, it makes felinity present in the intellect in which it inheres (i.e., it gives felinity "intelligible being," as Aquinas puts it). As I noted earlier, this presencing function need not be considered a mediation, although this is a controversial view.[62] But for our purposes it does not matter how the controversy is settled, because *in self-awareness the species does not play a presencing role* as the imported "similitude" or

---

[57] Aquinas mentions these two functions in, for instance, *ST* Ia.55.1, ad 2 [Leon. 5.54]: "Intellectus in actu dicitur intellectum in actu, non quod substantia intellectus sit ipsa similitudo per quam intelligit, sed quia illa similitudo est forma eius"; see also *SCG* 1.53; *ST* Ia.85.2. For further discussion see Chapter 6, pp. 153–5.

[58] See for instance *Sent* II.17.2.1; *SCG* 1.46, 1.53, 2.59, 3.42, 3.51; *ST* Ia.76.2, 85.1; *QDSC* 2; and for discussion see Leon Spruit, *Species intelligibilis: From Perception to Knowledge, vol. I, Classical Roots and Medieval Discussions* (Leiden: Brill, 1994), ch. 2.3.

[59] For the relationship between species and operation, see Chapter 5, p. 123.

[60] *DV* 10.8, ad 16 [Leon. 22/2.324:437–9]: "[I]d quod intelligitur accipitur ut simplicius ipso intellectu intelligente, sicut accipitur ut perfectio eius"; *SCG* 3.43 [Leon. 14.111]: "[I]ntellectus possibilis se habeat ad illas species sicut materia ad formam"; and texts cited in notes 60–2.

[61] See the discussion of *per essentiam* vs. *per speciem* cognition in the thirteenth century, in Chapter 1. Also see Aquinas's numerous references to the species as *similitudo* of the extramental object, for instance in *Sent* I.27.2.3; II.12.1.3, ad 5; *DV* 8.3, ad 17; *SCG* 1.53; *ST* Ia.14.2, ad 2; Ia.58.2; Ia.85.2; Ia 89.6; and *Quodl* 8.2.2, where he also describes the species as the *esse intelligibile* of the extramental object [Leon. 25/1.59:105–9]: "[U]nde species intelligibilis est similitudo ipsius essencie rei et est quodam modo ipsa quiddita et natura rei secundum esse intelligibile, non secundum esse naturale prout est in rebus." For discussion of the relationship between "likeness" and "intentional existence," see B. Carlos Bazán, "*Intellectum speculativum*: Averroes, Thomas Aquinas, and Siger of Brabant on the Intelligible Object," *Journal of the History of Philosophy* 19 (1981): 425–46; Deborah Black, "Mental Existence in Thomas Aquinas and Avicenna," *Mediaeval Studies* 61 (1999): 45–79; and Brower and Brower-Toland, "Aquinas on Mental Representation."

[62] See p. 98 above.

"likeness" of my mind. The intellectual soul does not need cat-species to make itself vicariously present to itself, as though it were foreign to itself – in fact, as we shall see in Chapter 5, it is naturally self-present.

The cat-species whereby I perceive myself thinking about cats, then, plays only a perfective role in my act of self-awareness. As Aquinas explains in *SCG* 2.98, in order to cognize itself, the intellect must be actually intelligible. Its intelligibility, like all intelligibility, depends on its actuality. And this actuality is precisely what the species-in-act contributes:

> Nothing is cognized insofar as it is in potency alone, but rather insofar as it is in act: whence the form is the principle of cognizing the thing that it actualizes. But in a similar way the cognitive power is made actually cognizing by some species. Therefore our possible intellect only cognizes itself by the intelligible species whereby it is rendered into act in intelligible being: and for this reason Aristotle says in *De anima* III that it is "cognizable like other things," namely, by species received from phantasms, as though by its proper forms.[63]

In short, as the intellect's form, cat-species-in-act makes the intellect *actually cognize cats*. In so doing, it transforms the intellect from a potential intellect to an actual, intelligible intellect. In asserting that self-awareness occurs "by a species," Aquinas is identifying the condition under which this actualization occurs.

Self-awareness thus turns out to be even more immediate than sensory or intellectual abstractive cognition. The latter acts require a species not only to perfect the intellect for action, but to make the object present, overcoming the metaphysical "distance" between the cognitive power and its object (I cannot have the paint's redness in my eye, so the redness can be there only "intentionally," by a species). But there is no distance between the intellect and itself – the only impediment to self-awareness is the intellect's natural lack of actuality. In its perfective role, the species-in-act removes this impediment, granting the intellect the stature of *actual intellect*. It thus cognizes itself by its own form, the informing species: "The intellect-in-act is that which it actually understands, because of the likeness of the understood thing, which is the form of the intellect-in-act.

---

[63] *SCG* 2.98 [Leon. 13.580]: "Nihil autem cognoscitur secundum quod est potentia tantum, sed secundum quod est actu: unde et forma est principium cognitionis rei quae per eam fit actu; similiter autem potentia cognoscitiva fit actu cognoscens per speciem aliquam. Intellectus igitur possibilis noster non cognoscit seipsum nisi per speciem intelligibilem, qua fit actu in esse intelligibili: et propter hoc dicit Aristoteles, in III *de Anima*, quod *est cognoscibilis sicut et alia*, scilicet per species a phantasmatibus acceptas, sicut per formas proprias"; and see the discussion of the identity account of implicit self-awareness in Chapter 6, pp. 153–60.

And thus the human intellect, which is actualized by the species of the understood thing, is understood by the same species, *as by its own form.*"[64] (In fact, as we will see in Chapter 6, actualization via a species is sufficient for actual self-awareness.)

The role that Aquinas assigns to the species in human self-awareness is thus analogous to the role he assigns to the divine essence in divine self-knowledge. Because the divine essence is already in act, it is in some sense its own species; i.e., the divine essence is itself the means by which God cognizes himself.[65] Similarly, once the human intellect is actualized by a species, it cognizes itself by its own actualizing form, which is the species-in-act of the cognized object. Thus the difference between divine and human self-knowledge is not a difference in the structure of their cognitive acts (i.e., as though one were immediate and the other were mediated by a species), but a difference in the metaphysical conditions of the divine and human intellects. Both intellects know themselves through their own actualized being, but whereas the divine intellect is already essentially in act, the human intellect needs to be actualized by a species from outside. Thus God knows himself *per essentiam*, and I know myself *per speciem*, but both acts of self-knowledge are immediate.[66]

To summarize, then: self-awareness is at least as immediate as ordinary abstractive cognition and sensation, and perhaps even more immediate. Whereas in abstractive cognition and sensation, the intelligible and sensible species play both a perfective and a presencing role, in self-awareness the species-in-act plays *only* a perfective role, making the intellect intelligible by giving it a "shape." In receiving the species-in-act, the human intellect is "lit up," so to speak, gaining actuality and therefore intelligibility, since nothing is understood except insofar as it is in act. Nothing in this arrangement can be described as a mediation.

---

[64] *ST* Ia.87.1, ad 3 [Leon. 14.356]: "[I]ntellectus in actu est intellectum in actu, propter similitudinem rei intellectae, quae est forma intellectus in actu. Et ideo intellectus humanus, qui fit in actu per speciem rei intellectae, per eandem speciem intelligitur, sicut per formam suam." See Romeyer, "Notre science de l'esprit humain," 44, n. 3.

[65] See *ST* Ia.14.2.

[66] Since according to Aquinas, angelic intellects are always in act, he makes a similar point in comparing angelic and human self-knowledge in *DV* 8.14, ad 6 [Leon. 22/2.265:247–57]: "Unde anima nostra non semper actualiter se intelligit; sed mens angeli semper actualiter se intelligit; quod ideo contingit quia mens angeli intelligit se per essentiam suam, qua semper informatur, mens autem nostra forte intelligit quodammodo per intentionem" – where the "intention" is the species-in-act that is the intellect's form. See also *InDA* III.3 [Leon. 45/1.216:87–217:106]; *ST* Ia.87.1; *SLDC* 15.

Implications of an intuitive self-awareness

By now it is clear that the answer to the intuition question (i.e., whether the mode of self-awareness in Aquinas parallels the directness and immediacy of sensation) is affirmative. As a result, Aquinas should not be taken too strictly when he employs the Aristotelian maxim that the intellectual soul is intelligible "like other things" (*sicut alia*). Although the same psychological mechanism (the intellect's species-informed act) is operative in self-awareness and cognition of "other things," it operates differently in self-awareness than in cognition of other things. Because the soul is already present to itself, it needs the species-informed act merely to "light it up" or "turn it on," so to speak. Once it is illuminated internally to itself, its intellectual potency has been actualized, enabling it to perform the acts proper to an intellect: cognizing itself and other things.

This account of intuitive self-awareness has significant implications. First, it gives Aquinas a way to account for the intermingling of certitude and self-opacity in the moment of self-awareness: Even though I intuitively grasp myself acting, I do not understand what the mind is or what kinds of hidden motivations generate those acts. In Chapter 3 we noted one reason for this persistent self-opacity: the mind initially grasps itself as a whole (a singular existent) and only later distinguishes its essential parts. But now we can consider the same idea from another angle: namely, each operation grants the thinker a temporary intellectuality-in-act by which she cognizes herself, but this intellectual actuality is limited by what the thinker is thinking about at any given moment.[67] Each act of cognition is only partially self-revelatory, manifesting a tiny sliver of human potential: I perceive myself admiring a piece of sculpture, reasoning through a philosophical problem, feeling a cold wind, squinting in the bright sun, or struggling to recall the tenth digit of *pi*. So the intellectual actuality received from sensation is only ever a partial cure for self-opacity, one individual puzzle-piece in a largely incomplete self-portrait. Gradually, over a lifetime of perceiving myself engaging in various cognitive acts that trigger various appetitive motions, passions, and choices, I can piece together a better understanding of myself as an individual – potentials, tendencies,

---

[67] See de Finance, "Cogito cartésien," 34: "The act whereby the soul perceives itself to be existing is itself specified by the structure of the object in which it terminates. It is under a foreign *species* that the soul cognizes itself" (my translation). In one sense, though, the species is not "foreign" to the soul, because the soul has a potency for it. In actualizing that potency, each species-formed thought manifests the soul's nature, as will become evident in Chapter 7.

good and bad habits, preferences, talents.[68] But since I cannot completely know everything that is (i.e., completely actualize the intellect's full potential), I can never completely know everything about myself.[69]

Second, the intuitive mode of self-awareness has significant implications for Aquinas's ontology of human selfhood. It is not anachronistic, in my view, to say that his account of self-awareness includes an early notion of what one might broadly call "selfhood" or "subjectivity" – namely, a notion of a first-person agent. De Libera has suggested that Aquinas occupies an important juncture in the history of the idea of the "subject as agent," on account of certain anthropological developments.[70] I would argue that this pattern is repeated in Aquinas's account of self-awareness as the perception of oneself dynamically engaged in some present action. Not only does he construe the subject ontologically as an agent, but he holds that the subject *perceives itself* only as a first-person agent-in-act.

---

[68] On cognizing our volitions, see *DV* 22.12; *ST* Ia.87.4; *DM* 6, ad 18. On cognizing our habits see *Sent* III.23.1.2; *DV* 10.9; *ST* Ia.87.2. On experiencing passions such as delight, suffering, anger, and sadness, see for instance *DeCar* I; *ST* Ia.81.3, ad 2; and *ST* IIa–IIae.154.11, ad 3.

[69] This is true of natural self-knowledge in this life, but perhaps Aquinas would also have to say that we cannot have absolutely perfect self-comprehension even in the next life, since such self-comprehension would require comprehending all being, including the divine essence, which is impossible for created minds – which would mean that I can never know my own mind as completely as God knows it.

[70] De Libera, *Archéologie du sujet* I, ch. 4.

CHAPTER FIVE

The significance of self-presence
Habitual self-awareness

Presence and self-presence

In arguing that actual self-awareness is dependent on cognition of other things, Aquinas provides a tidily unified account of both privileged self-access and self-opacity – but at a steep price. The notion of a dependent self-awareness runs counter to a basic intuition about the advantage of self-presence (ontological self-identity) in self-knowledge (cognitive self-identity). It makes sense that the mind has to fulfil certain conditions to become acquainted with extramental entities – but surely the mind, which already *is* itself, cannot naturally be as ignorant of itself as it is of, say, the multiplication table. The basic intuition that self-identity ought to provide an advantage in self-knowledge makes the experience of self-opacity especially galling. For thirteenth-century thinkers, this intuition was associated with the notion of natural self-knowledge, and was often cited either in support of supraconscious self-knowing or against dependent self-awareness.[1] Although Aquinas rejects the latter views, he nevertheless seeks to maintain their foundational intuition. His account of habitual self-awareness is designed to show that an account of dependent self-awareness grants the advantage of self-identity without having to explain away self-opacity in the process.

Now habitual self-awareness poses two main difficulties to interpreters. First, there is the question of explanatory value. Habitual self-awareness provides Aquinas not only with the means of preserving this intuition about the advantage of self-identity, but also with an account of the feeling of self-familiarity described by Augustine as *se nosse* and *memoria sui*. Its suspicious convenience in tying up so many loose threads has led some to conclude that it is merely a "strategy for deflating" inconvenient

---

[1] For supraconscious self-knowing, see William of Auvergne, *De anima* 3.12; for thinking about oneself at will, see Bonaventure, *Sent* III.33.1.2, ad 3, as discussed in Chapter 1.

Augustinian texts.[2] So does habitual self-awareness have genuine explanatory value in Aquinas's theory of self-knowledge?

Second, it is not even clear what habitual self-awareness *is*. From *DV* 10.8 – Aquinas's only detailed discussion of habitual self-awareness[3] – we can extract the following five-point description:

(1) Habitual self-awareness is properly habitual: in other words, the relationship between habitual and actual self-awareness is the relationship between a habit and its corresponding operation.[4]

(2) It is not an acquired or even innate habit (i.e., an accident in the category of quality), but rather belongs to the soul's very essence.[5]

(3) Habitual self-awareness is the mind's very self-presence pre-dating all cognitive acts.[6]

(4) To be habitually self-aware is to "see oneself by one's essence."[7]

(5) Habitual self-awareness does not involve any act of self-awareness, which occurs only when the soul "considers other things" (i.e., in its acts, as discussed in the previous chapters).[8]

How should we interpret the "essential self-presence" or "habitual self-seeing" described in (3) and (4)? To some readers, such language suggests that Aquinas is smuggling natural supraconscious self-knowing back into his theory. For instance, according to Armand Maurer: "Because the soul

[2] Pasnau, *Thomas Aquinas on Human Nature*, 455–6, n. 16; likewise Lambert, *Self Knowledge in Thomas Aquinas*, 114–15; and Still, "Aquinas's Theory of Human Self-Knowledge," 9 and 40.

[3] See especially the *respondeo* and replies to objections 1, 6, 9, 11, 14, 1 s.c., and 4 s.c. For other less-detailed discussions, see *Sent* I.3, qq. 4–5, in which the idea of a habitual self-knowledge, identified with the soul's natural self-memory or self-presence, is woven throughout, as discussed in Chapter 2, pp. 42–6; and *ST* Ia.93.7, ad 3–4. Habitual self-awareness also appears under different names in *DV* 10.2, and 5 (as "the soul's presence to itself"); *DV* 8.14, and 6 (as "interior memory"); and *DV* 10.3 (as *notitia*). Aquinas references the underlying concept obliquely when he speaks of actual self-awareness as cognizing oneself *per praesentiam* in *ST* Ia.87.1 and *per seipsam* in *SCG* 3.46 (see Chapter 2, pp. 60–3). For habitual knowledge of our own habits, see *DV* 10.9.

[4] See texts in notes 36, 39, and 40 below.

[5] *DV* 10.8 [Leon. 22/2.321:241–322:45]: "Ad hoc autem quod percipiat anima se esse, et quid in seipsa agatur attendat, non requiritur aliquis habitus; sed ad hoc sufficit sola essentia animae, quae menti est praesens"; and ad 14 (note 38 below).

[6] *DV* 10.8, ad 1 [Leon. 22/2.323:325–34]: "Sed essentia sua sibi innata est, ut non eam necesse habeat a phantasmatibus acquirere ... Et ideo mens antequam a phantasmatibus abstrahat, sui notitiam habitualem habet, qua possit percipere se esse"; and resp., in note 5 above.

[7] *DV* 10.8 [Leon. 22/2.321:234–6]: " Sed quantum ad habitualem cognitionem, sic dico, quod anima per essentiam suam se videt."

[8] *DV* 10.8, ad 1 s.c. [Leon. 22/2.324:441–7]: "[V]erbum Augustini est intelligendum quod mens seipsam per seipsam cognoscit, quod ex ipsa mente est ei unde possit in actum prodire, quo se actualiter cognoscat percipiendo se esse; sicut etiam ex specie habitualiter in mente retenta inest menti ut possit actualiter rem illam considerare"; and ad 4 s.c. [325:500–3]: "[A]nima est sibi ipsi praesens ut intelligibilis, idest ut intelligi possit; non autem ut per seipsam intelligatur, sed ex obiecto suo, ut dictum est."

is a spiritual substance it is always present to itself and aware of itself, at least subconsciously; and this 'habitual' grasp of itself comes to actual awareness through the mind's reflection on its object and activity."[9] Under this interpretation, it is hard to see how (3) and (4) could be compatible with (1) and (5). But if a "habitual self-seeing" is not some sort of intellectual actuality, then is it merely a sheer potency or "mere possibility" for self-cognition?[10] If so, of course, the explanatory value of habitual self-awareness comes under suspicion. The difficulty arises from an ambiguity that affects not only Aquinas's account of habitual self-awareness, but also his account of cognitive habits in general: namely, what is the status of a habitual cognition? He describes habits as occupying a "middle way"[11] between a sheer potency for operation and the operation itself, but such language gives the impression of a sliding scale between potentiality and actuality without specifying clearly what the "midpoint" of such a scale looks like, and how it is differentiated from operation and sheer potency.

Before tackling these two interpretive difficulties – the explanatory value and the nature of habitual self-awareness – we need to clarify Aquinas's concepts of "presence" and "habitual cognition." While such concepts would have been familiar to his thirteenth-century audience, they need additional explication today.

Let us begin with his concept of presence, which helps explain why he describes habitual self-awareness as a "self-seeing." Note that although Aquinas often describes *cognized objects* as having presence to sense or intellect, strictly speaking presence describes a feature of the *cognizer*, i.e., presence to an object. In other words, the statement "The apple is present to my mind" is true on account of a feature of the mind, not because of some change in the apple. Now in Aquinas, presence tends to be associated with vision, whether sensory or intellectual.[12] In discussing

---

[9] Armand Maurer, "Descartes and Aquinas on the Unity of a Human Being: Revisited," *American Catholic Philosophical Quarterly* 67 (1993): 497–511 (here at 505); see also Goehring, "St. Thomas Aquinas on Self-Knowledge," 12; Pierre Faucon de Boylesve, *Être et savoir: étude du fondement de l'intelligibilité dans la pensée médiévale* (Paris: Vrin, 1985), 169ff; and Gabriel Picard, "Le problème critique fondamental," *Archives de philosophie* 1.2 (1923): 1–94 (here at 55), n. 3 (arguing that habitual self-awareness is a tactile intuition in the soul's interior darkness). Even Gardeil spends some time describing the "immediacy" and "directness" of habitual self-awareness – terms which seem more appropriate for describing actual than habitual cognition ("Perception expérimentale," 225–7). The appeal of this interpretation is that, once construed this way, habitual self-awareness seems to provide an explanation of certain psychological phenomena; I argue against this view in Chapter 8.

[10] See Still, "Aquinas's Theory of Human Self-Knowledge," 40; Jordan, *Ordering Wisdom*, 129.

[11] See texts cited in note 17 below.

[12] *Sent* 1.3.4.5 [Mand. 1.122]: "Intelligere autem dicit nihil aliud quam simplicem intuitum intellectus in id quod sibi est praesens intelligibile ... intelligere nihil aliud dicit quam intuitum, qui nihil aliud est quam praesentia intelligibilis ad intellectum quocumque modo."

how God is present to all his creatures, *ST* Ia.8.3 clarifies the relevance of visual metaphors for understanding cognitive presence. Something is present, Aquinas explains, that is "within one's sight (*in prospectu ipsius*), just as everything in a house is said to be present to someone who nevertheless is not in any given part of the house in his substance." A little later, he repeats: "Something can be said to be present to someone insofar as it is subject to his gaze, even though he is distant from it in his substance."[13]

The term *prospectus* (a look-out point or field of vision) at first suggests that Aquinas is construing presence narrowly as "being actually cognized," e.g., actually seen within one's field of vision. But the example of homely objects that are present to the traveling homeowner suggests a broader interpretation: Items are present "within one's sight" or "subject to one's gaze" not only if I am *actually cognizing them*, but also if I *could cognize them*, should I choose to direct my attention toward them. For the sensory analogate, this broader construal means that objects are present to me if I *could* see them by directing my attention differently (e.g., by turning around). Something similar happens in the intellectual realm when my mind is habituated to consider a certain intelligible object. That object is now present to my intellectual gaze in the sense that an acquired habit gives my mind a "vantage point," so to speak, from which I can think about the object simply by directing my attention to it, without first having to go through a process of "searching" (*inquisitio*) or learning.[14]

---

[13] *ST* Ia.8.3 [Leon. 4.87]: "Per praesentiam vero suam, dicitur aliquid esse in omnibus quae in prospectu ipsius sunt; sicut omnia quae sunt in aliqua domo, dicuntur esse praesentia alicui, qui tamen non est secundum substantiam suam in qualibet parte domus. Secundum vero substantiam vel essentiam, dicitur aliquid esse in loco in quo eius substantia habetur"; and ad 2: "[A]liquid potest dici praesens alicui, inquantum subiacet eius conspectui, quod tamen distat ab eo secundum suam substantiam."

[14] See *DeVirtCom* 1. Aquinas draws the analogy between physical vision and intellectual habituation a little differently in *DV* 11.1, ad 12, comparing the state of the habituated intellect to the state of the unaided power of sight, which is properly equipped to be able to see *any* visible object. But the gist is generally the same as that of *ST* Ia.8.3 above, since presumably the visible object has to be within range of the viewer in order to be seen: "[N]on est omnino simile de intellectu et visu corporali: visus enim corporalis non est vis collativa, ut ex quibusdam suorum obiectorum in alia perveniat, sed omnia sua obiecta sunt ei visibilia, quam cito ad illa convertitur; unde habens potentiam visivam se habet hoc modo ad omnia visibilia intuenda, sicut habens habitum ad ea quae habitualiter scit consideranda, et ideo videns non indiget ab alio excitari ad videndum, nisi quatenus per alium eius visus dirigitur in aliquod visibile, ut digito, vel aliquo huiusmodi. Sed potentia intellectiva, cum sit vis collativa, ex quibusdam in alia devenit; unde non se habet aequaliter ad omnia intelligibilia consideranda … Doctor ergo excitat intellectum ad sciendum illa quae docet, sicut motor essentialis educens de potentia in actum; sed ostendens rem aliquam visui corporali, excitat eum sicut motor per accidens; prout etiam habens habitum scientiae potest excitari ad considerandum de aliquo" [Leon. 22/2.353:474–505]. See also *DV* 12.1, ad 11 [Leon. 22/2.369:341–4]: "[V]idere, secundum philosophum dupliciter dicitur: scilicet habitu, et actu; unde et visio actum et habitum

Consequently, the notion of "intellectual presence" or "having something intellectually within sight" in Aquinas is grounded in the intellect's being disposed toward a given object, whether or not it is currently thinking about that object. The notion of "habitually seeing" something, then, is not as peculiar as it initially seems: It simply refers to my subjective familiarity with that thing, i.e., my disposition for finding it without prompting. For instance, the items in my kitchen are present to me, or I "habitually see" them, in the sense that I am able to think about them without having to figure out what they are. I can retrieve cooking utensils without having to search for them, or direct someone over the phone where to find the plates. But if a visitor is helping me cook, he cannot find his way around the kitchen and must constantly ask where things are: they are not present to him, because *he* is not familiar with them. To say that "this kitchen is becoming quite familiar" is to affirm a developing disposition on *my* part, not some change in the kitchen itself. It is this state of subjective familiarity that lies at the heart of Aquinas's concept of presence.

When Aquinas says in *DV* 10.8 that the soul habitually "sees itself" by its essence because its essence is "present to the mind," then, he is simply applying his general understanding of habitual presence as subjective familiarity. For the mechanics of this presence-as-familiarity, we can now turn to his theory of habituation.

Habits in Aquinas[15]

Within Aquinas's wide-ranging and complex account of habituation in the "rational powers" of intellect and will,[16] two foundational characteristics

nominare potest" (referring to Aristotle's *Topics* I.15.106b18, which distinguishes having the power of sight from using the power of sight).

[15] Aquinas distinguishes between two ways in which something can be ordered toward an end: (1) changeable "dispositions" (*dispositiones*) such as temporary health or sickness; (2) deeply rooted and quasi-permanent "habits" (*habitus*) that are associated with the rational powers of intellect and will, such as generosity or knowledge of geometry (see text in note 18 below). In order to avoid confusion, I have chosen to translate both terms using the nearest English cognate. Thus "habit" as used here does not refer to a routine ("He was in the habit of eating breakfast alone"); rather, it loosely corresponds to the contemporary term "disposition," referring to a characteristic that originates predictably good or bad thoughts and actions.

[16] Intellect and will alone can be habituated (*DeVirtCom* 1); properly speaking, animals and the human sensory powers cannot have habits, except insofar as they are commanded by reason (*ST* Ia–IIae.50.3) For general treatments of habituation in Aquinas, see George P. Klubertanz, *Habits and Virtues* (New York: Appleton-Century-Crofts, 1965); B.R. Inagaki, "*Habitus* and *natura* in Aquinas," in *Studies in Medieval Philosophy*, ed. John F. Wippel (Washington, D.C.: The Catholic University of America Press, 1987), 159–75; and Bonnie Kent, "Habits and Virtues (Ia IIae, qq. 49–70)," in *The Ethics of Aquinas*, ed. Stephen Pope (Washington, D.C.: Georgetown

that he attributes to habits are especially useful for clarifying his theory of habitual self-awareness: (1) Habits occupy a place midway between potency and act; and (2) Habits are exercised "at will."

The midway point. Because Aquinas often describes habits as occupying the "middle" between potency and act, it is tempting to assume that a habit is some sort of embryonic operation arrested in development.[17] For Aquinas, however, there are no degrees of operation; the intellect is either thinking about something, or it is not. In fact, habits and operations are distinct kinds of accidental forms occupying distinct categories: i.e., habits are accidents in the category of quality that order a subject toward its proper operation, which is an accident in the category of action.[18] Compared to the rational power's default state, then, a habit is an actuality or "first perfection" (e.g., being generous) that, in turn, is in potency to a distinct kind of actuality, the power's operation or "second perfection" (e.g., choosing to act generously).[19] Aquinas illustrates this

University Press, 2002), 116–30. On the nature of intellectual habituation, see René Arnou, *L'homme a-t-il le pouvoir de connaître la vérité?* (Rome: Presses de l'Université Grégorienne, 1970); Joseph J. Romano, "Between Being and Nothingness: The Relevancy of Thomistic Habit," *The Thomist* 58 (1994): 427–40; Gregory M. Reichberg, "The Intellectual Virtues (Ia IIae, qq. 57–58)," in *The Ethics of Aquinas*, ed. Pope, esp. 131–5; and Tobias Hoffmann, "Intellectual Virtues," in *The Oxford Handbook to Aquinas*, ed. Brian Davies and Eleonore Stump (Oxford University Press, 2012), 327–36.

[17] For instance, *InDA* III.2 [Leon. 45/1.209:48–50]: "[C]um autem [intellectus] habet habitum sciencie, sunt species in intellectu medio modo inter potenciam puram et actum purum"; *DV* 10.2, ad 4; *SCG* 1.56; *ST* Ia.79.6, ad 3. For critique of this misinterpretation, see Arnou, *L'homme a-t-il le pouvoir?*, 19; and Inagaki, "*Habitus* and *natura*," 168, who describes this view as more Scotistic or Suarezian than Thomistic.

[18] *ST* Ia–IIae.54.2 [Leon. 6.342]: "[H]abitus et est forma quaedam, et est habitus … importat ordinem ad aliquid." The category of quality is divided into four species, of which the first is "habits and dispositions"; the former are "difficult to change" and the latter are fleeting (see *ST* Ia–IIae.49.1–2, and the detailed *InMet* V.16). On habit as ordered toward act, see Ia–IIae.49.3 and Ia–IIae.54. There has been some question about whether the intellectual operation belongs in the category of quality or action. Yves Simon, for instance, suggests that immanent acts like thinking and willing are qualities, in *An Introduction to the Metaphysics of Knowledge*, trans. Vukan Kuic and Richard J. Thompson (New York: Fordham University Press, 1990), 64–71. Pini however, contends that Aquinas places operation in the category of action ("Two Models of Thinking"). I believe Pini's interpretation is confirmed by *DeVirtCom* I, ad 8, where Aquinas states that dispositions need not be in the same category as "that to which they dispose," to undermine arg. 8's claim that virtues (a type of habit) must be in the category of act because they dispose to acts (the *respondeo* makes clear that the acts in question are the immanent acts of intellect and will).

[19] *ST* Ia–IIae.49.3, ad 1 [Leon. 6.312]: "[H]abitus est actus quidam, inquantum est qualitas, et secundum hoc potest esse principium operationis. Sed est in potentia per respectum ad operationem. Unde habitus dicitur *actus primus*, et operatio *actus secundus*"; *InEthic* VII.12 [Leon. 47/2.428:56–9]: "[H]orum autem operatio est sicut bonum perfectum, quia est perfectio secunda, habitus autem est sicut bonum imperfectum, quia est perfectio prima"; *DeVirtCom* I, ad 6; *InDA* III.2; and on perfection in general, *InMet* V.18.

relationship with reference to wet wood, which must be dried out (i.e., receive the form of dryness, itself in potency to the form of fire) in order to be burned.[20]

Once perfected by a habit, a rational power is inclined toward or equipped for a specific cognitive or appetitive object,[21] so that it can initiate thoughts and decisions about that object by itself.[22] By analogy, the fitness of an Olympic runner's body is an internal principle of his acts of running, equipping him to break spontaneously into a run. Like nature, then, habit is an internal principle of action, a "second nature" whose corresponding operations have the three characteristics of natural acts, i.e., consistency, facility, and pleasure.[23]

Exercise at will. Now one of these three properties – facility of exercise[24] – acquired special importance for medieval thinkers from Averroes' definition of habit: "One who has a habit understands by something that belongs to him [i.e., the informing habit], from himself and when he wills, without needing anything extrinsic."[25] But Aquinas introduces a modification that will be central to his account of habitual self-awareness. In *DeVirtCom* 1, quoting the Averroist definition of habit as "that by which someone can act when he wills," he replaces Averroes' final phrase ("without needing anything extrinsic") with an additional condition: "And Augustine says that habit is that by which someone acts *when*

---

[20] *ST* Ia–IIae.51.3; for discussion, see Inagaki, "*Habitus* and *natura*," 171.
[21] *InPhys* VII.3.6 [Leon. 2.344]: "Sciens maxime dicitur *ad aliquid*, scilicet ad scibile, cuius assimilatio in sciente, scientia est"; *ST* Ia–IIae.49.1 and Ia–IIae.54.
[22] *DV* 12.1, ad 1 s.c. [Leon. 22/2.369:354–70:355]: "[A]ctus totaliter ab habitu oritur."
[23] *ST* Ia–IIae.32.6 [Leon. 6.228]: "Aliud principium est habitus inclinans, secundum quem benefacere fit alicui connaturale"; *Sent* I.17,1,1, ad 1 [Mand. 1.395]: "[Q]uia etiam non est possibile aliquam operationem perfectam a creatura exire, nisi principium illius operationis sit perfectio potentiae operantis, prout dicimus habitum elicientem actum esse principium ejus"; see also *Sent* I.3.5.1, ad 5; *DV* 24.12, ad 9 s.c.; *ST* Ia.87.4; Ia–IIae.56.5; Ia–IIae.58.5; *InEthic* VII.10; *InPhys* VII.6; and *DeVirtCom* 9. On the three characteristics of natural acts, extended to habituated acts on account of their "connaturality," see *DV* 20.2; *DeVirtCom* 1, resp. and ad 13. On connatural knowledge, see Barry Miller, "Knowledge through Affective Connaturality" (PhD diss., Pontifical University Angelicum, 1959), 175–90; and Rafael Tomás Caldera, *Le jugement par inclination chez saint Thomas d'Aquin* (Paris: Vrin, 1980).
[24] See *DeVirtCom* 1; *Sent* III.33.1.1
[25] Averroes, *Commentarium magnum in De anima* III.18 [Crawford, 438:26–9]: "Hec enim est diffinitio habitus, scilicet ut habens habitum intelligat per ipsum illud quod est sibi proprium ex se et quando voluerit, absque eo quod indigeat in hoc aliquo extrinseco"; the corresponding text of Aristotle's *DA* III.4, 429b7 in the Latin Moerbeke translation states only, "Hoc autem confestim accidit cum possit operari per se ipsum" [Leon. 45/1.208]. Aquinas cites this definition in, for instance, *Sent* III.23.1.1; *DeVirtCom* 1; *DV* 12.1, ad 1; *ST* Ia–IIae.63.2, ad 2; IIa–IIae.171; *InEthic* VII.3 [Leon. 47/2.392:177–9]; and the texts on exercising cognitive habits in notes 31 and 32 below. For facility of exercise generally, see *Sent* III.33.1.1; *DV* 20.2; and Inagaki, "*Habitus* and *natura*," 162.

the time is favorable" (emphasis mine).[26] For Aquinas, willing to exercise
a habit is not sufficient for actually doing so. Rather, volition alone is
needed *on the part of the agent* for exercising the habit; but exercise may
still be impeded by external conditions. (No matter how generous I am,
I cannot perform a generous act if I am in solitary confinement.) For
Aquinas, then, a habit grants the agent only a conditional self-sufficiency
for action.

We can now restate our two foundational characteristics of habits more
precisely: (1) Habits are "midway between potency and act" in the sense
that they are *first perfections*, qualities ordered toward operations. In virtue
of this perfective role, (2) habits are exercised "at will" in the sense that
they *subjectively equip* the power to exercise the corresponding operation
at the command of the will, if circumstances permit. But these two characteristics deserve special attention in the case of cognitive habits, where
their applicability is not immediately evident.

First, *having* a habit of generosity and *performing* a generous act are easily recognized as different kinds of actualities, one of which is ordered to
the other. But it is harder to see that this is true also of habitual and actual
cognition, especially since in English and Latin the same verb can refer to
both ("he understands triangles"). Aquinas's own account of the conservation of intelligible species (the most common and basic kind of cognitive
habituation) makes this view all the more attractive.[27] Since the species *is*
the object's intentional presence in the intellect,[28] it becomes too easy to
think of habitual cognition as a partial, vague, or unconscious intellectual
act. This line of thinking, I believe, is responsible for the view that, for
Aquinas, the soul's self-presence in habitual self-awareness is an inchoate
or subconscious self-awareness.[29]

---

[26] *DeVirtCom* 1 [Marietti, 709]: "Sed sunt habitus, secundum quos potest quis agere cum voluerit ut
dicit Commentator in III *de Anima*. Et Augustinus in lib. *de Bono Coniugali* [= 21.25] dicit, quod
habitus est quo quis agit, cum tempus affuerit"; see also *InEthic* VII.3, where Aquinas speaks of habits being loosed vs. bound by external constraints: "[A]liquando autem est habitus ligatus ita quod
non possit exire in actum," on account of sleep or insanity or drunkenness or excessive passion
[Leon. 47/2.392:177–93].

[27] On intellectual memory, see for instance *Sent* I.3.4.1; *DV* 10.2–3 and 19.1; *ST* Ia.79.6–7; Ia.89.5;
Ia–IIae.67.2; *Quodl* 3.9.1; *InDA* III.2; and *InDMR* 2. Aquinas rarely calls the species habits (the
only exception I have found is in *DV* 19.1, ad 9). He prefers to say that they are retained habitually
(*DV* 10.2; 10.8, ad 1 s.c.; 19.1; *QDDA* 15, ad 17; *Quodl* 3.9.1), or that the retaining intellect is "in a
habitual state" (*ST* Ia.79.6, ad 3). *Sent* I.3.5.1, ad 1, suggests that the light of the agent intellect gives
species a habitual character.

[28] See the discussion of the "presencing role" of the species in Chapter 4, p. 110.

[29] See note 9 above.

But for Aquinas, the object's intentional presence via the species does not entail a quasi-thinking.[30] Instead, the species is a quality that "specifies" the intellect, equipping it for and ordering it toward consideration of a certain essence (say, triangularity).[31] This specification is only a necessary condition for the intellect's operation, which is the act of using the species to consider that object.[32] Like any other habit, then, habitual cognition is a way that the intellect *is* (a "first perfection" or quality), whereas thinking is something that the intellect *does* (a "second perfection" or operation).

Secondly, one might suppose that cognitive habits have greater facility of exercise than other habits, because whereas a jailer could stop me from performing a generous act by depriving me of persons toward whom I could exercise generosity, he cannot stop me from *thinking* about geometry, since the species of geometry is always present to my mind. It is true that for Aquinas, once my intellect is perfected by the species of geometry, I can think about geometry at will without "searching" (*inquisitio*):[33] i.e., my will simply moves my intellect to think about triangles and moves the imagination to present the corresponding phantasm.[34] Nevertheless, because the imagination is involved, my spontaneous consideration of geometry is dependent on a condition extrinsic to the intellect itself. For Aquinas, two conditions must be in place in order for me to think about an object:

> *The subjective equipping condition*: The intellect must be perfected and equipped for operation by the object's presence (recall that presence is rooted in a state of the *cognizing intellect*, not of the *cognized object*);
> *The objective availability condition*: The object must be available for cognition.

---

[30] He makes this particularly clear in responding to Avicenna's claim (*Liber de anima* V.6 [Van Riet 2.147–8]) that intentional presence is sufficient to cause the operation of thinking. See *DV* 10.2, *ST* Ia.79.6, *InDA* III.2, and *QDDA* 15.

[31] See *DV* 11.1, ad 2; *ST* Ia.79.6 and Ia.89.5; Ia–IIae.57.1; and *InPhys* VII.3 [Leon. 2.344], where Aquinas refers to *consideratio* as the proper act of the intellect and as the operation in which one exercises or "uses" a cognitive habit.

[32] On conservation vs. use of the species, see *ST* Ia.84.7, ad 1; Ia.89.6; *DM* 16.8; *InEthic* VII.3. On the operation as the "final perfection" of the intellect, see *ST* Ia.79.6, ad 3 and *SCG* I.56 [Leon. 13.162]: "Intellectus habitualiter tantum cognoscens non est in sua ultima perfectione"; and for discussion, Pini, "Two Models of Thinking."

[33] *DeVirtCom* I.

[34] For thinking at will, see *ST* Ia.57.4 [Leon. 5.76]: "Manifestum est autem quod ex sola voluntate dependet quod aliquis actu aliqua consideret: quia cum aliquis habet habitum scientiae, vel species intelligibiles in eo existentes, utitur eis cum vult"; as well as *DV* 10.2; 20.2; *DeVirtCom* 12, ad 15; *InDA* II.11 and III.2; *InEthic* VII.3; *ST* Ia.107.1; *ST* Ia–IIae.57.1; *DM* 16.8. On the role of imagination, see *Sent* III.31.2.4; *DV* 10.2, ad 7; *DV* 19.1; *ST* Ia.84.7 and Ia.89.1; *QDDA* 15. On the will's ability to move the other powers of the soul to their operations, see *DV* 22.12; *ST* Ia.82.4, ad 1; Ia–IIae.9.1.

Habituation satisfies the subjective equipping condition, providing perfect readiness-to-act *on the part of the intellect*. But there could be obstacles to *the object's availability*: namely, brain damage may prevent the power of imagination – whose organ is the brain – from presenting the appropriate phantasm.[35] (So for Aquinas memory loss is a failure of the imagination, not the intellect.) Assuming the brain's good functioning, however, cognitive habits can be exercised solely by an act of will, even in a state of sensory deprivation.

Habitual and yet not a habit

Now according to Aquinas, *the human soul's essence plays the same role with respect to self-awareness as a habit does for cognition of the corresponding extramental object* – i.e., the soul's essence is naturally perfected so as to be subjectively equipped to produce the operation of self-awareness:

> [F]rom the very fact that [the soul's] essence is present to it, it is able (*potens*) to go forth into an act of cognition of its own self; just as because someone has a habit of some science, he is able from the very presence of that habit to perceive those things that fall under that habit. But no habit is required for the soul to perceive that it exists and attend to what is occurring within it; rather, only the essence of the soul is required, which is present to the mind: for from acts proceed, in which it is actually perceived.[36]

Now of course Aquinas does not mean that the human soul *is* a habit in the category of quality.[37] At the same time he is adamant that habitual self-awareness is not an accidental acquired or innate habit for self-awareness inhering in the soul.[38] Rather, the essence of the soul *is functionally parallel to a habit for actual self-awareness*: It "has the character of a habit," or

---

[35] See Aquinas's discussion of how various conditions affecting the brain (insanity, inebriation, sleep, or violent passions) can impede imagination and thus prevent one from exercising cognitive habits; *ST* 1a.84.7; *InDA* II.11; *InEthic* VII.3.

[36] *DV* 10.8. See also ad 11 [Leon. 22/2.323:392–9]: "[S]icut non oportet ut semper intelligatur in actu, cuius notitia habitualiter habetur per aliquas species in intellectu existentes; ita etiam non oportet quod semper intelligatur actualiter ipsa mens, cuius cognitio inest nobis habitualiter, ex hoc quod ipsa eius essentia intellectui nostro est praesens"; ad 1 s.c.; and *Sent* 1.3.5.1, ad 1.

[37] See *QDSC* 11, ad 1.

[38] *DV* 10.8, ad 14 [Leon. 22/2.324:419–25]: "[N]otitia qua anima seipsam novit non est in genere accidentis quantum ad id quo habitualiter cognoscitur, sed solum quantum ad actum cognitionis qui est accidens quoddam; unde etiam Augustinus dicit quod notitia substantialiter inest menti, in IX *De Trinitate*, secundum quod mens novit se ipsam" (cf. *DeTrin* 9.4.5). Aquinas thus drops the traditional language of a "naturally inserted" habit of self-knowledge, in favor of a natural facility for self-awareness (a usage that is already in Bonaventure – see Chapter 1, p. 34). I thus cannot agree with Martín Federico Echavarría's interpretation that Aquinas views habitual self-awareness

"stands in the place of a habit" with respect to acts of self-awareness.[39] The reason is that the soul's ontological self-presence grants it the two above-mentioned characteristics of habits, relative to self-awareness: (1) Insofar as it is intellectual and self-identical it is intellectually present to itself and thus exists naturally in a state of "first perfection" for thinking about itself; (2) It is thereby essentially "subjectively equipped" to engage in the operation of thinking about itself at will. "From its own self, the mind has something whence it can go forth into the act in which it actually knows itself by perceiving that it exists – just as the mind has within itself, from the species habitually preserved therein, that which enables it to consider that thing actually."[40]

The notion that the soul's very essence functions as a "first perfection" and "subjective equipping principle" for self-awareness clears up the second interpretive difficulty raised at the beginning of this chapter: namely, the difficulty of understanding and harmonizing the various features that Aquinas ascribes to habitual self-awareness. As it turns out, there is nothing so strange after all in *DV* 10.8's assertion that the human soul "sees itself by its essence" with a "habitual familiarity (*notitia habitualis*) prior to any abstraction from phantasms." References to an essential vision or habitual cognition do not imply that habitual self-awareness occupies a "quantitative middle" between potency and act, like an inchoate background of self-awareness. Neither is it a mere potency like the natural sheer potency for cognizing tomatoes and the Pythagorean theorem.[41] Rather, habitual self-awareness stands in the "qualitative middle" between potency and the act of self-awareness: In other words, the soul naturally

---

as a habit lodged in intellectual memory, "Memoria e identidad según Santo Tomás de Aquino," *Sapientia* 62 (2002): 91–112 (here at 110).

[39] See especially *Sent* I.3.5.1, ad 1 [Mand. 1.124]: "[A]d esse habitus intellectivi duo concurrunt: scilicet species intelligibilis, et lumen intellectus agentis, quod facit eam intelligibilem in actu: unde si aliqua species esset quae in se haberet lumen, illud haberet rationem habitus, quantum pertinet ad hoc quod esset principium actus. Ita dico, quod quando ab anima cognoscitur aliquid quod est in ipsa non per sui similitudinem, sed per suam essentiam, ipsa essentia rei cognitae est loco habitus. Unde dico, quod ipsa essentia animae, prout est mota a seipsa, habet rationem habitus." The apparently contradictory *DV* 10.8, ad 6 s.c. actually refers to quidditative self-knowledge, not self-awareness: "[Q]uamvis anima nostra sit sibi ipsi simillima, non tamen potest esse principium cognoscendi seipsam ut species intelligibilis, sicut nec materia prima; eo quod hoc modo se habet intellectus noster in ordine intelligibilium sicut materia prima in ordine sensibilium" [Leon. 22/2.325:509–15] (compare arg. 6 and ad 6).

[40] *DV* 10.8, ad 1 s.c. It has been argued that Aquinas applies the language of "habit" to the soul's essence because of its facility for exercising self-awareness (see Lambert, "Habitual Knowledge," 11; Still, "Aquinas's Theory of Human Self-Knowledge," 33), but this interpretation confuses *being an intrinsic principle of operation* with the *facility* that accrues to operations elicited by such principles.

[41] See studies cited in notes 9 and 10 above.

exists in a state of perfection whereby it is ordered toward or subjectively equipped for self-awareness, without being naturally ordered in this way toward the cognition of any other object (more on this in a moment).[42]

In this natural state of being "equipped" for spontaneous operations of actual self-awareness, we can find an answer to a question that has puzzled some of Aquinas's modern readers and which could just as well have been articulated by his contemporaries: Why does he affirm that the soul is naturally subjectively equipped for self-awareness, yet deny that the self-present soul can cognize itself just by turning its attention inward?[43] In her in-depth study of this question, Brown proposes that habitual self-awareness is subject to a condition of exercise that does not apply to other habits: namely, as a habit for a second-order act, its exercise depends on the presence of a first-order act.[44] As we will see in Chapter 6, however, the language of second-order and first-order acts is misleading when applied to Aquinas's theory of actual self-awareness. I contend, rather, that the answer lies in his broader view about the exercise of habits, which applies equally to habitual self-awareness: namely, we can exercise our habits at will *only if the conditions are right*, which for a cognitive habit requires that the objective availability condition be fulfilled. Habitual self-awareness prepares the intellect-as-*cognizer* to think about itself at will – but does not grant sufficiency for action, since exercise of that habit still depends on the intellect-as-*object*'s being in the proper condition to be cognized. In order to turn its attention toward itself, then, the intellect-as-object must be rendered actually intelligible, which occurs only when it is thinking about something.

It may seem mere quibbling to distinguish between the cognizer's being-equipped-to-cognize and the object's availability-to-be-cognized, since in self-awareness, cognizer and cognized are numerically identical anyway. But for Aquinas, this fine distinction is the key to explaining how, although the intellect *is* itself, its self-awareness depends on cognition of extramental intelligibles. The intellect-as-cognizer *fulfils the subjective equipping condition* even when it is unactualized, because by its very essence it naturally has the "first perfection" of habitual self-awareness. But the unactualized intellect-as-cognized *fails to fulfil the objective availability*

---

[42] See *DV* 10.8, resp. and ad 1; *SCG* 3.46; compare to *ST* Ia.87.1, where the soul's presence is the "principle" of the act of perceiving one's own individual soul [Leon. 5.356]: "Nam ad primam cognitionem de mente habendam, sufficit ipsa mentis praesentia, quae est principium actus ex quo mens percipit seipsam."

[43] See Chapter 1, pp. 32 and 34–6.

[44] Brown, "Aquinas' Missing Flying Man," 26; see likewise de Finance, "Cogito cartésien," 34.

condition, because it lacks actual intelligibility due to the intellect's native lack of actuality. "The soul is present to itself as intelligible, namely, such that it *can* be understood, not such that it *is* understood by itself, but only from its object."[45] Hence actual self-awareness depends on the intellect's actualization by a species abstracted from sense. Once the intellect is in operation, the obstacle to self-awareness is removed, and self-consideration is now entirely in my power, so that I cognize myself "by myself."

Thus for Aquinas, the weakness of the human intellect-as-*cognizer* is not to blame for the fact that the human soul is by default only habitually self-aware. Instead, as Putallaz has pointed out against Gardeil and Ruane, the soul's natural self-awareness is merely habitual because of an obstacle on the side of the intellect-as-*cognized*, i.e., lack of intelligibility. This obstacle must be removed in order for the intellect to perceive itself existing.[46] Thus it is not true that habitual self-awareness is subject to more conditions of exercise than other habits, as Brown proposes; nor, conversely, does the soul's self-presence make the exercise of habitual self-awareness more spontaneous than that of other habits, as McKian argues.[47] Rather, the exercise of habitual self-awareness is subject to the object's cognitive availability, as is the exercise of any ordinary habit.

What conceptual work does habitual self-awareness do?

In response to our first interpretive difficulty at the beginning of the chapter – concerning the explanatory value of habitual self-awareness – we can now recognize the conceptual work it performs in two main areas of Aquinas's theory of self-knowledge.

First of all, Aquinas's account of habitual self-awareness allows him to accommodate the intuition with which the chapter began, i.e., that *being*

---

[45] *DV* 10.8, ad 4 s.c.; *ST* Ia.87.1 [Leon. 5.355]: "[Intellectus] in sua essentia consideratus, se habet ut potentia intelligens. Unde ex seipso habet virtutem ut intelligat, non autem ut intelligatur, nisi secundum quod fit actu" (note that for Aquinas to be actually understood is to be actually intelligible, as we shall see in Chapter 6). Along similar lines, see *DV* 24.4, ad 14 [Leon. 22/3.692:297–302]: "[N]otitia et amor dupliciter possunt comparari ad mentem. Uno modo ut ad amantem et cognoscentem; et sic ipsam mentem non excedunt, nec recedunt ab aliorum accidentium similitudine. Alio modo possunt comparari ad mentem ut ad amatam et cognitam; et sic excedunt mentem."

[46] See Putallaz, *Le sens de la réflexion*, 77–85, emphasizing that the obstacle originates in the sheer potency of the possible intellect; likewise McKian, "Metaphysics of Introspection," 97; Lambert, *Self Knowledge in Thomas Aquinas*, 106 and 109. (For the maturing of Aquinas's thought in the second and third phases of his writing on this point, see Chapter 2, especially pp. 60–3.) Putallaz is responding to interpretations placing the obstacle in the intellect's weakness, e.g., in Gardeil, "Examen de conscience," 161, and "Perception expérimentale," 223–24.

[47] See McKian, "Metaphysics of Introspection," 104.

oneself should entail some sort of unique advantage in cognizing oneself, as compared to cognizing extramentals. He agrees that because of its self-identity, the mind is better disposed toward itself than toward extramental objects. Habitual self-awareness is the only "first perfection" that the intellectual soul has by its essence, and actual self-awareness is the only cognitive act for which the soul is naturally equipped.[48] Thus the only entity to which the intellectual soul is naturally present is itself. Its natural relation to all other objects (which are made present only via abstracted species) is one of sheer undifferentiated potency.

In fact, since it is intellectual, the soul's *being itself* entails its natural *presence to itself*. But this self-presence is just a "first perfection" or "equipped state" in which the intellect is already essentially disposed to cognize itself. *The human soul, then, cannot be intellectual without also being "pre-equipped" for self-awareness.* The same idea can be rephrased in terms of the ontology of the human soul. Because the human soul is intellectual, its ontological self-identity is a cognitive self-presence (a habitual self-awareness). In other words, insofar as the human intellectual soul is ontologically self-identical, it is "equipped" or "ordered" toward actual self-awareness.[49] To put it another way, self-awareness is connatural to the human soul.[50] Habitual self-awareness, then, can be viewed not only as a cognitive state, but also as an ontological property: *What it is to be an intellectual soul includes being ordered to self-awareness.*[51]

---

[48] See Lambert, "Habitual Knowledge," 10–11, comparing the natural state of the human soul vis-à-vis self-awareness to the natural state of a sense-power vis-à-vis sensation. Aquinas explicitly acknowledges the privileged status of self-cognition in *DV* 24.4, ad 14 [Leon. 22/3.692:312–15]: "Sic ergo non oportet quod amor et notitia sint essentialia menti nisi secundum quod mens per suam essentiam cognoscitur et amatur." Although he also pairs a natural habitual cognition of God with habitual self-awareness in *Sent* 1.3.5.1 and *DV* 10.2, ad 5, this view does not seem to have persisted into his more mature writings.

[49] While this interpretation is very close to that of the Barcelona school of interpretation inspired by Jaume Bofill y Bofill (see "Ontología y libertad," in his *Obra filosófica*, 99–106), it differs in certain important respects. According to Bofill and others (for instance, Patricia Schell, "La doctrina tomista de la *memoria* espiritual: un punto de equilibrio ante las anomalías contemporánea," *Sapientia* 59 [2004]: 49–75 [here at 69]; and Tomar Romero, "La *memoria* como conocimiento," 104), habitual self-awareness *is* the soul's intellectual memory, i.e., the intellect *qua* retentive. In my view, however, Aquinas does not seem to think habitual self-awareness is identical with the intellect, let alone specifically the intellect under its retentive aspect. I would prefer to say that habitual self-awareness *belongs to the essence* of the intellectual soul.

[50] See note 23 above.

[51] Interestingly, in *Quodl* 7.1.4, Aquinas even goes so far as to permit referring to a "cognitive nature" as '*notitia*' or 'knowledge': "[N]oticia quatuor modis accipi potest: primo, pro ipsa natura cognoscitiua; secundo, pro potencia cognitiua; tercio, pro habitu cognoscitiuo; quarto, pro ipso cognitionis actu" [Leon. 25/1.15:22–35]; and see *SLDC* 15 for how self-knowledge completes subsisting entities. On the ontological significance of self-knowledge, see Putallaz, *Le sens de la réflexion*, 97–100; Still, "Aquinas's Theory of Human Self-Knowledge," 9; and Fetz, *Ontologie der*

The notion of the intellectual soul's essential self-presence as the functional equivalent of a habit for self-awareness, then, is Aquinas's version of the thirteenth-century notion of natural self-knowledge (see Chapter 1). He and his adversaries thus agree that the soul is closer to itself than to any other cognitive object, that self-presence grants an advantage in self-knowing, and that acts of self-awareness, when they happen, are the intellect's most natural acts. But his theory of habitual self-knowledge allows him to go further to reconcile two assertions that his contemporaries took to be incompatible: first, that the soul is naturally self-present (in line with the notion of natural self-knowledge); second, that actual self-knowledge depends on the intellect's actualization via a species (in line with the notion of dependent self-knowledge). For him, the first is true because by nature the intellectual soul is subjectively equipped for self-awareness, and the second is equally true because the intellectual soul naturally lacks objective availability, due to its sheer lack of intellectual actualization. He thus capitalizes on the explanatory value of the soul's self-presence, while blocking the inference to natural supraconscious self-knowing or to the independence of self-awareness from cognition of extramentals.

The second main explanatory function of habitual self-awareness is to account for certain experiential characteristics of actual self-awareness that Aquinas takes to be typical of acts that spring from habits. For one thing, as noted earlier, habits bestow on the corresponding acts a sense of familiarity. Acts of self-awareness are likewise marked by comfortable familiarity; I am already pre-equipped for self-awareness, so I never encounter myself as something strange and new.[52] For another thing, because habitual self-awareness constitutes the soul's natural "first-perfection" or "second-nature" aptitude for self-awareness, actual self-awareness – when it occurs – is like a natural act. So it is no coincidence that in various texts, Aquinas attributes to actual self-awareness each of the three characteristics of natural acts: pleasure, consistency, facility. Following Aristotle, Aquinas notes how "delightful" it is to experience oneself existing.[53] Self-awareness is "consistent" inasmuch as I am aware of myself whenever I have the opportunity, as we will see in Chapter 6. And the soul exercises

---

Innerlichkeit, 150–1 (the latter two go too far, in my opinion, by interpreting habitual self-presence as an ontological *rather than* a cognitive structure).

[52] A phenomenon famously discussed by Augustine; see Chapter 1, pp. 20–1.

[53] See *InEthic* IX.11 [Leon. 47/2.540:109–13]: "[Q]uod autem aliquis sentiat bonum esse in se ipso est delectabile. Et sic patet quod cum vivere sit eligibile et maxime bonis quibus est bonum esse et delectabile, quod etiam percipere se sentire et intelligere est eis delectabile, quia simul cum hoc sentiunt id quod est eis secundum se bonum, scilicet esse et vivere, et in hoc delectantur."

self-awareness with "facility" because it can cognize itself by itself (spontaneously) when the right conditions are met.[54] In the role of the "habit" whence all acts of self-awareness spring, *the soul's natural self-presence is responsible for these experiential characteristics in every act of self-awareness*[55] (though acquired memories can enrich later experiences, as I will discuss in a moment).

Certain experiential characteristics of actual self-awareness are traceable more specifically to the fact that habitual self-awareness belongs to the soul's *essence*, i.e., it is neither acquired nor even accidental. One minor repercussion is that since there is no initial habit-acquisition, the feeling of self-familiarity must extend even to a person's first act of self-awareness.[56] Thus this first act would not have *felt* like a first act, but rather like a recognition of something already familiar, known all along. (Of course, this hypothesis can never be corroborated, since no one remembers her first act of self-awareness!) But more importantly, the essential character of habitual self-awareness is necessary for the directness of self-awareness, and thus its first-person character, as discussed in Chapter 4. If the soul were not *already present to itself*, no sensation-based intervention could make it *directly* present to itself. The abstracted species of 'spider' makes spiderness present to the intellect and thus incidentally gives the intellect intelligibility. But if the intellect naturally lacked self-presence, only a species of 'intellect' could give the intellect *self-presence*. And because there are no sensory experiences of a soul, the latter could only be acquired indirectly, by reasoning or by constructing a third-person phantasm of 'intellect' from which to abstract a species. Habitual self-awareness thus plays an integral role in protecting the intuitive, first-person character of self-awareness in Aquinas's theory. To borrow Romeyer's clever financial metaphor:

> This disposition provides an original and essential capital, so to speak, that could never yield a return were it not stimulated by an understanding of external objects. Our soul only awakens to itself when it opens its eyes upon the outside world, but it is truly to *itself* that it awakes, and to which it is *habitually disposed by nature to awake*.[57]

---

[54] See Chapter 2, pp. 62–3.

[55] Note that this basic, essential habitual self-awareness is the principle for all our acts of self-awareness; at no point is there ever an acquired, accidental habit for self-awareness (see *DV* 10.8, ad 14 in note 38 above). This is why Aquinas says that the mind actually cognizes itself "by itself" or "by its presence" in *SCG* 3.46 and *ST* 1a.87.1, as discussed in Chapter 2, p. 62.

[56] Aquinas emphasizes the priority of habitual self-awareness to any act of actual self-awareness in connection with the mind's Trinitarian image; see *Sent* 1.3.4.1 and *DV* 10.2, ad 5.

[57] Romeyer, "Saint Thomas et notre connaissance," 59, my translation.

We will also see in Chapter 6 that habitual self-awareness makes implicit self-awareness possible.

Nevertheless, in discussing the contribution of habitual self-awareness to the phenomenal character of actual self-awareness, we should not overlook the additional contributions of acquired memories in shaping our self-experience. Like any other cognition, my awareness of myself as an individual is not monolithic, but improves with repeated experience and reflection over a lifetime. For instance, the more I reflect on my actions, the more insight I have into my motivations and interests, and the more clearly I understand myself as an individual. Even if I am not particularly self-reflective, my actions and experiences still quietly shape my self-image (e.g., someone's experiences of hiking and camping might lead her to think of herself as a "city person" even if she has never articulated this to herself).

In Aquinas, this lifetime development could perhaps be traced to the accumulation of self-experiences in an ever-more-complex acquired self-memory that reinforces and augments the basic effects of habitual self-awareness (familiarity, facility of exercise, etc.) and shapes my impression of myself as an individual ("city person"). Aquinas holds that self-awareness is part and parcel of every memory that the intellect stores, so that in recalling previously known objects I can recall my past acts and go on to draw conclusions about my motivations and personality that shape my self-image and future actions. There is no reason to think that these new memories or cognitive habits compete with or replace the soul's preexisting habitual self-presence. Rather, it seems more likely that, as the intellect receives and stores an ever-increasing number of species, each of which reveals to me a little more of my potential, it is "equipped" for increasingly distinct and sophisticated acts of self awareness over time. In fact, for Aquinas cognitive habits are simply modifications or "first perfections" of the intellect, so that one could simply say that my acts of self-awareness proceed from a much more "informed" mind now than at the age of two, and this difference would naturally shape the experiential character of those acts. In Chapter 8 we will discuss in detail how Aquinas thinks human memories incorporate self-awareness and contribute to a person's unified sense of self across time.

***

Before moving on, I would like to linger for a moment over a historical puzzle. Given the importance of habitual self-awareness to Aquinas's theory of self-knowledge, it is odd that he incorporates it into a formal schema of the types of self-knowledge only once, in *DV* 10.8. Habitual self-awareness is not absent from other texts, of course. It appears also in his earliest treatment of self-knowledge (*Sent* I.3.4–5), where he refers to it as a *notitia* or familiar knowledge "held" in memory (I.3.4.1, ad 5), a *notitia* stemming from the soul's self-presence (I.3.4.4), a consubstantial habit for self-knowledge (I.3.5.1), and the essence of the soul playing the role of a habit for self-understanding (I.3.5.1, ad 1). After *DV* 10.8, the underlying concept persists in some of the major treatments of self-knowledge; for instance in *SCG* 3.46 and *ST* Ia.87.1, we have seen Aquinas describe the self-present soul as internally equipped to think about itself on its own initiative (*per seipsam, per praesentiam suam*).[58] And the language of "habitual" cognition of one's own existence reappears again in *ST* Ia.93.7, ad 4, where he states that the soul always cognizes itself, "not actually, but habitually."

Nevertheless, why does Aquinas not include habitual self-awareness in any formal schemata of the types of self-knowledge after *DV* 10.8?[59] I suggest that the explanation lies in the shift that occurs in Aquinas's treatment of self-knowledge in the 1260s, from the end of his second phase to his third mature phase of writing about self-knowledge (see Chapter 2). At some point after *DV* 10, he begins to construe the flashpoint of disagreement with theories of supraconscious self-knowing differently. The earlier flashpoint concerns whether the self-presence of the intellect-as-cognizer is sufficient for actual self-knowledge; the later flashpoint concerns whether the intellect-as-cognized is essentially intelligible. It is no coincidence, I think, that after this shift, Aquinas no longer singles out habitual self-awareness as a separate subtype of self-knowledge. The fact is, even if he can convince his opponents that the intuitions and phenomena supposedly explained by supraconscious self-knowing can equally well be explained by a natural habitual self-awareness, his argument for the act-dependence of all actual self-knowledge really depends on two further premises: (1) The condition under which habits are exercised at will is the intelligibility of the cognitive object (i.e., the objective availability condition); (2) *Qua* object, the intellectual soul is essentially unintelligible to itself. Once he realized the importance of this second premise – later

---

[58] See Chapter 2, pp. 62–3.
[59] Scholarly attempts at explaining this peculiarity have been infrequent and generally perfunctory. Putallaz's *Le sens de la réflexion* does not mention it all. Romeyer, Gardeil, and Brown note it but do not explain it; they merely explain (correctly) in different ways that the reality that *DV* 10.8 identifies as habitual self-awareness does not really vanish, but remains in the background of *ST* Ia.87.1 (Romeyer, "Saint Thomas et notre connaissance," 72; Gardeil, "Perception expérimentale," 221, n. 1; Brown, "Aquinas' Missing Flying Man," 23).

elevated to prominence in arguing for the dependence of all actual self-knowledge on cognition of extramental objects – habitual self-awareness lost its centrality to his campaign against supraconscious self-knowing. Moreover, the claim that the soul's essence can play the role of a habit for self-awareness is distracting and easily misinterpreted. (Is there perhaps a hint of defensiveness in Aquinas's rare flash of frustration in *QDSC* 11, ad 1, written almost a decade after *DV* 10, when he says that nobody would hold that the soul's essence *is* a habit "unless they were insane"?[60])

The idea of the soul as naturally perfected or equipped for self-awareness, then, fits neatly into Aquinas's developing picture of the nature of the human soul as the lowest in the order of intelligibles, equivalent to prime matter in the order of sensibles. Because it is intellectual – essentially in potency to all intelligible form – its ontological self-presence translates into a psychological self-presence whereby it is equipped *qua* cognizer for cognizing itself. Yet due to this same essential potency to all forms, the soul *qua* cognized is unintelligible to itself, apart from its actualization in thinking about extramental objects. Naturally poised on the cusp of cognizing itself, the soul is barred from achieving perpetual actual self-awareness only by its own sheer potency to intelligible form – the same potency that grants it a habitual readiness to cognize itself. The structure of human self-awareness thus conforms to the status of the human soul, existing on the horizon of the physical and the intellectual, as a substantial form endowed with an intellectual power.

[60] See *QDSC* 11, ad 1 (composed *c.* 1267–68; see Torrell, *Saint Thomas Aquinas* 1:162).

CHAPTER SIX

Implicit vs. explicit self-awareness and the duality of conscious thought

The phenomena

As the preceding chapters have shown, Aquinas anchors his account of self-awareness in the principle that actual self-awareness depends on the intellect's being in act. But so far we have steered clear of a key question: Does engaging in intellectual activity merely provide the *opportunity* for me to consider myself, or do I *necessarily* cognize myself in all my mental acts? To put it another way, does Aquinas limit actual self-awareness to acts of thinking about myself, or can self-awareness also be concomitant to thinking about something else?

Consider the following phenomena. A gardener catches a glimpse of a toad under a leaf, and as she watches it devouring unsuspecting insects, her attention is entirely absorbed. Then she turns her attention to herself: "I'm seeing a real, live toad catching insects!" She has just had two distinct thoughts: one about the extramental toad, and one about herself in which she notices her own actions, emotions, and agency. (This second thought remains within the bounds of ordinary daily experience; it is not the philosopher's act of isolating the "I" from the experience in order to ponder the meaning of subjectivity.)

Now regardless of where attention is directed, subject and extramental object seem to be inextricably intertwined in the content of both thoughts. For instance, when the gardener turns her attention to herself, her awareness of herself continues to encompass the toad: "I'm seeing a toad!" Conversely, while engrossed in watching the toad, the gardener was nevertheless not wholly oblivious to herself. Suppose that she spends the whole time watching the toad and never once turns her attention to herself: If an onlooker then asks her what she had been doing in the garden, she will recall not just the toad but *herself watching the toad*, and she can articulate that experience as a statement *about herself*, the conscious subject. "Oh, just then? I was watching a toad eating insects." In order for this assertion to be possible at all, it seems that her cognition of the toad must have included some sort of embedded grasp of herself-as-thinker, which went unnoticed at the time but could be retrieved later in remembering the original experience.[1]

These phenomena suggest what we can call the "duality of conscious thought": namely, intellectual acts are "bipolar," co-manifesting both the thinker and the extramental object of thought in relation to each other. A broader version of the same idea, the indissociability of intentionality and consciousness, was famously defended by Brentano, Husserl, and Sartre.[2] Related ideas have elicited considerable debate in analytic circles, emerging most recently in Uriah Kriegel's self-representational theory of consciousness.[3] And the duality of conscious thought is loosely related to the ancient view that all knowing is in some sense self-knowing (Plato, Aristotle, Plotinus, Proclus, etc.), a view that takes on quite a different guise in early modern thought (Descartes, Berkeley, Kant).

In Aquinas, the duality of conscious thought shows up as a distinction between what we can call implicit and explicit self-awareness. Acts attentively directed toward extramental objects necessarily include some sort of self-awareness ("implicit self-awareness"). Conversely, acts attentively

---

[1] Consequently, I disagree with Pasnau that to "know that I am thinking about something" is merely to be *disposed* to notice later that I *was* thinking about that thing, in the sense in which "I [currently] know many things that I have never thought about, such as the answers to various trivial math problems" (*Thomas Aquinas on Human Nature*, 346–7). Noticing myself thinking is an entirely different sort of experience from answering a trivial math problem for the first time. No matter how instantly I grasp the answer to that math problem (whether by lightning-quick reasoning or even by intuition), it does not appear to me as something that was part of my *prior awareness of the world*. In recognizing that I was thinking about *toads*, in contrast, I remember *what it was like to observe them*, recapturing something that was already present in that original act.

[2] Franz Brentano, *Psychology from an Empirical Standpoint* II.8–12, referring to sound as "the primary object of the act of hearing," with the latter itself being "the secondary object" (ed. Oskar Kraus and Linda L. McAlister, and trans. Antos C. Rancurello, D.B. Terrell, and Linda L. McAlister [London: Routledge, 1995], 126–36, here 128); Edmund Husserl, *Cartesian Meditations: An Introduction to Phenomenology*, describes "the identical Ego, who, *as the active and affected subject of consciousness*, lives in all processes of consciousness and is related, *through* them, to all object-poles" (trans. Dorion Cairns [The Hague: Martinus Nijhoff, 1960], p. 66 and more generally chs. 4 and 5); Jean-Paul Sartre, *Being and Nothingness*: "The necessary and sufficient condition for a knowing consciousness to be knowledge of its object, is that it be consciousness of itself as being that knowledge" (trans. Hazel E. Barnes [New York: Philosophical Library, 1956], p. liv). For a comparison of Aquinas and Sartre that touches on this issue, see Wang, *Aquinas and Sartre*, esp. ch. 4. I cannot agree, however, with the author's claim that for Aquinas as for Sartre, we are conscious of the self as "a 'nothing,' a lack of form, a 'not being' the form of what is known" (73); see pp. 163–70 below and Chapter 8, pp. 202–5.

[3] Uriah Kriegel, *Subjective Consciousness: A Self-Representational Theory* (Oxford University Press, 2009); and the essays for and against in *Self-Representational Approaches to Consciousness*, ed. Uriah Kriegel and Kenneth Williford (Cambridge, Mass.: MIT Press, 2006).

directed toward oneself as thinking subject ("explicit self-awareness") necessarily include an implicit awareness of the extramental object. The reason is that the intelligible object and the thinking intellect are co-manifested in relation to each other in every intellectual act, whether attention is directed to the object or to the intellect itself.

This distinction has gone largely unnoticed in Aquinas, which is unfortunate – given the implications for his view of intellectual inten-tionality – but not inexplicable. He never developed technical terms for implicit and explicit self-awareness, depicting self-awareness instead in certain texts as intrinsic to every intellectual act, and in others as an explicit self-consideration (the "alpha" and "beta" texts discussed below). Consequently, among those few of his readers who have addressed the status of actual self-awareness,[4] some have read it as exclusively implicit, focusing on one group of texts (e.g., Putallaz),[5] while others have read it as exclusively explicit, focusing on the other group of texts (e.g., Gardeil, Maritain, Pasnau, and interestingly Brentano, who roundly critiqued Aquinas for, as he believed, neglecting implicit self-awareness).[6]

There have been some notable exceptions, such as Lonergan and Owens,[7] but their interpretations, which were not developed in detail, did not gain

---

[4] Many of Aquinas's readers simply have not inquired whether actual self-awareness is implicit or explicit. A group of early twentieth-century commentators on Aquinas even seems to have been unaware of the difference between these two phenomena of self-awareness in ordinary experience, which leads to some strangely jumbled descriptions of self-awareness; see Picard, "Le problème cri-tique fondamentale," 46–57; and the nearly identical view articulated in the same 1923 volume of *Archives de philosophie* by Romeyer ("Notre science de l'esprit humain," 44).

[5] See Putallaz, *Le sens de la réflexion*, 105–16, esp. 109, n. 17, and 167; and perhaps Reichmann, "The 'Cogito' in St. Thomas," 346–7. Putallaz posits an additional type of self-knowledge, "reflexion in the strict sense," that is not merely implicit, but not properly explicit either (*Le sens de la réflexion*, 148–208). For discussion and critique of this view, see Chapter 7, pp. 195–8.

[6] Gardeil, "Perception expérimentale," 220 and 231–6; Jacques Maritain, *Distinguish to Unite*, 4th edn, trans. Gregory B. Phelan (New York: Charles Scribner's Sons, 1959), 89–90, n. 1 (though see also note 7 below); Rabeau, Species, Verbum, 87–104; and Pasnau, *Thomas Aquinas on Human Nature*, 346, rejecting implicit self-awareness as discussed in note 1 above, though my notion of explicit self-awareness is somewhat different from his, as will be discussed below. For Brentano's critique, see *Psychology from an Empirical Standpoint*, 125–6 n.

[7] See Owens, "Aquinas on Cognition as Existence," 82 (applying to Aquinas a distinction he had located in Aristotle at 78–80), and *An Elementary Christian Metaphysics*, 223; Lonergan, "Christ as Subject," 243–70; Peillaube, "Avons-nous l'expérience du spirituel?" 264 (using the language of *in actu exercito*/*in actu signato*); de Finance, "Cogito cartésien," 37–41; Dhavamony, *Subjectivity and Knowledge*, 74–86; Toccafondi, "La spiritualità dell'anima"; Lambert, *Self Knowledge in Thomas Aquinas*, 133–52, based upon his earlier article, "Nonintentional Experience of Oneself" (though he argues that this distinction in Aquinas is ambiguous and in conflict with other aspects of his thought; see *Self Knowledge in Thomas Aquinas*, 117–18, 140–52); and tentatively, Wébert, "*Reflexio*," 319; and Wang, *Aquinas and Sartre*, 128. Note that although Maritain interprets Aquinas's texts on self-awareness as applying to explicit self-awareness, he thinks that implicit self-awareness can be found in Aquinas's theory of judgment, so he still ends up positing an implicit/explicit distinction in Aquinas (*Distinguish to Unite*, 89, n. 1, and 446).

much traction. Lonergan even discouragingly asserted that, although an experienced reader of Aquinas will recognize his sensitivity to "the facts of consciousness," the chasm between medieval approaches and modern expectations blocks any definitive confirmation of this interpretation.[8]

Luckily for us, the task of demonstrating Aquinas's commitment to a distinction between implicit and explicit self-awareness is not as hopeless as Lonergan would have it. The lynchpin is Aquinas's view of the intellect and the extramental object as co-manifested in intentional intellectual acts (his version of the duality of conscious thought). I will explore this view in unfolding his account of implicit self-awareness, but the same view also provides the framework for his account of explicit self-awareness. Once we have seen how he accounts for implicit self-awareness, then, we will already have seen (a) his adherence to the duality of conscious thought; and (b) his explanation of the psychological structure for explicit self-awareness. Nevertheless, we will still have to reckon with certain special difficulties posed by explicit self-awareness.

Where does implicit cognition fit?

Before showing that Aquinas provides a developed account of implicit self-awareness, I want to begin with the more modest project of establishing that he has a general account of implicit cognition. Now for Aquinas, there is no such thing as an implicit intellectual operation, because *the intellectual operation just is an act of attending.*[9] So if he is to admit the possibility of implicitly cognizing one thing in thinking about another, the explanation cannot be that some sort of implicit operation trails alongside an attentive operation. Rather, the actualized intelligibility of one entity must be *included implicitly* in the content of the operation of considering

---

[8] See Lonergan, "Christ as Subject," 249–50, esp. n. 11. At 257–9 he names the two relevant phenomena: "consciousness in the direct act" and "formal reflexion."

[9] *SCG* 1.55 [Leon. 13.159]: "Vis cognoscitiva non cognoscit aliquid actu nisi adsit intentio." Aquinas sometimes describes this attention as an inner "speaking," producing an interior "word" (*verbum*) or "concept" (*conceptus*); see e.g., *DV* 4.1, ad 1; *DV* 4.4; *ST* Ia.93.7, ad 3; Ia.107.1; *Quodl* 4.4.1 and 5.5.2; and *InIoan* I.1. For a study of Aquinas on the "inner word," see John Frederick Peifer, *The Concept in Thomism* (New York: Bookman Associates, 1952); and the exchange on this topic in John O'Callaghan, "*Verbum Mentis*: Philosophical or Theological Doctrine in Aquinas?" *Proceedings of the American Catholic Philosophical Association* 74 (2000): 103–17; James C. Doig, "O'Callaghan on *Verbum Mentis* in Aquinas," *American Catholic Philosophical Quarterly* 77 (2003): 233–55; John O'Callaghan, "More Words on the *Verbum*: A Response to James Doig," *American Catholic Philosophical Quarterly* 77 (2003): 257–68; and John Deely, "How To Go Nowhere with Language: Remarks on John O'Callaghan, *Thomist Realism and the Linguistic Turn*," *American Catholic Philosophical Quarterly* 82 (2008): 337–59.

some other entity. This sort of explanation, of course, requires that *what is actually manifested in the act* be more than just the precise object of attention.

Aquinas describes two cases in which an intellectual act encompasses intelligibles that are not the explicit objects of attention. We can call them, respectively, participated attention and implicit cognition. Although we are more interested in the latter, let us first briefly examine the former as a contrast point.

Participated attention

The notion of participated attention allows Aquinas to explain how we cognize complexes such as comparisons and propositions, even though the intellect is limited to cognizing one thing at a time.[10] His solution is that these complexes are themselves intelligible wholes that can be understood "as one." In formulating comparisons, affirming propositions, or grasping states of affairs, I conjoin multiple intelligibles into a single complex whole. And when I attend to this whole primarily as the object of cognition, I necessarily grasp each of the multiple component parts in virtue of their following upon that whole:

> Something can be understood by the intellect in two ways: primarily (*primo*) and by following [upon something understood primarily] (*ex consequenti*). Many are simultaneously understood by following [upon something else] inasmuch as they are ordered to one primary intelligible, and this happens in two ways. [One way occurs when many are understood by one species] … In another way, many are understood as one by the unity of that which is understood, for the whole itself is primarily understood and the many are understood by following upon the whole. For instance, when the intellect understands a line, it simultaneously understands the parts of the line as is said in III *De anima*; and likewise when it understands a proposition it simultaneously understands the subject and predicate; and when it understands the similarity or difference of various things, it simultaneously understands those things that are similar and different. But it is impossible for the intellect simultaneously to understand many intelligibles primarily and principally.[11]

---

[10] Because intellectual attention cannot point toward more than one object simultaneously, according to *DV* 8.14; or because the intellect cannot be perfected by more than one specifying form at a time, according to *ST* Ia.85.4 and *Quodl* 7.1.2. Both reasons appear in *SCG* I.55.

[11] *Quodl* 7.1.2; with parallel analysis in *SCG* I.55. See also *ST* Ia.85.4, ad 4 [Leon. 5.339]: "[Q]uando intellectus intelligit differentiam vel comparationem unius ad alterum, cognoscit utrumque differentium vel comparatorum sub ratione ipsius comparationis vel differentiae; sicut dictum est quod cognoscit partes sub ratione totius"; and texts in note 12.

Now even though the intellect is not considering the many parts in their own right (as "primary" objects of attention), it *actually understands* them in attending to the whole. When I am thinking about 'the relative sweetness of oranges and apples,' for example, neither oranges nor apples are objects of attention in their own right, since attention to one would exclude attention to the other.[12] But 'orange' and 'apple' are not cognized merely habitually, lying dormant in my intellect while I consider their relationship; they must be actualized as parts of my thought about 'the relative sweetness of oranges and apples.' "Those things that must fall under one intention must be simultaneously understood: for someone who considers a comparison of two things directs his intention to both and simultaneously beholds both."[13] (In fact, without an *actual* cognition of the parts, the cognition would merely be a thought about the indistinct whole 'sweet fruit,' containing only potentially the parts 'orange,' 'apple,' 'kiwi,' etc.[14] – which would not be a case of cognizing "many as one" in the first place.)

In cognition of complexes under a single intention, then, we have an example of a case in which the parts P_1 and P_2 *must be actually understood* in directing one's attention toward the whole, W. But this is not an implicit cognition because even though parts P_1 and P_2 are not the objects of attention in their own right (in which case thinking about P_1 would exclude thinking about P_2), they *receive attention as parts of a larger whole to which attention is directed* (hence "participated attention"). An analogy for participated attention is perhaps that of "seeing" the items within a scene at which I am "looking": i.e., in "looking out at the mountains" from a vantage point, I am necessarily "seeing" the waterfalls, cliffs, trees, birds, etc., within that chosen visual whole. Each of these parts is actually included in my visual experience, but I am not looking at any one of them

---

[12] *DV* 8.14 [Leon. 22/2.265:210–21]: "Et in huiusmodi intellectus vel sensus si feratur ut est unum, simul videtur, si autem ut est multa, quod est considerare unamquamque partem secundum se, sic non potest totum simul videri. Et sic etiam intellectus quando considerat propositionem, considerat multa ut unum; et ideo in quantum sunt unum, simul intelliguntur dum intelligitur una propositio quae ex eis constat; sed in quantum sunt multa, non possunt simul intelligi, ut scilicet intellectus simul se convertat ad rationes singulorum secundum se intuendas"; see also *ST* Ia.85.4, ad 3 [Leon. 5.339]: "[P]artes possunt intelligi dupliciter. Uno modo, sub quadam confusione, prout sunt in toto, et sic cognoscuntur per unam formam totius, et sic simul cognoscuntur. Alio modo, cognitione distincta, secundum quod quaelibet cognoscitur per suam speciem, et sic non simul intelliguntur."

[13] *SCG* I.55 [Leon. 13.157]: "Quae autem oportet sub una intentione cadere, oportet simul esse intellecta: qui enim comparationem duorum considerat, intentionem ad utrumque dirigit et simul intuetur utrumque."

[14] See p. 80, notes 46–7.

in particular, which would require focusing my attention on one so as to exclude the others.[15]

Implicit cognition

For Aquinas, there is another way in which the intellect actually understands something without making it the terminus of attention. For Aquinas, an entity affects a cognitive or appetitive power only *under a specific formality* (actual visibility, intelligibility, desirability) to which the power is oriented. Such forms constitute that entity *as operable object*. In other words, the object and the formal principle of its operability are related as matter and form, constituting a single actually visible or intelligible or desirable object, which is received in a single operation, under a single intention. This view can be stated as follows:

> The principle thesis: Whenever an intentional operation is directed to something, it *ipso facto* attains, implicitly, whatever formally actualizes that thing as a suitable object for such an operation.[16]

Aquinas's theories of human cognition and agency depend quite heavily on the principle thesis. The paradigm case is vision: Because physical light formally actualizes colors as visible (under a certain construal), in seeing a red apple I necessarily see the light that illuminates it.[17] Similarly, in desiring the apple I desire the end (e.g., satiating hunger) that formally constitutes this-apple-as-desirable-to-me.[18] Aquinas also applies this thesis more broadly, to explain why we can endorse a conclusion precisely *as* the conclusion of a certain set of premises,[19] why a bad intention can corrupt physical actions,[20] and why all love includes self-love.[21]

One particularly interesting application of the principle thesis occurs when Aquinas explains how species are cognized. As is well known, he holds that the essence is "that which" (*id quod cognoscitur*) I cognize, while the intelligible species, as the formal principle that makes the object intelligible to the intellect, is merely "that by which" (*id quo cognoscitur*)

---

[15] For the sensory analogy, see *DV* 8.14, in note 12 above.

[16] *SCG* I.76 [Leon. 13.217]: "Omnis enim virtus una operatione, vel uno actu, fertur in obiectum et in rationem formalem obiecti: sicut eadem visione videmus lumen et colorem, qui fit visibilis actu per lumen," and the texts in subsequent notes.

[17] See notes 37–41 below.

[18] See *Sent* I.17.1.5; II.38.1.4, ad 1; *SCG* I.76; *ST* Ia–IIae.12.4; Ia–IIae.18.7; *DM* 2.2, ad 11; and the texts in note 30 below.

[19] *SCG* I.76; *ST* Ia–IIae.57.2, ad 2.

[20] *DM* 2.2, ad 11.   [21] See texts in note 30 below.

I cognize.[22] *Per* the principle thesis, then, because the species is the formal principle of the object's intelligibility, it must be attained implicitly in attending to the object.[23] In other words, in using the species, I apprehend it implicitly, although later, I can consider it explicitly as a cognized object in its own right (*id quod cognoscitur*).[24] (Incidentally, this supports Pasnau's controversial claim that for Aquinas not just extramental objects but species themselves are "in a certain sense apprehended."[25])

In the principle thesis, then, we find Aquinas's rationale for implicit cognition: namely, if A_F is the formal principle that renders an object A intelligible, then every cognition of A necessarily includes A_F implicitly. Notice that A_F is not the object of attention, but neither is it cognized only habitually – A_F is included in A's intelligibility precisely as its *formal, actualizing principle.* Similar to participated attention, the intelligibility of A_F is built into the intelligibility of A so that in thinking about A, I necessarily actually grasp A_F. And similar to participated attention, the reason that A cannot be cognized without A_F is that the latter is an essential part

---

[22] See for instance *QDDA* 2, ad 5 [Leon. 24/119:389–20:392]: "Species enim intelligibilis est quo intellectus intelligit, non id quod intelligit, nisi per reflexionem, in quantum intelligit se intelligere id quo intelligit"; *DV* 2.6; *DP* 7.9; *SCG* 2.75 and 4.11; *ST* Ia.76.2, ad 4; *ST* Ia.85.2. For the scholarly debate on this issue, see p. 98, note 18.

[23] See *DV* 2.3, ad 3 [Leon. 22/1.52:341–50]: "Quando vero non alio actu fertur potentia cognoscitiva in medium quo cognoscit, et in rem cognitam tunc non est aliquis discursus in cognitione, sicut visus cognoscens lapidem per speciem lapidis in ipso existentem vel rem quae resultat in speculo per speculum non dicitur discurrere, quia idem est ei ferri in similitudinem rei, et in rem quae per talem similitudinem cognoscitur"; *Sent* I.27.2.3 [Mand. 1.663]: "[I]n speciem vel in imaginem contingit fieri conversionem dupliciter: vel secundum quod est species talis rei, et tunc est eadem conversio in rem et speciem rei; vel in speciem secundum quod est res quaedam; et sic non oportet quod eadem conversione convertatur quis per intellectum in speciem rei et in rem" (see also ad 4); *CT* I.85 [Leon. 42.110II36‑42]: "Vnde et species intelligibiles quia sunt immateriales, licet sint alie numero in me et in te, non propter hoc perdunt quin sint intelligibiles actu [= actually understood; see texts in notes 64 and 74 below]; sed intellectus intelligens per eas suum obiectum reflectitur supra se ipsum, intelligendo ipsum suum intelligere et speciem qua intelligit."

[24] This is not to say, however, that when I turn my attention explicitly to myself, I can identify the species as a distinct element in my experience, for reasons discussed on pp. 151–2 below.

[25] See Pasnau, *Theories of Cognition*, 195–219, esp. 212; and more recently, "Id quo cognoscimus," in *Theories of Perception in Medieval and Early Modern Thought*, ed. Simo Knuuttila and Pekka Kärkkäinen (Dordrecht: Springer, 2008), 131–49. Although I disagree with the conclusions he draws about the role of the species (e.g., the claim that "species actualize a cognitive power in virtue of being somehow apprehended by that cognitive power" seems to me to reverse the order in Aquinas's own theory), the texts cited above suggest that he is right to say that "the relationship between power and species is a cognitive one" ("Id quo cognoscimus," 146). Although O'Callaghan has critiqued Pasnau's view as "committing St. Thomas to what might be called 'shadow faculties,' a noncognitive *apprehensive* faculty for every cognitive *apprehensive* faculty a human being possesses" (*Thomist Realism and the Linguistic Turn*, 234–5), this problem disappears if the extramental object is considered and the species is grasped implicitly *in just one single act*. This line of reasoning could shed some interesting light on direct realism vs. representationalism in Aquinas, which I will pursue elsewhere.

of A. The key difference between implicit cognition and participated attention, however, is that in the latter, the complex whole W is composed of intelligible parts P_1 and P_2 as a toy tower is composed of blocks. Since I attend to W precisely *as a complex composed of these parts*, my cognition of W expresses these parts so that they share in the attention that W receives. By contrast, in implicit cognition, the principle of intelligibility A_F is related to the cognized object A as a form is related to the substance it constitutes (i.e., as a metaphysical principle). Consequently, it is not *expressed in* my cognition of A alongside other expressed parts; rather, it *constitutes* A as object of cognition. For this reason, while it is actually included in the cognition's content, it remains implicit, unarticulated.

Aquinas's account of implicit self-awareness

Two phenomena of self-awareness?

The principle thesis – coupled with the fact that for Aquinas the intellect is a principle of its objects' intelligibility – already provides some indications of how one might go about setting up an account of implicit self-awareness within such a framework. But I want to put forward a more ambitious claim, namely that Aquinas himself recognized implicit and explicit self-awareness as distinct phenomena and developed sophisticated accounts of each. The novelty of this interpretation demands special care. So the first task is to settle the factual question of whether he recognizes these two distinct phenomena, after which we can examine how he accounts for them.

Consider the following "alpha" and "beta" sets of texts. The "alpha" texts assert one or more of the following: (1) The human mind understands itself in *the numerically same act* in which it grasps an extramental; (2) Self-awareness accompanies *all* intellectual acts; (3) It is *impossible* to be ignorant of one's own agency in intentional acts.

Alpha texts
In the same operation (*eadem operatione*), I understand the intelligible and I understand that I understand. (*Sent* I.1.2.1, ad 1; see also *Sent* I.10.1.5, ad 2; *DV* 10.8, ad 9)

The soul always understands itself insofar as everything that is understood is only understood as illumined by the light of the agent intellect and received into the possible intellect. Just as in every color corporeal light is seen, so too in every intelligible, the light of the agent intellect is seen, not as object (*in ratione obiecti*), but as means of cognition (*in ratione medii cognoscendi*). (*Sent* I.3.4.5)

It is not necessary that he who cognizes something intelligible see the divine essence, but rather [it is necessary that] he perceive the intelligible light [viz., the agent intellect] which flows originally from God, insofar as by [that light] something is actually intelligible. (*DV* 18.1, ad 10; see also 10.8, ad 10 s.c.)

Whoever (*quicumque*) understands or is illuminated cognizes himself to understand or be illuminated, because he cognizes the thing to be manifest to himself. (*ST* Ia.III.1, ad 3; see also *Sent* 1.3.4.5; *ST* Ia.93.7, ad 4)

Clearly, one cannot be ignorant of who is performing [this moral act], because then one would be ignorant of oneself, which is impossible. (*InEthic* III.3)

In the "beta" texts, we find precisely the opposite claims: (4) The act of self-understanding is *numerically distinct from* and *posterior to* the extra-mentally directed act; (5) Self-awareness is the act of "considering" or "reflecting upon" oneself (and therefore happens only occasionally).

Beta texts

It is not necessary that whatever the intellect has by understanding, it understand by understanding; for it does not always reflect upon itself. (*DV* 1.5, ad 5)

But that which we cognize as the form of the cognizer need not be known (*notum*), for neither does the eye see the light that belongs to the eye's composition, nor the species by which it sees; and thus it is not necessary that whoever understands something, understand either his intellect by which he understands, or the intellectual light. (*Quodl* 10.4.1, ad 2)

There is one act by which the intellect understands a stone, and another act by which it understands itself understanding a stone, and so forth. (*ST* Ia.87.3, ad 2; see also *Sent* 1.17.5, ad 4; *DV* 10.9; *SCG* 4.11; *ST* Ia.16.4, ad 2; Ia.28.4, ad 2; Ia.87.3, *corp*. and ad 1; *InMet* XII.11, and *Quodl* 8.9.1)

[Texts in which the verbs explicitly connote attention]: Someone actually considers (*considerat*) that he has a soul … In order for the soul to perceive that it exists and attend (*attendat*) to the acts performed within itself. (*DV* 10.8) The soul does not always think about (*cogitat*) itself. (*ST* Ia.93.7, ad 4)

Now of course (4) is incompatible with (1), and (5) is incompatible with (2) and (3). So if we assume that both sets of texts are describing *the same phenomenon*, this divergence must result either from doctrinal development or from straightforward self-contradiction. Neither is plausible, however, since the texts in both lists are distributed across a twenty-year spread, and some of the same texts (*DV* and *ST*) appear in both lists. The more plausible alternative, then, is that each list addresses a different phenomenon: Alpha-list texts depict implicit self-awareness, while beta-list texts depict explicit self-awareness.

Aquinas spells out this distinction between implicit and explicit self-awareness in *ST* Ia.93.7, ad 4, which asserts (5) and (2), respectively, with reference to what are clearly two different kinds of actual self-awareness:

> Someone might respond to this [i.e., the argument that the Trinity is not always expressed in the soul's acts] by that which Augustine says in *De Trin.* XIV [= 14.6.6], that "the mind always remembers, always understands and loves itself" – which some take to mean that there is always actual understanding and love of itself in the soul. But Augustine excludes this meaning by adding that the soul "does not always think about (*cogitat*) itself as something discrete from those things that are not itself." And thus it is clear that the soul always understands and loves itself, not actually, but habitually. Although it can also be said that, by perceiving its act, [the soul] understands itself whenever it understands something.[26]

Here implicit self-awareness, habitual self-awareness, and explicit consideration of oneself are clearly distinct types of self-knowledge. Aquinas first rejects perpetual actual self-understanding because the "soul does not always think about itself" (claim 5, referring to explicit self-awareness). Instead, he interprets the Augustinian maxim "the mind always understands itself" as positing a perpetual habitual self-awareness. But he then proposes another acceptable interpretation, softening the "always" to "whenever we cognize anything": "It can also be said that, by perceiving its acts, [the soul] understands itself whenever it understands something" (claim 2, referring to implicit self-awareness).[27] Interestingly, his description of implicit self-awareness here presumes that cognizing one's act is cognizing oneself, as shown in Chapter 4, and that the intellect is aware of all its acts, as will be shown below.

Once we recognize this implicit/explicit distinction in Aquinas, it begins to stand out in various contexts. As early as *Sent* I.3.4.5 (in the "alpha" list), following Albert and the Aristotelian commentary tradition, he had cast

---

[26] See *ST* Ia.93.7, ad 4 [Leon. 5.409–10]: "[A]liquis respondere posset per hoc quod Augustinus dicit XIV de Trin., quod *mens semper sui meminit, semper se intelligit et amat.* Quod quidam sic intelligunt, quasi animae adsit actualis intelligentia et amor sui ipsius. Sed hunc intellectum excludit per hoc quod subdit, quod *non semper se cogitat discretam ab his quae non sunt quod ipsa.* Et sic patet quod anima semper intelligit et amat se, non actualiter, sed habitualiter. Quamvis etiam dici possit quod, percipiendo actum suum, seipsam intelligit quandocumque aliquid intelligit." Less clearly, *DV* 8.14, ad 6 also treats habitual self-awareness as different from actual implicit self-awareness; Aquinas interprets a similar Augustinian text as referring only to memory and then describes angels actually understanding themselves implicitly in cognizing other things (his ensuing discussion of implicit self-awareness is addressed on pp. 149–50 below).

[27] Compare to the two types of self-knowledge (supraconscious self-knowing and implicit self-awareness) in the solutions of Albert's *Sent* I.3.G.29 and Aquinas's *Sent* I.3.4.5, which address the same Augustinian concept of perpetual self-knowing, in the same context of the *imago Trinitatis*, as discussed in Chapter 2, pp. 42–6.

implicit self-awareness as the "philosophers' solution" to the problem of whether the mind always understands itself.[28] The language that he uses there (cognizing something as the means of cognizing, *in ratione medii cognoscendi*, not as object, *in ratione obiecti*) is the closest that we get to technical language for this distinction.[29] The same implicit/explicit distinction, with similar language, appears in connection with volition: Love directed toward the beloved also encompasses itself "as the principle of loving" (*ut ratio diligendis*), while some acts of love explicitly turn back upon themselves as objects (*ut obiectum*).[30]

So how does Aquinas account for implicit and explicit self-awareness? Let us begin with implicit self-awareness.

The light account

Aquinas provides two complementary explanations of implicit self-awareness. The first is grounded in a comparison to seeing physical light in the color it illuminates (the "light account," borrowed from the illuminationist tradition), and the second unfolds the implications of the identity of intellect and intelligible in the act of cognition (the "identity account," borrowed from the Aristotelian commentary tradition). They are rooted, respectively, in two complementary aspects of the intellect's role in cognition: Something is actually intelligible only insofar as it is (1) illuminated by the light of the agent intellect and (2) received by the possible intellect as its form.

The light account originates in a problem afflicting thirteenth-century illuminationist theories of cognition. Augustine had argued that our minds are illuminated by the light of divine truth, which enables the human mind to grasp unchangeable intelligibilities amidst the world of changeable objects. While Augustine's medieval followers differed about the details of this divine illumination, the theory commonly triggered a problem: If every thought involves an encounter with the divine light, how can the mind remain ignorant of God?[31]

---

[28] For his sources, see pp. 27–9 and 36; for *Sent* 1.3.4.5, see pp. 42–6.

[29] Compare also *DV* 10.8, ad 10 s.c.

[30] *Sent* I.17.1.5, ad 4 [Mand. 1.407]: "Quia vel dilectio fertur in actum dilectionis proprium, sicut in rationem dilectionis tantum; et sic constat quod eodem actu numero diligitur diligens et actus ejus; et sic idem actus diligitur per actum qui est ipse. Vel diligitur ut objectum dilectionis, et sic est alius actus dilectionis numero qui diligitur et quo diligitur; sicut patet planius in actu intellectus"; *ST* IIa–IIae.25.2; and the texts in note 18 above on desire as including the *ratio* of desirability.

[31] On Augustine's famous doctrine of divine illumination, see O'Daly, *Augustine's Philosophy of Mind*, 205–7. On medieval illuminationism, see Steven P. Marrone's excellent study, *The Light of Thy Countenance: Science and Knowledge of God in the Thirteenth Century*, 2 vols. (Leiden: Brill, 2001).

To accommodate the psychological possibility of atheism, medieval illuminationists had to explain how something can be intellectually "seen" without being noticed. Robert Grosseteste and Bonaventure propose the following solution (similar to Aquinas's principle thesis): Whenever I cognize anything, I also cognize the means by which that thing is visible, though not as a distinct perceptual object. Grosseteste draws a comparison to vision: Because sunlight makes color visible, I see it in seeing the objects it illuminates, but I do not see it in its own right as something perceptually distinct from colored bodies. In the same way, we grasp the divine light in apprehending the essences it illuminates – but only implicitly, because it is not perceptually distinguishable from them. The pure of heart, however, can behold this light in its own right.[32]

Now according to Aquinas's theory of cognition by abstraction, the "intellectual light" that illuminates intelligibles is not the divine light but the individual soul's own agent intellect.[33] Consequently, the explanation of perceiving *the divine light* in understanding essences neatly converts into an explanation of perceiving *the activity of one's own agent intellect*.[34] The result is his "light account" of implicit self-awareness, which can be summarized as follows: Just as I see physical light when I see the colors that it illuminates, so too I implicitly apprehend the light of my own agent intellect when I apprehend the essences that it illuminates.[35]

[32] Robert Grosseteste, *De veritate*, ed. Ludwig Baur in *Die philosophischen Werke des Robert Grosseteste, Bischofs von Lincoln* (Münster: Aschendorff, 1912), 137–8: "Veritas igitur etiam creata ostendit id, quod est, sed non in suo lumine, sed in luce veritatis summae, sicut color ostendit corpus, sed non nisi in luce superfusa … Hoc modo puto, quod etiam immundi multi summam veritatem vident et multi eorum nec percipiunt se videre eam aliquo modo, quemadmodum si aliquis primo videret corpora colorata in lumine solis, nec unquam deflecteret visum ad solem, nec didicisset ab aliquo, solem aut aliud lumen esse, quod illustraret corpora visa, nesciret omnino se videre corpora in lumine solis, ignoraret que se videre aliquid nisi corpus coloratum tantum. Mundicordes vero et perfecte purgati ipsam lucem veritatis in se conspiciunt, quod immundi facere nequeunt"; Bonaventure, *De scientia Christi* 4, ad 2 [Quar. 5.24]: "Dicendum, quod ad hoc, quod cognoscat per aeternas rationes, non oportet, quod in illis figatur, nisi in quantum cognoscit *sapientialiter*. Aliter enim attingit illas rationes *sapiens*, et aliter *sciens*: sciens attingit illas ut *moventes*, sapiens vero ut *quietantes*"; and corp.: "Sed quia in statu viae non est adhuc plene deiformis, ideo non attingit eas [rationes] clare et plene et distincte … attingit eas *ex parte* et *in aenigmate*."
[33] Encouraged by Aristotle's description of the agent intellect as "light" (*De anima* 430a10–16), a number of medieval thinkers sought to incorporate some sort of agent intellect into Augustinian illumination theory. Their strategies differed significantly, however, depending on how they conceived of the agent intellect's role in relation to the divine light. Aquinas goes so far as to insist that the divine light itself plays no role other than as the uncreated source in which the human agent intellect participates (*ST* 1a.84.5).
[34] He therefore dismisses the atheism problem: We do not cognize God first and in every act, because the light that we perceive illuminating our cognition is the light of our own minds, not the divine light itself (see *SBDT* 1.3, ad 1; *DV* 18.1, ad 10; and *ST* 1a.84.5).
[35] For this account see *SBDT* 1.3, ad 1; *Sent* 1.3.4.5; *DV* 8.14, ad 6; *DV* 10.8, ad 10 s.c.; *DV* 18.1, ad 10; *ST* 1a.87.1. On "seeing" the light of the agent intellect, see Bernard Lonergan, Verbum: *Word and Idea in Aquinas*, ed. David B. Burrell (Notre Dame, Ind.: University of Notre Dame Press, 1967), 79–81.

The key to this account of implicit self-awareness is the analogy to see-ing physical light. Aquinas inherits from the Islamic philosophical trad-ition two competing theories of how physical light facilitates vision: Avicenna's dissenting theory and the Averroist-Aristotelian theory.[36] He contrasts these two theories in *ST* Ia.79.3, ad 2. According to the Averroist-Aristotelian theory, which Aquinas endorses in his mature writings as the correct theory, physical light is "necessary for seeing" (*requiritur ad viden-dum*): namely, it makes the air actually transparent, allowing the visible species of color to pass through to the eye.[37] But *as a model for how intellec-tual light works*, he prefers Avicenna's theory of physical light as "necessary on account of the thing seen" (*requiritur ad visum*): namely, physical light actualizes the potentially visible color.[38]

According to this Avicennian theory, as Aquinas interprets it, color by itself has a mere potency for visibility, which must be actualized by light, the sheer form of visibility. By "formally completing" color, light grants it actual visibility, or Visibility.[39] (To avoid ambiguity, I will capitalize to designate actualized visibility, as distinct from merely potential visibility.) Light and the colored body are related as form and matter, together con-stituting the actually visible object, the Visible,[40] which affects the organ of sight precisely under the formal aspect of its Visibility. Thus in seeing a red car, I am seeing, not bare color, but *illuminated (Visible) color* – which is to say that I am seeing light as the form of the Visible.[41] For Aquinas,

---

[36] Avicenna, *Liber de anima* III; and Averroes, *Commentarium magnum in Aristotelis De anima* II.66–74. The background is Aristotle's *De anima* II.7 and *De sensu et sensato* 2–3. Aquinas initially employs the Avicennian view, but later, apparently around the time of *QDDA*, he adopted the Averroist-Aristotelian view; see note 76 below for details.

[37] *QDDA* 4, ad 4, *InDA* II.14; *InDS* 4–6; *ST* Ia.79.3, ad 2; Ia–IIae.57.2, ad 2.

[38] He discusses this theory of physical light in most detail in *Sent* II.13.1.3, and models his account of intellectual light thereon throughout his career, even after adopting the Averroist-Aristotelian view of physical light – a practice that he justifies in *QDDA* 4, ad 4 and again in *InDA* III.4 [Leon. 45/1.219.43–53; for a detailed discussion of how the agent intellect actualizes intelligibility, see 221:147–62].

[39] *Sent* III.24.1.1 [Moos 3.762]: "[I]n objecto alicujus potentiae contingit tria considerare: scilicet id quod est formale in objecto, et id quod est materiale, et id quod est accidentale; sicut patet in objecto visus: quia formale in ipso est lumen, quod facit colorem visibilem actu; materiale vero ipse color, qui est potentia visibilis; accidentale vero, sicut quantitas et alia hujusmodi, quae colorem comitantur"; III.34.2.3.1, ad 3 [Moos 3.1154]: "[I]llud quod est ratio alterius sicut formaliter com-plens objectum, non pertinet ad alium habitum vel potentiam, sicut lux et color"; I.45.1.2, ad 1; *DV* 10.8, ad 10 s.c. (note 49 below); *DV* 23.7; *SCG* 1.76.

[40] *DM* 2.2, ad 11 [Leon. 23.35:319–24]: "[O]mne quod comparatur ad alterum ut ratio eius, se habet ad ipsum sicut forma ad materiam; unde ex duobus fit unum sicut ex materia et forma. Et propter hoc color et lumen sunt unum visibile, quia color est visibilis propter lumen" (and see ad 5); *Sent* I.48.1.2, ad 1; and II.38.1.4, ad 1.

[41] *ST* Ia.87.1 [Leon. 5.355]: "[N]on enim visus percipit coloratum in potentia, sed solum coloratum in actu"; Ia–IIae.1.1, ad 2; Ia–IIae.10.2 [Leon. 6.82]: "Visibile enim movet visum sub ratione coloris actu visibilis."

the case of light is parallel to cases in which something affects a receiver in virtue of an accidental form. For instance, in receiving the accidental form (i.e., actuality) of heat, the iron becomes actually hot, a Hot Thing formally "completed" as such by heat, in virtue of which it burns the unlucky user. Again, the form of musicality is accidental to Paganini *qua* human, but constitutive of Paganini *qua* Musician, who delights audiences under that aspect. In the same way, physical light formally constitutes this red car *qua* Visible; consequently, to see the Visible is see something composed of light and color, something that affects my sense organ precisely under the formality of light.

Aquinas transfers this model to the intellectual realm to explain how intelligible light is apprehended implicitly whenever the intellect understands something. Because essences instantiated in material individuals (e.g., man instantiated as Socrates) are only potentially intelligible, they must be actualized as Intelligibles by the agent intellect's dematerializing "light." (For this chapter, I will continue my convention of capitalizing to designate actualization; thus 'Intelligible' replaces Aquinas's term 'intelligible-in-act' and 'Intellect' replaces 'intellect-in-act.') This intellectual "light" is the sheer form of Intelligibility just as physical light is the pure form of Visibility.[42] An essence is Intelligible, then, *qua* illuminated by the agent intellect, just as a colored object is Visible *qua* illuminated by sunlight and candlelight. And thus just as we see physical light implicitly in seeing the Visible, we apprehend the light of the agent intellect implicitly in understanding the Intelligible.

Aquinas articulates this account of implicit self-awareness as early as *Sent* I.3.4.5:

> According to the philosophers, the soul always understands itself in the sense that everything that is understood is understood only as illuminated by the light of the agent intellect and received into the possible intellect. Whence just as in every color the corporeal light is seen, so too in every intelligible the light of the agent intellect is seen (*in omni intelligibili videtur lumen intellectus agentis*) – although not as object (*in ratione objecti*), but as the means of cognizing (*in ratione medii cognoscendi*).[43]

---

[42] See *DV* 18.8, ad 3 (note 49 below) for the agent intellect's bestowing the "form of intelligibility." For Aquinas, the role of the agent intellect is to make things Intelligible (see e.g., *QDDA* 4–5; *InDA* III.4; *ST* Ia.79.3–5).

[43] *Sent* I.3.4.5; compare *DV* 18.1, ad 10 [Leon. 22/2.534:364–78]: "[I]mmediatum principium et proximum quo ea quae sunt in potentia, fiunt intelligibilia actu, est intellectus agens; sed primum principium quo omnia intelligibilia fiunt, est ipsa lux increata. Et ita ipsa essentia divina comparatur ad intelligibilia, sicut substantia solis ad visibilia corporalia. Non est autem necesse ut ille qui videt colorem aliquem, videat substantiam solis; sed ut videat lumen solis, prout eo color illustratur.

Underlying this account is the principle thesis: i.e., the reason that the illuminating light is implicitly cognized in explicit cognition of the Intelligible is that, as the formal principle of the object's Intelligibility (the "means of cognizing"), this light formally constitutes the Intelligible as such.

In *DV* 8.14, ad 6, Aquinas examines in depth the form–matter composition of the Intelligible, in the course of examining whether angels can understand many things at the same time. Wielding the Augustinian maxim that the mind "always remembers itself, knows itself, and loves itself," the objector in arg. 6 had concluded that since angels are always cognizing themselves and must sometimes cognize other things, they must (at least sometimes) cognize two things at once. Aquinas's response reaffirms his abovementioned rule that simultaneous cognition of "many" is only possible if they are cognized as "one" in some way. This rule holds equally true, he insists, for simultaneous cognition of the mind and other things. Since the mind is the principle of cognition, it is related to the object as form to matter, composing a single Intelligible that is understood "as one":

> When the mind of an angel understands itself and something else, it understands many only as one; which is clear from the following: If there are two things such that one is the principle for understanding the other (*ratio intelligendi aliud*), one of them is as though formal (*quasi formale*), and the other is as though material (*quasi materiale*); and thus those two are one intelligible [= the Intelligible], because it is constituted as one thing by form and matter. So when the intellect understands one thing by another, it understands one intelligible alone, as is clear in sight: for light is that by which color is seen, whence it is related to color as formal (*ut formale*); and thus color and light are only one single visible [= the Visible], and are seen at once. But for the angel, its own essence is the principle of its cognizing anything that it cognizes ... Thus when it understands itself and others, it does not understand many things at the same time except as one.[44]

Aquinas makes clear that in cognizing an Intelligible, the angelic intellect *actually understands itself* as the formal principle of the Intelligible. And although he focuses on the angelic intellect, his reasoning (grounded in

Similiter etiam non est necessarium ut ille qui cognoscit aliquod intelligibile, videat essentiam divinam; sed quod percipiat lumen intelligibile, quod a Deo originaliter manat, prout ipso est aliquid intelligibile actu" (note that Aquinas agrees that we cognize the intellectual light in grasping illuminated Intelligibles; his disagreement is with identifying it as the divine light, since it is the light of our own agent intellect that is necessarily cognized in every Intelligible); and *ST* Ia.87.1 [Leon. 5.355–6]: "[C]onsequens est ut sic seipsum intelligat intellectus noster, secundum quod fit actu per species a sensibilibus abstractas per lumen intellectus agentis, quod est actus ipsorum intelligibilium, et eis mediantibus intellectus possibilis." For a parallel account in Albert, see pp. 36 and 44; and Kennedy, "The Nature of the Human Intellect," 126–9.

[44] *DV* 8.14, ad 6.

the principle thesis) applies equally to the light of the human agent intellect, which is the formal principle of Intelligibility in human cognition.[45] In ad 16, in fact, he proposes as a general principle applicable to any intellect: "The one understanding and what is actually understood are in some way one (*unum quodammodo*); therefore when someone understands himself understanding something, he understands many as one."[46]

But if we ask *how intellectual light formally constitutes the Intelligible*, the analogy to physical light breaks down. Colored objects acquire Visibility in the physical world when sunlight shines on them. But in illuminating 'dogness,' the agent intellect cannot shine outside the mind on Spot; and dogness-instantiated-as-Spot cannot itself take on the form of Intelligibility, because materiality is incompatible with Intelligibility.[47] In fact, when speaking more precisely, Aquinas describes the light of the agent intellect as the *form of the species* that intramentally manifests the extramental essence: "The light of the agent intellect in us ... informs received species as light informs colors."[48] The "form" of the intelligible species 'triangle' is sheer Intelligibility (the light of the agent intellect), and its "matter" is the content from my phantasm of the triangle sketched on the chalkboard.[49] Thus speaking more precisely, intellectual light "informs" the Intelligible

---

[45] The difference is that the angelic intellect is by its very nature always acting as a principle of cognition, whereas the human agent intellect, while it is by nature an act, has nothing to *act on* without the presence of a species, and is thus not always *illuminating*. But this difference affects the frequency with which angelic vs. human intellects cognize themselves as principles of cognition, not the way in which this cognition occurs.

[46] *DV* 8.14, ad 16 (note 99 below).

[47] See texts in note 66 below.

[48] *Sent* II.3.3.4, ad 4. See also *Sent* II.20.2.2, ad 2 [Mand. 2.514]: "[P]erfectio intellectus possibilis est per receptionem objecti sui, quod est species intelligibilis in actu. Sicut autem in objecto visus est aliquid quasi materiale, quod accipitur ex parte rei coloratae, sed complementum formale visibilis inquantum hujusmodi est ex parte lucis, quae facit visibile in potentia esse visibile in actu: ita etiam objectum intellectus quasi materialiter administratur vel offertur a virtute imaginativa; sed in esse formali intelligibili completur ex lumine intellectus agentis, et secundum hanc formam habet quod sit perfectio in actu intellectus possibilis: et ita non sequitur deordinatio in partibus animae, si intellectus possibilis perficiatur per species a phantasmatibus acceptas, inquantum illustrantur lumine intellectus agentis, quae est potentia altior quam intellectus possibilis"; *Sent* III.14.un.1.3; and texts in note 49.

[49] *DV* 18.8, ad 3 [Leon. 22/2.559:118–28]: "[S]pecies intelligibilis id quod in ea formale est, per quod est intelligibilis actu, habet ab intellectu agente qui est potentia superior intellectu possibili quamvis id quod in ea materiale est a phantasmatibus abstrahatur. Et ideo magis proprie intellectus possibilis a superiori accipit quam ab inferiori, cum id quod ab inferiori est non possit accipi ab intellectu possibili nisi secundum quod accipit formam intelligibilitatis ab intellectu agente"; *DV* 10.8, ad 10 s.c. [Leon. 22/2.325:535–47]: "[L]ux corporalis non videtur per se ipsam, nisi quatenus fit ratio visibilitatis visibilium, et forma quaedam dans esse eis visibile actu. Ipsa vero lux quae est in sole, non videtur a nobis nisi per eius similitudinem in visu nostro existentem. Sicut enim species lapidis non est in oculo, sed similitudo eius, ita non potest esse quod forma lucis quae est in sole, ipsa eadem sit in oculo. Et similiter etiam lumen intellectus agentis per seipsum a nobis intelligitur,

by proxy: The intellectual light is the form of the intelligible species, which in turn is the formal principle whereby the extramental essence is cognized. Thus the extramental essence is Intelligible, informed by intellectual light, only *qua* cognized via an illuminated species. Thus when Aquinas asserts that the light of the agent intellect is cognized "insofar as it is the principle (*ratio*) of the intelligible species, making them intelligible in act," he is articulating more precisely how intellectual light serves as the form of the Intelligible.[50]

But how can the "informing" of the species with intellectual light guarantee that I see my own intellectual light in every act, unless the *species itself* is that which is cognized in place of the extramental object – which Aquinas strenuously denies?[51] Perhaps an analogy can help. In looking through a spyglass at a ship, I see the ship *only as conveyed to my gaze by the lenses*. Although I am certainly not looking at the lenses, it is untrue that they have no part in what I see. Indeed, they serve as the means of my seeing the ship precisely *because* their curvature, transparency, and spacing bring an otherwise too-distant ship into my range of vision. Other properties of the lenses also affect how the ship is manifested to me: A clean, well-made spyglass conveys the ship to my gaze crisply, whereas a poorly crafted or dirty spyglass distorts my view. All the while, of course, the object of vision is the ship, regardless of which spyglass I use.

Similarly, for Aquinas, triangularity is Intelligible *only as conveyed to the intellect immaterially via the illuminated species*, even though properly speaking, what I am understanding (*id quod cognoscitur*) is triangularity in extramental triangles.[52] The illuminated species is able to serve as the means of cognition because it has a property – the actualizing "form" of

---

inquantum est ratio specierum intelligibilium, faciens eas intelligibiles actu" (note that the visual analogue here to cognizing the intellectual light is not seeing the sun, but seeing *ambient light emanated from the sun*; the sun is seen not in some special way but via its own species, just as a stone is seen via its own species); and *ST* Ia.84.6.

[50] For the agent intellect as illuminating the Intelligible, see the texts in note 43 above.

[51] See pp. 140–1 above.

[52] *ST* Ia.14.5, ad 2 [Leon. 4.173]: "[I]ntellectum est perfectio intelligentis, non quidem secundum suam substantiam, sed secundum suam speciem, secundum quam est in intellectu, ut forma et perfectio eius"; and see texts in note 69 below. For Aquinas, "being understood," "being abstracted," and "universality" are modes of being that exist only intramentally, and thus are attributed to the object only incidentally insofar as its species is present in the intellect – but *what is understood* by that presence is the extramental object: "[C]um dicitur intellectum in actu, duo importantur, scilicet res quae intelligitur, et hoc quod est ipsum intelligi. Et similiter cum dicitur universale abstractum, duo intelliguntur, scilicet ipsa natura rei, et abstractio seu universalitas. Ipsa igitur natura cui accidit vel intelligi vel abstrahi, vel intentio universalitatis, non est nisi in singularibus; sed hoc ipsum quod est intelligi vel abstrahi, vel intentio universalitatis, est in intellectu" (*ST* Ia.85.2, ad 2 [Leon. 6.334]).

Intelligibility, roughly analogous to the curvature, transparency, and spacing of the lenses – that makes triangularity manifest to the mind (i.e., Intelligible). The reason that the light of the agent intellect is seen in every Intelligible is simply that it is the formal constituent of the Intelligible, communicated to the Intelligible insofar as the latter is understood via the illuminated species. As he explains in *ST* Ia.87.1: "Our intellect understands itself insofar as it is rendered in act by species abstracted from sensibles by the light of the agent intellect, *which is the act of the intelligibles themselves*." (Recall too that for Aquinas, *per* the principle thesis, the species is grasped implicitly as means of cognition when used to consider the corresponding object.)

Before turning to Aquinas's other account of implicit self-awareness, we should add a final clarification to the light account. If the Intelligible I apprehend is composed of the agent intellect's light and abstracted triangularity, why is my attention drawn to triangles explicitly while I grasp myself only implicitly? The answer, I think, is that as the Intelligible's formal and material principles, the intellectual light and the cognized essence are asymmetrically related to the Intelligible. This asymmetry is reflected in the differing modes in which they are manifest to the intellect. For instance – returning to the analogue of vision – suppose a strand of hair is caught in a beam of green light. It is true that the green light and the hair make each other Visible; the hair cannot be seen unless it is illuminated, and the light cannot be seen unless it is illuminating something. But their relationship is asymmetrical: the strand of hair is the *material subject* to which Visibility accrues – it is *that which* the light formally illuminates. Thus *what* I see is an illuminated hair, not a hairy light. Similarly, *what* I cognize is Intelligible triangularity (*in ratione objecti*), because the content abstracted from the phantasm of a triangle is the material principle that "determines" or "specifies" what this particular thought is about.[53] In providing Intelligibility to that "matter," the agent intellect is therefore cognized implicitly as that which makes triangularity manifest (*in ratione medii cognoscendi*).[54]

On its own, the analogy to "seeing light" seems to push Aquinas in a Humean direction: Just as I cannot look at light in its own right, but only see it incidentally in color, so too, presumably, I cannot "look at" my own

---

[53] *QDDA* 5, ad 6 [Leon. 24/1.44:317–25]: "Et primo quidem requiruntur fantasmata a sensibilibus accepta, per que represententur intellectui rerum determinatarum similitudines, nam intellectus agens non est talis actus in quo omnium rerum species determinate accipi possunt ad cognoscendum, sicut nec lumen determinare potest uisum ad species determinatas colorum, nisi assint colores determinantes uisum"; *ST* Ia.14.5, ad 3; *CT* I.88.
[54] For the language of *in ratione objecti*, etc., see pp. 144–5 above.

intellectual light in its own right – in which case it seems that I could never intellectually "see" *myself* as an explicit object of experience.[55] In order for Aquinas to be able to account for both implicit *and* explicit self-awareness, as we will see, the light account needs to be completed by the identity account.

The identity account

Aquinas's "identity account" of implicit self-awareness takes its cue from the *De anima* commentary tradition. As we saw in Chapter 1, some of Aristotle's Greek and Arabic commentators drew an explanation of self-knowledge from *De anima* III.4's cryptic comments about the mind's identity with its objects: In receiving intelligibles as its own form, the intellect itself acquires intelligibility. On some readings, (e.g., in Alexander, Themistius) the intellect's identity with intelligibles means that cognizing the intelligible *is* cognizing oneself – a strain of thought that Aquinas picks up via Albert and Averroes.

In miniature, Aquinas's version of this account runs as follows: The intellect-in-act (Intellect) is one with the intelligible-object-in-act (Intelligible) at the moment of cognition (one, in the sense of formal sameness, not numerical identity).[56] But if the thinking Intellect *is* the Intelligible, cognition of any Intelligible must be in some sense a self-cognition. Every thought, in fact, includes an implicit grasp of oneself thinking.

The inner workings of this identity account of implicit self-awareness hinge on the twofold function of the species-in-act (i.e., the species "illuminated" by Intelligibility and used in an intellectual operation) in

---

[55] See for instance *DV* 14.8, ad 4 [Leon. 22/3.460:188–95]: "[L]umen quodammodo est obiectum visus et quodammodo non. In quantum enim lux non videtur nostris visibus nisi per hoc quod ad aliquod corpus terminatum, per reflexionem, vel alio modo coniungitur, dicitur non esse per se visus obiectum, sed magis color, qui semper est in corpore terminato"; although *DM* 2.2, ad 5 reverses this position.

[56] For the maxim, "The intellect-in-act and the intelligible-in-act are one" – or the equivalent formulation, "The intellect-in-act and the actually understood thing are one" – see for instance *DV* 8.14, ad 16; *SCG* 2.59 and 74–6; *ST* 1a.14.2; 1a.55.1, ad 2; 1a.85.2, ad 1, etc. For a helpful review of various interpretations on Aquinas on this point, see Brower and Brower-Toland, "Aquinas on Mental Representation," 212–15. There is considerable controversy over how the form that the intellect adopts relates to a specific object's individualized substantial form. See for example ibid.; John Haldane, "Aquinas and the Active Intellect," *Philosophy* 67 (1992): 208; Owens, "Aquinas on Cognition as Existence"; Stump, *Aquinas*, 270–5; Black, "Mental Existence"; Peter King, "Rethinking Representation in the Middle Ages: A Vade-Mecum to Mediaeval Theories of Mental Representation," in *Representation and Objects of Thought in Medieval Philosophy*, ed. H. Lagerlund (Aldershot: Ashgate, 2007); Pasnau, *Theories of Cognition*, 31–60; Panaccio, "Aquinas on Intellectual Representation"; and O'Callaghan, *Thomist Realism and the Linguistic Turn*, 237–54, etc. We need not resolve this issue here, since my contention that the intellect apprehends itself in apprehending its object does not depend on interpreting the species–object relationship in one specific way.

unifying the Intellect and Intelligible. By itself, the intellect is a sheer potency for intelligible form, analogous to prime matter; but as informed by the species-in-act, it is constituted as the intellect-in-the-act-of-thinking, or Intellect.[57] (This is the "perfective" role of the species discussed in Chapter 4.) Similarly, toadness as instantiated in this material toad is merely potentially intelligible; but when toad-species-in-act actualizes the Intellect, toadness acquires intentional existence as the intelligible-in-the-act-of-being-understood, or Intelligible.[58] (This is the "presencing" role of the species discussed in Chapter 4.) The intellect and the intelligible are thus co-actualized by a single species in a single operation, together constituting a single reality: the Intellect/Intelligible.[59] *ST* Ia.85.2, ad 1, aptly summarizes: "The understood is in the one understanding by its likeness. And in this way it is said that the thing actually understood (*intellectum in actu*) is the intellect-in-act (*intellectus in actu*), insofar as the likeness of the thing understood is the form of the intellect."[60]

As a result, the species-in-act is the principle of Intelligibility not only for the object, but also for the Intellect itself. For instance, when I am thinking about toads, toad-species-in-act is not just the formal likeness of Intelligible toadness: It is also equally the form of the Intellect, the only form that the Intellect has at that moment.[61] In the instant of thinking, "being an Intellect" just is "to be thinking about Intelligible toadness," in the same way that "being an actual musician" just is "to be playing this

---

[57] See for instance *Sent* IV.49.2.1 [Parma 7.1199]: "In intellectu autem oportet accipere ipsum intellectum in potentia quasi materiam, et speciem intelligibilem quasi formam; et intellectus in actu intelligens erit quasi compositum ex utroque"; and the texts in notes 60–2 below.

[58] See texts in note 69 below. Aquinas goes so far as to say that the Intelligible is instantiated in the Intellect, for instance in *QDSC* 9, ad 6 [Leon. 24/2.97:415–40]: "Intellectum autem, sive res intellecta, se habet [ad intellectum possibilem] ut constitutum vel formatum per operationem intellectus … Res igitur intellecta a duobus intellectibus est quodammodo una et eadem, et quodammodo multae: quia ex parte rei quae cognoscitur est una et eadem, ex parte vero ipsius cognitionis est alia et alia"; and *Quodl* 8.2.2. (Recall, however, that for Aquinas, this does not mean that *what I cognize* is merely intramental; see the discussions on pp. 140–1 and 151–2 above.) On intentional existence or *esse intentionale / intelligibile*, see *ST* Ia.56.2, ad 3; and Ia–IIae.50.4, ad 2; with somewhat different analyses in Bazán, "*Intellectum Speculativum*"; Black, "Mental Existence"; and Brower and Brower-Toland, "Aquinas on Mental Representation."

[59] On the intellect and intelligible as two principles of cognition that are in potency to each other and jointly actualized, see *DV* 8.6 [Leon. 22/2.238:123–6]: "Sed intelligens et intellectum, prout ex eis est effectum unum quid, quod est intellectus in actu, sunt unum principium huius actus quod est intelligere"; ad 3 and ad 11; *DV* 8.7, ad 6 s.c.; *QDSC* 10, ad 4; *InDA* III.4 [Leon. 45.221:136–62].

[60] *ST* Ia.85.2, ad 1 [Leon. 5.334]: "[I]ntellectum est in intelligente per suam similitudinem. Et per hunc modum dicitur quod intellectum in actu est intellectus in actu, inquantum similitudo rei intellectae est forma intellectus."

[61] *SCG* 2.76 [Leon. 13.480]: "Sicut materia prima perficitur per formas naturales, quae sunt extra animam, ita intellectus possibilis perficitur per formas intellectas in actu"; *QDDA* 18, ad 5 [Leon. 24/1.159:411–14]: "Comparatur igitur forma intellectiua ad intellectum possibilem sicut forma naturalis ad materiam primam, prout est intellecta in actu, non prout est habitualiter"; *InDA* III.1 [Leon.

Rachmaninoff concerto." In that moment, toad-species is *just as much the intellectual manifestation of the Intellect-thinking-about-toad-nature as it is the intellectual manifestation of toadness*:

> Just as the sense-in-act is sensible on account of the likeness of the sensible object that is the form of the sense-in-act, so too the intellect-in-act is actually understood on account of the likeness of the understood thing, which is the form of the intellect-in-act. And therefore the human intellect, which is rendered into act by the species of the understood thing, is understood by that same species, as though by its own form.[62]

Thus the reception of toad-species-in-act not only lights up Intelligible toadness to the Intellect, but it also lights up the Intellect to itself.

> It belongs to the nature of the intellect that it understand itself insofar as it assumes or conceives in itself something intelligible; for the intellect itself becomes intelligible by attaining something intelligible. And therefore, because the intellect becomes intelligible in conceiving something intelligible, it follows that the intellect and the intelligible are the same.[63]

45/1.206:323–5]: "[S]pecies igitur intelligibilis non est forma intellectus possibilis nisi secundum quod est intelligibilis actu"; *ST* Ia.14.2, ad 2 [Leon. 4.169]: "[P]er hoc quod [intellectus] est in potentia, differt ab intelligibili, et assimilatur ei per speciem intelligibilem, quae est similitudo rei intellectae; et perficitur per ipsam, sicut potentia per actum"; Ia.55.1, ad 2; and the texts in note 62.

[62] *ST* Ia.87.1, ad 3 [Leon. 5.356]: "Sicut enim sensu in actu est sensibile, propter similitudinem sensibilis, qua est forma sensus in actu; ita intellectus in actu est intellectum in actu, propter similitudinem rei intellectae, quae est forma intellectus in actu. Et ideo intellectus humanus, qui fit in actu per speciem rei intellectae, per eandem speciem intelligitur, sicut per formam suam"; *DV* 10.8, ad 16 (note 90 below); *SCG* 2.98 [Leon. 13.580]: "[F]orma est principium cognitionis rei quae per eam fit actu; similiter autem potentia cognoscitiva fit actu cognoscens per speciem aliquam. Intellectus igitur possibilis noster non cognoscit seipsum nisi per speciem intelligibilem, qua fit actu in esse intelligibili: et propter hoc dicit Aristoteles, in III *de Anima*, quod *est cognoscibilis sicut et alia*, scilicet per species a phantasmatibus acceptas, sicut per formas proprias"; *QDDA* 16, ad 8 [Leon. 24/1.147:405–10]: "Vnde, cum intellectus possibilis sit potentia tantum in esse intelligibili, non potest intelligi nisi per formam suam per quam fit actu, que est species a fantasmatibus accepta; sicut et quelibet alia res intelligitur per formam suam"; *InDA* III.3 [Leon. 45/1.216:80–2]: "Species igitur rei intellecte in actu est species ipsius intellectus, et sic per eam se ipsum intelligere potest"; *SLDC* 15 [Saffrey, 92]: "[I]n substantia sua [anima intellectiva] non habet nisi vim intellectualitatis; unde intelligit substantiam suam, non per essentiam suam, sed … secundum Aristotelem autem, in III° *De anima*, per intelligibiles species quae efficiuntur quodammodo formae in quantum per eas fit actu." As Lonergan puts it, "one and the same act is at once the act of the object and the act of the subject; inasmuch as there is … an *intelligibile actu*, an object is known; inasmuch as there is … an *intellectus actu*, the subject in act and his act are constituted and known" ("Christ as Subject," 254; see also Owens, "Aquinas on Cognition as Existence," 79).

[63] See *InMet* XII.8, no. 2539 [Marietti, 594]: "Et dicit, quod hoc est de ratione intellectus, quod intelligat seipsum inquantum transumit vel concipit in se aliquid intelligibile; fit enim intellectus intelligibilis per hoc quod attingit aliquod intelligibile. Et ideo, cum ipse intellectus fiat intelligibilis concipiendo aliquod intelligibile, sequetur quod idem sit intellectus et intelligibile"; see also *ST* Ia.93.7, ad 4, in note 26 above.

Here the path forward is blocked by an important objection: This is all very well, but how do we know that for Aquinas intellectual actualization is sufficient for actual self-awareness? One might argue, for instance, that formulations such as "the intellect cannot be understood except by the species that is its form" or "the intellect becomes intelligible by receiving the species" only specify a necessary condition for the Intellect to think about itself explicitly in a subsequent act. I contend, however, that for Aquinas intellectual actualization is both necessary and sufficient for the Intellect's actual self-awareness: i.e., just by being in act, the Intellect must at least implicitly understand itself as subject of that act. Simply in virtue of thinking about toadness, I understand myself at that moment as the one-thinking-about-toadness. I will call this view the "sufficiency view," and the opposing view the "necessity view."

Now according to Aquinas, *to be actually intelligible (Intelligible) to some Intellect is to be actually understood by that Intellect.*[64] Consequently, if we can show that he thinks the Intellect meets the conditions for *Intelligibility* in the moment of operation, then we can conclude that the Intellect must be *actually understood by itself* in that moment, even if it is not yet thinking about itself. Before unpacking this positive argument for the sufficiency view, however, let us first see why the necessity view falls short.

The necessity view must show that by cognizing extramental objects, the Intellect acquires an intelligibility that it naturally lacks and that is necessary for actual self-awareness – but which is not Intelligibility, viz., actual intelligibility or being-actually-understood. (In other words, the Intellect's reception of toad-species would make toadness *Intelligible*, but would only make the Intellect *intelligible*.) But what could such an intelligibility be? For Aquinas, intelligibility is only either potential or actual. There is no third option, such as habitual intelligibility: As we saw in Chapter 5, habit is a perfection of the cognizer, not of the object, and in any case he holds that habituation for self-awareness belongs to the soul's essence *before* any intellectual acts occur.

A defender of the necessity view, however, might object that perhaps 'intelligibility' merely refers to *some degree of accessibility* – in other words, actualization makes the Intellect more accessible to itself without yet granting it Intelligibility. Now it seems to me improbable that Aquinas would

---

[64] *DV* 8.6 (note 74 below); and *ST* 1a.87.4 [Leon. 5.363]: "Quod autem intelligibiliter est in aliquo intelligente, consequens est ut ab eo intelligatur." See also *QDDA* 15, ad 17, where Aquinas appears to be in agreement with the objector's claim that "the Intellect (*intellectus in actu*) understands all those things whose intelligible species are in act in it."

have applied the term 'intelligibility' to the Intellect in the loose sense of 'accessibility,' in the same texts in which he uses the same term in a precise technical sense to designate an entity's condition of actually-being-understood or sheer potency thereto. Nevertheless, let us consider two senses in which an object could be more or less accessible to an intellect. In one sense, the closer an object is to a cognizer, the more accessible it is to that cognizer. For instance, if a Monet painting is donated by a private collector to my local art museum, that painting is now more accessible to me than it was in the collector's private home. But this increase in accessibility is nothing more than my increased likelihood for encountering the painting. In any case it is hard to see how there could be any parallels to this sort of "relocation increasing the likelihood of encounter" in the case of self-awareness, since the object to be cognized *already is* the intellect itself.

In another sense, accessibility to a cognizer increases in proportion to the object's readiness to be illuminated by the agent intellect. In this sense, "toad-nature in this pond-dwelling individual" and "my phantasm of this toad" are both equally potentially intelligible, but the latter is more accessible to the intellect. The reason is that the human psychological–neurological system has refined the phantasm to the point at which it is properly disposed for illumination by the agent intellect as the next step in the cognitive process. But Aquinas cannot mean that actualization brings the Intellect to the *penultimate stage of preparation* before actual self-awareness. The reason that there *is* a penultimate stage before Intelligibility in the case of the toad is that the phantasm is still a material form. But the intellect never was material to begin with.

The necessity view thus fails to explain what kind of intelligibility the Intellect gains by acting, if not Intelligibility. We can now argue positively for the sufficiency view, by showing that the Intellect meets all the conditions for Intelligibility and thus actually understands itself in the moment of actualization.

According to Aquinas, something is Intelligible if and only if (a) it is immaterial, (b) it is present to an Intellect, typically by its species, and (c) it – or its species – is "in act" in that Intellect.[65] (These are individually necessary and jointly sufficient conditions for Intelligibility.) Immateriality ensures the compatibility of intellect and intelligible, since material objects

---

[65] *Sent* I.35.1.1, ad 3 encapsulates all three conditions: "[A]d hoc quod sit intelligens in actu, oportet quod intelligibile in potentia fiat intelligibile in actu per hoc quod species ejus denudatur ab omnibus appenditiis materiae per virtutem intellectus agentis [= immateriality]; et oportet quod haec species, quae est intellecta in actu [= actuality], perficiat intellectum in potentia [= presence]: ex quorum conjunctione efficitur unum perfectum, quod est intellectus in actu" [Mand. 1.820].

cannot inform the immaterial mind. It is so important to Aquinas's conception of Intelligibility that he sometimes simply states that something is Intelligible "insofar as" it has immaterial being.[66] Presence is necessary because the intellect is undetermined with respect to its objects, so that it must be specified, either by the object itself or by an abstracted species, to cognize *this* rather than *that* essence.[67] Finally, the condition of "being in act" is related to Aquinas's defense of intellectual memory against Avicenna (for whom the intellect must actually cognize everything that is present within it, in which case the first two criteria alone would be sufficient for Intelligibility). Habitual presence, for Aquinas, is not enough for an object's Intelligibility; the present object must have *actual* intentional or intelligible being (*esse intelligibile, esse intentionale*), guaranteeing the Intellect's *actual* (and not merely habitual) conformity to the Intelligible.[68] For objects made present by species, this criterion is fulfilled when the species is "in act" as the actualizing form of the Intellect, i.e., when it is being used in an operation, like a circuit that is actually conducting electricity. In fact, on the assumption that the intellectual presence of the species already satisfies the first two conditions, Aquinas sometimes condenses these three conditions into one: A thing is Intelligible if and only if its species-in-act informs the Intellect.[69]

Now the human intellect is in the unique situation of *automatically meeting the first two conditions by its nature*, since it is immaterial and present to itself (in other words, it naturally has habitual self-awareness).[70] Consequently, to attain Intelligibility, it is sufficient that it meet the third condition. This occurs when it is constituted as an Intellect by engaging

[66] For instance: *Sent* III.14.un.1.2, ad 2 [Moos 3.437]: "[N]on omnes res, prout sunt in sui natura, sunt actu intelligibiles; sed solum res immateriales. Unde et res materiales intelligibiles efficiuntur per hoc quod abstrahuntur a materia particulari et a conditionibus ejus, ut sic quodammodo intellectui qui immaterialis est, assimilentur"; *SCG* I.44 and 2.62; *QDDA* 2, ad 5; *QDDA* 4–5; *ST* Ia.55.1, ad 2; Ia.58.2; Ia.79.3, corp. and ad 3; Ia.87.1, ad 3; *InDA* III.4, etc. In fact, Aquinas frequently describes the role of the agent intellect as that of causing Intelligibility by dematerializing (e.g., in *ST* Ia.79.3).

[67] For instance: *SCG* I.53; *ST* Ia.14.2, 58.2, and 79.3; see also the discussion of the species's "presencing" role in Chapter 4, pp. 110–11; as well as the discussions of presence and self-presence throughout Chapter 5.

[68] For instance: *DV* 8.6, ad 9 [22/2.239:239–42]: "Causa cognitionis est illud quod facit cognoscibile esse actu in cognoscente"; *Sent* II.20.2.2, ad 2 (note 48 above); *SCG* 2.76 and *QDDA* 18, ad 5 (both in note 61 above).

[69] For instance: *ST* Ia.14.2 [Leon. 4.168]: "Ex hoc enim aliquid in actu sentimus vel intelligimus, quod intellectus noster vel sensus informatur in actu per speciem sensibilis vel intelligibilis"; *Sent* I.35.1.1, ad 3; II.20.2.2, ad 2; *DV* 8.6 and 10.6, ad 7; *SCG* I.53; *QDDA* 15, arg. 17 (note 64 above); *ST* Ia.58.2; Ia79.6, ad 3; Ia.84.7, ad 1.

[70] Habitual self-awareness thus plays an important role in the psychological mechanism underlying implicit self-awareness – see p. 172.

in the act of thinking about something: At that moment it is "in act" in an Intellect, i.e., itself. "Our possible intellect does not cognize itself except by an intelligible species *by which it is rendered into act in intelligible being.*"[71] The same idea can be rephrased in terms of the species's contribution: i.e., the Intellect satisfies this third condition when its species is "in act" in itself. As we saw earlier, toad-species-in-act is just as much the form or species of the Intellect thinking about toadness, as it is the species of Intelligible toadness. So when the Intellect is thinking about toadness, *a species of the informed Intellect itself is in act in the Intellect,* making the Intellect Intelligible to itself.[72] As Aquinas explains in *InMet* XII.8, "It belongs to the nature of the intellect that it understand itself insofar as it assumes or conceives in itself something intelligible; for the intellect itself becomes intelligible by attaining something intelligible (*per hoc quod attingit aliquod intelligibile*)."

To put it another way, since the human intellect is already immaterial and self-present, the sole obstacle to its Intelligibility is its natural lack of actuality – an obstacle that is removed when it cognizes anything at all. This is precisely the line of reasoning adopted in *ST* Ia.87.1. Appealing to the principle that "each thing is cognizable insofar as it is in act and not insofar as it is in potency," Aquinas explains that the reason the divine and angelic intellects perpetually cognize themselves by their essence is that they are always in act. Conversely, lack of actuality is the reason that the human intellect cognizes itself only intermittently:

> The human intellect is related to the genus of intelligible things as a mere being-in-potency, just as prime matter is related to the genus of sensibles: whence it is called "possible." Thus from itself the human intellect has the power to understand but not to be understood, except insofar as it is made actual ... So our intellect understands itself insofar as it is rendered into act by a species abstracted from sensible things by the light of the agent intellect, which is the act of those intelligibles and [the act] of the possible intellect with [those intelligibles] mediating.[73]

---

[71] *SCG* 2.98.   [72] See note 62 above.

[73] *ST* Ia.87.1. Note that if Aquinas had thought intellectual actualization were sufficient for Divine and angelic self-knowledge but not for human self-knowledge, the appropriate next step should have been to show that actualization and self-cognition are related *differently* in God and angels than in the human intellect, i.e., perhaps by identifying some feature that causes the human intellect to fail to cognize itself even though it is actualized. Instead, he proceeds as though divine, angelic, and human self-knowledge are all governed by the same relationship between actualization and self-cognition, arguing that their different modes of self-knowledge are traceable to the fact that the Divine and angelic intellects are always in act, but the human intellect is not.

The human intellect, then, becomes a member of the "genus of Intelligibles" when it is informed by any species-in-act.[74] In other words, its act of cognizing removes the obstacle of non-actuality, so that it acquires Intelligibility.

The argument for the sufficiency view is now complete. Whatever is Intelligible is actually understood; and the Intellect becomes Intelligible by understanding anything at all. So the Intellect's actualization in cognizing an object is sufficient for actual (though only implicit) self-awareness. Aquinas's identity account of implicit self-awareness can be summarized, then, as follows. Because the Intellect and the Intelligible are one in the act of cognition, the Intelligibility of one is the Intelligibility of the other. Consequently they are co-manifested in the act of cognition: I grasp toadness as the object of *my* cognition, and I grasp myself as the one cognizing *toadness*. In this way, I cognize, not bare toadness, but toadness-as-manifest-to-me. "Whoever understands or is enlightened cognizes that he is understanding and being enlightened, because he cognizes the thing as manifest to himself."[75] This experience of objects as manifest to *me* is the work of implicit self-awareness.

Two complementary accounts

The light and identity accounts of implicit self-awareness lead to the same conclusion: No intellectual operation is completely devoid of self-awareness. But why does Aquinas use two different accounts to make the same point? Historical development cannot be the answer. While the light account appears to predominate in earlier texts, both accounts appear together in *Sent* 1.3.4.5.[76] The identity account appears as late as *SLDC* 15;

---

[74] The same reasoning appears in *DV* 8.6 [Leon. 22/2.238:137–77]: "Sicut ergo corpus lucidum lucet quando est lux actu in ipso, ita intellectus intelligit omne illud quod est actu intelligibile in ipso ... Sicut igitur materia prima non potest agere aliquam actionem nisi perficiatur per formam – et tunc actio illa est quaedam emanatio ipsius formae magis quam materiae – res autem existentes actu possunt agere actiones secundum quod sunt actu, ita intellectus possibilis noster nihil potest intelligere antequam perficiatur forma intelligibili in actu: tunc enim intelligit rem cuius est illa forma; nec potest se intelligere nisi per formam intelligibilem actu in se existentem. Intellectus vero Angeli, quia habet essentiam suam quae est ut actus in genere intelligibilium sibi praesentem, potest intelligere id quod est intelligibile apud ipsum, id est essentiam suam, non per aliquam similitudinem, sed per se ipsam." (Notice that *potest se intelligere* in this case apparently does not refer to a mere aptitude for Intelligibility, since it is said here not only about human self-awareness but also about angelic self-awareness, and as we already know from *DV* 8.14, ad 6, Aquinas holds that angels are always Intelligible.)

[75] *ST* 1a.111.1, ad 3 [Leon. 5.516]: "[Q]uicumque intelligit vel illuminatur, cognoscit se intelligere vel illuminari; quia cognoscit rem sibi esse manifestam."

[76] B. Carlos Bazán argues that in writing his commentary on *De anima*, Aquinas became aware of the Averroist-Aristotelian view of physical light, and thereafter abandoned his earlier view of physical light as the actual visibility of color (see his "Introduction," 3.3, in Leon. 24/1.20*– 21*; some of the

and the light account appears at least as late as *ST* Ia.87.1, with its essential components (e.g., the use of the Avicennian theory of physical light's role in vision, to model the agent intellect's role in understanding) preserved unchanged right up into such late works as *DM* and *DUI*.

The privileging of one or the other account in different contexts seems to be related to their diverse historical origins in Augustinian illumina-tionism and the Aristotelian commentary tradition. It is Aquinas's practice to tailor his vocabulary, problem-structure, and imagery, to the tradition with which he is dealing in a given text. In addressing themes that are dear to illuminationists, such as Augustine's theory of mind in *DV* 10, he naturally emphasizes the light account. And in expositing themes from the Aristotelian psychological tradition (abstraction, species, identity), he gravitates toward the identity account.

Nevertheless, the light and identity accounts are not different formula-tions of the same account, but two partial accounts that complete each other. They depict, respectively, the contributions of the agent and possible intellects in implicit self-awareness. Now for Aquinas, the agent intellect's illumination of the Intelligible and the possible intellect's reception thereof are not two separate events, but two activities concurring in *one intellectual operation*.[77] (In a sense, the activities of agent and possible intellect are two sides of the same coin; in formally constituting the Intelligible as such, the agent intellect generates something that can only exist as received into the possible intellect.) The light and identity accounts explain, respectively, how these complementary activities contribute to the Intellect's implicit self-manifestation in its operations: "Our intellect understands itself inso-far as it is rendered into act by a species abstracted from sensible things by the light of the agent intellect, which is the act of those intelligibles and [the act] of the possible intellect with [those species] mediating."[78] In other words, the species-in-act is the vehicle by which the agent intellect

---

relevant texts are cited in notes 36–38 above). The shift seems to have taken place earlier than Bazán suggests, since there is a detailed discussion of the Aristotelian-Averroist view already in *QDDA* 4, ad 4. Nevertheless, Aquinas's turn toward the Averroist-Aristotelian view of physical light could be responsible for a lessening emphasis on the light account, although it does not prevent him from referencing the latter in connection with self-knowledge as late as *ST* Ia.87.1.

[77] *QDDA* 4, ad 8 [Leon. 24/1.36:255–37:262]: "[D]uorum intellectuum, scilicet possibilis et agentis, sunt duae actiones. Nam actus intellectus possibilis est recipere intelligibilia; actio autem intellectus agentis est abstrahere intelligibilia. Nec tamen sequitur quod sit duplex intelligere in homine, quia ad unum intelligere oportet quod utraque harum actionum concurrat." See also *Sent* II.24.2.2, ad 1; and *DV* 10.8, ad 11 s.c.

[78] *ST* Ia.87.1 (note 43 above). See also *Sent* I.3.4.5 [Mand. 1.122]: "Alio tamen modo, secundum phi-losophos, intelligitur quod anima semper se intelligit, eo quod omne quod intelligitur, non intel-ligitur nisi illustratum lumine intellectus agentis, et receptum in intellectu possibili."

imparts actualization and hence Intelligibility to the possible intellect.[79]
The agent and possible intellects, then, are responsible for different aspects
of the Intellect's acquisition of Intelligibility in the act of cognition. In
implicit self-awareness, we "see" the agent intellect as the formal principle bestowing Intelligibility on the essence via the species (*per* the light
account), but we also "see" the possible intellect acquiring Intelligibility
via the informing species (*per* the identity account). One could arguably
associate each account with a distinct aspect of the experience of oneself
in implicit self-awareness: The light account captures the aspect of agency,
i.e., the experience of thinking as an activity that I perform; whereas the
identity account captures the aspect of subjectivity, i.e., the experience of
thinking as a passive reception of insight.[80]

The complementarity of these two accounts is important for another
reason, too. As I noted earlier, the light account cannot adequately explain
the possibility of explicitly attending to myself. If physical or intellectual
light is only grasped as the formal principle of the Visible or Intelligible,
how can it be "seen" in its own right? The juxtaposing of the light and identity accounts, however, shows that by the same stroke, intellectual light
also thereby serves as the formal principle of the Intellect's Intelligibility,
via the illuminated species. Consequently, my thinking intellect is not
manifested in its acts merely as the formal aspect of the Intelligible, but
rather as a complete actualized intellectual being, composed of the possible
intellect as its "matter" and the illuminated species-in-act as its "form."
For this reason, the Intellect-thinking-about-toads is something complete
that can become the explicit object of attention. And for the same reason,
the distinctness of the agent intellect, possible intellect, and the species are
not manifested to me in implicit or explicit self-awareness, but can only
be established later by reason. Just as the matter and form of a toad cannot be perceived separately, but are manifested to sensation as one toad, so
too the metaphysical parts of the Intellect-thinking-about-toads are manifested in the act of thinking as one actualized composite entity, which
shows up implicitly or explicitly in my experience as "myself." To explicit
self-awareness we now turn.

[79] *ST* 1a.84.4, ad 3 [Leon. 5.321]: "[I]ntellectus noster possibilis reducitur de potentia ad actum per
aliquod ens actu, idest per intellectum agentem"; *QDDA* 18, ad 11 [Leon. 24/1.159:451–8]: "Et si
quis recte consideret, intellectus agens, secundum ea quae Philosophus de ipso tradit, non est acti-
uum respectu intellectus possibilis directe, set magis respectu fantasmatum que facit intelligibilia
actu, per que intellectus possibilis reducitur in actum quando aspectus eius inclinatur ad inferiora
ex unione corporis." Compare to Albert, *InDA* III.2.17.
[80] On these two aspects of the act of understanding, see *DV* 8.6 [Leon. 22/2.238:104–32].

Deciphering explicit self-awareness

By this point, we already have a rough picture of Aquinas's account of explicit self-awareness. The list of "beta" texts showed that he thinks the intellect can explicitly "consider" or "think about" or "attend to" itself-as-thinking-about-something. And his explanation of implicit self-awareness provides the requisite psychological structure. Since the Intellect and Intelligible are necessarily understood in relation to each other, not only must explicit attention to the extramental Intelligible include implicit self-awareness, but any explicit attention to myself must also include an implicit grasp of the extramental Intelligible.[81] This is why, as I hinted in earlier chapters, Aquinas's theory of dependent self-awareness means that we apprehend ourselves not only as cognizing, but more specifically as cognizing this or that.[82]

But can Aquinas consistently hold an account of *explicit self-awareness* that is *also dependent on cognition of extramental objects*? To see why such an account could be problematic, consider a student sitting in class, working a tedious math problem. First her mind drifts to a toad she sees outside the window; then she turns her attention again to the problem; and suddenly, she realizes that she is having an intellectual breakthrough: "I understand the Pythagorean theorem!" These three distinct intellectual operations terminate in different objects. The first operation (O_1) terminates in the essence of toads; the second (O_2) in triangularity; the third (O_3) in the thinking Intellect itself. As Aquinas would see it, operations O_1 and O_2 use *different* species (toad-species and triangle-species, respectively), whereas O_2 and O_3 use the *same* species (triangle-species); further, O_3 is an act in which *the Intellect in the act of understanding the Pythagorean theorem* becomes the object of its own attention.

This portrait of explicit self-awareness poses three problems. First, if O_2 and O_3 use the same species, it seems impossible to differentiate them psychologically as two distinct operations terminating in two distinct entities.[83] Second, the content of triangle-species seems insufficient to

---

[81] See *DV* 10.8, where he refers to acts of "considering oneself" as dependent on the intellect's actualization in cognizing an extramental object.

[82] See Chapter 3, pp. 119–20, and Chapter 4, pp. 113–14.

[83] This sort of concern, more broadly, underlies the assumption that in Aquinas, for every change of attention (viz., change in intentionality) there has to be a change of species. In the context of self-awareness, this assumption produces the two opposite views of Lambert and Gardeil. For the latter, explicit self-awareness is "non-intentional" because it involves no second species representing the soul ("Perception expérimentale," 234–6). For Lambert, all self-awareness, implicit and explicit,

support my thinking about myself (O_3). Third, any attempt to parse the structure of O_3 seems to threaten either Aquinas's claim that the intellect cannot be engaged in two acts at once, or the truly experiential character of explicit self-awareness. How is it possible to think about triangles and think about oneself thinking about triangles, all at the same time? Aquinas does not directly address these problems, but we can reconstruct solutions using his principles.

The first problem can be solved by getting a clearer perspective on the relationship between species and the direction of attention. Now for Aquinas, the intentionality of a given intellectual act is governed by two principles, both of which sometimes go under the name 'intention' (*intentio*): the species being used (which specifies a range of intelligible content[84]), and the direction of intellectual attention (which determines the intellect to some aspect of the intelligibility made present via the species).[85] A single species-intention can support many attention-intentions, like a multipurpose instrument. For instance, one might think of man as rational, teachable, living, mammalian, in distinct acts, all using a single species of man.[86] Aquinas explains, "From one species that is in the intellect, the intellect embarks upon diverse thoughts (*in diversas cogitationes prodit*), just as by the species 'man,' one can think (*cogitare*) various things

---

must be intentional, and thus must involve a second species representing the soul (*Self Knowledge in Thomas Aquinas*, 151).

[84] On the term 'content' as used here, see Chapter 3, pp. 69–70.

[85] According to Schütz, '*intentio*' for Aquinas more usually signifies attention or direction of gaze; less often but still quite frequently, it signifies a species or phantasm; see Ludwig Schütz, *Thomas-Lexikon: Sammlung, Übersetzung und Erkläung der in sämtlichen Werken des h. Thomas von Aquin vorkommenden Kunstausdrücke und wissenschaftlichen Aussprüche*, 2nd edn (Paderborn: Schöningh, 1895; reprint, New York: Musurgia Publishers, 1948), s.v. *intentio*, pp. 419–22; and A. Hayen, *L'intentionnel dans la philosophie de Saint Thomas* (Paris: Desclée de Brouwer, 1942), 212. This is more than an etymological triviality, however; for Aquinas, intention-attention is the operation of using, i.e., actualizing, the intention-species. The medieval term *intentio* is in general puzzling. Noting that "most authors before Thomas used 'intention' and 'species' interchangeably," Spruit interprets intention in Aquinas as "what is grasped in a concept: it is *terminus* rather than *principium* of intellectual knowledge" (Species intelligibilis 1:161), citing a text in which Aquinas uses *intentio* to refer to the concept. Intention in the sense of attention, however, *picks out* the terminus, as George P. Klubertanz suggests: For medieval thinkers, cognition is intentional in the sense that it has "a direction (finality, or tendency) toward an object" (*The Discursive Power: Sources and Doctrine of the* 'Vis Cogitativa' *according to St. Thomas Aquinas* [Carthagena, Oh.: Messenger Press, 1952], 232). For intentionality in medieval thinkers, see Dominik Perler, *Théories de l'intentionnalité au moyen âge* (Paris: Vrin, 2003), 17–41; and *Theorien der Intentionalität im Mittelalter*, 2nd edn (Frankfurt am Main: Klostermann, 2004).

[86] Aquinas explains that a single object, rendered intelligible by a single species, can be considered under distinct aspects. See *ST* 1a.76.3, ad 4 [Leon. 5.221]: "[N]on oportet secundum diversas rationes vel intentiones logicas, quae consequuntur modum intelligendi, diversitatem in rebus naturalibus accipere, quia ratio unum et idem secundum diversos modos apprehendere potest."

concerning man." This is true to such an extent that he adds, "Even if an angel sees our intellect being shaped (*figurari*) according to the species 'man,' it does not follow that the angel cognizes determinately the thought of the heart."[87] In short, the range of thoughts that I can have is delimited by the species I use, but *what I think about within that specified range* (the object-under-a-specific-aspect) is determined by how I choose to direct my attention.

I contend that the same principles govern the shift from O_2 (thinking about triangularity, with an attendant implicit self-awareness) to O_3 (explicitly thinking about oneself). Not only triangularity but also the *Intellect itself* becomes Intelligible when the Intellect is using triangle-species in its operation. Consequently, informed by that single triangle-species, I can choose to consider either triangularity-as-known-by-me, or myself-as-knowing-triangularity, merely by willing to direct my attention differently. Implicit and explicit self-awareness differ in their "intention" in the sense of attention, not in the sense of using different species.

But here our second problem rears its head: It is one thing to use triangle-species to think about various aspects of triangles and even to sustain an implicit self-awareness in thoughts about triangles. But it seems quite another thing to use triangle-species to *think about something non-triangular*, namely, my own Intellect. We have already seen, however, that for Aquinas triangle-species is not simply a bearer of pure extramental content. It is formally constituted by the light of the agent intellect (as emphasized in the light account). As used in an operation, it is the form and likeness of the Intellect just as much as of the Intelligible (as emphasized in the identity account). In fact, Aquinas holds that just as natural form is individuated by matter, so too the species is individuated by my intellect.[88] It belongs to the character of this species, then, to *be mine*; it exists only as "instantiated" in the "matter" of my own intellect.

---

[87] *DV* 8.13, ad 2; and *DM* 16.8.

[88] For just a few examples, see *SCG* 2.75; *QDSC* 9, ad 6 [Leon. 24/2.97:415–40]: "Intellectum autem siue res intellecta se habet ut constitutum uel formatum per operationem intellectus ... Res igitur intellecta a duobus intellectibus est quodammodo una et eadem et quodammodo multe, quia ex parte rei que cognoscitur est una et eadem, ex parte uero ipsius cognitionis est alia et alia"; ad 13 [100:563–7]: "[A]ccidit enim homini aut intentioni speciei quod intelligatur a me; unde non oportet quod de intellectu hominis aut intentionis speciei sit quod intelligatur a me uel ab illo"; 10, ad 14 [114:586–90]: "[U]niuersale quod facit intellectus agens est unum in omnibus a quibus ipsum abstrahitur; unde intellectus agens non diuersificatur secundum eorum diuersitatem. Diuersificatur autem secundum diuersitatem intellectuum, quia et universale non ex ea parte habet unitatem, qua est a me et a te intellectum: intelligi enim a me et a te accidit universali"; *DUI* 5 [Leon. 43.312:226–42]. Kenny has critiqued Aquinas for holding that what makes my thoughts *mine* is their connection to my body (see *Aquinas on Mind*, 122–5); but as we can see from these texts, in fact for Aquinas, my thoughts are mine because they are instantiated in my intellect.

Consequently, it is not the case that in explicit self-awareness, triangle-species is being used to think about something wholly non-triangular, because for Aquinas, the Intellect thinking about triangles *is in some sense triangular*. Triangle-species-in-act is not only the likeness of extramental triangles, enabling the student to think about triangles (O_2), but also the "likeness" of the Intellect engaged in a particular act, enabling her to notice herself thinking about triangles (O_3).[89] "The soul is cognized ... by a species of its object, which is also *its own form insofar as it is actually understanding*."[90] Neither, conversely, is it the case that triangle-species purely manifests the triangular. In its individuation in *my intellect* as *my species*, triangle-species refers to my intellect as its "matter" or subject. Triangle-species-in-act, then, should be able to support not only a thought about triangles in O_2, but also the student's thought about herself understanding the Pythagorean theorem in O_3.

With the two species-related problems out of the way, however, we are still left with the third and most difficult problem: namely, whether Aquinas can legitimately defend the act-dependence of explicit self-awareness without violating his own stricture against multiple simultaneous intellectual operations. It seems that any explanation of noticing oneself *in the very act* of thinking about triangles will have to posit two concurrent operations: O_2 directed at triangles and – dependent thereon – O_3 directed at myself. In discussing a kind of self-knowledge that he names "reflexion in the strict sense" (*réflexion au sens strict*),[91] Putallaz takes the bull by the horns, arguing that for Aquinas, O_2 and O_3 are concurrent operations. In this special case, he explains, there is no violation of the stricture against concurrent intellectual operations, because both operations are about the same object, under different intentional aspects: O_3 "grasps the extramental thing in its real quiddity," and O_2 "attains the same thing, but in its intelligibility as conceived by the intellect."[92] But for Aquinas, differences in intentional aspect require differently directed acts of attention. Indeed, the impossibility of "pointing" intellectual attention in two directions simultaneously is precisely one of the reasons he cites

---

[89] Though not in the sense of a likeness that makes present something absent, but only in the sense in which a thing's own form is its likeness.

[90] *DV* 10.8, ad 16 [Leon. 22/2.325:504–7]: "[A]nima non cognoscitur per aliam speciem abstractam a se, sed per speciem obiecti sui, quae etiam fit forma eius secundum quod est intelligens actu"; and texts in notes 61 and 62 above.

[91] See Putallaz, *Le sens de la réflexion*, 148–208. This type of self-knowledge is not a sheer implicit self-awareness, but it does not quite qualify as an explicit self-awareness either, for reasons discussed in note 98 below. For discussion of his view, see Chapter 7, pp. 195–8.

[92] See Putallaz, *Le sens de la réflexion*, 154, my translation.

for rejecting simultaneous intellectual operations. Although his theory of cognition thus allows for cognizing two things simultaneously *under the same aspect in one act*, it does not permit cognizing one thing under *two different aspects in two simultaneous acts*.[93]

Pasnau proposes a different solution, arguing that the intellect is not involved in two operations at once, because O_2 and O_3 are not concurrent. The present-tense "I am thinking about ..." is, in his view, misleading; one ought rather to say "I *was* thinking about ..."[94] (Interestingly, Brentano likewise reads Aquinas as holding that one can only reflect on *past* acts – a view that he takes to be fatally flawed because it destroys the possibility of implicit self-awareness.[95]) Like Putallaz, Pasnau takes O_3 to be an act of "attending to external things in a special reflective manner ... not an introspective turning away from external things, but a certain way of looking at external things: it is an outward look that is reflected back within."[96] He describes the move from O_2 to O_3 as a simple "shift of attention" that is comparable to the shift from looking at an object in a mirror, to looking at the mirror itself.[97]

Although in my view Putallaz's and Pasnau's solutions are ultimately unsuccessful, they capture an important insight into how Aquinas construes the shift from explicitly considering extramental objects to explicitly considering oneself. In noticing that "I finally understand triangles," I do not appear to myself as a *new thing*; rather, I am focusing on *another aspect* of what I am actually already understanding. The shift from simply thinking about triangles (O_2) to noticing oneself thinking about triangles (O_3) is less like the shift from thinking about toads (O_1) to thinking about triangles (O_2), and more like the shift from thinking about man-as-rational to thinking about rationality-as-distinctively human.

The underlying flaw in Putallaz's and Pasnau's solutions, however, is their reliance on two assumptions that Aquinas does not share: (1) that for self-awareness to depend on cognition of triangularity, O_3 must be a

---

[93] See p. 138 above. Putallaz's solution seems to me unsatisfactory also because explicit self-awareness would thus be reducible to cognition of the extramental object.

[94] Pasnau, *Thomas Aquinas on Human Nature*, 346–7.

[95] Brentano, *Psychology from an Empirical Standpoint*, 125–6 n. The idea behind his critique is that if O_3 cannot include a reference to an *ongoing* cognition of triangles and can only target a past O_2, then O_2 could not really have included a present, implicit self-awareness either. Interestingly, Pasnau apparently accepts this implication: see note 1 above.

[96] Pasnau, *Thomas Aquinas on Human Nature*, 343. If O_3 is really just another thought about the extramental object, however, it is hard to see how he can go on to say that O_3 is a higher-order thought with O_2 as its content (345). The concern that underlies both formulations seems to be to exclude a Lockean-style introspection of one's thoughts.

[97] Pasnau, *Thomas Aquinas on Human Nature*, 345–6.

higher-order act parasitical on O_2, the act in which the student is thinking about the Pythagorean theorem;[98] and (2) that there can be no truly attentive experience of *myself* – for Putallaz because this parasitical relationship is only possible inasmuch as O_3 and O_2 are thoughts *about the extramental object*, triangularity, and for Pasnau because an experiential explicit self-awareness would involve an introspective "turning away" from extramental reality.

The first assumption misconstrues the nature of "dependence" on cognition of extramental objects in Aquinas. I would argue that, for Aquinas, the student noticing herself thinking about the Pythagorean theorem ("Now I finally understand the Pythagorean theorem!") is engaged in just one single operation (O_3) with a present-tense object, not two operations that must be creatively stacked or nested, nor a backward-looking operation "hooked into" a previous operation. The dependence in question occurs *within that one operation O_3*, insofar as that *the Intellect's Intelligibility* in that operation is borrowed from the species-in-act of Intelligible triangularity, which informs the Intellect in O_2 and again in O_3. Thus the content of O_3, 'myself thinking about triangles,' does not refer to some *distinct past or present act of attending to triangles*. Rather, the element of 'thinking about triangles' is a *present aspect* under which the thinker grasps the one object of attention, 'myself'; just as in O_2 the element of 'being thought by me' was the *present aspect* under which she grasped the object of attention, 'triangularity.' The structure of O_3, then, is exactly like that of any act of thinking about many under a single unifying aspect: "The one understanding and what is actually understood are in some way one; therefore when someone understands herself understanding something, she understands many as one."[99]

Thus in O_3 our student thinks about herself as *presently* actually understanding triangularity, not as having *previously* thought about triangularity. Although O_2 and O_3 are distinct, sequentially occurring operations, Aquinas's account of both implicit and explicit self-awareness assumes

[98] See also Wang, *Aquinas and Sartre*, 128, who speaks of "standing outside" our mental processes to observe them. Putallaz's effort to avoid the latter sort of higher-order monitoring in explaining O_3's relationship to O_2 seems to be what motivates him to insist that O_3 and O_2 have the same object. He assumes that if the intellect turned its attention to *itself* as the explicit terminus (object) of cognition, it would necessarily "objectify" itself, resulting in a cognition that is no longer first-personal, but that is rather an "abstract analysis" (*Le sens de la réflexion*, 111 and 165–6). Aquinas, however, does not share this assumption, as we shall see in Chapter 8.

[99] *DV* 8.14, ad 16 [Leon. 22/2.266:341–3]: "[I]ntelligens et intellectum in actu sunt unum quodam modo; unde quando aliquis intelligit se intelligere aliquid, intelligit multa ut unum," and on understanding many as one, see pp. 138–42 above.

that the *entire intellectual content* of the Intelligible (manifesting both the object and the thinking Intellect) remains in act during both operations. The student explicitly thinks about triangularity as presently manifest to her in O_2; conversely, she thinks about herself as presently understanding triangularity in O_3.[100] For this reason, O_2 does not target a bare extramental, but an extramental-as-apprehended. And likewise, O_3 does not target a bare self, but an agent-in-act.

Consequently, *contra* the second assumption, O_3 is a truly attentive experience of myself in relation to the extramental object. It is not a thought *about the same object* as O_2; and although attention turns inward to myself as thinker, extramental reality remains a part of the content of the act. Certainly for Aquinas the Intellect is actualized in both operations as *the same Intelligible*. But in each operation it directs its attention differently, and thus *what each operation is about* is different. In O_2 I attend to *triangularity as understood by me*, in which case my attention terminates in the extramental object, whereas in O_3 I attend to *myself as understanding triangularity*, in which case my attention terminates intramentally, in myself. (Recall that for Aquinas while the species "specifies" the form of the Intellect as a given Intelligible, it is the direction of attention that determines what a given operation is "about."[101]) For Aquinas, then, O_3 is a genuine experience of myself as agent-in-act, engaged with a given Intelligible extramental object.

Thus explicit self-awareness in Aquinas should not be interpreted as a second-order thought piggybacking on a more basic first-order act. O_2 is completely replaced by a new thought, O_3, which is genuinely a thought *about* myself. But since O_2 already included implicit self-awareness, O_3 is merely raising to explicit attention a different aspect of an already-actually-understood whole, pushing other aspects of the same whole out of the spotlight of intellectual attention even though they remain Intelligible. Perhaps the best analogy to this experience is gazing at a framed portrait for several minutes and then pointing out a detail that one had already seen a hundred times without noticing it. In attending to triangularity, the "scene" that is present to my gaze is *not* just bare triangularity, but the whole of what is Intelligible, i.e., triangularity-as-understood-by-me. And the "detail" that I notice in shifting to explicit self-awareness is my own agency, which I perceive as an aspect of the larger, still-actually-understood Intelligible whole.

---

[100] See *ST* Ia.III.I, ad 3, in note 75 above.
[101] See the discussion at note 85 above.

For Aquinas, then, this prephilosophical act of attention to oneself is merely an attentive intensification of self-awareness as part of a continuous experience of extramental reality. Lonergan is apparently driving at a similar point when he states that "consciousness can be heightened by shifting attention from the content to the act; but consciousness is not constituted by that shift of attention."[102] The shift from implicit to explicit self-awareness is so easy, so spontaneous, that it does not disrupt the even flow of prephilosophical experience. And thus in describing an ongoing experience, we can shift smoothly between the third person ("This sunset is amazing") and the first person ("I'm particularly struck by how dark the clouds are against the mountains").

Aquinas and the bare 'ego'

Implicit and explicit self-awareness, as described in the above account, inhabit the realm of prephilosophical experience. Here, as compared to Descartes on the one hand and Hume on the other, Aquinas turns out to be defending a unique middle position. Unlike Descartes, he insists that the experience of a first-person thinker is indissociable from the experience of extramental objects of thought. There is no encounter with or observation of a bare "I" or even a bare "I think," but only an encounter with myself, the agent-in-act, presently thinking about or understanding *this thing*. And unlike Hume, he insists that the Intellect directly intuits *itself* (explicitly or implicitly) as really Intelligible within its experience of extramental Intelligibles.[103]

Nevertheless, Aquinas could grant somewhat more to Descartes than the previous discussion might suggest. Given his broader views on intellectual abstraction, there seems to be no reason that he would deny the possibility of moving from prephilosophical self-awareness to a philosophical act of considering "myself" in isolation from the experiential context. While I

---

[102] Bernard J. Lonergan, *Insight: A Study of Human Understanding*, rev. edn, (New York: Longmans, 1958), 321.

[103] One might thus recognize certain affinities between Aquinas's position and John J. Drummond's proposal that "the experience to be explained, however, is not the experience of an 'I.' I am not prereflectively aware that *I* am perceiving an object; I am aware of *my perceiving an object*. The case-structure is properly genitive, not nominative"; "The Case(s) of (Self-)Awareness," in *Self-Representational Approaches to Consciousness*, ed. Kriegel and Williford, 199–220 (here at 212) – at least in the sense in which both rule out the experience of an 'I' as a introspected thing isolated from its activity. As I have said before, Aquinas does not think that an explicit awareness of oneself in act, articulated in the nominative 'I,' is necessarily an objectification of the subject.

cannot *experience* myself apart from my intentional acts of thinking about extramental objects, I can presumably isolate a bare notion of 'myself,'[104] by means of the conceptual "separation" (*separatio*) used in discovering metaphysical notions like 'substance' and 'being.' "Separation" is a negative judgment ("*A* is not *B*"), whereby one "explicitly acknowledges and asserts that that by reason of which something is recognized as being need not be identified with that by reason of which it is recognized as enjoying a given kind of being, for instance, material being, or changing being, or living being."[105] For example, although we acquire our prephilosophical notion of 'being' from material existents, we can arrive at a philosophical grasp of 'being *qua* being,' by affirming that being is not necessarily restricted to material being. Thus although Aquinas holds that I only ever encounter myself *in the mode of thinking about something*, he could grant that by separation, I can philosophically consider myself as a bare I, as something that can exist apart from the act of thinking. This separated notion of 'myself' would make it possible to consider the nature of first-personality in experience, or the meaning of the term 'I.'

It is no surprise that when I attempt to consider myself as a 'bare I' in this way, I find 'myself' abstract and remote, just as difficult to grasp as notions like 'being' and 'substance.' This does not mean that my notion of 'myself' is empty, but rather that I am grasping a reality that is inaccessible to imagination. The first-personality of this notion, however, is essential. Within Aquinas's system, an abstract notion of 'the Self' or 'the Ego' would make little sense, because for him there is no such entity distinct from the composite human individual. From this perspective, there are only two paths available for philosophical inquiry into the nature of 'myself': One could consider the nature of the mind or more generally the nature of the human agent to whom 'I' refers; or one could examine the conditions for the character of first-personality that clings to human experience.

***

Looking back over the last four chapters, we can now see how Aquinas handles one of the most contentious elements in the Neoplatonic legacy

---

[104] See for instance Picard's distinction between an "experiential I" inextricable from a particular experience, and the abstract "notion of me" (*la notion du moi*) ("Le problème critique fondamental," 48).

[105] Wippel, *Metaphysical Thought*, 23–62, here 48–9; the key text for Aquinas's doctrine of *separatio* (part of a larger discussion of abstraction) is *SBDT* 5.3.

of self-knowledge in the thirteenth century: the claim that "the mind always remembers, understands, and loves itself" (the second Augustinian maxim from Chapter 1). His strategy is to interpret the 'always' in different ways, as we saw earlier in connection with *ST* Ia.97.3, ad 4.[106] Taking 'always' in the strongest sense – at every instant of one's existence – he affirms that the soul always understands itself in the sense of being habitually prepared or subjectively equipped for acts of self-awareness. This habitual self-knowledge is a genuinely *natural self-knowledge* belonging to the soul's essence. But taking 'always' in the weaker sense of 'in every intentional act,' he allows that the soul always understands itself actually, in the sense that it implicitly apprehends itself whenever it knows or senses anything at all. By distinguishing habitual and implicit actual self-awareness, Aquinas clears a space in the Augustinian texts for a key Aristotelian insight: namely, that the soul is manifested to itself in all its acts, as a necessary result of explaining understanding as an illumination and reception of the Intelligible.

The resulting tightly integrated theory of self-awareness represents a new level of sophistication in medieval theories of self-knowledge. The entire theory unfolds from the claim that the human soul is a hylomorphic form that is habitually self-present and only potentially intellecting. In fact, we can now see that in addition to its other explanatory functions,[107] habitual self-awareness also makes implicit self-awareness possible. Because the mind is already immaterial and habitually present to itself, the only obstacle to the mind's Intelligibility is its essential lack of actuality. Removal of this obstacle (which occurs whenever the mind cognizes something) is sufficient for actual self-awareness – and thus I cognize myself implicitly in all intellectual acts. While my attention is normally drawn outwards to the objects that specify these acts, the "bipolar" nature of the intellectual act means that I can always turn my attention inward to notice myself as the agent engaged in thinking about those objects.

Explicit self-awareness, in turn, serves as the gateway to the philosophical modes of self-knowledge considered in the next chapter. It is in considering myself as the singular agent thinking about this mathematical theorem or enjoying this sunset, that I first generate the interior word or concept 'I.' This experience is the springboard for further inquiry, because one cannot inquire into the nature of a thing before explicitly recognizing

---

[106] See p. 144 above.   [107] See Chapter 5, pp. 127-31.

that there is something there to be investigated. When my mind turns back upon itself, noticing itself engaged in some act, it is already taking the first step on the path toward a science of the soul.[108]

---

[108] See *SCG* 2.75, where Aquinas equates "considering the intellect" with pondering the nature of the intellect: "Suum autem intelligere intelligit dupliciter: uno modo in particulari, intelligit enim se nunc intelligere; alio modo in universali, secundum quod ratiocinatur de ipsius actus natura. Unde et intellectum et speciem intelligibilem intelligit eodem modo dupliciter: et percipiendo se esse et habere speciem intelligibilem, quod est cognoscere in particulari; et considerando suam et speciei intelligibilis naturam, quod est cognoscere in universali. Et secundum hoc de intellectu et intelligibili tractatur in scientiis" [Leon. 13.475].

CHAPTER SEVEN

Discovering the soul's nature
Quidditative self-knowledge

From prephilosophical self-awareness to a definition

From the soul's cognition *that* it exists, we turn now to the soul's cognition of *what* it is. For Aquinas, his predecessors' theories of supraconscious self-knowing – some of which held that the soul innately comprehends not only its existence, but its whole nature – are undermined by widespread ignorance about the nature of the soul. The obstacles in the path to quidditative self-knowledge are, in his view, due to the dependence of self-awareness on cognition of extramental objects. The soul only catches glimpses of itself engaged in various intentional acts, none of which singlehandedly reveals its whole nature, because each represents a mere sliver of its actualized potential. "When the acts of the soul are perceived, the principle of such acts is perceived to inhere ... yet from this the nature of the soul is not known."[1] Even once engaged in various acts, the information that I glean about myself from self-perception is raw and disorganized. When I catch myself thinking, sensing, or falling asleep, nothing in these self-perceptions tells me which of these capacities differentiates the human soul from other kinds of souls. Consequently, the human soul's essence can only be known by the same process that yields knowledge of "other things' essences," i.e., by engaging in discursive argumentation.[2]

Unfortunately, the process of discursive reasoning carries the risk of error. And in fact, Aquinas thinks that reasoning about the human soul usually goes wrong – which is why the proverbial Man on the Street cannot articulate what he means by terms like "soul," "mind," or "intellect," and why even seasoned philosophers vehemently disagree about the nature

---

[1] *DV* 10.9 [Leon. 22/2.328:173–8]: "Sed anima non est principium actuum per essentiam suam sed per suas vires, unde perceptis actibus animae, percipitur inesse principium talium actuum, utpote motus et sensus, non tamen ex hoc natura animae scitur."

[2] The reasoning process is necessary because although the soul has a natural habitual self-awareness, it has no natural habitual *quidditative* self-knowledge; see *DV* 10.8, ad 6, ad 1 s.c., and ad 6 s.c.

of the soul or mind or intellect.³ The problem extends also to the natures of internal accidents, such as our own acts, habits, and motivations. For instance, when I perceive myself engaged in some act, I may be able to identify that act nominally as "thinking," but it is no small undertaking to ascertain whether thinking is a sort of sophisticated generalizing imagination, or an apprehension of a genuinely dematerialized essence. Again, we feel ourselves drawn to certain choices, but considerable reflection is needed to ascertain whether those impulses arose, say, from genuine prudence or a self-excusing cowardice.⁴ For Aquinas, the difficulty of reasoning well is to blame, not only for the difficulty of establishing the nature of the mind and of mental acts, but also for the prevalence of ethical self-deception.

Nevertheless, Aquinas does not want to go so far as to deny the possibility of acquiring quidditative self-knowledge altogether. As we will see, he holds that the soul reasons to its essence "by a species" of the extramental object, and he seems to be acutely aware of the *prima facie* implausibility of arguing that extramental intelligibilities can be the principles for understanding the essence of the mind. So he is especially intent on showing that this cognition-dependence does not prevent the soul from attaining true and definitive knowledge of its own essence,⁵ and even a "science of the soul." (The terms *scire* or *scientia* refer to the epistemological gold standard for medieval thinkers, i.e., knowledge reached as the conclusion of demonstrative argument; depending on the context, they may indicate either dispositional or occurrent knowledge.) In fact, for those few who do achieve it, the "science of the soul" is the most certain science of all, because the experiential data that grounds it is most certain.⁶ We live, so to speak, in the lab of human nature, and if our conclusions about the soul's nature are correct, we should see them confirmed daily.

---

³ As he points out in *SCG* 3.46.

⁴ See the discussions of how we cognize our own habits in *Sent* III.23.1.2; *DV* 10.9–10; and *ST* Ia.87.2, for instance.

⁵ See *SCG* 3.46 [Leon. 14.123], where Aquinas explains that to know what the soul is, is to know the definition that distinguishes it from other things: "Unde et in hoc dicit aliquos errasse, quod animam non distinxerunt ab illis quae sunt ab ipsa diversa. Per hoc autem quod scitur de re quid est, scitur res prout est ab aliis distincta: unde et definitio, quae significat quid est res, distinguit definitum ab omnibus aliis"; and *ST* Ia.87.1. On the definition as signifying the quiddity, essence, or nature; see *InPostAn* II.2; *Quodl* 2.2.2, etc.; and Chapter 3 for discussion.

⁶ *DV* 10.8, ad 8 s.c. [Leon. 22/2.325:521–4]: "[S]ecundum hoc scientia de anima est certissima, quod unusquisque in se ipso experitur se animam habere, et actus animae sibi inesse"; *InDA* I.1 [Leon. 45/1.5:92–5]: "Hec autem sciencia, scilicet de anima … certa est (hoc enim quilibet experitur in se ipso, quod scilicet habeat animam et quod anima uiuificet)." Aquinas repeatedly uses *scire* to refer to knowledge of what the soul is (*quid est*); see note 58 below.

For Aquinas, the cure for ignorance of the soul's quiddity is to be found in the very phenomenon whose partiality hinders easy quidditative self-knowledge in the first place: namely, my individual experiences of myself. The philosophical quest to understand the soul's nature is much like the quest to understand any other nature: It begins with raw experiential data that becomes organized over time by reasoning, until we identify the genus and difference and distinguish the essential properties from the accidents, arriving at a definition that sets this essence apart from every other essence.[7]

In the quest for quidditative self-knowledge, the raw experiential data is provided by prephilosophical self-awareness.[8] Thus one does not discover the essence of the intellectual soul by observing it from the outside, as it were, but rather by reflecting on *one's own intellectual activity as experienced from the inside*.[9] In fact, as noted in Chapter 3, Aquinas's account of self-awareness allows for each person to develop over time a fairly rich understanding of herself as an individual, with nominal and descriptive content taken from the various acts that she has perceived herself performing. So by the time she embarks on a philosophical inquiry into the soul's nature, she already has a store of indisputably certain experiential self-observations to serve as the basis for investigation.

---

[7] For further discussion, see Chapter 3.

[8] *DV* 10.8, ad 8 s.c.; *InDA* I.1; III.3 [Leon. 45/1.216:82–6]: "Philosophus per ipsum intelligere et per id quod intelligitur scrutatus est naturam intellectus possibilis: non enim cognoscimus intellectum nostrum nisi per hoc quod intelligimus nos intelligere." Aquinas applies this idea in developing his own cognition theory, repeatedly calling upon experience of our own acts to support his explanation of how cognition works (for one example see *ST* Ia.79.4). For discussion of self-awareness as the starting-point for the quest for quidditative self-knowledge, see Lambert, *Self Knowledge in Thomas Aquinas*, 225; Romeyer, "Saint Thomas et notre connaissance," 77–9; and Wébert, "*Reflexio*," 324–5. In contrast, Reichmann, among others, holds that for Aquinas "this primitive, connatural knowledge [self-awareness] cannot function as the first principle of inquiry into the nature of the self, etc.," for such a "Cartesian" claim would mean that we "instantaneously possess full and unerring knowledge of the self" ("The 'Cogito' in St. Thomas," 348) – but as we have already seen on pp. 87–9 above, this does not follow. For an interesting discussion of how the appeal to individual self-awareness factors into Aquinas's argument for the unicity of the possible intellect in *ST* Ia, 76.1, see Black, "Consciousness and Self-Knowledge," 354–56.

[9] Thus for Aquinas, I do not come to understand the nature of my own mind by observing other minds, but the reverse: I consider the natures of other minds by comparison to the mind-nature I discover within myself: "[I]ntellectus noster cognoscendo se ipsum cognoscit alios intellectus in quantum ipsemet est similitudo aliorum intellectuum" (*DV* 2.3, ad 1 [Leon. 22/1.51:271–4]). Cornelio Fabro puts it well: "Thus the soul's perception of itself by its acts constitutes a source of original content, the content of the life of the spirit. The Lockian '*nihil est in intellectu quod prius non fuerit in sensu*' is only valid in Thomism for the objects that are cognized by species received from phantasms, namely, the essences of material things. The cognition of spiritual reality has its own new point of departure, even though it occurs in continuity with and dependence on the other cognition" ("Coscienza e autocoscienza dell'anima," *Doctor communis* 11 [1958]: 112, translation mine).

As a philosopher reasons from this basic self-experience, her path leads from what is best known but farthest from oneself (i.e., sensible objects), to what is most obscure but most intimate (one's own nature): "It is necessary that in cognition of the soul we proceed from those things that are more external, from which intelligible species are abstracted, through which [species] the intellect understands itself – in other words, so that through objects we may know acts and through acts, powers, and through powers, the essence of the soul."[10] This quest instantiates the methodology described in Aristotle's *De anima* II: namely, the one who seeks science of the soul must reason from its objects to its acts to its powers to its essence, inasmuch as objects differentiate acts, which differentiate powers, which specify the nature of the soul.[11] Construed this way, the broad project of inquiring into the human soul's nature is daunting. One must examine *all* the vital acts characterizing living humans – nutritive acts supporting bodily integration and healthy functioning, sensation and its neurological underpinnings, imagination, appetites and passions, acts of grasping intelligibles and making choices, etc. – and differentiate them in terms of their objects. In order to comprehend what kind of thing the soul is, one must comprehensively study what it can do, a project that perhaps can never be completed in a lifetime.

Here, however, I will focus on a more narrowly defined version of this project, which Aquinas outlines in his main texts on self-knowledge. There, he traces a path from *the nature of objects of intellectual acts* through the nature of the intellectual power, to the intellectual soul's *immaterial nature*.[12] (The sequence sometimes varies: In *DV* 10.8, Aquinas replaces

---

[10] *InDA* II.6 [Leon. 45/1.94:176–86]: "[N]ichil autem cognoscitur nisi secundum quod est actu; unde intellectus possibilis noster cognoscit se ipsum per speciem intelligibilem, ut in III habebitur, non autem intuendo essenciam suam directe. Et ideo oportet, quod in cognitionem anime procedamus ab hiis que sunt magis extrinseca, a quibus abstrahuntur species intelligibiles, per quas intellectus intelligit se ipsum; ut scilicet per obiecta cognoscamus actus et per actus potencias et per potencias essenciam anime." See Putallaz, *Le sens de la réflexion*, 130–1; and Fabro, "Coscienza e autocoscienza," 110.

[11] See Aristotle *De anima* 415a15–22; and in Aquinas, *Sent* I.3.1.2, ad 3; *Sent* I.17.1.4, ad 4; *Sent* III.23.1.2, ad 3; *DV* 2.2, ad 2 (where it is presented as a path for "returning to oneself"); *SCG* 3.46; *QDDA* 16, ad 8; *InDA* II.6; *ST* Ia.77.3. On this methodology, see Pasnau, *Thomas Aquinas on Human Nature*, 336–41; and Lambert, *Self Knowledge in Thomas Aquinas*, 211–24.

[12] See *Sent* III.23.1.2, ad 3, where Aquinas presents knowledge of the intellect's nature as the first topic of inquiry into the human soul's nature [Moos 3.703]: "[A]nimam reflecti per cognitionem supra seipsam, vel supra ea quae ipsius sunt, contingit dupliciter. Uno modo secundum quod potentia cognoscitiva cognoscit naturam sui, vel eorum quae in ipsa sunt; et hoc est tantum intellectus cujus est quidditates rerum cognoscere. Intellectus autem, ut dicitur in III *De anima*, sicut alia, cognoscit seipsum, quia scilicet per speciem non quidem sui, sed objecti, quae est forma ejus; ex qua cognoscit actus sui naturam, et ex natura actus naturam potentiae cognoscentis, et ex natura potentiae naturam essentiae, et per consequens aliarum potentiarum"; *DV* 10.8 [22/2.322:277–86]:

"acts" with "species"; in *DV* 10.9 he adds "species" and "habits" to the sequence, but this does not seem to make a significant philosophical difference.[13]) This more narrowly specified four-stage sequence, "intelligible object → species-informed act → intellect → soul's essence," has a familiar ring. In fact, it discursively retraces, step by step, the logical structure of a single act of prephilosophical self-awareness: i.e., by grasping an extramental object, I grasp my act of thinking, which manifests my thinking intellect, which manifests my soul as the principle of thought. (Putallaz observes that the similarity between this train of reasoning and the structure of an act of self-awareness confused Aquinas's thirteenth-century readers, most of whom erroneously thought that he was describing a drawn-out, discursive process for reaching *self-awareness!*[14])

Now it is not surprising that Aquinas would have construed the project of quidditative self-knowledge more narrowly as a process of reasoning about the *intellectual* soul. Quidditative self-knowledge involves defining the soul's essence so as to distinguish it from everything else – which is not the same as comprehending the nature of the soul. Because for Aquinas the human soul's distinctive feature is its intellectual power, an accurate concept of the intellect is crucial to defining the human soul. This is not to say that other vital acts are unimportant to his conception of the human soul (and in fact, as we will see in the next section, he seems to think that a philosopher will already have some sort of grasp of the soul's other vital activities before turning to the nature of intellectual understanding). But since the intellect is key to distinguishing the human soul properly from other kinds of soul, the path to *quidditative self-knowledge* (as distinct from thorough comprehension) passes through the nature of the intellect.[15]

"[E]x hoc enim quod anima humana universales rerum naturas cognoscit, perceperunt quod species qua intelligimus est immaterialis, alias esset individuata et sic non duceret in cognitionem universalis; ex hoc autem quod species intelligibilis est immaterialis, perceperunt quod intellectus est res quaedam non dependens a materia, et ex hoc ad alias proprietates cognoscendas intellectivae animae processerunt"; *DV* 10.9 [Leon. 22/2.328:202–7]: "Unde actio intellectus nostri primo tendit in ea quae per phantasmata apprehenduntur et deinde redit ad actum suum cognoscendum, et ulterius in species et habitus et potentias et essentiam ipsius mentis"; *SCG* 3.46 [Leon. 14.123], where cognizing the immaterial nature of the intellect ("[Aristoteles] ex ipso intelligere demonstrat naturam intellectus possibilis, scilicet quod sit *immixtus et incorruptibilis*") is treated as interchangeable with cognizing the nature of the soul ("[Q]uid autem [anima] sit, inquirimus ex actibus et obiectis"). For condensed versions of this project, see texts in note 20 below.

[13] Although for an argument that knowledge of habits is an important part in developing one's understanding of human nature, see Inagaki, "*Habitus* and *natura.*"

[14] See Putallaz, *Le sens de la réflexion*, 131, n. 50; Pasnau likewise rejects this misreading in *Thomas Aquinas on Human Nature*, 341. Two texts that are particularly susceptible to this misreading are *QDDA* 16, ad 8; and *InDA* II.6.

[15] *SCG* 3.46 [Leon. 14.123]: "Unde et in hoc dicit aliquos errasse, quod animam non distinxerunt ab illis quae sunt ab ipsa diversa. Per hoc autem quod scitur de re quid est, scitur res prout est ab aliis distincta: unde et definitio, quae significat quid est res, distinguit definitum ab omnibus aliis."

Let us look more closely at this narrower four-stage sequence, which sheds light on how Aquinas thinks information about the *human soul's* nature can be gotten from reflecting on the natures of *extramental objects as attained by the intellect.* This four-stage schema is not itself an argument for the human soul's immateriality, but merely spells out a program for any such argument, in order to justify the possibility of making claims about the soul's nature. It reveals what is missing from self-awareness and left to reason to discover, and highlights the main challenges that must be overcome to define the human soul. Aquinas will implement this program in his various well-known arguments for the human soul's immateriality, but I will not discuss the latter here, since they would take us too far afield from the study of the psychology of self-knowledge.[16]

The first stage in the journey toward quidditative self-knowledge consists in determining the nature of the object of thought – not the nature of some extramental intelligible (toadness), but rather *what it is to be an object of thought as such.* "It is common to all powers of the soul that acts are cognized by objects, and powers by acts, and the soul by its powers. In this way too, then, the intellective soul is cognized by its intelligible [object] (*per suum intelligibile*)."[17] The goal is to get beyond merely noticing oneself thinking about triangles, and investigate what it means for 'triangle' to be the object of thought. By pondering the difference between seeing a particular triangle and thinking about what triangles are, one can eventually define the object of thought as a "universal nature" (as opposed to, say, a sensible particular or a generalized image).

The second stage is to determine what the intellectual act must be like in order to be able to grasp such objects. "From the fact that the human soul cognizes the universal natures of things, it perceives that the species by which we understand is immaterial."[18] For Aquinas, this hurdle is cleared when one

---

[16] For studies skeptical of Aquinas's arguments for the immateriality and consequent incorruptibility of the soul, see Pasnau, *Thomas Aquinas on Human Nature*, 48–57 and 361–6; Joseph A. Novak, "Aquinas on the Incorruptibility of Soul," *History of Philosophy Quarterly* 4 (1987): 405–21; Richard Cross, "Is Aquinas's Proof for the Indestructibility of the Soul Successful?" *British Journal of Philosophy* 5 (1997): 1–20. For studies defending Aquinas, see Herbert McCabe, "The Immortality of the Soul," in *Aquinas*, ed. Anthony Kenny (London: Macmillan, 1969), 297–306; and Joseph Owens, "Aquinas on the Inseparability of Soul from Existence," *The New Scholasticism* 61 (1987): 249–70. An interesting debate on this topic took place between Gyula Klima and Robert Pasnau during the 2001 meeting of the Society for Medieval Logic and Metaphysics, which was published in *The Immateriality of the Human Mind, the Semantics of Analogy, and the Conceivability of God*, ed. Gyula Klima and Alexander W. Hall, Proceedings of the Society for Medieval Logic and Metaphysics 1 (Newcastle upon Tyne: Cambridge Scholars Publishing, 2011), 25–60.

[17] *QDDA* 16, ad 8.

[18] *DV* 10.8; and see the other texts cited above in note 12.

concludes that these essences of material things can only be understood in a dematerialized and universalized way, and thus that the intellect's act must be immaterial.[19] For Aquinas, proving this conclusion is apparently the most difficult leg of the journey, and he devotes special attention to it in fleshing out his own arguments for the immateriality of the human soul. In fact, when he abbreviates the sequence of stages leading up to quidditative self-knowledge, he invariably retains at least this second stage.[20]

If the immateriality of intellectual cognition can be proven, however, the rest is smooth sailing. The third stage consists in reasoning that if the intellect produces an immaterial act, then it must itself be immaterial, i.e., it does not operate by means of a material organ.[21] The journey concludes with a fourth stage, in which the inquirer reasons from the immaterial nature of the intellect "to the essence of the [human] soul." Sometimes Aquinas identifies this conclusion more specifically as a recognition of the soul's immateriality: Because an immaterial power could not be present in a wholly corporeal being, the intellective soul itself must be immaterial and therefore subsistent.[22] (In the next section we will see why immateriality acquires such a central role in this schema.)

This program for argumentation sheds light on Aquinas's conception of how cognition of extramental objects assists in overcoming self-opacity. When the mind perceives itself in act, its own essence remains opaque to itself. Nevertheless, in this prephilosophical self-perception it is already beginning to acquire – from within – what it needs to dispel this more resilient self-opacity. Because the human mind has no form other than the form of the extramental essence, that essence and the mind itself are complicit in rendering each other intelligible. The species whereby the mind knows itself is *the species of the extramental object*. This is just as true in quidditative self-knowledge as in self-awareness:

> Our possible intellect understands itself, not by directly apprehending its essence, but by a species received from the phantasms. Whence the

---

[19] For examples of Aquinas fleshing out this second stage in his own treatment of the soul, see *ST* 1a.75.2; *InDA* III.1; *QDDA* 1; and *DUI* 1.

[20] See for instance in *SCG* 3.46 ("the act of understanding demonstrates the nature of the possible intellect"); *QDDA* 16, ad 8 and *InDA* II.6 (where the condensed strategy for discovering the nature of the intellective soul is presented as an application of the general methodology for inquiry into the soul); *ST* 1a.87.1 ("we consider the nature of the human mind from its act"), and *InDA* III.3 [Leon. 45/1.216:80–6] ("by that understanding itself and by that which is understood, Aristotle probes the nature of the possible intellect") – not to mention Aquinas' abbreviations of the entire process in passing as cognizing the nature of the intellect or soul "by its species" (e.g., *QDDA* 3, ad 4, etc.).

[21] For an example of this third stage fleshed out as an argument, see *ST* 1a.75.2.

[22] See texts cited in note 26 below.

philosopher says in III *De Anima* that the possible intellect is intelligible just like other things ... Whence, because the possible intellect is only in potency in intelligible being, it cannot be understood except by its form, through which it is rendered into act, which is the species received from the phantasms ... And this is common in all powers of the soul, that acts are cognized by objects, and powers by acts, and the soul by its powers. In this way, then, the intellective soul is cognized by its intelligible too [object].[23]

We can now see why Aquinas insists that any attempt to define the intellect's essence (and hence the quest for quidditative self-knowledge, more narrowly construed) begins by considering the object of cognition *qua* object of cognition. As we saw in Chapter 6, the actual intelligibility (Intelligibility) that the intellect gains from the species-in-act is all the Intelligibility that it has at that moment. As the form instantiated in the "matter" of the possible intellect (constituting the intellect-in-act or Intellect), the species-in-act of 'triangle' serves as the source of information about the being of triangularity *and* intellectual being. In the act of cognizing some essence – triangles, trees, and toads – my own capacity for cognizing that essence is manifested. "The human soul understands itself by its understanding, which is its proper act, perfectly demonstrating its power and nature."[24] To put it another way, because of the same co-manifesting of cognizer and cognized in the act of cognition, when I explore *what it is that I am cognizing* when I think about triangles, trees, and toads, I learn *what it is for me to cognize such things.*[25]

Just as the mere fact of thinking about extramental objects implicitly manifests the thinker as agent-in-act, then, so too the reasoned exploration of what it is to be an object ultimately reveals what that agent-in-act is. For Aquinas, this is certainly no easy project, but it would be impossible if self-awareness were not an intuitive perception of oneself-in-act (see Chapter 4). In fact, this argumentative procedure would look very different if we were reasoning from the human soul's sensible *effects* such as heartbeats, spoken speech, or artistic creations. It is only because we experience ourselves from the inside performing different acts like thinking, sensing, desiring, that we can even recognize that there *are* different

[23] *QDDA* 16, ad 8; *Sent* III.23.1.2, ad 3; *QDDA* 3, ad 4 [Leon. 24/1.28:338–42]: "Set intellectus possibilis dicitur intelligibilis sicut et alia intelligibilia, quia per speciem intelligibilem intelligibilium aliorum se intelligit. Ex obiecto enim cognoscit suam operationem per quam deuenit in cognitionem sui ipsius"; *InDA* III.3; *ST* Ia.87.1. Compare also the following, where it is not entirely clear whether he is referring to self-awareness or quidditative self-knowledge or both: *DV* 10.8, ad 5 s.c.; *DV* 10.9, ad 4, ad 10, and ad 2 s.c.; and *SCG* 2.98.
[24] *ST* Ia.88.2, ad 3.
[25] See Romeyer, "Saint Thomas et notre connaissance," 84–5.

kinds of mental acts, and eventually come to know which of them distinguishes the human soul from other kinds of souls.

The case of the missing definition

Curiously, when Aquinas occasionally describes more precisely the endpoint of the journey to quidditative self-knowledge, he presents this as the conclusion that "the intellect is a kind of thing that does not depend on matter," from which "the other properties of the intellective soul" (such as self-subsistence) can be inferred.[26] But why should the path to quidditative self-knowledge be designed to arrive at the immateriality of the intellectual soul via the immateriality of the intellect? The human soul is not exclusively intellectual; it is a hylomorphic form that is responsible for bodily life, nutrition, growth, sensation, appetite, etc. Moreover, the statement "The human soul is immaterial" cannot be a proper definition of the soul, since it lacks a genus and specifying difference. Aquinas's own definitions of the human soul "from above" and "from below" in other texts do not even mention immateriality. Viewed from below, the human soul is the highest organic life-principle, defined as the intellectual form of a potentially living physical organic body.[27] Viewed from above, the human soul is the lowest of intellectual beings, defined as the intellectual being that tends toward completion by organic matter.[28] Neither of these definitions mention immateriality, and it is not immediately obvious whether either is implied in Aquinas's description of attaining quidditative self-knowledge.

Now certainly there are strong historical influences behind Aquinas's granting such a pivotal place to the intellect's immateriality in the

---

[26] *DV* 10.8 [Leon. 22/2.322:281–6]: "[E]x hoc autem quod species intelligibilis est immaterialis, perceperunt quod intellectus est res quaedam non dependens a materia; et ex hoc ad alias proprietates cognoscendas intellectivae animae processerunt"; *SCG* 3.46 [Leon. 14.123]: "Unde et Aristoteles … ex ipso intelligere demonstrat naturam intellectus possibilis, scilicet quod sit *immixtus et incorruptibilis*."

[27] See for instance *ST* 1a.76.3, ad 4, where he identifies the genus of the human soul as sensate soul, with the specific difference of intellectuality. He is relying on Aristotle's definition of soul in general as the first act of a physical organic body that has life potentially (*De anima* 412b4–5); see *InDA* II.1; *ST* 1a.76.4, ad 1; 1a.76.5, s.c.

[28] This definition results from adding to the genus of intellectual being the specific difference of informing a material body, as suggested for instance in *ST* 1a.75.7, ad 3; 1a.76.5; and 1a.89.1. On these two approaches to defining the soul, see B. Carlos Bazán, "On Angels and Human Beings," *Archives d'histoire doctrinale et littéraire du moyen âge* 77 (2010): 47–85. The existence of two ways of defining the human soul is certainly puzzling, since according to an Aristotelian conception of definition, a thing can have only one definition, properly speaking. Is one a proper definition and the other only a description? Or is the soul a special case due to its place on the "horizon" of the corporeal and incorporeal realms (see *Sent* III, prooem., and *SCG* 2.68)?

argument for the soul's nature. Prior to the advent of Aristotelian hylomorphism, twelfth-century treatises on the soul focused on awakening the reader to the human soul's metaphysical nobility, namely, its immaterial nature by which it reflects the image of God. According to this traditional discourse, to "know what the soul is" is simply to recognize its immateriality, usually by meditating on the kinds of acts that it performs.[29] Decades later, thinkers such as Jean de la Rochelle and William of Auvergne, reinforced by Avicenna's "Flying Man," continued to frame ignorance of the soul's nature as an ignorance of its immateriality.[30] Aquinas is very likely influenced by this traditional pattern of discourse. Moreover, given the tendency among defenders of supraconscious self-knowing to hold that the soul innately grasps its own independence from matter, it is no surprise that Aquinas makes a point of insisting that the *immateriality* of the soul is inaccessible to direct perception and can only be reached by a fallible process of reasoning.

Nevertheless, the historical background does not tell the whole story. Given Aquinas's intense commitment to perfecting what was then a novel hylomorphic account of the human soul, it seems unlikely that he blindly adopts his predecessors' approach in discussions of self-knowledge without considering the effects on his theory of the human soul. More likely, he accepts this approach because it aptly accords with his conception of how one typically goes about seeking quidditative self-knowledge. I contend that Aquinas schematizes the quest for quidditative self-knowledge in the way he does, not because he thinks quidditative self-knowledge *is* knowledge of the human soul's immateriality, but because he takes the argument for intellectual immateriality to be *the clinching step* in attaining quidditative self-knowledge – the final piece in the puzzle of the soul's nature. In fact, the schema he outlines makes perfect sense if we assume that the quest for quidditative self-knowledge aims at a definition of the human soul from below, a definition whose components are already readily available via prephilosophical experience.

Recall that, for Aquinas, in an act of explicit self-awareness the soul perceives itself as agent-in-act, the source or first principle of its thinking, willing, sensing, etc. So the philosopher embarking on the quest for quidditative self-knowledge already indistinctly cognizes the genus in the

---

[29] See for instance three twelfth-century Cistercian treatises on the soul: William of St. Thierry's *Physica animae*, Isaac of Stella's *Epistola de anima*, and the *Liber de spiritu et anima*, translated by McGinn, in *Three Treatises on Man* (see pp. 22–3 above).

[30] See William of Auvergne, *De anima*, esp. 3.12–13; and the first two of the seven definitions of the soul given in Jean de la Rochelle, *Summa de anima* 1.2. For the "Flying Man," see pp. 24–6 above.

human soul's "definition from below," because she grasps the actions as
hers, i.e., as stemming from an internal principle of action. By inquiring
into the soul, she is already asking about what it means to be the principle
of one's own operations. "In order to seek the nature of the soul, one must
presuppose that the soul is called the first principle of life in those things
that we take to be alive; for we say that animate things are living, but that
inanimate things lack life."[31] "Everyone experiences in himself that he has
a soul and that the soul gives life."[32]

In explicit self-awareness, one also indistinctly grasps the specific difference of a definition from below, namely, intellectuality. Aquinas identifies the basic experience that undergirds the quest for quidditative
self-knowledge as the experience of oneself *thinking*. "From the fact that
it apprehends other things, it arrives at a cognition of itself [i.e., of its
nature]."[33] From these prephilosophical self-experiences, most people recognize at least nominally what the word 'thinking' refers to: "No one is
ignorant of possessing memory, intellect, and will."[34] Most can even readily identify *thinking* as the most distinctively human feature, even if they
cannot explain what it means to think.

Consequently, for Aquinas, the conceptual framework for a "bottom-
up" definition of the human soul is already present in actual self-awareness.
He presupposes that anyone who sets out to define the human soul *is
already familiar with its genus and specifying difference*, though only indistinctly. Very little philosophical work is required to articulate this knowledge in a preliminary (still indistinct but basically correct) definition of
the soul as an organic life-principle capable of thought. Nevertheless, to
have genuine quidditative knowledge it is not enough to memorize and
repeat the correct definition; one must understand the essence distinctly,
which requires that one distinctly understand both the genus and the specifying difference.

---

[31] *ST* Ia.75.1 [Leon. 5.194]: "[A]d inquirendum de natura animae, oportet praesupponere quod anima
dicitur esse primum principium vitae in his quae apud nos vivunt: animata enim viventia dicimus,
res vero inanimatas vita carentes"; for other texts describing a prephilosophical grasp of soul as life-
principle (agent-in-act), see *DV* 10.8; *ST* Ia.76.1; and *ST* Ia–IIae.112.5, ad 1.

[32] *InDA* I.1, cited in note 6 above.

[33] *DV* 10.8 [Leon. 22/2.322:272–3]: "[E]x hoc quod apprehendit alia devenit in suam cognitionem";
DV 10.8, ad 8 s.c.; *InDA* III.3. See also *Sent* III.23.1.2; *SCG* 2.98 and 3.46; *QDDA* 3, ad 4; and *QDDA*
16, ad 8, where Aquinas describes quidditative self-knowledge as depending on a cognition of the
act (apparently meaning the nature of the act).

[34] *ST* Ia.93.7, ad 2 [Leon. 5.409]: "[A]ccipit in anima tria quaedam propria mentis, scilicet memoriam, intelligentiam et voluntatem, quae nullus ignorat se habere, et in istis tribus potius imaginem
Trinitatis assignat, quasi prima assignatio sit quodammodo deficiens."

So now we can see why Aquinas insists that quidditative self-knowledge is achieved by recognizing the soul's immateriality: He thinks that the major obstacle to quidditative self-knowledge is a failure to understand the human soul's specifying difference distinctly, i.e., *a failure to recognize that immateriality is essential to intellectuality.* The immaterial nature of thought is not evident in prephilosophical experience, and one can discover it only by reasoned argument (as Aquinas himself repeatedly seeks to do). Without grasping the immateriality of thought, one cannot understand distinctly what it is to think. Someone who defines the human soul as a "life-principle capable of thought," while conceiving of thought as something material, is unwittingly conceiving of the human soul as a "life-principle capable of imagination."

Thus for Aquinas, it is only when the philosopher understands thinking as the immaterial act of grasping dematerialized essences, that she distinctly understands what it means to be intellectual. And only then does she achieve quidditative knowledge of the soul as the intellectual form of a potentially living organic body, properly understood so as to distinguish the human soul from other life-principles.[35] The process of attaining quidditative self-knowledge, then, is simply a process of gaining distinct knowledge of the indistinctly understood prephilosophical description of the human soul with which the philosopher begins her inquiry.[36]

Judging the soul in the light of divine truth

In just two texts, after discussing how the philosopher acquires knowledge of the soul's definition, Aquinas includes a relatively lengthy and rather puzzling discussion of a judgment of the soul's nature. In *DV* 10.8, he presents what initially appears to be a subdivision of quidditative self-knowledge into apprehension of the soul's definition and judgment of the latter's veracity:

> But if we speak of the cognition of the soul when the human mind is defined by species or genus, it seems that we must again distinguish. Just as

[35] If the immateriality of thought is the main obstacle to achieving proper quidditative self-knowledge, then, it is no surprise to find him alternating, even in the same sentence, between characterizing quidditative self-knowledge as a knowledge of what the *soul* is, and characterizing it as a knowledge of what the *mind* or *intellect* is; see especially *DV* 10.8, *SCG* 3.46, and *ST* 1a.87.1. I should also emphasize here that the attainment of quidditative self-knowledge in no way constitutes *comprehension* of the soul; it is simply the ability to define what the soul is (*quid est*) in such a way as to distinguish it from everything else.

[36] See for instance *SCG* 3.46 and *ST* 1a.87.1, and the discussion of indistinctness vs. distinctness in Chapter 3 pp. 77–81.

two things must concur for cognition, namely apprehension and judgment of the apprehended thing, so too the cognition by which the nature of the soul is cognized can be considered with respect to apprehension, and with respect to judgment. [A discussion of the reasoning by which one apprehends the soul's immateriality, as above, ensues] ... But if one considers our cognition of the soul's nature with respect to the judgment whereby we pronounce that it is such (*sententiamus ita esse*) as it had been apprehended by the previous deduction, we have knowledge of the soul insofar as "we behold (*intuemur*) inviolable truth, from which we define as perfectly as we can, not what sort of mind each man has, but what sort of mind it ought to be in the eternal reasons," as Augustine says in *De Trin.* IX. But we behold this inviolable truth in its likeness impressed on our mind, insofar as we naturally know certain things as *per se* known, according to which we examine all other things, judging about all things according to them.[37]

Judgment of the soul's nature reappears in *ST* Ia.87.1:

[The intellect cognizes itself by its act] in the universal, insofar as it considers the nature of the human mind from the intellect's act. But it is true that the judgment and efficacy of this knowledge by which we know the nature of the soul belongs to us according to the derivation of the light of our intellect from the divine truth, in which the reasons of all things are contained, as was said above. Whence also Augustine says, in *De Trin.* IX, that we behold inviolable truth from which we define as perfectly as we can, not what sort of mind each man has, but what sort of mind it ought to be in the eternal reasons.[38]

What is this judgment, and how should we understand its references to the divine light or inviolable truth, taken from an Augustinian theory of divine illumination that Aquinas himself rejects? Does it contribute anything to Aquinas's theory of self-knowledge, and if so, why does it appear only in two texts? Various interpretations have been suggested. Pasnau proposes that Aquinas is appealing to divine illumination in order to fill a conceptual hole in his theory of self-knowledge. McKian interprets the discussion of judgment as a further argument for the soul's immateriality.[39]

Putallaz, however, has argued very persuasively that judgment of the soul's nature verifies one's conclusion about the soul's essence according to the standard of first principles.[40] Building on this interpretation,

---

[37] *DV* 10.8, referring to Augustine, *De Trin* 9.6.9 (for Latin text, see p. 194, note 59 below).

[38] *ST* Ia.87.1.

[39] Pasnau, *Thomas Aquinas on Human Nature*, 349; and McKian, "Metaphysics of Introspection," 108–9 (Lambert, *Self Knowledge in Thomas Aquinas*, 250, shares McKian's view).

[40] For Putallaz's discussion of the relevant texts and detailed analysis of how first principles are known, see *Le sens de la réflexion*, 131–48. See a similar but less-developed interpretation in Jordan, *Ordering Wisdom*, 128–9.

I want to propose that Aquinas includes this judgment in his theory of self-knowledge because it elevates quidditative self-knowledge to the level of a "science of the soul." Apprehension of the reasoned definition and judgment of that definition are not two distinct *types* of quidditative self-knowledge, but rather two *stages* in the attainment of the "science of the soul." In fact, counterintuitively, the key role of judgment in the science of the soul is the reason that most of his texts on self-knowledge do not discuss it explicitly. And as we shall see, Aquinas is motivated to distinguish apprehension and judgment of the soul's essence only as part of a broader strategy of showing how his thought on self-knowledge accommodates Augustinian intuitions.

Verificational judgment and the agent intellect

Let us begin by sketching Aquinas's general account of verificational judgment, which sheds light on his mysterious phrase "judgment [of the soul's nature] by the eternal reasons." As we saw in Chapter 3, judgment is the intellectual operation of "assenting," pronouncing whether an apprehended nature "is or is not so in a real thing (*ita esse vel non esse in re*)." Interestingly, however, Aquinas does not think that judgment is merely an assent to what has *already been verified*. Rather, to verify *is* to assent to the truth of what is apprehended.[41] (I use "verify" here in a non-technical sense to mean "confirming the truth of one's understanding," without implying any particular method for confirmation.)

The epistemological function of judgment in Aquinas has already been the topic of numerous studies,[42] so here I want to focus on his standards for verification, which are central to his account of the "judgment of the

---

[41] *InPerierm* 1.3 [Leon. 1*/1.17:167–72]: "Cognoscere autem predictam conformitatis habitudinem nichil est aliud quam iudicare ita esse in re uel non esse, quod est componere et diuidere, et ideo intellectus non cognoscit ueritatem nisi componendo uel diuidendo per suum iudicium"; *DV* 1.9 [Leon. 22/1.29:18–22]: "In intellectu enim est [ueritas] sicut consequens actum intellectus et sicut cognita per intellectum: consequitur namque intellectus operationem secundum quod iudicium intellectus est de re secundum quod est."

[42] For the debate about whether judgment involves some sort of perception of a sensory object's existence, between Maritain, Gilson, Wippel, Owens and Knasas on the one hand, and Régis and Cunningham on the other, see p. 75, note 24 above. On logical verification, see Julien Péghaire, Intellectus *et* ratio *selon S. Thomas d'Aquin* (Paris: Vrin, 1936), 269–72; and Putallaz, *Le sens de la réflexion*, 135–42. Sometimes judgment of truth is linked to the reflexivity of judgment: see Scott MacDonald, "Theory of Knowledge," in *The Cambridge Companion to Aquinas*, ed. Norman Kretzmann and Eleonore Stump (Cambridge University Press, 1993), 162–3; Putallaz, *Le sens de la réflexion*, 172–208; Charles Boyer, "Le sens d'un texte de Saint Thomas," *Gregorianum* 5 (1924): 424–43. Stump argues persuasively against a foundationalist reading of Aquinas's epistemology in *Aquinas*, ch. 7.

188 Phenomena and problems

soul's essence." For Aquinas, a verificational judgment involves measuring one's thoughts according to the appropriate standard: e.g., sensory experience or "eternal truth."[43] When the entity to be measured is a universal abstracted directly from sensory experience, such as 'dog,' the intellect verifies it according to the "standard" of my remembered or current sensory experiences of dogs.[44] (For Aquinas, this verification hinges on an intellectual "connection" or *continuatio* to the particular, established by the agent intellect in abstracting the species from the phantasm; but as this is not relevant to self-knowledge, we need not go into details here.[45])

A different standard of verification is needed, however, for reasoned conclusions like "The soul is immaterial" or "Socrates is mortal," because they were apprehended indirectly via argumentation rather than directly via sensory experience. In order to verify the truth of a reasoned conclusion, one must measure the logical validity of the argument form that produces this conclusion against the standard of "the first principles by which we judge all things." Aquinas calls this measuring "resolution to first principles" for an Aristotelian audience and "consultation with first or eternal truth" for an Augustinian audience (we can call it "logical verification").[46]

Aquinas's usual examples of the common, *per se* known, immediate propositions that serve as the standard for logical verification are "Being and non-being are not the same," "A whole is greater than its part," and "Two things equal to the same thing are equal to each other."[47] These first

---

[43] *DV* 10.9 [Leon. 22/2.329:226–30]: "Unde iudicium in quo completur cognitio de natura habitus, vel est secundum id quod sensu accipimus, vel secundum quod increatam consulimus veritatem." See also a more detailed division in *SBDT* 6.2. In fact, Aquinas says that judgment *is* an act of measuring and that the name *mens* derives from this activity; see *ST* Ia.79.9, ad 4.

[44] See for instance *ST* Ia.21.2 [Leon. 4.260]: "Quando igitur res sunt mensura et regula intellectus, veritas consistit in hoc, quod intellectus adaequatur rei, ut in nobis accidit, ex eo enim quod res est vel non est, opinio nostra et oratio vera vel falsa est"; *InPerierm* I.3 [Leon. 1*/1.16:149–51].

[45] *DV* 2.6 [Leon. 22/1.66:62–7]: "[S]icut species quae est in sensu, abstrahitur a rebus ipsis et per eam cognitio sensus continuatur ad ipsas res sensibiles, ita intellectus noster abstrahit speciem a phantasmatibus et per eam eius cognitio quodammodo ad phantasmata continuatur"; see also *DV* 10.5; *SCG* 2.59; and *ST* Ia.84.7. This procedure is more familiarly known as the "turn to the phantasms" (see p. 11 above). Interestingly, Klubertanz even goes so far as to say that the turn is a judgment ("St. Thomas and the Knowledge of the Singular," 165).

[46] *DV* 10.6, ad 6 [Leon. 22/2.313.265–70]: "[P]rima principia quorum cognitio est nobis innata, sunt quaedam similitudo increatae veritatis; unde secundum quod per ea de aliis iudicamus, dicimur iudicare de rebus per rationes incommutabiles vel per veritatem increatam"; *SCG* 4.92 [Leon. 15.288]: "Intellectus noster circa conclusiones aliquas errare potest antequam in prima principia resolutio fiat, in quae resolutione iam facta, scientia de conclusionibus habetur, quae falsa esse non potest"; *DV* 1.4, ad 5; *ST* Ia.16.6, ad 1; and *InPostAn* I.1, cited in note 56 below.

[47] See *InPostAn* I.5 [Leon. 1*/2.25:116–30] and I.43 [165:310–11], *InMet* IV.5; *ST* Ia–IIae.94.2, etc. For further discussion, see Péghaire, *Intellectus et ratio*, 269–72, which helpfully lists the key texts; and Putallaz, *Le sens de la réflexion*, 135–42. On *per se* known propositions in Aquinas generally, see Luca

principles are universally or "naturally" known (*naturaliter nota*), because their subject terms are known to everyone as the basic intelligibles grasped in every act of cognition ('being,' 'one,' etc.), and the predicates are contained in their subjects. Consequently, *per se* known propositions are grasped instantly (*statim*) when their terms are grasped.[48] To put it another way, in grasping the notion of 'whole,' 'part,' 'being,' and 'equal,' as part of every intelligibility, the intellect instantly grasps how parts and wholes, etc., *are necessarily related to each other.* (These principles should not be confused with *per se* known, immediate principles whose terms are not known to everyone, such as definitions;[49] or with the first principles that a given discipline presupposes as the basis for its reasoning.)

So what does this logical verification, or "measuring truth according to first principles," look like from the perspective of the thinker? We can get a clue from the fact that these three universally known first principles (Aquinas intimates that there could be more, but he does not identify them) articulate the basic necessary relationships that are at the core of Aristotelian syllogistic logic: affirmation–negation, part–whole, equality–inequality. The grasp of first principles thus grants a basic familiarity[50] with the relationships that are presumed in logical reasoning. All thinkers (not just logicians) acquire this familiarity by merely apprehending beings, whether or not they ever spell out these first principles consciously. I would suggest that, for Aquinas, verification "in light of these principles," in its simplest form, is nothing more than the everyday exercise of this familiarity, an act of *recognizing necessity in an inference's part–whole and affirmation–negation relationships, in congruence with these basic familiar*

F. Tuninetti, *Per se notum*; *Die logische Beschaffenheit des Selbstverständlichen im Denken des Thomas von Aquinas* (Leiden: Brill, 1996), esp. 24–6 and 165–85.

[48] *SCG* I.10 [Leon. 13.23]: "Illa enim per se esse nota dicuntur quae statim notis terminis cognoscuntur: sicut, cognito quid est totum et quid est pars, statim cognoscitur quod omne totum est maius sua parte"; *DV* 10.12 [Leon. 22/2.341:154–63]: "[A]d hoc autem quod sit per se notum nobis, oportet quod nobis sit cognita ratio subiecti in qua includitur praedicatum. Et inde est quod quaedam per se nota sunt omnibus, quando scilicet propositiones huiusmodi habent talia subiecta quorum ratio omnibus nota est, ut omne totum maius est sua parte: quilibet enim scit quid est totum et quid est pars; quaedam vero sunt per se nota sapientibus tantum ..." *ST* Ia–IIae.57.2 [Leon. 6.365]: "Quod autem est per se notum, se habet ut principium; et percipitur statim ab intellectu. Et ideo habitus perficiens intellectum ad huiusmodi veri considerationem, vocatur *intellectus*, qui est habitus principiorum"; Ia–IIe.58.4.

[49] As Aquinas points out in *ST* Ia–IIae.94.2, though some principles are self-evident in themselves to everyone, such as the latter principles, others, though self-evident in themselves, are not self-evident to everyone, so that some people can only attain them by reasoning. A classic example is the existence of God, which is self-evident in itself but not self-evident to any human being, because due to our inability to grasp the divine essence, we cannot grasp the definition of the term "God": see *ST* Ia.2.1. For a helpful discussion, see Tuninetti, *Per se notum*, especially 24–6; and Stump, *Aquinas*, 227–8.

[50] The "habit of principles"; see *ST* Ia–IIae.57.2 in note 48 above.

relationships. It is not an act of working out whether an argument adheres to a set of explicitly articulated first principles. Nor is it a project of reducing an argument to a set of basic axioms. Rather, it is a simple everyday insight into the necessity of the part–whole and affirmation–negation relationships among the propositions in an argument.

As such, "measuring the argument by the standard of first principles" is less like a painter checking his landscape against the original, and more like a singer with perfect pitch instinctively hearing that the song has started on the right note, or a batter realizing by the crack of the ball on the bat that he has hit a home run. That is to say, logical verification is an insight into or recognition of "rightness," based in a habitual experience of the ideal that serves as standard of measurement: namely, the basic structure of being itself. Of course, this instinct or insight is often wrong; its accuracy, like that of any other skill gained by experience, will vary depending on intellectual ability and training. Nevertheless, everyone capable of understanding the concepts 'part,' 'whole,' 'being,' etc. should be able to recognize the validity of the simplest forms, such as a categorical syllogism or *modus ponens*. In fact, any child who can respond to a parent's promise of reward or threat of punishment already grasps the validity of a practical syllogism. Even the logician's laborious verification of a complex argument is reducible to a series of these instantaneous insights into the logical validity of the inferences that compose the larger argument.

For Aquinas, it is the agent intellect, as the intramental principle of intelligibility, that gives us the basic ability to "see" *per se* relationships in logical forms and propositions (especially those articulated in the first indemonstrable principles, but, to varying degrees, also those in other *per se* known propositions). "The intellective power judges concerning truth, not through some intelligibles existing outside, but through the light of the agent intellect, which makes intelligibles."[51] Thus whether the mind is verifying its apprehensions by the measure of sensation or of the first principles, the agent intellect is at work illuminating the standard for verification.

---

[51] *SBDT* 1.1, ad 8; *QDSC* 10, ad 8 [Leon. 24/2.113:538–41]: "[S]upra sensum est uirtus intellectiua, que iudicat de ueritate, non per aliqua intelligibilia extra existentia, set per lumen intellectus agentis, quod facit intelligibilia"; *ST* 1a.88.3, ad 1 [Leon. 5.368]: "[I]n luce primae veritatis omnia intelligimus et iudicamus, inquantum ipsum lumen intellectus nostri, sive naturale sive gratuitum, nihil aliud est quam quaedam impressio veritatis primae"; IIa–IIae.173.2; *InDA* II.11 [Leon. 45/1.113:229–34]; *InEthic* VI.5 [Leon. 47/2.349:50–63]: "Accipitur autem hic intellectus ... pro habitu quodam quo homo ex virtute luminis intellectus agentis naturaliter cognoscit principia indemonstrabilia. Et satis congruit nomen: huiusmodi enim principia statim cognoscuntur cognitis terminis, cognito enim quid est totum et quid pars statim scitur quod omne totum est maius sua parte; dicitur autem intellectus ex eo quod intus legit intuendo essentiam rei."

The illuminative role of the agent intellect in logical verification is especially important for our purposes, because it explains the language of Augustinian illuminationism ("eternal reasons," "immutable truth," "first truth," etc.) that Aquinas often employs in discussing how we cognize the truth of a conclusion. For him, the reason that the human mind is capable of grasping these principles is that its native light-source, the agent intellect, participates in the divine light that actually contains the eternal reasons.[52] Thus Aquinas can say that in verifying the truth of a reasoned conclusion, *the intellect "sees" that conclusion in the light of immutable truth and the divine reasons* – which is precisely how he describes the judgment of the soul's nature.

Verificational judgment of the soul's nature

So how does this account of verification apply to self-knowledge? In verifying reasoned conclusions, the intellect ordinarily performs both verifications described above, measuring the premises against sensory experience and measuring the reasoning against first principles. But for the judgment that the soul's nature "exists in the way that it has apprehended," the first verification occurs somewhat differently. Since the premises in the argument for the soul's definition are taken from one's self-aware experiences of one's acts, there is no sensory experience against which I can check the premise "I am thinking." These premises, then, are presumably verified simply *by the experiences of self-awareness themselves*. For Aquinas, a thinker cannot be mistaken about the fact of her mental acts or the fact of her own existence. "No one ever erred by failing to perceive himself living, because it pertains to the cognition by which someone individually cognizes what is happening in his own soul."[53] In fact, it is on account of the certitude of these experiences that the "science of the soul" acquires its special degree of certitude.[54] (Here we see an important corollary of Aquinas's insistence

---

[52] *ST* Ia.84.5 [Leon. 5.322]: "Ipsum enim lumen intellectuale quod est in nobis, nihil est aliud quam quaedam participata similitudo luminis increati, in quo continentur rationes aeternae"; *DV* 11.3 [Leon. 22/2:359:236–48]: "Sic igitur homo ignotorum cognitionem per duo accipit: scilicet per lumen intellectuale et per primas conceptiones per se notas quae comparantur ad istud lumen quod est intellectus agentis sicut instrumenta ad artificem. Quantum igitur ad utrumque Deus hominis scientiae causa est excellentissimo modo quia et ipsam animam intellectuali lumine insignivit et notitiam primorum principiorum ei impressit quae sunt quasi seminaria scientiarum"; *ST* Ia.88.3, ad 1; IIa–IIae.2.3, ad 2; and IIa–IIae.171.2.

[53] *DV* 10.8, ad 2 [Leon. 22/2.323:335–9]: "[N]ullus unquam erravit in hoc quod non perciperet se vivere, quod pertinet ad cognitionem qua aliquis singulariter cognoscit quid in anima sua agatur."

[54] See texts on p. 175, note 6.

on the directness of self-awareness. Without a direct experiential awareness of our acts, the premises of the argument would have to be verified by
external sensory observations, which could not provide insight into *what
it is like to think* and thus could not ground the kind of science of the soul
that Aquinas seeks.)

Thus in order to know with certitude that the soul really *is* the intellectual first act of a physical organic body, the philosopher need only perform
the second verification, i.e., confirming that the reasoning that generated
the soul's definition was valid according to first principles.[55] This judgment of the soul's nature, then, presumably occurs like any other logical
verification, as described above: namely, the philosopher recognizes that
the part–whole, affirmation–negation, and equality–inequality relationships are organized in her argument exactly as they *ought to be*. She recognizes this *rightness* or *necessity* in the argument structure on the basis of
her familiarity with the necessary relationships in the structure of being,
which are instantly apprehended in every act of understanding as the "first
principles of reason." The need for this second verification highlights the
epistemological difference between self-awareness and quidditative self-
knowledge. While I cannot doubt the reality of my directly experienced
existence and acts, error can enter in when I argue for attributing a certain
nature to these acts; hence the need for logical verification.

The contribution of judgment of the soul's nature in Aquinas's theory
of self-knowledge now comes clearly into view. By affirming the necessity
of the logical relationships in the argument, this judgment grants quidditative self-knowledge certitude and raises it to the level of a "science of the
soul."[56] "To have scientific knowledge of something is to know it perfectly,

---

[55] Still denies that judgment of the soul's nature is carried out with reference to the first principles,
concluding that the soul judges its nature by verifying its knowledge against the basic experience of self-awareness ("Aquinas's Theory of Human Self-Knowledge," 86–90). This interpretation, however, apparently stems from a misapprehension of what "resolution to first principles"
entails.

[56] For the "science of the soul," see p. 175, note 6 and p. 193, note 58. Fabro, who describes judgment
of the soul's nature as "a technical treatment according to propositions (judgments) scientifically
organized so as to produce objective certainty about a given nature" ("Coscienza e autocoscienza,"
109, translation mine; note though that I would not agree with Fabro's characterization of apprehension vs. judgment as confused vs. distinct knowledge). For the role of judgment in establishing
scientific certitude, see *InPostAn* I.1 [Leon. 1*/2.5:75–6:87]: "Pars autem logice que primo deseruit
processui pars iudicatiua dicitur, eo quod iudicium est cum certitudine sciencie; et, quia iudicium
certum de effectibus haberi non potest nisi resoluendo in prima principia, pars hec analetica uoca-
tur, id est resolutoria. Certitudo autem iudicii que per resolutionem habetur est uel ex ipsa forma
sillogismi tantum, et ad hoc ordinatur liber Priorum analeticorum, qui est de sillogismo simpliciter, uel etiam cum hoc ex materia, quia sumuntur propositiones per se et necessarie, et ad hoc
ordinatur liber Posteriorum analeticorum, qui est de sillogismo demonstratiuo." Notice that the

which is to apprehend its truth perfectly."[57] In order to hold the soul's definition as demonstrably true – in order for quidditative self-knowledge to count as "scientific knowledge" – the intellect must judge that the human soul does indeed exist in reality "as apprehended" (*DV* 10.8). If he had not defended the possibility of such verification, Aquinas would have had to hold that arguments about the soul's nature were merely probable at best, and idle speculation at worst. Of course, one could judge falsely if one's habit of recognizing logical patterns is poorly developed. Nevertheless, Aquinas seems to be confident that the cautious and well-trained mind will be able to distinguish merely speculative conclusions from those that unfold necessarily from the premises.

In any case, if the philosopher does perform this verification successfully, her activity will be due to the light of the agent intellect that illuminates the first principles in rendering being intelligible. Thus there is nothing particularly unusual about Aquinas's references to "inviolable truth," the "derivation of the divine light," and the "eternal reasons" in discussing the judgment of the soul's nature. Insofar as it is able to make judgments at all, the mind does so because its own native light participates in the divine source of intelligibility. It is thus able to actualize the intelligibility of an extramental essence, or of the possible intellect itself, or of the necessary relationships among propositions in a demonstrative argument.

We can now see why, apart from *DV* 10.8 and *ST* Ia.87.1, Aquinas does not single out the judgment of the soul's nature in treating quidditative self-knowledge. Apprehension and judgment of the soul's essence are not actually two separate kinds of self-knowledge, but two stages in the acquisition of the "science of the soul." So when he describes quidditative self-knowledge as the soul's "scientifically knowing what it is" – as he frequently does – apprehension and judgment are both included in this *scientia*.[58] (In fact, once we realize that the judgment of the soul's nature

<hr/>

philosopher who seeks to meet the requirements for Aristotelian *demonstrative* science must verify not only the argument structure, but also the "*per se* and necessary" character of the premises.

[57] *InPostAn* I.4 [Leon. 1*/2.19:82–4]: "[S]cire aliquid est perfecte cognoscere ipsum, hoc autem est perfecte apprehendere ueritatem ipsius." I.7 distinguishes two senses of "science," both of which would apply to Aquinas's science of the soul: "[S]ciendum tamen quod hic Aristotiles large accipit scienciam pro qualibet certitudinali cognitione, et non secundum quod sciencia diuiditur contra intellectum, prout dicitur quod sciencia est conclusionum et intellectus principiorum" [Leon. 1*/2.31:64–9].

[58] For *scire* applied specifically to quidditative self-knowledge, see *Sent* I.3.4.5; I.17.1.4, ad 2; *DV* 10.9 (for both quidditative self-knowledge and quidditative knowledge of one's own habits); *SCG* 3.46; *SLDC* 15. For the *scientia de anima*, see *DV* 10.8, ad 8 s.c.; and *InDA* I.1. Sometimes *scire* is applied to cognition of one's acts, but it is hard to tell whether Aquinas is using the term merely to indicate the certitude of the experience or to indicate quidditative knowledge of the act (as

is an ordinary logical verification, it is clear that it is referenced obliquely elsewhere besides *DV* 10.8 and *ST* Ia.87.1, e.g., in *SCG* 3.46: "We inquire into what the soul is from its acts and objects, by the principles of the speculative sciences.")

Nevertheless, I think there is an interesting reason that in *DV* 10.8 and *ST* Ia.87.1 Aquinas *does* treat judgment of the soul's nature separately. In both cases, his treatment of judgment quotes extensively from Augustine's *DeTrin* 9.6.9, according to which knowledge of the mind's nature is acquired not by gathering information from the senses, but by "beholding inviolable truth, from which we perfectly define to the best of our abilities not what the mind of each man is like, but what sort of mind it *ought* to be in the sempiternal reasons."[59] It is no coincidence, I believe, that earlier in the same two texts (and only in those two texts) Aquinas had referenced Augustine's distinction from a few sentences earlier in *DeTrin* 9.6.9, between a private cognition of what is proper to one's own mind vs. a universally accessible cognition of the definition of the mind "according to species or genus"[60] – a passage that lends authority to Aquinas's main distinction between "cognizing that the soul is" vs. "cognizing what the soul is."

This little detail offers a fascinating glimpse of Aquinas's handling of his sources in a tricky situation. On the one hand, here was a little-known Augustinian text defending the very distinction that Aquinas wished to introduced to the self-knowledge debate as part of a campaign against supraconscious self-knowing. An appeal to *DeTrin* 9.6.9 had the

---

distinguished in the preceding footnote). Nevertheless, for Aquinas, scientifically knowing that one's act proceeds from a certain kind of habit (*scire se habere fidem, gratiam*, etc.) requires that one already cognize the nature of that habit in order to be able to recognize it correctly; in that case, scientific certitude about the reality of the act *as belonging to a certain kind* already implies quidditative knowledge of the habit (see for instance *DV* 10.9 and 10.10, ad 5; *InMet* XII.11; *ST* Ia.87.1; Ia–IIae.112.5, etc.).

[59] Augustine, *DeTrin* 9.6.9 [*CCSL* 50.301]: "Aliterque unusquisque homo loquendo enuntiat mentem suam quid in se ipso agatur attendens; aliter autem humanam mentem speciali aut generali cognitione definit. Itaque cum mihi de sua propria loquitur, utrum intellegat hoc aut illud an non intellegat, et utrum uelit an nolit hoc aut illud, credo; cum uero de humana specialiter aut generaliter uerum dicit, agnosco et approbo. Vnde manifestum est aliud unumquemque uidere in se quod sibi alius dicenti credat, non tamen uideat; aliud autem in ipsa ueritate quod alius quoque possit intueri, quorum alterum mutari per tempora, alterum incommutabili aeternitate consistere. Neque enim oculis corporeis multas mentes uidendo per similitudinem colligimus generalem uel specialem mentis humanae notitiam, sed intuemur inuiolabilem ueritatem ex qua perfecte quantum possumus definiamus non qualis sit uniuscuiusque hominis mens, sed qualis esse sempiternis rationibus debeat."

[60] *DV* 10.8 explicitly cites Augustine; while *ST* Ia.87.1 merely adopts, without attribution, the Augustinian terminology, distinguishing between knowledge of oneself "in the particular" vs. "in the universal" (rather than between knowledge that the soul exists vs. what the soul is, as is Aquinas's more usual practice).

additional advantage of highlighting the similarities between Augustine's account of self-awareness as a private, from-the-inside awareness of acting, and the Aristotelian notion of self-awareness as dependent on a cognition of extramental objects. But practically in the next breath, Augustine outlines an unmistakably illuminationist account of cognizing the soul's nature, not in dependence on sensation, but "by beholding eternal truth," which reveals "what sort of mind it ought to be." For Augustine, to cognize the mind's essence is to be illuminated by the divine idea of Mind in which individual human minds participate, enabling me to know the eternally true definition of Mind.[61] But of course for Aquinas, in contrast, the human mind cognizes its essence "by a species," i.e., by reasoning about its own potential, glimpsed in the act of cognizing extramental objects.

In *DV* 10.8 and *ST* Ia.87.1, then, seeking to enlist the support of *De Trin* 9.6.9 for his main division of self-knowledge without subscribing to its illuminationist account of quidditative self-knowledge, Aquinas deploys his usual tactic for dealing with illuminationist texts: namely, reinterpreting them as references to the light of the mind's own agent intellect. In this case, Augustine's reference to cognizing the mind's nature by beholding divine truth is assimilated to a verificational judgment according to first principles illuminated by the agent intellect, a judgment that grants scientific certitude to one's reasoning about the soul's essence. The "inviolable truth" by which we judge what the soul "ought" to be (*debeat esse*) thus becomes the "likeness of that truth impressed on our mind" (i.e., the habit of first principles), which enables us to "know certain things naturally, such as those that are *per se* known, according to which we examine all other things, judging about all things according to them."[62] For Aquinas, then, the "ought" (*debeat*) in Augustine's cognition of "what the mind ought to be in the eternal reasons" refers to the necessity of one's reasoning about the nature of the soul, not to some ideal essence that individual minds strive to approximate.[63]

Another type of self-knowledge? Putallaz's "reflexion in the strict sense"

We have now examined all the kinds of self-knowledge that Aquinas schematizes: habitual self-awareness, actual self-awareness (which may

---

[61] See note 63 below. [62] *DV* 10.8.
[63] Compare his broader statement about necessity and certitude in *InEthic* VI.3 [Leon. 47/2.340:53–6]: "Sed certa ratio scientiae hinc accipitur, quod omnes suspicamur de eo quod scimus quod non

be implicit or explicit), and the science of the soul with its two stages of apprehension and judgment. But Putallaz has defended the existence of another kind of self-knowledge, which he calls "reflexion in the strict sense" (*réflexion au sens strict*, hereafter "reflexion$_{ss}$"), and which he identifies with what Aquinas names *reditio completa* (the "complete return" from the *Liber de causis*, prop. 15).[64] Reflexion$_{ss}$ consists in a special kind of act in which the intellect grasps its act of understanding some extramental object, and in doing so, recognizes that it has a natural aptitude for this act, i.e., that it is "made to attain that which is true."[65] Putallaz argues that this recognition grounds our everyday judgments; indeed, he goes so far as to say that reflexion$_{ss}$ *just is* the intellect's judgment of its own conformity to its objects (i.e., its judgment of truth, or verificational judgment).[66]

Putallaz makes a strong case that judgment in Aquinas relies on some sort of self-awareness. But there are significant textual and philosophical difficulties with his account of reflexion$_{ss}$ and its proposed epistemological role. Space does not permit detailed analysis of his position here, so I will limit myself to proposing two reasons for rejecting the view that reflexion$_{ss}$ is an additional kind of self-knowledge beyond those we have already seen. (1) Reflexion$_{ss}$ as Putallaz describes it cannot be identified with the "complete return," because the latter involves reaching scientific self-knowledge; (2) Reflexion$_{ss}$ is not convincingly distinguished from actual self-awareness.

In arguing that reflexion$_{ss}$ is identical with Aquinas's "complete return" or *reditio completa*, Putallaz appeals to *DV* 1.9. There, Aquinas explains:

> The intellect cognizes truth by reflecting upon its act, inasmuch as it cognizes not only its act but also its proportion to the thing, which indeed

contingit illud aliter se habere: alioquin non esset certitudo scientis, sed dubitatio opinantis." The interpretation of Augustine in *DV* 10.8 and *ST* Ia.87.1, though forced, is not as distorting as it might seem at first glance. In fact, it has long been a matter of scholarly debate whether for Augustine, illumination applies to the apprehension of essences, or to the judgment of eternal truths, or both. Gilson, for instance, defines Augustinian illumination almost exclusively as a matter of judgment (*The Christian Philosophy of St. Augustine*, ch. 5, especially pp. 84 and 89). O'Daly, however, argues that for Augustine, the Divine light renders both apprehension *and* judgment of eternal truths possible (*Augustine's Philosophy of Mind*, 205–6). For a brief analysis of the scholarly debate, see 206–7, n. 122; as well as the very thorough schema of the nine ways of interpreting Augustine, in F. Cayré, *Initiation à la philosophie de saint Augustin* (Paris: Desclée de Brouwer, 1947), 215–43.

[64] Putallaz, *Le sens de la réflexion*, 148–208. His interpretation is inspired by Boyer's much earlier article, "Le sens d'un texte de Saint Thomas"; but I will focus on Putallaz's better-developed and more philosophically rigorous interpretation here.

[65] Putallaz, *Le sens de la réflexion*, 189–96 and 198–202 (here 199).

[66] See ibid., 182–9, esp. 188. On the judgment of truth, see *InPerierm* I.3 [Leon. 1*/1.17:167–9]; *InMet* VI.4; and *ST* Ia.16.2.

cannot be cognized without cognizing the nature of that act, which cannot be cognized without cognizing the nature of the active principle, which is the intellect itself, whose nature is to conform to things.

The text goes on to explain that the reason intellect – but not sense – can cognize the truth whereby it judges is that intellectual beings are the most perfect entities and thus "return to their essence by a complete return (*reditio completa*)."[67]

But *DV* 1.9 does not equate the "complete return" with the judgment of truth/reflexion$_{ss}$, as Putallaz would have it. Rather, it introduces the "return" as evidence that intellectual beings are fully reflexive; this full reflexivity, in turn, explains why the *intellect* can reflect on its conformity to reality whereas the senses cannot. In fact, as we have already seen in Chapter 2, Aquinas interprets the Neoplatonic complete return in *SLDC* 15 as the achieving of teleological completeness, which occurs when the soul "operationally returns" to itself by knowing (*scire*) its own essence, "completing" the "substantial return" of its self-subsistence.[68] This operational return is clearly a quidditative – or even scientific – self-knowledge.[69] Indeed, *DV* 2.2 and 10.9 confirm that for Aquinas, the complete return is achieved by reasoning discursively from object to act to power to essence, which is precisely the four-stage process for attaining quidditative self-knowledge that we saw earlier in this chapter.[70] The complete return, then, is not a separate kind of self-knowledge, but a condition of perfection achieved by engaging in scientific self-knowledge. Consequently, it cannot be identical with reflexion$_{ss}$, which Putallaz characterizes as a concrete experiential self-cognition, not an abstract quidditative self-knowledge.[71]

Second, I am not convinced by Putallaz's arguments for distinguishing reflexion$_{ss}$ from the actual self-awareness that Aquinas includes in his "standard" kinds of self-knowledge. Putallaz argues that actual

---

[67] *DV* 1.9 [Leon. 22/1.29:22–55]: "[Veritas] cognoscitur autem ab intellectu secundum quod intellectus reflectitur super actum suum, non solum secundum quod cognoscit actum suum sed secundum quod cognoscit proportionem eius ad rem … Cuius ratio est, quia illa quae sunt perfectissima in entibus, ut substantiae intellectuales, redeunt ad essentiam suam reditione completa … sed reditus iste completur secundum quod cognoscunt essentias proprias: unde dicitur in libro De causis quod 'omnis sciens essentiam suam est rediens ad essentiam suam reditione completa.'"

[68] See pp. 57–60 above.

[69] See also Still, "Aquinas's Theory of Human Self-Knowledge," 124–5 and 139.

[70] *DV* 2.2, ad 2; and *DV* 10.9 [Leon. 22/2.328:194–207]: "Sed ista reditio incomplete quidem est in sensu, complete autem in intellectu qui reditione completa redit ad sciendum essentiam suam … Unde actio intellectus nostri primo tendit in ea quae per phantasmata apprehenduntur, et deinde redit ad actum suum cognoscendum; et ulterius in species et habitus et potentias et essentiam ipsius mentis."

[71] Indeed, he describes reflexion$_{ss}$ as the foundation for quidditative self-knowledge (which he calls "abstract analysis"; see *Le sens de la réflexion*, 149 and 166–7).

self-awareness (which he calls "prereflexive consciousness") "is not a distinct act from our vital, affective, or cognitive operations," whereas reflexion_{ss} is a grasp of the intentional operation "in its exercise determined by the other [i.e., the extramental object]."[72] But as we saw in Chapter 6, for Aquinas actual self-awareness is either implicitly embedded in an extramentally directed act, or made explicit by turning one's attention toward oneself as the agent of that act. Aquinas's cognition theory has no way of accommodating two superimposed acts; it is *from within an act* that I attend to that same act itself.[73]

In my view, then, there is no reason to single out the "reflexion on one's act" involved in judgment, and that Putallaz describes as reflexion_{ss}, as a separate kind of self-knowledge. Rather, I would argue that Aquinas's theory of actual self-awareness provides adequate resources for explaining the relationship between verification and intellectual reflexivity. But that task will have to be left for another time.

***

"The soul is intelligible like other things." Aquinas elegantly develops his account of quidditative self-knowledge in conformity with the structure of quidditative knowledge in his general theory of cognition. Throughout, he makes almost no accommodations to the fact that in this case the inquirer is seeking the nature of *his own soul*, a metaphysical principle that is part of him. Even though the soul is itself, definitive knowledge of its nature is just as inaccessible as definitive knowledge of any other nature. The quest for quidditative self-knowledge differs from the quest for quidditative knowledge of other things only in one respect: namely, its starting point is the experience of oneself from the inside in one's acts. It is from these partial glimpses of actualized intellectual potential, revealed in each species-informed act, that the lucky philosopher may eventually be able to put together a complete and distinct picture of the human soul's essence.

---

[72] Ibid., 149, 155–6, and 167.   [73] See Chapter 6, pp. 163–70.

CHAPTER EIGHT

Self-knowledge and psychological personhood

Metaphysical vs. psychological personhood

The preceding chapters have shown that Aquinas's theory of self-knowledge offers a nuanced account of the relevant phenomena by means of a serious, thoughtful, and original appropriation of his Latin, Greek, and Arabic sources. This final chapter adopts a more speculative approach, unfolding the implications of his thought on self-knowledge for what it means to be a self. There is a pervasive assumption that medieval thinkers have only the crudest understanding of subjectivity and selfhood.[1] This assumption has recently been dealt a blow by Alain de Libera, who has shown that the so-called "modern subject" has its roots not in modernity, but in various mid-thirteenth-century models of the mind that spawned the notion of the "subject-as-agent."[2] We can take this idea even further: In Aquinas, this metaphysical view of the subject-as-agent is paired with a psychological view of what it is to be such a subject. As we have seen, in addressing self-knowledge, Aquinas is not merely adding another item to the list of things that we cognize (God, angels, our minds, material essences), but grappling with an experiential tension between self-opacity and privileged self-access in the everyday life of first-person agents. The resulting theory, I argue, opens up possibilities for addressing all sorts of interesting and complex psychological phenomena associated with selfhood.

We will explore three ways in which Aquinas's theory of self-knowledge grounds three key phenomena of selfhood: the subject-viewpoint, the use of the first person, and diachronic unity of consciousness. Aquinas himself does not explicitly discuss any of these phenomena in their own right;

---

[1] See Charles Taylor's seminal *Sources of the Self: The Making of the Modern Identity* (Cambridge, Mass.: Harvard University Press, 1989), which glosses over the medieval period in silence. Similarly, medieval thinkers receive little attention in Richard Sorabji's *Self: Ancient and Modern Insights about Individuality. Life and Death* (University of Chicago Press, 2006).

[2] Alain de Libera, "When Did the Modern Subject Emerge?" *American Catholic Philosophical Quarterly* 82 (2008): 181–220; see also his *Archéologie du sujet* 1, chs. 3 and 4.

but as we shall see, he was aware of them and makes room for them in his theory of self-knowledge. My goal is not to construct complete accounts of them on the basis of his theory of self-knowledge (which would certainly be impossible in such a short space), nor even to analyze how they compare to other possible accounts. Instead, I simply want to excavate the bare bones of what I take to be an interesting and sophisticated approach to human selfhood embedded within his treatment of self-knowledge – particularly in his account of implicit self-awareness – in order to show that there are insights here worth pursuing.

Since Aquinas employs the term "person" differently from his present-day readers, let us begin by clarifying the conceptual framework. The contemporary paradigm for thinking about the human individual as a "person" is primarily psychological, associated with being a self, a subject of experience, a self-conscious agent, an "I."[3] We can call this "psychological personhood" or "selfhood." When Aquinas identifies humans as persons, however, he is making a metaphysical claim: i.e., that a human is (in his famous definition of personhood) "an individual of a rational nature."[4] We can call this "metaphysical personhood." To be a subsisting rational entity is not sufficient for being a person, for Aquinas. Persons must "have the complete nature of the species. Whence a hand or foot cannot be called a hypostasis or person. And in the same way, neither can the soul [be called a person] because it is a part of the human species."[5]

---

[3] For instance, in contemporary ethics, the term "personhood" is frequently equated with the developed capacity to conceive oneself as a distinct individual existing across time. A strain of "personalist" phenomenology tends in the same direction. Crosby, for instance, argues that one ought to study human beings "not only in terms of substance, potentiality, rationality, and the like, but also in terms of subjectivity, that is, in terms such as self-presence, inwardness, self-donation. Only by probing the subjectivity of human beings can we understand them in all their personhood"; see John F. Crosby, *The Selfhood of the Human Person* (Washington, D.C.: The Catholic University of America Press, 1996), 84; relying on Karol Wojtyla, "Subjectivity and the Irreducible in Man," in *Analecta Husserliana*, vol. 7 (Dordrecht: D. Reidel, 1978), 107–14. For an example of how far one could take the notion of subjectivity as definitive of personhood, see Romano Guardini, *The World and the Person*, trans. Stella Lange (Chicago: Regnery, 1965), 216, who even asks, "We can count figures, individuals, personalities – but can we, while doing justice to the concept of 'person,' say 'two persons' and have the statement mean anything?"

[4] See *ST* Ia.29, here a. 3 [Leon. 4.331]: "[P]ersona significat id quod est perfectissimum in tota natura, scilicet subsistens in rationali natura"; and *DP* 9.2. The source is Boethius *Liber de persona et duabus naturis contra Eutychen et Nestorium* III, defining 'person' as "naturae rationabilis individua substantia" (*Opuscula theologica*, ed. C. Moreschini [Leipzig: Saur, 2000], 214). For a discussion of the theological background of Boethius's definition and Aquinas's appropriation and modification thereof, see Joseph W. Koterski, "Boethius and the Theological Origins of the Concept of Person," *American Catholic Philosophical Quarterly* 78 (1994): 203–24; a general summary of the development of the notion of personhood up to Aquinas can be found in Mary T. Clark, "An Inquiry into Personhood," *Review of Metaphysics* 46 (1992): 3–27.

[5] *ST* Ia.75.4, ad 2; see also *Sent* III.5.3.2; III.6.1.1.1, ad s.c.; *SCG* 4.26 and 4.38; and *QDDA* 1.

Thus for Aquinas, although the soul of Socrates can exist separately from the body after death, it is not the *person* of Socrates, because it does not fully express what it is to be human and remains metaphysically incomplete apart from the body.[6]

This theory of metaphysical personhood, of course, raises all sorts of psychological questions about selfhood and personal identity. But Aquinas's texts on personhood remain disappointingly silent about such topics, and his silence can give the impression that he has no theory of selfhood at all. The fact is that it simply does not occur to him to treat selfhood in addressing the metaphysics of the human person. The notion of a reified "Self" – whether a transcendent entity or a mere epiphenomenal bundle – is still centuries away in the future. He thus does not conceive of a Self as a *psychological entity associated with the human individual*; for him, there is simply the human individual Socrates, who instantiates a complete rational nature.[7]

Nevertheless, Aquinas is fully aware that the intellectual activity of such "individuals of a rational nature" manifests what one might call *attributes of selfhood*: subjectivity, the first person, a sense of personal identity existing across time, etc. His texts on "the person" are simply not the place to look for his account of psychological personhood, nor even for any hint that he recognizes metaphysical persons as enjoying a unique mode of experience. Instead, I propose that such an account is rather to be found in his theory of self-awareness, because for him, the structure of self-awareness is the basis for the human knower's approaching the world as a single, stable "I." As we will see, in the rare instances in which readers of Aquinas have drawn implications for selfhood from his theory of self-awareness, they have focused on habitual self-awareness. But I will contend that it

---

[6] *ST* Ia.29.1, ad 5 [Leon. 4.328]: "[A]nima est pars humanae speciei, et ideo, licet sit separata, quia tamen retinet naturam unibilitatis, non potest dici substantia individua quae est hypostasis vel substantia prima; sicut nec manus, nec quaecumque alia partium hominis. Et sic non competit ei neque definitio personae, neque nomen"; Ia.75.4, ad 2; *InCor I* 15.2; *DP* 9.2, ad 14. On the human soul's metaphysical orientation toward matter, see for instance *SCG* 2.80–1; and *QDDA* 1, ad 10. Note that Aquinas distinguishes two senses in which something can be called a subsistent or "this something" (*hoc aliquid*): i.e., simply insofar as it subsists, or insofar as it is a "complete subsistent in the nature of some species" (see *ST* Ia.75.2, ad 1; *QDDA* 1). When he describes the soul as subsisting or a *hoc aliquid*, then, he means it in the first sense; see B. Carlos Bazán, "The Human Soul: Form *and* Substance? Thomas Aquinas's Critique of Eclectic Aristotelianism," *Archives d'histoire doctrine et littéraire du moyen âge* 64 (1997): 95–126 (here at 122–6). For the scholarly debate on the status of the separated soul in Aquinas, see p. 90, note 80 above.

[7] Nevertheless, metaphysical and psychological personhood are related in Aquinas. Human nature implies selfhood at the appropriate stage of development (barring trauma to the brain), and selfhood belongs to the human being precisely because one of the constituents of human nature, the rational soul, is immaterial and therefore reflexive.

is *implicit actual self-awareness*, grounded in his view of the immateriality and receptivity of the human intellect, that provides the access point to his thought on selfhood.

The subject-viewpoint: the self and the other

Chapter 6 discussed the phenomenon of the duality of conscious thought: Subject and object are indissociably co-manifested in relation to each other, in a single intentional act of intellect. (For instance, when I am thinking about the toad explicitly, I implicitly grasp myself; conversely, when I explicitly notice myself in that act, I implicitly grasp the toad.) Now, however, we can take a closer look at a peculiar facet of this experience, which we can call "the subject-viewpoint." Whether I am thinking about myself-as-toad-thinker, or thinking about toad-as-manifest-to-me, a clear distinction is preserved between myself as subject and the toad as object. I never confuse the toad with myself, despite the fact that both of us are co-manifested in the same cognition. This distinction is so basic to our experience that it is hard even to imagine how things could be otherwise. Yet at first glance there seems to be nothing in the content of my cognition that would consistently guarantee that subject and object are never confused. Why do the tree, the coffee mug, the dog, all consistently appear in my experience as "other," i.e., as *not me*? And why do I consistently appear in my own experience as their cognizer, i.e., as *not any of those things*? The bright line between subject and object in ordinary experience is what makes it possible to have a "viewpoint" from which one experiences reality. In fact, to have a subject-viewpoint is to have an inerrant sense of who is performing the thinking ("I") and what is being thought of ("it"), experiencing each in relation to the other.[8]

We can find a way of accounting for this subject-viewpoint in the considerations that led Aquinas to his theory of implicit self-awareness. The reason that I perceive myself in *all* my acts is that in receiving any intelligible species the human intellect thereby gains its own intelligible actuality (see Chapter 6). This single intelligible actuality is bipolar, establishing a relation between the one cognizing and what is cognized. Accordingly, the only way that I appear to myself experientially is *as the one cognizing something*; conversely, the only way that things appear to me experientially is *as*

---

[8] Or in interpersonal perception, as "you," a point that I will not address here, as I have not found an account of it in Aquinas.

things that are cognized by me.[9] (This is why Aquinas takes self-awareness to be a perception of oneself-as-agent, and not as a bare self, as we saw in Chapter 4.) Consequently, subject and object are necessarily conceived as correlatives, like double and half, part and whole, or father and son. For Aquinas, to be aware of some entity, implicitly or explicitly, is to be aware of it as "other," which is just to say that it is *not-me, because it is being cognized by me.* Conversely, to be aware of myself, implicitly or explicitly, is to be aware of myself as subject, which is just to say that I am *not-that, because I am the one cognizing that.*[10] The correlativity of the subject and object, experienced over against each other, is what gives me a "viewpoint" as subject, from which I cognize everything that I cognize. (Incidentally, this means that Aquinas would reject Plotinus's claim that an experience can be so absorbing that one loses the sense of oneself as subject.[11]) As Wilhelmsen observes: "To be conscious is to be conscious of another. Consciousness, in Thomistic terms, is always relation and the term of the relation is the other."[12]

A benefit of this relational approach to subjectivity is that it sidesteps the concern that by thinking explicitly about oneself, one would "object-ify" the self, making it into something foreign and third-personal, or per-haps a bare entity for introspection. Concern to avoid this objectification leads Putallaz, for instance, to deny that there can be a properly explicit self-awareness in which I become the object of my own cognitive acts.[13] Objectification becomes a problem, however, only when one assumes that to think about something as "the object of cognition" is necessarily

---

[9] See *ST* Ia.III.I, ad 3 (for Latin text, p. 205, note 18 below); *InEthic* III.3 [Leon. 47/1.127:165–7]: "[M]anifes-tum est, quod non potest ignorare quis sit operans, quia sic ignoraret se ipsum, quod est impossibile."

[10] This is not to say, however, that for Aquinas we are "conscious of [the self as] not another 'thing' (with a form) but a 'nothing,' a lack of form, a 'not being' the form of what is known," as Wang proposes (*Aquinas and Sartre*, 73). The relationality that defines the experienced difference between subject and object does not mean that we have only negative knowledge of the subject, as I have argued in Chapters 4 and 6.

[11] See for instance Plotinus *Ennead* VI.9. This premise is commonly raised as an objection to duality-of-consciousness views (see for instance Lambert, *Self Knowledge in Thomas Aquinas*, 118–19). But in fact Aquinas insists that even in the most powerful of all experiences of the Divine, the beatific vision, the angels and separated souls cognize other things without being thereby distracted from their experience of God, because union with God is of a different order from other cognitive acts and is the *ratio* for all these lesser acts (*Quodl* 9.4.2 [Leon. 25/1.104:75–85]).

[12] Frederick D. Wilhelmsen, "The 'I' and Aquinas," *Proceedings of the American Catholic Philosophical Association* 51 (1977): 47–54; and Reichmann, "The 'Cogito' in St. Thomas."

[13] "In reality, in every act of cognition, there is no other object than the entramental thing; the 'self' is not an ob-ject [*ob-jet*]; it is not conceived as other" (Putallaz, *Le sens de la réflexion*, 111, my transla-tion; see also 166–7). Compare to the similar interpretation adopted by Pasnau to distance Aquinas from a Lockean theory of introspection (*Thomas Aquinas on Human Nature*, 343–47), as discussed on pp. 166–9.

to conceive it as 'other' than oneself (not-me) – whereas from Aquinas's perspective, something is conceived as 'other' only *against the backdrop* of the subject. Consequently, I *cannot* think about myself as other, because even when I direct my attention explicitly to myself, I still grasp myself in relation to some extramental intelligible, as the one cognizing that thing. Certainly when I think about myself, I am the "object" of my own cognition in the sense of being the terminus of attention, the *id quod cognoscitur*. But Aquinas would deny that this entails perceiving myself as 'not-myself,' an abstract third-person 'other.' Whether a given act is directed towards the intellect itself or towards the other, this dimension of duality remains.[14]

In Aquinas, then, intellectuality entails the capacity to experience the world from one's own "viewpoint" as subject, because intellectual cognition is always ineliminably twofold, illuminating the knowing intellect and its known object in relation to each other.[15] The necessary correlation of subject and other in intellectual cognition opens up a new perspective on intellectual intentionality as Aquinas construes it. If subject and other are necessarily experienced correlatively, then not only do we experience ourselves subjectively in contrast to the "other," but also the reverse, i.e., we experience the other as object of thought in contrast to ourselves as subjects. In other words, not only does every intellectual act include self-awareness, but its *inclusion of self-awareness is essential to its intentionality*.[16] To attend to items in the world around us is to grasp them as other, as Aquinas points out: "To intend means stretching, as it were, toward something other (*Intendere enim dicitur, quasi in aliud tendere*)."[17] To

---

[14] Dhavamony unfolds a similar view in *Subjectivity and Knowledge*, 82–3, esp. n. 113, although he denies that the intellect is the object of cognition on the assumption that 'objects' are grasped "as *aliud in aliud*" (82). As I use the term here, 'object' simply refers to the terminus of attention.

[15] Interestingly, this seems to be true not only for the human intellect, but for higher intellects as well, though in different ways. At the bottom of the intellectual hierarchy the human intellect, which is like prime matter in its potency to form, is only illuminated to itself when it is actualized in cognizing some other entity. Aquinas holds that the reverse is true for the pure intellectual actuality at the pinnacle of the intellectual hierarchy, i.e., God, whose very essence is an act of self-cognition that includes a cognition of all creatures insofar as he cognizes the ways that the divine essence can be imitated; see *ST* 1a.14.5 [Leon. 5.172]: "Deus seipsum videt in seipso, quia seipsum videt per essentiam suam. Alia autem a se videt non in ipsis, sed in seipso, inquantum essentia sua continet similitudinem aliorum ab ipso."

[16] One might compare Kriegel's approach to consciousness in *Subjective Consciousness*; see also the discussion in *Self-Representational Approaches to Consciousness*, ed. Kriegel and Williford.

[17] *Sent* II.38.1.3; *ST* Ia–IIae.12.5. Note that in both texts Aquinas restricts the proper meaning of *intendere* to appetitive acts, which strive for an end not yet attained. But since elsewhere he frequently describes intellectual attention as the intellect's *intentio* (see p. 164, note 85 above), it seems that he holds for an analogous sense in which the intellectual act "tends toward another" – not in the sense that the intelligible object is not yet attained (since the intellectual operation is precisely the act of being united with the intelligible object), but in the sense that the object is the target toward which attention is directed. See Perler, *Théories de l'intentionnalité*, 8.

perceive something as 'other' is precisely to perceive it in relation to one-self: "Whoever understands or is illuminated cognizes himself to understand or be illuminated; because he cognizes the thing to be manifest to himself."[18] Conversely, to perceive 'myself' is to perceive the first-person subject in relation to the third-person other. Thus while the intelligible species determines what I am thinking about in a given intentional act (triangles or trees), the experience of thinking *as intentionally directed toward something* originates from the bipolarity of the act: Triangularity or tree-ness is manifest *to me*.[19] To be a subject is precisely to be that to which something is manifest; conversely, to be manifest is precisely to be manifest to a subject.

The first person

Not only are the subject and the other experienced in relation to each other, but the subject is experienced in *the first person*, as "I" distinct from the other, "it." As we saw in Chapter 4, Aquinas avoids the problems posed by indirect self-awareness (which would eviscerate the possibility of cognition in the first person), by casting self-awareness as a direct experience of oneself acting. And as we saw in Chapter 3, Aquinas clearly construes self-awareness as having first-personal content, a position that we have accepted at face value so far. But we can now investigate why, in his view, self-awareness has a first-person character. Mere correlativity does not prevent two correlatives from being experienced in the third person as "it" and "it."[20] So why, in ordinary cases at least,[21] is one member of the "subject–other" pair of correlatives experienced in the first person, as "I"?

---

[18] *ST* Ia.III.I, ad 3 [Leon. 5.516]: "[E]x parte rei intellectae … quicumque intelligit vel illuminatur, cognoscit se intelligere vel illuminari; quia cognoscit rem sibi esse manifestam."

[19] Thus I would agree with Brower and Brower-Toland that intentionality is an irreducible feature of mental acts in Aquinas, although I do not think this notion can be separated from his account of cognition by formal identity, as they propose ("Aquinas on Mental Representation," 225ff., which provides a helpful overview of other approaches to intentionality in Aquinas; see also the studies by Haldane, Owens, Stump, Black, King, Pasnau, Panaccio, and O'Callaghan, cited on p. 153 above, note 56).

[20] Recall Martin's critique that "nothing that Aquinas says shows how my awareness of my act of understanding can be either an awareness that the act is *my* act or that it is an act of *understanding*" ("Self-Knowledge and Cognitive Ascent," 98–9, discussed in Chapter 4), pp. 98–109.

[21] Schizophrenia sometimes involves referring to oneself in the third person, though it is not clear whether the patient actually experiences himself this way. Louis Arnorsson Sass, "Self and World in Schizophrenia: Three Classic Approaches," *Philosophy, Psychiatry, and Psychology* 8 (2001): 251–68, argues that schizophrenia involves an excessively heightened self-awareness; see the other articles in this issue for interesting discussions of this question from a phenomenological perspective.

Some readers have interpreted habitual self-awareness as the key to the first-person character of our experience in Aquinas.[22] Now certainly habitual self-awareness is necessary for the *directness* of self-awareness; and direct self-awareness is necessary for the first-person character of our cognition. But mere aptitude or habituation for perceiving oneself is not enough to explain why we perceive ourselves *in the first person*. After all, habits for cognizing extramental objects generate acts of cognizing them as third-person objects. Why should a habit for cognizing one's own intellect be any different?

In my view, Aquinas's account of the reflexivity of immaterial acts provides a more fruitful approach to the first-personal character of experience. The first-person character of self-awareness (whether implicit or explicit) is the experiential manifestation of the completely reflexive character of intellectual cognition. As we already saw in Chapter 6, even in explicitly thinking about myself, for Aquinas, I do not "stand outside" myself and look back on myself in a second-order act directed at a first-order act. There simply is no outside vantage point from which the intellect could look at itself as "other." Consequently, if the intellect is to cognize itself at all, it must cognize itself from the *inside*. (By analogy, one could imagine that a self-seeing eye would have to see itself from the inside, not by getting some sort of outside perspective on itself.) This necessarily "insider" character is arguably experienced as the first person, giving self-awareness the feel of intimate, privileged self-access.

For Aquinas, this sort of insider self-appropriation is possible only for immaterial powers like intellect and will. Following Avicenna and the *Liber de causis*,[23] he points out that corporeal entities and powers, on account of their extension in matter, cannot return to themselves completely. Each part of a body can turn back upon another part (as when I touch my head), but not upon itself, since matter is extended and has parts outside of parts. Only an indivisible and incorporeal being can be made wholly present to itself since it has no parts that get in the way of each other. What is immaterial can be placed in contact, so to speak, with the whole of itself.[24] And in fact this complete self-reversion occurs, at

---

[22] Goehring, for instance, cites habitual self-awareness as the source of "the ability to attribute acts or functions to myself" ("St. Thomas Aquinas on Self-Knowledge," 11); Gardeil likewise states that "without habitual consciousness, the soul would doubtless attain the principle of its acts by actual reflexion, but it could not grasp itself directly, experience itself as this principle, and say 'It is *I* who am thinking'" ("Perception expérimentale," 220, translation mine; see also 226–7).

[23] See *Liber de causis* 7 and 15, and Avicenna, *Liber de anima* V.2 [Van Riet, 2.93–4].

[24] *SLDC* 7 [Saffrey, 52]: "Et haec quidem probatio hic subditur satis confuse, cum dicitur: *Et significatio quidem illius*, scilicet quod intelligentia non sit corpus, *est reditio super essentiam suam*, id est quia convertitur supra seipsam intelligendo se, quod convenit sibi quia non est corpus vel

least implicitly, whenever the intellect is thinking about anything: "The intellect reflects upon itself by acting, for it understands itself not part-by-part, but according to the whole."[25] The intellect *must* take a first-person perspective of itself: in perceiving itself, it cannot step outside itself and perceive itself as other, because it simply cannot leave any of itself behind to look at from outside.[26]

Underlying this approach to first-person cognition is the claim that in its acts the whole mind grasps itself *as a whole*, rather than one part grasping another part. It is difficult to understand what it means for an immaterial being to see itself acting from the inside, since our experience of material objects offers no comparable examples. But for Aquinas, we experience this kind of full reflexivity when we perceive our own existence or cognize the mind's essence; and to be immaterial is precisely to be capable of performing such acts. The mechanics of this "from-the-inside" self-awareness can also be understood in terms of Aquinas's identity account of implicit self-awareness. As seen in Chapter 6, for Aquinas the possible intellect is informed by the species-in-act in a matter–form relationship, together constituting the intellect-in-act (Intellect) that is the intelligible-in-act (Intelligible). Because it is the matter or subject in this Intellect/Intelligible, the intellect is manifested in cognition *differently* than the extramental object, as the one cognizing, the thinker – regardless of where attention is directed. The difference between the fixed roles of the intellect and the extramental object in actualizing the Intellect/Intelligible is, perhaps, experientially manifested by the distinction between the first and third person.

Unity of consciousness across time

Not only do we have a subject-viewpoint in which the subject itself is experienced in the first person as "I," but that "I-viewpoint" remains consistent and stable throughout one's experience – a phenomenon known

---

magnitudo habens unam partem ab alia distantem. Et hoc est quod subdit: *scilicet quia non extenditur*, extentione scilicet magnitudinis, *cum re extensa*, id est magnitudinem habente, *ita* quod *sit una suarum extremitatum secunda ab alia*, id est ordine situs ab alia distincta." See also *Sent* I.17.1.5, ad 3; *Sent* II.19.1.1; *Sent* III.23.1.2, ad 3; *DV* 1.9; *DV* 10.9; *SCG* 2.49; *InDA* II.26; *SLDC* 15; and for discussion, Ruane, "Self-Knowledge and the Spirituality of the Soul," 40–2. Interestingly, in the texts from *Sent*, Aquinas denies that the senses have any reflexivity whatsoever, whereas in the texts from *DV* he affirms that the senses can reflect "partially" on their own acts, but not on themselves.

[25] *SCG* 2.49 [Leon. 13.381]: "Intellectus autem supra seipsum agendo reflectitur: intelligit enim seipsum non secundum partem, sed secundum totum. Non est igitur corpus"; *ST* Ia.93.7, ad 2 [Leon. 5.409]: "Sed quia mens, etsi se totam quodammodo cognoscat, etiam quodammodo se ignorat, prout scilicet est ab aliis distincta."

[26] As Galen Strawson argues, there is "no such thing as the use [of the word 'I'] merely 'as object'"; see *Selves: An Essay in Revisionary Metaphysics* (Oxford University Press, 2009), 32.

as the diachronic unity of consciousness. There is a basic continuity in my experiences, insofar as I experience and remember them as *mine*. The same "I" appears as the subject of all my conscious acts across time. Each individual perception takes its place in a larger web of personal experience that is tied together by belonging to one and the same subject across time. But how exactly are these disparate experiences held together?[27]

Aquinas's account of habitual self-awareness has seemed to some readers to provide an answer: The soul's native aptitude for self-awareness binds together all our experiences.[28] Here again, it seems to me that this line of reasoning leads to a dead end. Habitual self-awareness is certainly essential to the psychological structure that makes unity of consciousness possible, given its role in facilitating implicit self-awareness.[29] But habitual self-awareness by itself does not explain why I perceive myself as *one and the same "I"* across all these acts, experiencing things from a single continuous viewpoint. To trace diachronic unity to habitual self-awareness is essentially to argue that my acts are unified because they all proceed from the same mind – that is to say, I *perceive* all my experiences as belonging to a single "I," because they *do* belong to a single "I." The identity of the source in itself does not seem adequate to secure the *experience* of continuity among all my acts.

I contend that an account of diachronically unified consciousness can be found, instead, in Aquinas's account of implicit self-awareness as the

---

[27] Philosophical approaches to the diachronic unity of consciousness have varied widely. One general strategy is to posit a single all-encompassing matrix of awareness into which individual conscious acts are set, like the essentially self-knowing soul of Avicenna's Flying Man (*Liber de anima* I.1 and V.7), the perpetually available self discovered in Descartes's *Cogito* (*Meditation* 2), or Kant's transcendental unity of apperception (*Critique of Pure Reason*, A104–10). Another strategy is to look for some property that "bundles" multiple experiences, à la Hume (*Treatise on Human Understanding* I.IV). Galen Strawson has argued against long-lasting diachronic unity, in favor of the view of the human self as a string of consecutive selves (see his *Selves*).

[28] See Echavarría, who argues that "the true root of self-identity is found in the soul, which always remembers itself (habitually), and which is always ready … to recognize itself (actually) at every moment" ("Memoria e identidad," 110–11, my translation); and McKian, "Metaphysics of Introspection," 105. Some of these interpretations tend toward making habitual self-awareness into an undifferentiated background self-awareness; see Rabeau, Species, Verbum, 90: "The actual grasp of the *species* is, in fact, surrounded by the habitual cognition of my soul, as though by a halo. If there were only the presence of a *species* – immobile, limited, exclusive – there would be no cognition of myself"; and Tomar Romero, "La *memoria* como conocimiento," 104: "This third Augustinian faculty of memory is recognized by St. Thomas as *self-cognition*. Consequently, memory is not so much a particular faculty of the subject, but a general faculty of *self-presence*, that is, the constancy of the psychic subject in its self-identity across time, as principle of its activity and substrate for its becoming" (my translations). But regardless of the philosophical plausibility of such an approach, it cannot be attributed to Aquinas, for whom habitual self-awareness is not an undifferentiated background awareness (the latter view is closer to an Avicennian supraconscious self-knowing).

[29] See Chapter 6, p. 172.

foundation for the possibility of memory in an intellect that transcends temporality.[30] This account offers resources to fulfil what I take to be two key conditions for obtaining diachronic unity of consciousness: (1) Each present and past act must be cognized, not as bare acts, but as belonging to a subject (the ownership of acts condition); (2) The subject of those past and present acts must be perceived as a single identical subject, the present "I" (the continuity of ownership condition).

The ownership of acts condition is satisfied by the contribution of implicit self-awareness to Aquinas's theory of intellectual memory.[31] According to Aquinas, to remember something is to store and apprehend it under the aspect of *having-been-previously-cognized-by-me*: "Memory is of things that are past with respect to our apprehension, namely, we have previously sensed or understood things, whether those things considered in themselves exist in the present or not."[32] Thus even though intelligibles (e.g., triangularity) are in themselves indifferent to time, they can be objects of intellectual memory insofar as they are conceived as objects of my previous act of cognition. There is no "past or present" Pythagorean theorem, strictly speaking, but I can *remember* it insofar as I *think of it as something I cognized before*, as Aquinas explains in *ST* Ia.79.6, ad 2:

> As for an act, [its] being-past can be grasped by the intellect just as well as by the sense. For the understanding of our soul is a particular act, existing in this or that time, according to which as a man is said to understand now

---

[30] I here sketch his account only briefly; for a more detailed analysis and comparison to Augustine, see my "Diachronically Unified Consciousness in Augustine and Aquinas," *Vivarium* 50 (2012): 554–81.

[31] For Aquinas, the human being has two retentive powers: intellectual memory, which is the possible intellect insofar as it retains previously understood intelligible essences, and imaginative memory, which retains previously sensed particulars (see p. 10 above). The main texts on imaginative memory and intellectual memory in Aquinas are *Sent* 1.3.4.1, *DV* 10.2–3, *ST* Ia.79.6–7, *Quodl* 3.9.1, and *InDMR* (for intellectual memory esp. c. 2). For discussion of imaginative memory, see Stump, *Aquinas*, ch. 8; and Pasnau, *Thomas Aquinas on Human Nature*, 280–1. For intellectual memory, see Klubertanz, *The Discursive Power*, 160–2; J. Castonguay, *Psychologie de la mémoire: sources et doctrine de la memoria chez saint Thomas d'Aquin*, 1st edn (Montreal: Lévrier, 1963); Marcos F. Manzanedo, *La imaginación y la memoria según santo Tomás* (Rome: Herder, 1978), 275–382; Merriell, *To the Image of the Trinity* (which returns throughout to the ways in which Aquinas develops Augustine's account of memory); Héctor Hernando Salinas, "El problema de la memoria intelectiva en Tomás de Aquino," *Universitas Philosophica* 42 (2004): 87–115; Schell, "La doctrina tomista de la *memoria* espiritual"; and Kevin White, notes to *Commentaries on Aristotle's "On Sense and What is Sensed" and "On Memory and Recollection,"* trans. Kevin White and Edward M. Macierowski (Washington, DC: The Catholic University of America Press, 2005). For discussion of the relation between memory and personal identity, see Echavarría, "Memoria e identidad," 91–112.

[32] *InDMR* 1 [Leon. 45/2.106:161–77]: "*Semper enim, cum* anima memoratur, pronunciat se *prius* audiuisse aliquid uel sensisse uel intellexisse ... Set intentio Philosophi est dicere quod memoria est preteritorum quantum ad nostram apprehensionem, id est quod prius sensimus uel intelleximus aliqua, indifferenter siue ille res secundum se considerate sunt in presenti siue non."

or yesterday or tomorrow. And this is not incompatible with intellectuality, because to know in this way, although it is a certain particular, is yet
an immaterial act ... and therefore just as the intellect understands itself,
although it is itself a certain singular intellect, so too it understands its
understanding, which is a singular act existing in the past or in the present
or in the future. Therefore in this way the account (*ratio*) of memory as
concerning past things, is preserved in the intellect insofar as it understands
itself to have understood previously, but [it is not preserved] insofar as it
understands the past thing precisely as being here and now.[33]

Aquinas explains that to remember an intellectual object is to understand
it *as the object of my past intellectual act*. Elsewhere, he carefully specifies
what it means for the activity of an immaterial intellect to exist in the
past or present. Intellectual acts are not temporal, in the sense that due to
their indivisibility, they have no duration (except accidentally on account
of their connection to the physical phantasm in the imagination).[34]
Nevertheless, they do have temporality in the restricted sense of occurring
in a sequence of priority and posteriority.[35] In cognizing an intelligible
object (*A*) as the object of a past act, then, I recognize that *A* was cognized
by an act that is prior to my present act in the sequence of my thoughts.

[33] *ST* Ia.79.6, ad 2. Note his admission here that in one sense, the character (*ratio*) of memory is not
preserved in the intellect insofar as its objects are not in themselves timebound (see also *DV* 10.2;
and *InDMR* 2). Some take this too far to argue that intellectual memory is memory only ana-
logically (see Castonguay, *Psychologie de la mémoire*, 182–4; Salinas, "El problema de la memoria
intelectiva," 106–7). I read Aquinas, rather, as acknowledging that in common usage memory is
considered as the power of remembering *past things* as objects of a past cognition, but that its minimal defining feature from a philosophical perspective is the manifesting of something as the object
of a past cognition (as stated in *DV* 10.2, ad 2 s.c., and repeatedly throughout *InDMR*).
[34] On the indivisibility of intellectual acts, see for instance *InDA* III.5. On the connection to duration via the imagination, see *InDMR* 2 [Leon. 45/2.108:51–7]: "*[N]ichil* homo potest *intelligere
sine continuo* <et> tempore. Quod quidem accidit in quantum nichil potest homo intelligere sine
fantasmate: fantasma enim oportet quod sit cum continuo et tempore, eo quod est similitudo rei
singularis que est hic et nunc"; *SCG* I.102 [Leon. 13.268]: "Divinum autem intelligere est absque
successione totum simul aeternaliter existens: nostrum autem intelligere successionem habet,
inquantum adiungitur ei per accidens continuum et tempus." On cognition of time generally, see
InDMR 2 [Leon. 45/2.109:127–30]: "[T]empus autem cognoscitur in quantum cognoscitur prius et
posterius in motu; unde hec tria sensu percipi possunt"; and *InPhys* IV.16–17, especially 17 [Leon.
2.203]: "Et hoc ideo, quia tempus nihil aliud est quam *numerus motus secundum prius et posterius*:
tempus enim percipimus, ut dictum est, cum numeramus prius et posterius in motu."
[35] *ST* Ia.85.4, ad 1 [Leon. 5.339]: "[I]ntellectus est supra tempus quod est numerus motus corporalium
rerum. Sed ipsa pluralitas specierum intelligibilium causat vicissitudinem quandam intelligibilium
operationum, secundum quam una operatio est prior altera. Et hanc vicissitudinem Augustinus
nominat tempus, cum dicit, VIII super Gen. ad Litt., quod *Deus movet creaturam spiritualem per
tempus.*" On intellectual "time" in Aquinas, see Steven Snyder, "Thomas Aquinas and the Reality
of Time," *Sapientia* 55 (2000): 371–84; J.J. Macintosh, "St. Thomas on Angelic Time and Motion,"
The Thomist 59 (1995): 547–75. Armand Maurer offers an intriguing reflection on the way in which
human beings exist and act in time, with special emphasis on Aquinas, in "Time and the Person,"
Proceedings of the American Catholic Philosophical Association 53 (1979): 182–93.

Implicit self-awareness plays an important role in this theory of intellectual memory. The reason that I now recall *A* as previously-cognized-by-me is precisely that I first cognized *A* as manifest *to me*, as the object of *my* present thought. Implicit self-awareness is so thoroughly part of my understanding of *A* that the habitually retained species of *A* is stamped, so to speak, with a reference to myself cognizing *A* in that act. As we saw in Chapter 6, in manifesting *A* the species also manifests the Intellect-thinking-about-*A*, insofar as the species is instantiated in the thinking Intellect as its form. Thus the habitually retained species does not merely store bare *A*, but *A*-as-understood-by-me-then. When I think about *A* again later, it appears to me under the aspect of that relation to my intellect in a prior act.[36] In other words, "remembering the Pythagorean theorem" involves *the intellect's grasping the theorem not only as manifested to me now, but as having been manifested to me previously, i.e., as the object of two intellectual acts under the aspect of their relation of priority and posteriority.*[37] Because implicit reference to the thinker is embedded in all intellectual cognition in such a way as to be retained and recalled via the corresponding species, Aquinas's theory of self-awareness meets the ownership of acts condition.

But how is this memory of A-as-previously-understood-by-me unified with my experience of *myself* as the one presently remembering? As the continuity of ownership condition stipulates, in order to have diachronically unified consciousness I must perceive my past and present acts as belonging to one and the same subject, the *presently experiencing or remembering me*. Now one way of fulfilling this condition would be to posit that diachronic unity relies on a judgment of identity, as follows: (1) via

---

[36] *InDMR* 4 [Leon. 45/2.118:110–17]: "[R]eminiscentia non est resumptio memórie, *sed cum resumit* aliquis id quod *prius* scivit vel sensit sensu proprio vel communi, *cuius habitum* dicimus esse *memoriam* (sicut enim memorari refertur ad prius factam noticiam, ita et reminisci), *et tunc est reminisci*, scilicet cum aliquo modo resumimus priorem apprehensionem"; and 1 [Leon. 45/2.105:150–106:162]: "*Cum* aliquis autem habet *scienciam* habitualem et potenciam sensituam *sine actibus uel operibus* eorum, tunc dicitur memorari preteritorum actuum, puta cum considerauit intellectu triangulum habere tres angulos *duobus rectis equales* et forte sensibiliter descriptionem figure uidit: et ex parte *quidem* operationis intellectualis memoratur aliquis *quia didicit* ab alio uel quia *speculatus* est per se ipsum, ex parte *uero* sensibilis apprehensionis memoratur quia *audiuit* uel *uidit* uel aliquo alio sensu percepit. *Semper enim, cum* anima memoratur, pronunciat se *prius* audiuisse aliquid uel sensisse uel intellexisse."

[37] See *InDMR* 2, here discussing imaginative memory [Leon. 45/2.109:159–65]: "[A]d memoriam autem pertinet apprehensio temporis secundum determinationem quandam, secundum scilicet distanciam in preterito ab hoc presenti nunc; unde per se pertinet memoria ad apparitionem fantasmatis, per accidens autem ad iudicium intellectus." This could be applied to intellectual acts if "distance from the present" (which implies duration) is replaced with "order prior to the present"; see p. 210, note 35 above.

intellectual memory, I remember the "past me" (S_{-1}) as the subject of a past act (C_{-1}); (2) I perceive the "present me" (S_0) as the subject of a present act (C_0); (3) I perceive that S_{-1} is identical with S_0. Here one encounters two subjects, a past and a present subject, and judges that both are identical. While the reliability of this identity judgment could be called into question, one might perhaps respond that the possibility of memory presupposes a basic intellectual ability to perceive identity reliably.

The notion of distinguishing past subjects from the present subject, however, is not congruent with Aquinas's conception of the intellect as not subject to time except accidentally insofar as it is bound to the imagination. It is hard to see what the notion of "past vs. present selves" would even mean for such a theory. Interestingly, in the text cited above from *ST* Ia.79.6, ad 2, he insists upon the pastness of the intellectual *act*, without ever suggesting that the *thinking intellect* can be construed as past or present in itself:

> The understanding of our soul is a particular act, existing in this or that time, according to which a man is said to understand now or yesterday or tomorrow … Just as the intellect understands itself, although it is a certain singular intellect, so too it understands its understanding, which is a singular act existing in the past or in the present or in the future.

In concluding his argument, Aquinas again emphasizes that the key to intellectual memory is not the apprehension of things-as-past (among which we might include the subject itself) but past *acts*, thus things-as-objects-of-past-acts: "The intellect understands itself to have understood before (*se prius intellexisse*)."[38] I would argue that the "itself" refers to the intellect's *present* self (S_0) rather than to some past self (S_{-1}) that must then be identified with S_0.[39]

A way of satisfying the continuity of ownership condition in a way that is consistent with Aquinas's thinking on the intellect, then, could look something like this: Although I apprehend the pastness of the act C_{-1} in which A was previously manifested to me, I do not apprehend it as the act of a *past subject*, S_{-1}, which must be then be identified with myself, the present subject S_0. Instead, I apprehend it as the past act of *my present self – my* past act, where the first-person pronoun refers to myself, S_0. In other words, the problem of

---

[38] See *ST* Ia.79.6, ad 2 (pp. 209–10 above), as well as *InDMR* 1 (p. 209, note 32 above).

[39] Knasas seems to have something like this in mind when he says, "For Aquinas the psychic situation is read in substrate-determination terms. One introspectively experiences not a bundle of perceptions, but a multitude of acts of one subject. Since the subject lasts despite the varying acts in and of the subject, there is no need to enlist the imagination to connect discrete 'bundles'" (*Being and Some Twentieth-Century Thomists*, 88, n. 28). I would add that this subject is always present-tense.

how to identify the past subject, S_{-1}, with the present subject, S_0, is actually a false problem. Intellectual memory is only possible in the first place if a single subject-perspective, that of S_0, encompasses C_{-1} and C_0, grasping their order in the sequence of one's mental acts.[40] Such an account of diachronically unified consciousness would involve not the identification of successively experienced "selves," but the experience of a single trans-temporal subject anchoring past and present acts. Thus when I articulate my experience of remembering *A* ("I remember that I learned *A* before"), *both* first-person pronouns have the same referent, the present speaker S_0. Similarly, when I say, "I should not have eaten so much dinner," I ascribe responsibility to myself, the *present subject*, not some past subject whose blame I am shouldering in the present.

For Aquinas, then, the intellectual soul is the unifying principle of the human being, not only metaphysically, but also psychologically. As a hylomorphic entity, the human being exists in time.[41] Nevertheless, the human intellectual soul is not swept along by the flux of time, but has a sort of fixity or stability, as an immaterial, self-subsisting entity. The self-aware intellect is like a root sticking out into a river, a single subject-perspective upon which bits of time-bound flotsam are caught, the past and present preserved in the sequential order of acts of a single subject. Collecting these time-bound experiences, it holds them together in a temporal sequence, according to a single unifying viewpoint.

***

It is not habitual self-awareness, then, but rather implicit self-awareness that is mainly responsible for the various phenomena characteristic of psychological personhood in Aquinas. Habitual self-awareness contributes to psychological personhood only because it grants the soul an ontological structure that necessitates an implicit self-awareness in every intellectual act. Implicit self-awareness itself provides the building-blocks for an account of psychological personhood, as follows. First, we can trace the fact that each human person approaches the world as a subject, to the ineliminable duality of all conscious thought, such that in every intellectual act the cognizer and the cognized are co-manifested as correlatives. Second, we can trace the fact that this subject is always experienced in

---

[40] This account has interesting similarities to Augustine's description of memory as a *distentio animi* in *Confessions* XI, which I have explored elsewhere in more detail (see p. 209, note 30 above).

[41] See *Sent* I.8.1.1 [Mand. 1.195]: "Esse autem nostrum habet aliquid sui extra se: deest enim aliquid quod jam de ipso praeteriit, et quod futurum est"; and discussion in Maurer, "Time and Person," 182–3.

the first person as "I," to the fact that the immaterial intellect is wholly reflexive, so that when it acts, it wholly reappropriates itself cognitively from the inside, whereas it cognizes everything else from the outside as third-person objects. Thus in cognizing other things, it cognizes itself from a wholly different, internal perspective. Third, consciousness is diachronically unified insofar as the intellect not only perceives its objects as manifest-to-itself (implicit self-awareness), but *remembers* them as having-been-manifest-to-itself (intellectual memory). The implicit reference in all past and present acts to a single present "subject" draws together a temporally ordered set of experiences into the unity of a single, first-person subject-viewpoint.

Conclusion
Self-knowledge at the core of intellectual being

Medieval theories of self-knowledge have long been the victims of a certain mythology according to which premodern thinkers are supposed to have nothing interesting to say about human subjectivity, the latter being an early modern invention. Superficial readings of Aquinas have helped perpetuate the myth. Indeed, his simple schemata of different types of self-knowledge, coupled with his insistence that the mind cognizes itself "by a species, like other things," easily give the impression of a theory too rigidly conceived in terms of cognitive dependence on sensation to account for complex psychological phenomena.

It is time for the myth to be laid to rest. Ironically, the two features that perhaps doomed Aquinas's theory of self-knowledge to centuries of undervaluing are in fact his two most original contributions to the medieval debate: namely, his distinction between cognizing the mind's existence vs. cognizing its essence; and his account of all actual human self-knowledge as dependent on cognition that begins in the senses. What is more, they are arguably the signal philosophical accomplishments of his theory.

I. Aquinas's key distinction between knowing *that the mind is* (*an est*) and *what the mind is* (*quid est*) is the backbone of a sophisticated solution to the tension between self-opacity and privileged self-access. For Aquinas, the mysteriousness of the human mind, impenetrable even to itself, is grounded in its nature: (1) It is a sheer potency for intelligible form, and each form that actualizes it only "lights up" a sliver of its potential; (2) It acquires its understanding of essences (including its own and those of its own thoughts, passions, desires, and motivations) from individual instances that do not manifest their essences distinctly or completely, so that we can only define these essences by reasoning about the content of experience; and (3) The weak human agent intellect cannot light up essences comprehensively.

As a result, the *what-it-is* of the mind is opaque to ordinary experience. No matter how direct and intimate our self-experiences are, they cannot reveal how a mind, an act of thinking, or the emotion of revenge are each distinguished as a *kind* of entity from other kinds of entities – in other words, I perceive the existence of my existing mental acts and mind only indistinctly. I may be able to develop relatively good descriptions of the mind and various kinds of mental acts, and even name them correctly. But acquisition of quidditative self-knowledge, articulable in a true definition of the mind, demands considerable philosophical effort with high risk of error. To go even farther, beyond quidditative self-knowledge to a genuine comprehensive knowledge of our minds and mental acts, is likely beyond our abilities, given the weakness of our agent intellects.

But when it comes to the *existence* of my mental acts or my mind or myself, matters are quite different. In thinking about something, I am certain of the reality of my act, and of my own reality as the one thinking. This certitude comes from "seeing" or "feeling" these realities intellectually from the inside, rather than cognizing them via a referred vision (as though in the "mirror" of the extramental object), or via discursive reasoning (as one reasons to the existence of God). For Aquinas, the mind's privileged access to itself in its acts is grounded in its nature: (1) It is a sheer potency for intelligible form, so that in its cognitive acts, it takes on the form of the extramental object as its own form; (2) It is always habitually present to itself; (3) It is immaterial. Consequently, the mind merely needs to be "lit up" by its act in order to perceive itself from the inside. When it is in act, its self-identity becomes the foundation for a cognitive self-appropriation, which may be explicit or (as is more often the case) implicit while the mind's attention is directed toward extramentals.

As a result, Aquinas's theory of self-knowledge carves out a middle ground between Descartes and Hume. Certain aspects of his theory resonate well with Humean intuitions. Because the mind's actual intelligibility is the actual intelligibility of trees, toads, or the Pythagorean theorem, extramental objects dominate our conscious life, such that I can perceive myself only as shaped by these intelligibilities, as 'myself-cognizing-*that.*' Thus Aquinas would agree with Hume, against Descartes, that it is sheer fantasy to suppose that we can experience a bare self. But he could not agree with Hume's conclusion that the self cannot be an object of experience at all. Rather, for Aquinas, I genuinely experience *myself* as the direct object of perception, as actualized or determined by my engagement with extramental reality. The mind is not veiled from itself by its acts, but is revealed to itself in its acts.

At the same time, Aquinas can grant to Descartes (and Augustine or Avicenna) that our cognition of ourselves has a special clarity, certitude, and intimacy. Because I am myself, I can attend to myself whenever I want (as long as I am already thinking), perceiving myself from the inside of my acts, and occupying a single, first-person subjective viewpoint. He could very well agree with Descartes's claim that "I think; I exist," in the sense that the mere act of thinking manifests my existence to me as thinking subject. But he would reject the idea that such moments of explicit self-awareness can occur apart from the mind's actualization in cognizing extramentals. For Aquinas, there is no Self in the core of the soul that can be perceived by introspectively withdrawing from the senses. He also rejects the Cartesian (and Avicennian) view that in perceiving myself-in-act, I grasp *what* I am. In implicit or explicit self-awareness, I understand myself as a whole (this individual existent, I), but I do not understand myself wholly, for the reasons mentioned above. From glimpsing myself in these prephilosophical self-perceptions, I cannot determine which of the glimpsed aspects is relevant to the definition of my essence; I thus grasp myself as "a thinking thing" in perceiving myself thinking, but only descriptively. Without further reasoning, I cannot know what the significance of "thinking" is for my essence, or even what thought is, or whether the "I" is identical with the mind.

II. Aquinas's hylomorphic anthropology anchors his signature claim that *all actual human self-knowledge* depends on cognition originating in sensation: The human mind cognizes itself "by a species, like other things." For him, embodiment only makes sense for the human intellect (or conversely, intellectuality only makes sense for a hylomorphic composite), if the human intellect is a sheer potency for abstracted intelligible forms and thus benefits from being oriented toward sensible reality. And thus as was forecast in the Introduction to this book, the fundamental challenge that Aquinas faces in developing his theory of human self-knowledge is to show that the cognitive structures responsible for abstractive knowledge of the essences of sensed material individuals can accommodate (a) a first-personal, intuitive awareness and even (b) a properly quidditative knowledge of the immaterial mind itself.

In response to this challenge, Aquinas cashes out the implications of viewing the human intellect as a sheer potency for intelligible forms: *Insofar as it is a potential cognizer by nature, the human intellect must likewise be a habitual self-cognizer by nature.*[1] The reason is that as a sheer

---

[1] *ST* Ia.87.1 [Leon. 5.355]: "[Intellectus] in sua essentia consideratus, se habet ut potentia intelligens. Unde ex seipso habet virtutem ut intelligat, non autem ut intelligatur, nisi secundum quod fit actu."

potency for intelligible form, the intellect already fulfils *qua* cognizer all the subjective conditions for self-knowledge – i.e., it is immaterial and self-present in virtue of its ontological self-identity. But, likewise as a potency for intelligible form, it does not fulfil *qua* cognized object the objective conditions for self-knowledge (i.e., it is not actually intelligible). Thus the intellect's natural potency to extramental objects entails a natural disposition for self-awareness – or to put it another way, prior to all cognition the intellect is related *differently* to extramental objects (to which it is in sheer potency) and to itself (to which it is habitually disposed). Both the potency and the disposition are brought to actualization in a single event, by the intellect's receiving the species-in-act of extramental objects.

The result is that *Aquinas's theory of the human intellect demands, in the very stroke of orienting the human intellect to sense-dependent cognition, that it enjoy precisely the sort of self-knowledge that we have seen him describe.* Not only does his theory of self-knowledge pose no threat to the core principles of his general theory of cognition, but it also reveals the nuance in his theory of human cognition and in his hylomorphic anthropology. In fact, it forestalls crude interpretations of the human person's orientation toward the sensory realm.

For instance, in insisting on the sense-dependence of all human cognition, Aquinas does not mean to say that we can only cognize things that can be sensed, but rather that sensation is the point of departure for all embodied human cognition, the source whence the human intellect acquires the "material" for intelligible forms. Thus the intellect's self-knowledge depends on sensation inasmuch as its actualization (caused by the intelligible form abstracted ultimately from sensory experience) is the sufficient condition for it to be made actually intelligible to itself. Consequently, the requirement of cognizing oneself "like other things" does not mean that the mind must pass through its own abstractive mechanism, as though a species of the mind were to be abstracted from some sensory experience, rendered intelligible by the agent intellect, and received by the possible intellect. Rather, it means that one's own existence is manifested *within* the ordinary process of cognizing extramentals, by the species *of an extramental object* (self-awareness), and that this ordinary process reveals crucial information about the soul that can serve as the starting-point for reasoning to its essence (quidditative self-knowledge).

Again, although Aquinas holds that, as hylomorphic beings, our attention is naturally directed toward the extramental realities from which we abstract intelligible universals, his theory of cognition does not exclude intuitive experiences of my individually existing mind. Immaterial singulars – such as the mind itself – do not have to be dematerialized in order to be cognized. They can be apprehended individually, in their concrete, singular existence. Consequently, the structure of Aquinas's theory of cognition does not preclude my being manifested to myself in my acts intuitively (directly and immediately) as an individually existing agent-in-act. Respecting the integrity of self-opacity, however, Aquinas excludes intuitive knowledge of the soul's essence by arguing that these self-experiences are insufficient to provide quidditative knowledge of the mind's definition.

Finally, and most importantly, Aquinas's theory of self-knowledge sheds light on a little-known aspect of his broader theory of cognition: namely the fundamental duality of all conscious thought. The intellect can only catch itself in the act of cognizing something else; there is no explicit self-awareness without an implicit awareness of extramental realities. Yet neither is there explicit awareness of extramental realities without implicit self-awareness. Objects appear to me only as positioned over and against my subjectivity. This fundamental duality of experience grounds psychological personhood or selfhood, making it possible to explain how every act of knowing the other is also an experience of "I," the subject of experience, encountering that which is other from a single unified viewpoint.

Aquinas's insistence on the dependence of human self-knowledge, rooted in his hylomorphic anthropology, can give the impression of a wholesale rejection of Neoplatonism in favor of Aristotle. But this is not the case. While his psychological framework is broadly Aristotelian, Aquinas adapts it flexibly to the types of self-knowledge and first-person phenomena described by Augustine, Avicenna, and other Neoplatonic sources: the private insider "feel" of experiencing one's own acts; the apprehension of oneself in the first person, equated with an indistinct apprehension of the soul; the sense of deep familiarity that accompanies self-awareness; the intuition that nothing can be closer to the mind than the mind itself; the notion of a natural self-presence that equips the soul habitually for self-awareness. He thus orchestrates a masterful rapprochement between the Aristotelian notion of human self-knowledge as dependent on borrowed intelligibility, and the Neoplatonic insight – especially prominent in the *Liber de causis* – that self-knowledge is a basic property of intellectual beings. Nevertheless, he conducts this synthesis with an eye to a philosophically coherent outcome. Thus in two respects his reading of Augustine, though respectful, is deliberately corrective. Where the Augustinian maxim that the mind knows itself by itself interferes with the ontological boundary between separate and embodied intellects, Aquinas allows that the soul can know itself by itself only in the sense of being the spontaneous originator of the act in which it is rendered intelligible-in-act. And where Augustine's appeal to knowledge of one's nature in the eternal types clashes with Aquinas's rejection of illuminationism, Aquinas reinterprets the text as describing a verificational judgment of the soul's nature.

In the end, then, Aquinas's theory of self-knowledge is not wholly Aristotelian; nor is it an awkward grafting of Neoplatonism onto an Aristotelian stem. Rather, he takes ownership of insights from both traditions, weaving strands of their thought together into his own original theory. The sophistication of this endeavor went largely unappreciated among subsequent medieval thinkers, who were mainly hostile to (and indeed usually misread) his solution. Yet his way of drawing the fault lines in the debate would shape future medieval discussions of self-knowledge.[2]

Let us conclude by singling out two aspects of Aquinas's theory of self-knowledge that could be fruitfully placed into dialogue with contemporary inquiry. First, it underscores the intrinsic reflexivity of the mind: "But since the intellect reflects upon itself, according to this same reflexion it understands both its understanding and the species by which it understands" (ST Ia.85.2). This reflexivity – the ability of the whole to "bend back" or "turn back" upon the whole, rather than part-by-part – is an intrinsic property of immaterial being, the foundation for what we now call the conscious "I" or the human self. Although these lines of inquiry could not be pursued here, I suspect that further study will expose a leading role for reflexivity in many other areas of Aquinas's theories of human cognition and action, including knowledge of the transcendentals, free choice, and epistemological certitude. His theory opens a path for a "metaphysics of mind" that would investigate the structures supporting full or partial reflexivity.

Second, Aquinas presents the human mind as inherently relational, experiencing itself only in its engagement with extramental objects. What the human intellect first cognizes is not itself: I do not appear to myself as some solitary self-enclosed being and then proceed to reach out towards the external world. Rather, I first encounter myself only *in the act of apprehending that which is other*. Aquinas's theory thus opens the door to further reflection on the role of embodiment in human self-knowledge, and on the philosophical implications of conceiving the "I," not as a bare "self," but as a first-person agent.

---

[2] This story is told by Putallaz, *La connaissance de soi*.

Bibliography

Note: Abbreviations have been designated for the most frequently cited editions of Latin texts used in this book; these appear, together with full bibliographic references, in the list of abbreviations on pp. ix–xi.

Alexander of Aphrodisias. *The* De anima *of Alexander of Aphrodisias*. Trans. and comm. Athanasios P. Fotinis. Washington, D.C.: University Press of America, Inc., 1979.

Alexander of Aphrodisias and Themistius. *Two Greek Aristotelian Commentators on the Intellect: The* De intellectu *Attributed to Alexander of Aphrodisias and Themistius' Paraphrase of Aristotle* De anima *3.4–8*. Trans. and comm. Frederic M. Schroeder and Robert B. Todd. Toronto: Pontifical Institute of Mediaeval Studies, 1990.

Alwishah, Ahmed. "Avicenna's Philosophy of Mind: Self-Awareness and Intentionality." PhD diss., University of California, Los Angeles, 2006.

Aminrazavi, Mehdi. "Avicenna's (Ibn Sīnā) Phenomenological Analysis of How the Soul (*Nafs*) Knows Itself (*'ilm al-ḥuḍūrī*)." In *The Passions of the Soul in the Metamorphosis of Becoming*, ed. Anna-Teresa Tymieniecka, 91–100. Dordrecht: Kluwer, 2003.

Aristotle. *Aristotelis Opera*. Ed. Immanuel Bekker. Prussian Academy edition. 5 vols. Berlin: G. Reimerum, 1831–70. Reprint. Berlin: W. De Gruyter, 1960–87.

The Basic Works of Aristotle. Ed. Richard McKeon. New York: Random House, 1941.

De anima Books II and III. Trans. with notes by D.W. Hamlyn. Oxford University Press, 1993.

De anima. Ed. W.D. Ross. Oxford University Press, n.d.

Arnou, René. *L'homme a-t-il le pouvoir de connaître la vérité? Réponse de Saint Thomas: La connaissance par habitus*. Rome: Presses de l'Université Grégorienne, 1970.

Arroyabe, Estanislao. *Das Reflektierende Subjekt: Zur Erkenntnistheorie des Thomas von Aquin*. Frankfurt am Main: Athenäum, 1988.

Averroes. *Long Commentary on the* De anima. Trans. Richard C. Taylor. New Haven, Conn.: Yale University Press, 2009.

Ayres, Lewis. "The Discipline of Self-Knowledge in Augustine's *De trinitate* Book X." In *The Passionate Intellect: Essays on the Transformation of Classical Traditions*, ed. Lewis Ayres, 261–96. London: Transaction Publishers, 1995.

Bazán, B. Carlos. "On Angels and Human Beings." *Archives d'histoire doctrinale et littéraire du moyen âge* 77 (2010): 47–85.

———. "Le dialogue philosophique entre Siger de Brabant et Thomas d'Aquin: à propos d'un ouvrage récent de E.H. Wéber." *Revue philosophique de Louvain* 72 (1974): 55–155.

———. "The Human Soul: Form *and* Substance? Thomas Aquinas' Critique of Eclectic Aristotelianism." *Archives d'histoire doctrine et littéraire du moyen âge* 64 (1997): 95–126.

———. "*Intellectum speculativum*: Averroes, Thomas Aquinas, and Siger of Brabant on the Intelligible Object." *Journal of the History of Philosophy* 19 (1981): 425–46.

Bérubé, Camille. *La connaissance de l'individuel au moyen âge*. Paris: Presses universitaires de France, 1964.

Black, Deborah L. "Avicenna on Self-Awareness and Knowing that One Knows." In *The Unity of Science in the Arabic Tradition*, ed. S. Rahman, T. Hassan, T. Street, 63–87. Dordrecht: Springer, 2008.

———. "Consciousness and Self-Knowledge in Aquinas's Critique of Averroes's Psychology." *Journal of the History of Philosophy* 31 (1993): 349–85.

———. "Mental Existence in Thomas Aquinas and Avicenna." *Mediaeval Studies* 61 (1999): 45–79.

Blankenhorn, Bernhard. "How the Early Albertus Magnus Transformed Augustinian Interiority." *Freiburger Zeitschrift für Philosophie und Theologie* 58 (2011): 351–86.

Boethius, Manlius Severinus. *Opuscula theologica*. Ed. C. Moreschini. Leipzig: Saur, 2000.

Bofill y Bofill, Jaume. *Obra filosófica*. Barcelona: Ariel, 1967.

Boiadjiev, Tzotcho, Georgi Kapriev, and Andreas Speer, eds. *Die Dionysius-Rezeption im Mittelalter: Internationales Kolloquium in Sofia vom 8. bis 11. April 1999*. Turnhout: Brepols, 2000.

Booth, Edward. "St. Augustine's '*notitia sui*' Related to Aristotle and the Early Neo-Platonists." 4 pts. *Augustiniana* 27 (1977): 70–132, 364–401; 28 (1978): 183–221; 29 (1979): 97–124.

Bougerol, Jacques Guy. "Jean de la Rochelle: les oeuvres et les manuscrits." *Archivum Franciscanum historicum* 87 (1994): 205–15.

Boulnois, Olivier. *Être et représentation: une généalogie de la métaphysique moderne à l'époque de Duns Scot, XIIIe–XIVe siècle*. Paris: Presses universitaires de France, 1999.

Boyer, Charles. "Le sens d'un texte de Saint Thomas: 'De Veritate, q. 1, a. 9.'" *Gregorianum* 5 (1924): 424–43.

Brachtendorf, Johannes. "Selbsterkenntnis: Thomas von Aquin als Kritiker Augustins?" *Philosophisches Jahrbuch* 109.2 (2002): 255–70.

Brennan, Robert Edward. *Thomistic Psychology: A Philosophic Analysis of the Nature of Man*. New York: Macmillan, 1941.

Brentano, Franz. *Psychology from an Empirical Standpoint*. Ed. Oskar Kraus and Linda L. McAlister, and trans. Antos C. Rancurello, D.B. Terrell, and Linda L. McAlister. London: Routledge, 1995.

Brown, Deborah J. "Aquinas' Missing Flying Man." *Sophia* 40 (2001): 17–31.

Brower, Jeffrey, and Susan Brower-Toland. "Aquinas on Mental Representation: Concepts and Intentionality." *Philosophical Review* 117 (2003): 193–243.

Brower-Toland, Susan. "Olivi on Consciousness and Self-Knowledge: The Phenomenology, Metaphysics, and Epistemology of Mind's Reflexivity." In *Oxford Studies in Medieval Philosophy*, ed. Robert Pasnau, vol. 1. Oxford University Press, forthcoming.

    "Self-Knowledge, Self-Consciousness, and Reflexivity." In *Companion to Cognitive Theory in the Later Middle Ages*, ed. Russell Friedman and Martin Pickavé. Leuven University Press, forthcoming.

Burnett, Charles. "Arabic into Latin: The Reception of Arabic Philosophy into Western Europe." In *The Cambridge Companion to Arabic Philosophy*, ed. Peter Adamson and Richard C. Taylor, 370–404. Cambridge University Press, 2005.

Caldera, Rafael Tomás. *Le jugement par inclination chez saint Thomas d'Aquin*. Paris: Vrin, 1980.

Cary, Phillip. *Augustine's Invention of the Inner Self: The Legacy of a Christian Platonist*. Oxford University Press, 2000.

Cassam, Quassim, ed. *Self-Knowledge*. Oxford University Press, 1994.

Caston, Victor. "Aristotle on Consciousness." *Mind*, n.s., 111 (2002): 751–815.

Castonguay, J. *Psychologie de la mémoire: sources et doctrine de la memoria chez saint Thomas d'Aquin*. 1st edn. Montreal: Lévrier, 1963; 2nd edn, 1964.

Cayré, F. *Initiation à la philosophie de saint Augustin*. Paris: Desclée de Brouwer, 1947.

Centi, Tito. "L'autocoscienza immediata nel pensiero di S. Tommaso." *Sapienza* 3 (1950): 220–42.

Chenu, M.-D. *Das Werk des Hl. Thomas von Aquin*. Trans. Otto M. Pesch. Heidelberg: Kerle, 1960.

Chisholm, Roderick M. "On the Observability of the Self." *Philosophy and Phenomenological Research* 30 (1969): 7–21.

Clark, Mary T. "An Inquiry into Personhood." *Review of Metaphysics* 46 (1992): 3–27.

Clarke, W. Norris. "What Is Most and Least Relevant in the Metaphysics of St. Thomas Today?" *International Philosophical Quarterly* 14 (1974): 411–34.

Cohen, Sheldon M. "St. Thomas Aquinas on the Immaterial Reception of Sensible Forms." *Philosophical Review* 91 (1982): 193–210.

Cory, Therese Scarpelli. "Diachronically Unified Consciousness in Augustine and Aquinas." *Vivarium* 50 (2012): 554–81.

Crosby, John F. *The Selfhood of the Human Person*. Washington, D.C.: The Catholic University of America Press, 1996.

Cross, Richard. "Accidents, Substantial Forms, and Causal Powers in the Late Thirteenth Century: Some Reflections on the Axiom *actiones sunt suppositorum.*" In *Compléments de substance: études sur les propriétés accidentelles offertes à Alain de Libera* ed. C. Erismann and A. Schniewind, 133–46. Paris: Vrin, 2008.

"Is Aquinas's Proof for the Indestructibility of the Soul Successful?" *British Journal of Philosophy* 5 (1997): 1–20.

Cunningham, Francis A. *Essence and Existence in Thomism.* Lanham, Md.: University Press of America, 1988.

Davies, Brien, and Eleonore Stump, eds. *The Oxford Handbook of Aquinas.* Oxford University Press, 2012.

de Almeida Sampaio, Lara Frage. *L'intuition dans la philosophie de Jacques Maritain.* Paris: Vrin, 1963.

de Finance, Joseph. "'Cogito' cartésien et réflexion thomiste." *Archives de philosophie* 16.2 (1946): 3–185.

Connaissance de l'être: traité d'ontologie. Paris: Desclée de Brouwer, 1966.

de Libera, Alain. "Les actions appartiennent aux sujets: Petite archéologie d'un principe leibnizien." In *Ad Ingenii Acuitionem: Studies in Honour of Alfonso Maierù*, ed. S. Caroti *et al.*, 199–220. Louvain-La-Neuve: Fédération Internationale des Instituts d'Etudes Médiévales, 2007.

Archéologie du sujet. 2 vols. Paris: Vrin, 2007–8.

"When Did the Modern Subject Emerge?" *American Catholic Philosophical Quarterly* 82 (2008): 181–220.

Deely, John. "How to Go Nowhere with Language: Remarks on John O'Callaghan, *Thomist Realism and the Linguistic Turn.*" *American Catholic Philosophical Quarterly* 82 (2008): 337–59.

Deferrari, Roy J., and Inviolata M. Barry, *A Lexicon of St. Thomas Aquinas.* Washington, D.C.: The Catholic University of America Press, 1949.

Dewan, Lawrence. "St. Albert, St. Thomas, and Knowledge." *American Catholic Philosophical Quarterly* 70 (1996): 121–35.

"Saint Thomas, Ideas, and Immediate Knowledge." *Dialogue* 18 (1979): 392–404.

Dhavamony, Mariasusai. *Subjectivity and Knowledge in the Philosophy of Saint Thomas Aquinas.* Rome: Typis Pontificiae Universitatis Gregorianae, 1965.

Doig, James C. "O'Callaghan on *Verbum Mentis* in Aquinas." *American Catholic Philosophical Quarterly* 77 (2003): 233–55.

Druart, T.-A. "The Soul and Body Problem: Avicenna and Descartes." In *Arabic Philosophy and the West: Continuity and Interaction*, ed. Druart, 27–48. Washington, D.C.: Center for Contemporary Arab Studies, Georgetown Univ., 1998.

Drummond, John D. "The Case(s) of (Self-)Awareness." In *Self-Representational Approaches to Consciousness*, ed. Kriegel and Williford, 199–220.

Eberl, Jason T. "Do Human Persons Persist between Death and Resurrection?" In *Metaphysics and God: Essays in Honor of Eleonore Stump*, ed. Kevin Timpe, 188–205. New York: Routledge, 2009.

"The Metaphysics of Resurrection: Issues of Identity." *Proceedings of the American Catholic Philosophical Association* 74 (2000): 215–30.

Echavarría, Martín Federico. "Memoria e identidad según Santo Tomás de Aquino." *Sapientia* 62 (2002): 91–112.

Émery, Gilles. "L'unité de l'homme, âme et corps, chez S. Thomas d'Aquin." *Nova et Vetera* 75.2 (2000): 53–76.

Fabro, Cornelio. "Coscienza e autocoscienza dell'anima." *Doctor communis* 11 (1958): 97–123.

Faucon de Boylesve, Pierre. *Être et savoir: étude du fondement de l'intelligibilité dans la pensée médiévale.* Paris: Vrin, 1985.

Fay, Thomas A. "The Problem of Intellectual Intuition in the Metaphysics of Thomas Aquinas." *Sapienza: Rivista di filosofia e di teologia* 27 (1974): 352–9.

Fetz, R. *Ontologie der Innerlichkeit:* Reditio completa *und* processio interior *bei Thomas von Aquin.* Fribourg: Universitätsverlag Freiburg Schweiz, 1975.

Fidora, Alexander, and Andreas Niederberger. *Von Bagdad nach Toledo: Das 'Buch der Ursache' und seine Rezeption im Mittelalter.* Mainz: Dieterich'sche Verlagsbuchhandlung, 2001.

Friedman, Russell L. *Medieval Trinitarian Thought from Aquinas to Ockham.* Cambridge University Press, 2010.

Führer, Markus L. "Albertus Magnus' Theory of Divine Illumination." In *Albertus Magnus: Zum Gedenken nach 800 Jahren: Neue Zugänge, Aspekte und Perspektiven,* ed. Walter Senner *et al.*, 141–55. Berlin: Akademie Verlag, 2001.

"The Contemplative Function of the Agent Intellect in the Psychology of Albert the Great." In *Historia Philosophiae Medii Aevi: Studien zur Geschichte der Philosophie des Mittelalters,* ed. B. Mojsisch and O. Pluta, 305–19. Amsterdam: Grüner, 1991.

Gaetani, F. "Come l'anima conosca se stesa. Controversie speculative e contributi sperimentali." *Civiltà Cattolica* 86 (1935): 465–80.

Gardeil, Ambroise. "Examen de conscience." *Revue thomiste* 33 (1928): 156–80.

"L'habitation de Dieu en nous, et la structure interne de l'âme." *Revue thomiste* 28 (1923): 238–60.

"La perception expérimentale de l'âme par elle-même d'après saint Thomas." In *Mélanges Thomistes,* 219–36. Le Saulchoir: Kain, 1923.

"À propos d'un cahier du R.P. Romeyer." *Revue thomiste,* n.s., 12 (1929): 520–32.

La structure de l'âme et l'expérience mystique. 2nd edn. 2 vols. Paris: J. Gabalda, 1927.

Garrigou-Lagrange, Reginald. "Utrum mens seipsam per essentiam cognoscat, an per aliquam speciem." *Angelicum* 5 (1928): 37–54.

Gerson, Lloyd P. "*Epistrophe pros heauton*: History and Meaning." *Documenti e studi sulla tradizione filosofica medievale* 8 (1997): 1–32.

Gilson, Étienne. *Being and Some Philosophers.* Toronto: Pontifical Institute of Mediaeval Studies, 1949.

The Christian Philosophy of St. Augustine. Trans. L.E.M. Lynch. New York: Vintage, 1967.

History of Christian Philosophy in the Middle Ages. New York: Random House, 1955.

The Philosophy of St. Bonaventure. Trans. Illtyd Trethowan and Frank J. Sheed. Paterson, N.J.: Desclée, 1965.

"Les sources gréco-arabe de l'augustinisme avicennisant." *Archives d'histoire doctrinale et littéraire du moyen âge* 4 (1929–30): 5–149.

Gioia, Luigi. *The Theological Epistemology of Augustine's* De Trinitate. Oxford University Press, 2008.

Goehring, Bernd. "St. Thomas Aquinas on Self-Knowledge and Self-Awareness." *Cithara* 42 (2003): 3–14.

Grabmann, Martin. *Thomas Aquinas: His Personality and Thought.* Trans. Virgil Michel. New York: Longmans, Green, & Co., 1928.

Gracia, Jorge J. and Timothy B. Noone, eds. *A Companion to Philosophy in the Middle Ages.* Oxford: Blackwell, 2003.

Grégoire, Franz. "Notes sur les termes 'intuition,' et 'expérience.'" *Revue philosophique de Louvain* 44 (1946): 401–15.

Grosseteste, Robert. *Die philosophischen Werke des Robert Grosseteste, Bischofs von Lincoln.* Ed. Ludwig Baur. Münster: Aschendorff, 1912.

Guardini, Romano. *The World and the Person.* Trans. Stella Lange. Chicago: Regnery, 1965.

Haldane, John. "Aquinas and the Active Intellect." *Philosophy* 67 (1992): 199–210.

Hankey, W. J. "Between and Beyond Augustine and Descartes: More than a Source of the Self." *Augustinian Studies* 32 (2001): 65–88.

Hasse, Dag Nikolaus. *Avicenna's* De anima *in the Latin West: The Formation of a Peripatetic Philosophy of the Soul 1160–1300.* Warburg Institute Studies and Texts 1. London: The Warburg Institute, 2000.

Hayen, A. *L'intentionnel dans la philosophie de Saint Thomas.* Paris: Desclée de Brouwer, 1942.

Hoenen, Marten. *Reality and Judgment according to St. Thomas.* Trans. Henry F. Tiblier. Chicago: Regnery, 1952.

Hoffmann, Tobias. "Intellectual Virtues." In *The Oxford Handbook to Aquinas,* ed. Davies and Stump, 327–36.

Husserl, Edmund. *Cartesian Meditations: An Introduction to Phenomenology.* Trans. Dorion Cairns. The Hague: Martinus Nijhoff, 1960.

Inagaki, B.R. "*Habitus* and *natura* in Aquinas." In *Studies in Medieval Philosophy,* ed. John F. Wippel, 159–75. Washington, D.C.: The Catholic University of America Press, 1987.

Jean de la Rochelle. *Johannes von la Rochelle, Summa de anima, Tractatus de viribus animae, Lateinisch–Deutsch.* Ed. and trans. Jörg Alejandro Tellkamp. Freiburg: Herder, 2010.

Jolivet, Régis. "Étude critique: Saint Thomas et notre connaissance de l'esprit humain." *Revue de philosophie,* n.s., 4 (1933): 295–311.

"L'intuition intellectuelle." *Revue thomiste* (1932): 52–71.

Jordan, Mark. *Ordering Wisdom: The Hierarchy of Philosophical Discourses in Aquinas.* Notre Dame, Ind.: University of Notre Dame Press, 1986.

Kahn, Charles H. "Aristotle on Thinking." In *Essays on Aristotle's* De anima, ed. M.C. Nussbaum and A.O. Rorty, 359–79. Oxford: Clarendon Press, 1992.

"Sensation and Consciousness in Aristotle." In *Articles on Aristotle*, ed. Jonathan Barnes *et al.* Vol. IV, *Psychology and Aesthetics*, 1–31. London: Duckworth, 1978.

Kaukua, Jari. "Avicenna on Subjectivity: A Philosophical Study." PhD diss., University of Jyväskylä, 2007.

Kennedy, Leonard A. "The Nature of the Human Intellect According to St. Albert the Great," *Modern Schoolman* 37 (1960): 121–37.

"The Soul's Knowledge of Itself: An Unpublished Work Attributed to St. Thomas Aquinas." *Vivarium* 15 (1977): 31–45.

Kenny, Anthony J.P. "Aquinas on Knowledge of Self." In *Language, Meaning, and God: Essays in Honor of Herbert McCabe*, ed. Brian Davies, 104–19. London: Chapman, 1987.

Aquinas on Mind. New York: Routledge, 1993.

Kent, Bonnie. "Habits and Virtues (Ia IIae, qq. 49–70)." In *The Ethics of Aquinas*, ed. Pope, 116–30.

Kenzeler, A.M. "Une prétendue dispute de saint Thomas." *Angelicum* 33 (1956): 172–81.

King, Peter. "Rethinking Representation in the Middle Ages: A Vade-Mecum to Mediaeval Theories of Mental Representation." In *Representation and Objects of Thought in Medieval Philosophy*, ed. H. Lagerlund 81–100. Aldershot: Ashgate, 2007.

Klima, Gyula. "Man = Body + Soul: Aquinas's Arithmetic of Human Nature." In *Thomas Aquinas: Contemporary Philosophical Perspectives*, ed. Brian Davies, 257–73. Oxford University Press, 2002.

Klima, Gyula, and Alexander W. Hall, eds. *The Immateriality of the Human Mind, the Semantics of Analogy, and the Conceivability of God*. Proceedings of the Society for Medieval Logic and Metaphysics 1. Newcastle upon Tyne: Cambridge Scholars Publishing, 2011.

Klubertanz, George P. *The Discursive Power: Sources and Doctrine of the* vis cogitativa *according to St. Thomas Aquinas*. Carthagena, Oh.: The Messenger Press, 1952.

Habits and Virtues. New York: Appleton-Century-Crofts, 1965.

"St. Thomas and the Knowledge of the Singular." *The New Scholasticism* 26 (1952): 135–66.

Klünker, W.U. *Selbsterkenntnis der Seele: zur Anthropologie des Thomas von Aquin*. Beiträge zur Bewusstseinsgeschichte, 7. Stuttgart: Edition Hardenberg in Verlag Freies Geistesleben, 1990.

Knasas, John F.X. *Being and Some Twentieth-Century Thomists*. New York: Fordham University Press, 2003.

Koterski, Joseph W. "Boethius and the Theological Origins of the Concept of Person." *American Catholic Philosophical Quarterly* 78 (1994): 203–24.

Kretzmann, Norman, and Eleonore Stump, eds. *The Cambridge Companion to Aquinas*. Cambridge University Press, 1993.

Kriegel, Uriah. *Subjective Consciousness: A Self-Representational Theory*. Oxford University Press, 2009.

Kriegel, Uriah, and Kenneth Williford, eds. *Self-Representational Approaches to Consciousness*. Cambridge, Mass.: MIT Press, 2006.

Lalande, André. *Vocabulaire technique et critique de la philosophie.* 9th edn. Paris: Presses Universitaires de France, 1962.

Lambert, Richard T. "Habitual Knowledge of the Soul in Thomas Aquinas." *The Modern Schoolman* 60 (1982): 1–19.

"Nonintentional Experience of Oneself in Thomas Aquinas." *The New Scholasticism* 59 (1985): 253–75.

Self Knowledge in Thomas Aquinas: The Angelic Doctor on the Soul's Knowledge of Itself. Bloomington, Ind.: AuthorHouse, 2007.

"A Textual Study of Aquinas' Comparison of the Intellect to Prime Matter." *The New Scholasticism* 56 (1982): 80–99.

Leuret, Simonne. "Saint Thomas et *Notre science de l'esprit humain.*" *Revue thomiste* 28 (1923): 368–86.

Liber de spiritu et anima. In *Patrologia cursus completus, series Latina,* ed. J.-P. Migne. Vol. XL, 779–832. Paris: Garnier, 1844.

Lloyd, A.C. "*Nosce teipsum* and *conscientia.*" *Archiv für Geschichte der Philosophie* 46 (1964): 188–200.

Lonergan, Bernard J. "Christ as Subject: A Reply." *Gregorianum* 40 (1959): 242–70.

De constitutione Christi ontologica et psychologia. 4th edn. Rome: Gregorian University Press, 1964.

Insight: A Study of Human Understanding, rev. edn. New York: Longmans, 1958.

Verbum. *Word and Idea in Aquinas.* Ed. David B. Burrell. Notre Dame, Ind.: University of Notre Dame Press, 1967.

López-Farjeat, Luis Xavier. "Self-Awareness (Al-Shu'Ûr Bi-Al-Dhât) in Human and Non-Human Animals in Avicenna's Psychological Writings." In *Oikeiosis and the Natural Bases of Morality: From Classical Stoicism to Modern Philosophy,* ed. Alexander Vigo, 121–40. New York: Georg Olms Verlag, 2012.

Lottin, Odon. *Psychologie et morale aux XIIe et XIIIe siècles.* 6 vols. Louvain: Abbaye du Mont César/Gebloux: Duculot, 1942–60.

McCabe, Herbert. "The Immortality of the Soul." In *Aquinas,* ed. Anthony Kenny, 297–306. London: Macmillan, 1969.

MacDonald, Scott. "Theory of Knowledge." In *The Cambridge Companion to Aquinas,* ed. Kretzmann and Stump, 160–95.

McGinn, Bernard. *Three Treatises on Man: A Cistercian Anthropology.* Kalamazoo, Mich.: Cistercian Publications, 1977.

Macintosh, J.J. "St. Thomas on Angelic Time and Motion." *The Thomist* 59 (1995): 547–75.

McKian, John D. "The Metaphysics of Introspection According to St. Thomas." *The New Scholasticism* 15 (1941): 89–117.

Manzanedo, Marcos F. *La imaginación y la memoria según santo Tomás.* Rome: Herder, 1978.

Maritain, Jacques. *Distinguish to Unite, or The Degrees of Knowledge.* 4th edn. Trans. G. B. Phelan. Notre Dame, Ind.: University of Notre Dame Press, 1959.

Existence and the Existent. Trans. Lewis Galantiere and Gerald B. Phelan. New York: Pantheon Books, 1948.

Marmura, M.E. "Avicenna's 'Flying Man' in Context." *Monist* 69 (1986): 383–95.

Marrone, Steven P. *The Light of Thy Countenance: Science and Knowledge of God in the Thirteenth Century*. 2 vols. Leiden: Brill, 2001.

William of Auvergne and Robert Grosseteste: New Ideas of Truth in the Early Thirteenth Century. Princeton University Press, 1983.

Martin, Christopher. J. "Self-Knowledge and Cognitive Ascent: Thomas Aquinas and Peter Olivi on the KK-Thesis." In *Forming the Mind: Essays on the Internal Senses and the Mind/Body Problem from Avicenna to the Medical Enlightenment*, ed. H. Lagerlund, 93–108. Dordrecht: Springer, 2007.

Matthews, Gareth B. "Si Fallor, Sum." In *Augustine: A Collection of Critical Essays*, ed. R.A. Markus, 151–67. New York: Anchor Books, 1972.

Thought's Ego in Augustine and Descartes. Ithaca, N.Y.: Cornell University Press, 1992.

Maurer, Armand. "Descartes and Aquinas on the Unity of a Human Being: Revisited." *American Catholic Philosophical Quarterly* 67 (1993): 497–511.

"Time and the Person." *Proceedings of the American Catholic Philosophical Association* 53 (1979): 182–93.

Menn, Stephen. *Descartes and Augustine*. Cambridge University Press, 1988.

Mensching, Gunter, ed. *Selbstbewußtsein und Person im Mittelalter*. Würzburg: Königshausen, 2005.

Merriell, D. Juvenal. *To the Image of the Trinity: A Study in the Development of Aquinas' Teaching*. Toronto: Pontifical Institute of Mediaeval Studies, 1990.

Michaud-Quantin, P. "Les puissances de l'âme chez Jean de la Rochelle." *Antonianum* 24 (1949): 489–505.

Miller, Barry. "Knowledge through Affective Connaturality." PhD diss., Pontifical University Angelicum, 1959.

Modrak, Deborah. *Aristotle: The Power of Perception*. University of Chicago Press, 1987.

Moody, Ernest A. "William of Auvergne and His Treatise *De anima*." In idem *Studies in Medieval Philosophy, Science, and Logic, Collected Papers 1933–1969*, 1–109. Berkeley: University of California Press, 1975.

Moreau, Joseph. *De la connaissance selon S. Thomas d'Aquin*. Paris: Beauchesne, 1976.

Mulchahey, M. Michèle. *"First the Bow is Bent in Study": Dominican Education before 1350*. Toronto: Pontifical Institute of Mediaeval Studies, 1998.

Müller, Jörn. "La vie humaine comme un tout hiérarchique: Félicité contemplative et vie active chez Albert le Grand." In *Vie active et vie contemplative au Moyen Age et au seuil de la Renaissance*, ed. C. Trottmann, 241–63. Rome: École Française de Rome, 2009.

Nodé-Langlois, M. "L'intuitivité de l'intellect selon Thomas d'Aquin." *Revue thomiste* 100 (2000): 179–203.

Novak, Joseph A. "Aquinas on the Incorruptibility of Soul." *History of Philosophy Quarterly* 4 (1987): 405–21.

O'Callaghan, John. "More Words on the *Verbum*: A Response to James Doig." *American Catholic Philosophical Quarterly* 77 (2003): 257–68.

"The Problem of Language and Mental Representation in Aristotle and St. Thomas." *Review of Metaphysics* 50 (1997): 499–545.

Thomist Realism and the Linguistic Turn: Toward a More Perfect Form of Existence. Notre Dame, Ind.: Notre Dame Press, 2003.

"*Verbum Mentis*: Philosophical or Theological Doctrine in Aquinas?" *Proceedings of the American Catholic Philosophical Association* 74 (2000): 103–17.

O'Daly, Gerard. *Augustine's Philosophy of Mind.* Berkeley: University of California Press, 1987.

Oderberg, David. "Hylemorphic Dualism." In *Personal Identity*, ed. Eleanor Franken Paul, Fred Dycus Miller, and Jeffrey Paul, 70–99. Cambridge University Press, 1995.

Owens, Joseph. "Aquinas on Cognition as Existence." In *Thomas and Bonaventure: A Septicentenary Commemoration*, ed. George F. McLean, 74–85. Proceedings of the American Catholic Philosophical Association 48. Washington, D.C.: The Catholic University of America Press, 1974.

"Aquinas on the Inseparability of Soul from Existence." *The New Scholasticism* 61 (1987): 249–70.

"Aquinas on Knowing Existence." *Review of Metaphysics* 29 (1976): 670–90.

An Elementary Christian Metaphysics. Milwaukee, Wis.: Bruce Publishing Co., 1983.

An Interpretation of Existence. Milwaukee, Wis.: Bruce Publishing Co., 1968.

"Maritain's Three Concepts of Existence." *American Catholic Philosophical Quarterly* 49 (1975): 295–308.

"A Note on Aristotle, *De anima* 3.4, 429b9." *Phoenix* 30.2 (1976): 107–18.

"The Self in Aristotle." *Review of Metaphysics* 41 (1988): 707–22.

Panaccio, Claude. "Aquinas on Intellectual Representation." In *Ancient and Medieval Theories of Intentionality*, ed. Perler, 185–202.

Pasnau, Robert. "Id quo cognoscimus." In *Theories of Perception in Medieval and Early Modern Thought*, ed. Simo Knuuttila and Pekka Kärkkäinen, 131–49. Dordrecht: Springer, 2008.

Theories of Cognition in the Later Middle Ages. Cambridge University Press, 1997.

Thomas Aquinas on Human Nature: A Philosophical Study of Summa theologiae Ia 75–89. Cambridge University Press, 2002.

trans. *The Treatise on Human Nature: Summa theologiae 1a 75–89, with Introduction and Commentary.* Indianapolis, Ind.: Hackett, 2002.

Pedrazzini, Gidone Gabriel. *Anima in conscientia sui secundum S. Thomam: excerpta ex dissertatione ad Lauream in Facultate Philosophica Pontificiae Universitatis Gregorianae.* Gallarate: Dominico Ferrario, 1948.

Péghaire, Julien. Intellectus *et ratio selon S. Thomas d'Aquin.* Paris: Vrin, 1936.

Pégis, Anton C. "The Separated Soul and Its Nature in St. Thomas." In *St. Thomas Aquinas 1274–1974: Commemorative Studies*, ed. A. Maurer. Vol. I, 131–58. Toronto: Pontifical Institute of Mediaeval Studies, 1974.

Peifer, John Frederick. *The Concept in Thomism.* New York: Bookman Associates, 1952.

Peillaube, E. "Avons-nous expérience du spirituel?" 2 pts. *Revue de philosophie* 36 (1929): 245–67, 660–85.

Pelster, F. "Eine ungedruckte Quaestio des hl. Thomas von Aquin über die Erkenntnis der Wesenheit der Seele." *Gregorianum* 36 (1955): 618–25.

Perkams, Matthias. *Selbstbewusstsein in der Spätantike: Die neuplatonischen Kommentare zu Aristoteles' De anima.* Berlin: de Gruyter, 2008.

Perler, Dominik, ed. *Ancient and Medieval Theories of Intentionality.* Leiden: Brill, 2001.

Theorien der Intentionalität im Mittelalter. 2nd edn. Frankfurt am Main: Klostermann, 2004.

Théories de l'intentionnalité au moyen âge. Paris: Vrin, 2003.

Perry, John. "The Problem of the Essential Indexical." *Noûs* 13 (1979): 3–20.

Philoponus, John. *Commentaire sur le* De anima *d'Aristote, traduction de Guillaume de Moerbeke.* Ed. G. Verbeke. Corpus Latinum Commentariorum in Aristotelem Graecorum 3. Paris: Editions Béatrice-Nauwelaerts, 1966.

Picard, Gabriel. "Le problème critique fondamental." *Archives de philosophie* 1.2 (1923): 1–94.

"Réflexions sur le problème critique fondamental." *Archives de philosophie* 13.1 (1937): 1–78.

Pines, S. "La conception de la conscience de soi chez Avicenne et chez Abū'l-Barakāt al-Baghdādī." *Archives d'histoire doctrinale et littéraire du moyen âge* 29 (1954): 21–56.

Pini, Giorgio. "Intentions and Modes of Understanding in Thomas Aquinas." In *Categories and Logic in Duns Scotus: An Interpretation of Aristotle's Categories in the Late Thirteenth Century,* 45–67. Leiden: Brill, 2002.

"Two Models of Thinking: Thomas Aquinas and John Duns Scotus." In *Intentionality, Cognition and Representation in the Middle Ages,* ed. Gyula Klima. New York: Fordham University Press, forthcoming. It is available online at http://faculty.fordham.edu/pini/pini/Blank_files/Two%20Models%20of%20Thinking.pdf (accessed June 19, 2013).

Plotinus. *The Essential Plotinus.* Trans. Elmer O'Brien. Indianapolis: Hackett, 1964.

Pope, Stephen, ed. *The Ethics of Aquinas.* Washington, D.C.: Georgetown University Press, 2002.

Proclus. "Procli *Elementatio Theologica* translata a Guilelmo de Moerbeke." Ed. C. Vansteenkiste. *Tijdschrift voor philosophie* 13 (1951): 263–302, 491–531.

Putallaz, François-Xavier. *La connaissance de soi au XIIIe siècle: De Matthieu d'Aquasparta à Thierry de Freiberg.* Paris: Vrin, 1991.

Le sens de la réflexion chez Thomas d'Aquin. Paris: Vrin, 1991.

Rabeau, Gaston. Species, Verbum: *L'activité intellectuelle élémentaire selon S. Thomas d'Aquin.* Paris: Vrin, 1938.

Régis, Louis-Marie. *Epistemology.* Trans. Imelda Choquette Byrne. New York: Macmillan, 1959.

Reichberg, Gregory M. "The Intellectual Virtues (Ia IIae, qq. 57–58)." In *The Ethics of Aquinas*, ed. Pope, 131–50.

Reichmann, James. "The 'Cogito' in St. Thomas: Truth in Aquinas and Descartes." *International Philosophical Quarterly* 26 (1986): 341–52.

Rist, John M. *Augustine: Ancient Thought Baptized*. Cambridge University Press, 1996.

Roland-Gosselin, Marie-Dominique. "Peut-on parler d'intuition intellectuelle dans la philosophie thomiste?" In *Philosophia Perennis*, ed. F.-J. von Rintelen. Vol. II, 709–30. 729–30. Regensburg: Habbel, 1930.

Review of "Notre science de l'esprit humain, d'après S. Thomas d'Aquin," by Blaise Romeyer. *Bulletin thomiste* 1.4 (1924): 113–15.

Review of "Saint Thomas et notre connaissance de l'esprit humain," by Blaise Romeyer. *Bulletin thomiste* 6.2 (1929): 469–74.

Romano, Joseph J. "Between Being and Nothingness: The Relevancy of Thomistic Habit." *The Thomist* 58 (1994): 427–40.

Romeyer, Blaise. "La doctrine de saint Thomas sur la vérité." *Archives de philosophie* 3.2 (1925): 1–54.

"Notre science de l'esprit humain, d'après saint Thomas d'Aquin." *Archives de philosophie* 1.1 (1923): 32–55.

"À propos de S. Thomas et notre connaissance de l'esprit humain." *Revue de philosophie* 36 (1929): 551–73.

"Saint Thomas et notre connaissance de l'esprit humain." *Archives de philosophie* 6.2 (1928): 1–114.

Ruane, John. "Self-Knowledge and the Spirituality of the Soul in St. Thomas." *The New Scholasticism* 32 (1958): 425–42.

Salinas, Héctor Hernando. "El problema de la memoria intelectiva en Tomás de Aquino." *Universitas Philosophica* 42 (2004): 87–115.

Sartre, Jean-Paul. *Being and Nothingness*. Trans. Hazel E. Barnes. New York: Philosophical Library, 1956.

Sass, Louis Arnorsson. "Self and World in Schizophrenia: Three Classic Approaches." *Philosophy, Psychiatry, and Psychology* 8 (2001): 251–68.

Schell, Patricia. "La doctrina tomista de la *memoria* espiritual: un punto de equilibrio ante las anomalías contemporánea." *Sapientia* 59 (2004): 49–75.

Schmidt, Robert W. "The Evidence Grounding Judgments of Existence." In *An Étienne Gilson Tribute*, ed. Charles J. O'Neil. 228–44. Milwaukee, Wis.: Marquette University Press, 1959.

Schneider, Arthur. *Die Psychologie Alberts des Grossen*. Beiträge zur Geschichte der Philosophie des Mittelalters 4, parts 5–6. Münster: Aschendorff, 1903/1906.

Schütz, Ludwig. *Thomas-Lexikon: Sammlung, Übersetzung und Erklärung der in sämtlichen Werken des h. Thomas von Aquin vorkommenden Kunstausdrücke und wissenschaftlichen Aussprüche*. Paderborn: Schöningh, 1895. Reprint. New York: Musurgia Publishers, 1948.

Sertillanges, A.-D. *Foundations of Thomistic Philosophy*. Trans. Godfrey Anstruther. St. Louis: Herder, 1931.

S. Thomas d'Aquin. 4th edn. 2 vols. Paris: Alcan, 1925.

Shoemaker, Sydney. "Introspection and the Self." In *Self-Knowledge*, ed. Cassam, 118–39.

Simon, Yves. *An Introduction to the Metaphysics of Knowledge*. Trans. Vukan Kuic and Richard J. Thompson. New York: Fordham University Press, 1990.

Simplicius. *On Aristotle's* On the Soul *3.1–5*. Trans. H.J. Blumenthal. Ithaca, N.Y.: Cornell University Press, 2000.

Snyder, Steven. "Thomas Aquinas and the Reality of Time." *Sapientia* 55 (2000): 371–84.

Sorabji, Richard. *The Philosophy of the Commentators 200–600 AD: A Sourcebook*. Vol. 1, *Psychology (with Ethics and Religion)*. Ithaca, N.Y.: Cornell University Press, 2005.

—— *Self: Ancient and Modern Insights about Individuality, Life, and Death*. Oxford University Press, 2006.

Spruit, Leon. Species intelligibilis: *From Perception to Knowledge*. 2 vols. Leiden: Brill, 1994.

Still, Carl N. "Aquinas's Theory of Human Self-Knowledge." PhD diss., University of Toronto, Centre for Medieval Studies, 1999.

Stock, Brian. *Augustine the Reader: Meditation, Self-Knowledge, and the Ethics of Interpretation*. Cambridge, Mass.: Belknap Press, 1996.

Stock, Michael. "Sense Consciousness According to St. Thomas." *The Thomist* 21 (1958): 415–86.

Strawson, Galen. *Selves: An Essay in Revisionary Metaphysics*. Oxford University Press, 2009.

Stump, Eleonore. *Aquinas*. New York: Routledge, 2003.

—— "Non-Cartesian Dualism and Materialism without Reductionism." *Faith and Philosophy* 12 (1995): 505–31

—— "Resurrection, Reassembly, and Reconstitution: Aquinas on the Soul." In *Die menschliche Seele: Brauchen wir den Dualismus?*, ed. Bruno Niederberger and Edmund Runggaldier, 153–74. Frankfurt: Ontos Verlag, 2006.

Suchla, Beate Regina. *Dionysius Areopagita: Leben, Werk, Wirkung*. Freiburg: Herder, 2008.

Swinburne, Richard. *The Evolution of the Soul*. Rev. edn. New York: Oxford University Press, 1997.

Szaif, Jan. "Selbsterkenntnis: Thomas contra Augustinum." *Theologie und Philosophie: Vierteljahresschrift* 74 (1999): 321–37.

Taylor, Charles. *Sources of the Self: The Making of the Modern Identity*. Cambridge, Mass.: Harvard University Press, 1989.

Taylor, R.C. "A Critical Analysis of the Structure of the *Kalām fī mahd al-khair (Liber de causis)*." In *Neoplatonism and Islamic Thought*, ed. Parviz Morewedge, 11–40. Albany, N.Y.: State University of New York Press, 1992.

Teske, Roland. "William of Auvergne's Debt to Avicenna." In *Studies in the Philosophy of William of Auvergne, Bishop of Paris 1228–1249*, ed. Roland Teske, 217–37. Milwaukee, Wis.: Marquette University Press, 2006.

—— "William of Auvergne's Spiritualist Concept of the Human Being." In *Autour de Guillaume d'Auvergne († 1249)*, ed. Franco Morenzoni and Jean-Yves Tilliette, 35–53. Turnhout: Brepols, 2005.

Themistius (see Alexander of Aphrodisias).

Thomas Aquinas. *Commentaries on Aristotle's "On Sense and What is Sensed" and "On Memory and Recollection."* Trans. Kevin White and Edward M. Macierowski. Washington, D.C.: The Catholic University of America Press, 2005.

Commentary on the Book of Causes. Trans. Vincent A. Guagliardo, Charles R. Hess, and Richard C. Taylor. Washington, DC: The Catholic University of America Press, 1996.

Toccafondi, Eugenio T. "La spiritualità dell'anima e la coscienza dell'io." *Doctor communis* 11 (1958): 155–77.

Tomar Romero, Francisca. "La *memoria* como conocimiento y amor de sí." *Revista española de filosofia medieval* 8 (2001): 95–110.

Torrell, Jean-Pierre. *Saint Thomas Aquinas.* Vol. 1, *The Person and His Work,* rev. edn. Trans. Robert Royal. Washington, DC: The Catholic University of America Press, 2005.

Tuninetti, Luca F. Per se notum: *Die logische Beschaffenheit des Selbstverständlichen im Denken des Thomas von Aquinas.* Leiden: Brill, 1996.

Van Dyke, Christina. "Not Properly a Person: The Rational Soul and 'Thomistic Substance Dualism.'" *Faith and Philosophy* 26 (2009): 186–204.

van Inwagen, Peter. *Routledge Encyclopedia of Philosophy.* London: Routledge, 1998.

Verbeke, Gerard. "Connaissance de soi et connaissance de Dieu chez saint Augustin." *Augustiniana* 4 (1954): 495–515.

"A Crisis of Individual Consciousness: Aquinas' View." *The Modern Schoolman* 69 (1992): 379–94.

Wang, Stephen. *Aquinas and Sartre on Freedom, Personal Identity, and the Possibility of Happiness.* Washington, D.C.: The Catholic University of America Press, 2009.

Wéber, E.-H. *La controverse de 1270 à l'Université de Paris et son retentissement sur la pensée de S. Thomas d'Aquin.* Paris: Vrin, 1970.

La personne humaine au XIIIe siècle. Paris, Vrin: 1991.

Wébert, Jourdain. "'*Reflexio*': Études sur les opérations réflexives dans la psychologie de saint Thomas d'Aquin." In *Mélanges Mandonnet.* Vol. 1, 286–325. Paris: Vrin, 1930.

Weisheipl, James A. *Friar Thomas d'Aquino: His Life, Thought, and Works.* 2nd edn. Washington, D.C.: The Catholic University of America Press, 1983.

Wilhelmsen, Frederick D. "The 'I' and Aquinas." *Proceedings of the American Catholic Philosophical Association* 51 (1977): 47–54.

William of Auvergne. *The Soul.* Trans. Roland J. Teske. Milwaukee, Wis.: Marquette University Press, 2000.

Williams, Rowan. "The Paradoxes of Self-Knowledge in the *De Trinitate.*" In *Augustine: Presbyter factus sum,* ed. J.T. Lienhard, 121–34. New York: Lang, 1993.

Wippel, John F. *The Metaphysical Thought of Thomas Aquinas: From Finite Being to Uncreated Being.* Washington, D.C.: The Catholic University of America Press, 2000.

"Thomas Aquinas on the Separated Soul and Its Natural Knowledge." In *Thomas Aquinas: Approaches to Truth*, ed. James McEvoy and Michael Dunne, 114–40. Dublin: Four Courts Press, 2002.

Wojtyla, Karol. "Subjectivity and the Irreducible in Man." In *Analecta Husserliana*. Vol. VII, 107–14. Dordrecht: D. Reidel, 1978.

Index

abstraction, 10–12, 146
access to myself, cognitive, *see* privileged
    self-access
acts
    as compared to effects, 102
    cognizing the existence of my own, 32–3,
        47–9, 85, 89, 98–109, 184, 191–2, 207–13
    cognizing the essences of my own, 47–9,
        88–9, 174–5, 179–80, 193n53
    intellect cannot engage in two simultaneously,
        see under intellect
    as manifesting agents, 102–6
    as means of self-knowledge, *see* self-
        knowledge, by one's acts
    metaphysical status of, 120
actual self-awareness, 47, 50, 52, 56, 63
    apprehension in, 74–5, 83–6
    certitude of, *see* certitude of self-knowledge
    content of, *see* content of self-awareness
    as dependent on acts, *see* self-knowledge, by
        one's acts
    described as a "perceiving" (*percipere*), 51,
        70–4
    experiential character of, 70–3, 106–9, 129–31,
        195–8
    first-personality of, 4, 48, 51, 64, 70–3, 84,
        89–91, 98–109, 130, 205–7
    as foundation for quidditative self-knowledge,
        55, 83–9, 174–7, 198
    indistinctness of, 20, 46, 76–7, 83–9, 183–5
    intuitive character of, 75–6, 92–114, 130, 170,
        218–9
    judgment in, 75, 83–6, 171
    obstacles to, 126–7
    phenomena corresponding to, 70–3
    role of species in, *see* self-knowledge, by a
        species
    with or without attention, *see* explicit self-
        awareness; implicit self-awareness
    actuality as condition for intelligibility, 104,
        157–60

agent, *see under* acts; subject
agent intellect, 11, 161–2, 187–91
    contribution to self-knowledge, 36, 44–5, 56,
        145–53, 160–2, 193
    as intellectual light, 146, 150, 193
Albert the Great, 3, 29, 35–7, 41, 56, 144, 149,
    162n79
    influence on Aquinas, 29, 41–7, 144, 153
Alexander of Aphrodisias, 2, 28, 36, 56n43, 153
Alexander of Hales, 30n49, 43n8, 45n13, 47n18
angels, *see* substances, separate
anthropology, Aquinas's, 9–12, 64–5, 114, 182–3,
    213
    relevance to self-knowledge, 12, 39,
        40–1, 49–65, 126–9, 131–3, 153–5, 158–60,
        172–3, 217–19
apprehension (first operation of intellect),
    75, 81–3, *see also* actual self-awareness;
    quidditative self-knowledge
Arabic philosophy, *see names of individual
    authors or works*
Aristotle
    cognition in, 78, 135, 209
    commentary tradition on, 2, 26–9, 38, 144,
        153, 161
    habits in, 121n25
    maxim concerning intellect's intelligibility,
        see under intellect
    physical light in, 147
    self-knowledge in, 27, 50–1, 54, 64, 129, 177
    soul in, 182n27
    thirteenth-century influence of, 1–3, 17–18,
        26–9, 35–8, 44, 48, 50, 53–6, 58–60, 90,
        146n33, 219–20
attention
    Aquinas's account of, 7, 49, 137–42, 163–70,
        204–5
    participated, 138–40
    to myself, *see* explicit self-awareness
Augustine
    habits in, 121

236